*Crossing Boundaries
in the Americas, Vietnam,
and the Middle East*

Crossing Boundaries
in the Americas, Vietnam, and the Middle East

A Memoir

Ron Young

Preface by
David K. Shipler

RESOURCE *Publications* · Eugene, Oregon

CROSSING BOUNDARIES IN THE AMERICAS, VIETNAM, AND THE MIDDLE EAST
A Memoir

Wipf and Stock
An Imprint of Wipf and Stock Publishers
199 W. 8th Ave., Suite 3
Eugene, OR 97401

www.wipfandstock.com

ISBN 13: 978-1-62564-765-8

Manufactured in the U.S.A.   10/07/2014

To John David Maguire,
a Southern Freedom Rider in 1961,
who taught and inspired many of us
at Wesleyan University with his course,
Religious Currents in Contemporary Literature.
When I decided to leave college for a year in Fall 1962,
John arranged for me to work with Rev. Jim Lawson in Memphis.
That boundary crossing profoundly influenced the course of my life.
John and his wife, Billie have remained lifelong friends.

Even in the darkest of times we have the right to expect some illumination, and that such illumination may come less from theories and concepts than from the uncertain, flickering, and often weak light that some men and women, in their lives and works, will kindle under almost all circumstances and shed over the time span that was given them on earth.

HANNAH ARENDT, *MEN IN DARK TIMES*

Contents

Preface

David K. Shipler

HISTORY IS WRITTEN BY the victors, as Winston Churchill observed. It is then interpreted by the powerful, and periodically reinterpreted as values mature and new voices are heard. In other words, history is malleable. Russians under communism used to joke about the disappearance of important figures from official recollections: "What is the definition of a Soviet historian?" The answer: "A person who can predict the past."

We Americans like to think we're more truthful than autocracies, and we are, but only to a degree. While no central government dictates what we learn about our history, we have multiple versions manipulated instead by a thousand points of institutional bias, from the Texas school board's textbook requirements to the museums and monuments scattered across the country. In democracies, too, what is taught and known about the past is shaped by the cultural consensus of the present.

Not long ago, Native Americans (then called "Indians") appeared in classrooms and films as ruthless primitives. If they were occasionally admired, it was only for their savage nobility—their exotic rituals and canny self-reliance—or as collaborators with the white man against their own. I went to school in the 1950s, and I cannot remember reading a line in a textbook or hearing a sentence from a teacher about the atrocities visited upon them.

Nor was slavery sufficiently woven into the American story. Not until the waning years of the twentieth century did visitors to Monticello, Mount Vernon, and other plantations see anything of the majority of residents who had lived there—the enslaved blacks who built and labored on the land. Tours concentrated on the owners' elaborate mansions, furniture, silverware, and china.

That this has changed—that the powerless are now seen—is a tribute to America's sporadic capacity for self-correction. We hail Martin Luther King, Jr. and the civil rights movement that were so vilified and spied upon by J. Edgar Hoover's FBI. What an FBI memo called a "demagogic speech" that made King "the most dangerous and effective Negro leader in the country" we now celebrate as one of the most inspiring pieces of eloquence in our history: "I have a dream."

Yet even this evolving self-portrait underestimates a whole subculture of America's sons and daughters who struggled against established policies and norms. They include whites who journeyed south during the civil rights movement, defied the military draft to campaign against the war in Vietnam, protested United States aid for Latin American dictatorships, urged nuclear disarmament, demanded protection of the environment, and called broadly on their country to stand for peace and humane justice—not easy standards for a superpower to achieve, evidently.

We need to fill gaps in what we understand about ourselves, for these Americans have been the backbone of our conscience. If we sing of their achievements too softly, we miss essential ingredients of our country's greatness.

Ron Young is one of those Americans. I first met him when he and his wife, Carol Jensen, visited Jerusalem, where I was a correspondent, from their home base of Amman, Jordan. Their task, for the American Friends Service Committee, was to cross the rigid boundaries that divided Israelis and Arabs—and the internal boundaries that divided Israelis and Arabs among themselves—so they could report to Quakers back home on the state of the Middle East and its faltering peace process.

Being a reporter was my job, too. But Ron and Carol seemed to be doing much more. In harvesting competing perspectives, they were also seeding a measure of interaction and dialogue. They were carrying the contrasting views across those boundaries and leaving them for contemplation by the other side. To believe that this would make a difference took enormous faith in people's good sense and their capacity to listen, especially to voices different from their own.

Given the absence of Israeli-Palestinian peace more than thirty years after their efforts, you might conclude that their faith was misplaced. But they never struck me as naïve. They honored the decency in people, respected their need for dignity, and looked at hard truths with a clear gaze. We need more of this realistic idealism. Lofty goals cannot be reached by cynicism.

So this personal memoir of Ron's is more significant than simple autobiography. His story is the country's story—or, a part of the country's story not usually told vividly. Because he came of age by following pathways that led through the most momentous protest movements in the nation's postwar experience, his personal narrative helps to fill in the picture of a turbulent society reaching for moral poise.

He told me little of this during our long conversations about the Israeli-Palestinian conflict during those years in Jerusalem. Well, perhaps I never asked—a grievous failing for a reporter. But he also never volunteered, a measure of his humility. He is not a man obsessed with himself.

But he is a man driven by the desire to see injustice made right—not with the flashing rhetoric of hyperbole, not with unprovable accusations of conspiracy or venality, but with the quiet assurance that understanding can be nourished from those seeds of listening.

At a time when organized religion is most publicized for its intolerance, it's worthwhile noting the spotlight that Ron shines on the American religious leaders from various faiths. If there has been a common denominator to his work, it is his regard for clergy as catalysts of change.

That began at the height of efforts to topple Jim Crow segregation, when he dropped out of Wesleyan to work at a black church in Memphis under the Reverend J.M. Lawson Jr., who set him to reading and thinking about topics far beyond the immediate racial conflicts, including the threat of nuclear war.

He visited the Dominican Republic after the United States invasion, went to Uruguay for a conference on nonviolence and social change, and would have been drawn more deeply into Latin America were it not for the escalation of the war in Vietnam.

Ron worked for the religious and pacifist organization, the Fellowship of Reconciliation. He burned his draft card, became active in the peace movement, and led a delegation including religious leaders for discussions with non-communist South Vietnamese who opposed the war. His anti-war credentials enabled him to visit North Vietnam in 1970 as part of a small group of religious figures to deliver mail to and from American prisoners and their families.

In later years he has translated those early contacts with religious leaders into a longterm effort toward Middle East peace. It's hard to think of anyone else with his deep experience who could mobilize Muslim, Jewish, and Christian clergy in the way that he has done, to keep pressing the United States to keep the Israeli-Palestinian peace negotiations alive.

If you are ever tempted to despair that Americans have lost their moral compass, look into Ron Young's generous life of activism. He has not been alone.

David K. Shipler is a journalist and author. His books include:

A Country of Strangers: Blacks and Whites in America and

Arab and Jew: Wounded Sprits in A Promised Land,

for which he won a Pulitzer Prize.

Acknowledgments

Thanks to family members and friends who
read earlier versions of *Crossing Boundaries*,
helped me to tell my story more clearly and,
more importantly, over many years, helped me live it.
Thanks to Heidi Favour for design of the cover and
to John Goodwin for several of the photographs.
Special thanks to my editor, Claire Gorfinkel,
who sharpened and shortened the telling of my story
in ways that make it more interesting and readable.
Ways it's improved are a credit to Claire's skills.
Errors of fact and opinions expressed that
may be controversial are completely my doing.

Introduction

From the time I was a young man, thanks to a combination of fortuitous circumstances and personal choices, I was privileged to participate and play leadership roles in movements for civil rights, against the Vietnam War, and for Arab-Israeli-Palestinian peace. One day, listening to yet another story from my life experiences, our older son turned to me smiling and said, "Dad, you're the Forrest Gump of the American peace movement."

Reflecting on extraordinary experiences I have had, I realized that starting with a decision I made when I was twenty, "crossing boundaries" has been an important and blessed, if sometimes serendipitous theme of my life's journey. I crossed racial and regional boundaries in America, travelled back and forth across international borders to meet with people and parties on different sides of two wars; and I traversed boundaries of three religious communities to engage in interreligious work for peace. I crisscrossed this country a hundred or more times to speak at high schools, colleges, congregations, and community forums, working for fifty years as a national community organizer for justice and peace.

In the fall of 1962, as a student at Wesleyan University in Connecticut, with the encouragement of my religion professor, I moved to Memphis, Tennessee, to live in the black community and work with Rev. J.M. Lawson Jr., a major leader in the civil rights movement, devoted teacher of nonviolence, and close colleague of Martin Luther King Jr. As riots greeted James Meredith's enrollment at Ole Miss and the Cuban missile crisis brought the world to the brink of nuclear war, I experienced living in the black community and being tutored by Jim Lawson as my "second baptism," this one by full immersion. I returned to Wesleyan, and then left again in spring 1965 to support the voting rights campaign in Selma, Alabama.

In June 1965, I joined the national staff of the Fellowship of Reconciliation as director of youth work. Following the US invasion of the Dominican Republic, I travelled to Santo Domingo, where I met with Juan Bosch, the country's first democratically elected president who had been ousted by a military coup and then was prevented from returning to the presidency by the US invasion and occupation. During the American war in Vietnam, I made two visits to both the South and the North, leading an interracial, interreligious delegation focused on repression in Saigon, and carrying mail between their families and American POWs in Hanoi. In March, 1980 I participated in an ecumenical delegation to El Salvador that met with Archbishop Oscar Romero shortly after he urged the United States to cut off aid to the Salvadoran military and one day before he was assassinated. In 1982, along with my wife and son, I moved to Jordan, and traveled regularly in Israel, the West Bank and Gaza, Egypt, Syria and Lebanon, to listen to Arabs and Israelis about opportunities and obstacles for achieving peace, and what the United States could do to help.

Not all my challenging boundary crossing experiences were geographical. In 1967, having decided that I could no longer conscientiously cooperate with the draft, I burned my draft card. A year later I received a federal indictment that read "THE UNITED STATES OF AMERICA vs. RONALD JAMES YOUNG." In Bratislava, Czechoslovakia, I met North and South Vietnamese whom my government had declared to be "enemies." In 1969 and 1970, I served as coordinator of national marches on Washington for peace in Vietnam.

After three years living and working for the Quakers in the Middle East, I wrote a book, *Missed Opportunities for Peace: U.S. Middle East Policy, 1981-86*, that was praised by supporters of both sides in the conflict and was accepted as my senior thesis for graduation from Wesleyan at the age of forty-four. From 1985 to the present, I have worked with American Jewish, Christian and Muslim religious leaders coordinating a dozen interfaith trips to the Middle East; organizing interfaith convocations for peace in Washington, DC and several other cities; meeting with senior government officials including four Secretaries of State; authoring a score of op-ed articles; and advocating for US policies to achieve Arab-Israeli-Palestinian peace.

Crossing Boundaries focuses on my experiences after I moved to Memphis in 1962, but my journey didn't start there. My involvement in these struggles for social change reflected influences of my parents and grandparents, and my experiences growing up in a modest middle class family in New Jersey in the 1940s and 1950s. My dad wanted me to go to the US Military Academy at West Point, while mom encouraged my interest in becoming a Christian minister. My involvement with movements for justice and peace was intertwined with two marriages and parenting two sons. While other books provide more political analyses of these times and movements, *Crossing Boundaries* weaves together my personal memories of people and experiences with my firsthand account of major events in three social change movements over five decades. I hope this book will make a contribution to understanding the issues and movements in which I participated, and to informing and encouraging young people as they find their own paths to participating in building a better future for us all.

We live in a time when technology and communications media expose us every day to events and people's experiences around the world. Facebook, Twitter, You-Tube, and other social media enable us to communicate easily and instantly across some gaps. At the same time, other gaps, most notably between rich and poor—in our country and around the world—are growing wider; wars and threats of terrorism continue; patterns of consumption and development, combined with global warming, endanger the earth's future; and politics in America have become bitterly contentious. My personal boundary crossing experiences related to race and the civil rights movement, conflict in Latin America, wars in Vietnam and the Middle East, and the role of religion in resolving or perpetuating conflict reflect the times in which I've lived and choices I've made. I believe that my experiences offer relevant lessons for different situations going forward. By literally, not just virtually, crossing boundaries, I believe we can walk with people who face very different and often much more difficult circumstances than our own. Then, hopefully, we can work together creatively and courageously for a more just, participatory, peaceful and sustainable future. I hope my life story makes a contribution to this process.

Ron Young lives in Everett, Washington.

He can be contacted by email at ronyoungwa@gmail.com

Growing Up: From Playing War
to Following Jesus

Living near New York City; war was heroic and war was a game we played; grow-ing up Christian and going forward at a Billy Graham rally; encountering preju-dice at seven and fifteen years old; realizing our family struggled to make ends meet; attending College High School where every student was headed to college; learning about the Civil Rights Movement; starting to ask the questions, who am I? and what am I meant to be?; driving across our big, beautiful country and see-ing some awful poverty; choosing Wesleyan University over West Point; and being the first in my family to go away to college.

MY EARLIEST BOUNDARY CROSSING, other than being born which I don't remember, was riding on a bus, passing the double, thick, vertical lines painted on the wall in the Lin-coln Tunnel under the Hudson River. Big, bright, black printed words, all in upper case letters, marked this border: NEW JERSEY on the west side of the lines and NEW YORK on the east. From our apartment in West New York, New Jersey, we could look across the Hudson and see New York City. My family did not own an automobile until 1950 and we didn't have a lot of money, so to make our semi-annual family visits to New York City, we would travel by bus through the Lincoln Tunnel. I remember my excitement as a young boy when we crossed that boundary.

I loved going into New York City, with its skyscrapers, bright lights, crowded buses and subways, and mind boggling mass of people from different countries and cultures. Whenever we were in the City, our family enjoyed walking a lot. On one of our long walks I learned from my dad that crossing twenty-one numbered streets go-ing North or South along one of the city's canyon-like avenues meant we had walked a mile. I also loved riding the subways. I especially liked riding in the first car of an

Express Train where I could stand next to the engineer's booth, with my face pressed against the front window, and watch as the train sped forward, swallowing the tube of black space, shiny rails, signal lights, and stations. I loved seeing people in New York from all over the world. On one occasion, riding the A Train—made famous in Duke Ellington's jazz tune—I saw people in just one subway car reading newspapers in half a dozen different languages.

Dad and mom had deeper, positive connections with New York City from before I was born. In the 1930s my father James (Jim) Young commuted from New Jersey into the Bronx to attend Fordham University. I remember his smile as he told me how some nights after class, he and a few other male students would go out to drink beer and discuss philosophy with their favorite priest professor. My mother, Edith (Edie) Young (maiden name Hofer) talked about how before I was born, she enjoyed working in New York City as an executive secretary at American Power & Light, located downtown by Wall Street near to where the World Trade Towers later stood. On nice days, she would eat her lunch outdoors in the gardens by Trinity Church, and enjoy seeing people from many different cultures. Before I was born, dad and mom occasionally took a bus into New York City in the evening to have dinner at the Horn & Hardart automat and go dancing.

In contrast with some children who experience New York City as overwhelming, intimidating or even threatening, thanks to our parents and the times, my sister Judy and I loved visiting New York: the Empire State Building, Times Square, the Museum of Natural History, Hayden Planetarium, Central Park Zoo, the Statue of Liberty, Rockefeller Center, and Radio City Music Hall. My earliest memories of sexy girls were the Rockettes at Radio City Music Hall and the street walkers on 42nd Street in tawdry Times Square. As a young boy, all these girls seemed unapproachable and forbidding. I remember Thanksgiving Day parades, sitting on the curb leaning back and looking up to view the huge balloon comic book characters held by long ropes floating by high overhead.

As a special treat at Thanksgiving or Christmas, a few times dad took our family to have dinner at the old Astor Hotel in Times Square. I thought it was awesome to be served by several waiters, wearing perfectly pressed black pants and trim red jackets with gold buttons. I think that experience may have inspired my taste for pleasures that exceed my means. As I recall, we all ordered chopped steaks or chicken—the least expensive entrees on the menu—and dad seemed relieved when I announced that all I wanted for dessert was a dish of vanilla ice cream. Usually we ate at the closet-sized and more affordable Gaiety Delicatessen on 46th Street, just west of Broadway, where several burly, hairy armed men dispensed fat deli sandwiches accompanied by huge garlic pickles, and where dad allowed me to sip his Heineken beer. I loved going to special places in New York City, but I also just loved being there, walking the streets and riding the subways, seeing all the different people. To me as a child, visits to New

York City, like the name of the restaurant atop the fated Trade Towers, offered wonder-filled windows on the world.

West New York, New Jersey

I was born September 9, 1942 at St. Mary's Hospital in Hoboken, New Jersey, where my sister, Judy, was born four years later. We liked to brag that we were born in the same city as Frank Sinatra. Until I was nine, my family lived in West New York, New Jersey in a three room apartment with a great view across the Hudson River to midtown Manhattan. On many evenings the sunset would turn the windows on the west side of Manhattan copper colored. In spring, Forsythia bushes formed a bright yellow border between the water and the West Side Highway along the New York waterfront. From our windows, I could watch the busy boat traffic, including the bulky, old West Shore Ferries plowing back and forth across the river. Occasionally I got to see the magnificent Queen Mary luxury liner departing or docking.

In 1948, when I was six, the battleship USS Missouri anchored in the Hudson River across from our apartment. Dad took me on a Navy launch to visit this famous warship and view the deck plaque commemorating where three years earlier emissaries of Japan had surrendered to General Douglas MacArthur. According to my mother, right after Japan's attack on Pearl Harbor, dad tried to join the Navy but was rejected because of a small heart murmur. I remember mom telling me that dad felt badly that he hadn't been able to serve. One Saturday in the fall when I was seven and again when I was eight, dad took me up the Hudson River to visit the Military Academy at West Point. We watched the Corps of Cadets dress parade and attended the Army football game. Those visits inspired my interest in going to college at West Point, an interest dad encouraged and I pursued until I was fifteen and decided I wanted to go to a liberal arts college.

My first world war was the Korean War. I remember following the war in the New *York Daily News* on full page printed maps with names of places I didn't know: Seoul, Inchon, Busan, and Pyongyang. Broad, blunt, black arrows showed American and South Korean forces sweeping north or North Korean and Chinese forces sweeping south. Our country didn't win that war, but it didn't lose it either; and it's a war that still hasn't ended. My friends and I used to play Korean War in an empty dirt lot on the street where I lived.

Decades later, I was deeply moved by reading David Halberstam's book, *The Coldest Winter: America and the Korean War* (2007), published six months after Halberstam's tragic death. Sadly, veterans from the Korean War seem forgotten in an historical amnesia and ambivalence between our nation's sense of pride over the allied victory in World War II, the so called "good war," and the controversy and sense of shame many Americans experienced about the Vietnam War. For a very different, if controversial, perspective on World War II, I urge you to read *Human Smoke* by Nicholson Baker.

In West New York, my sister and I shared the apartment's only bedroom with my parents until I was nine and Judy was five. I slept in a day bed that my tall, skinny body outgrew by the time I was seven or eight years old. From my earliest memory, our parents always slept in separate beds. As I grew older and realized that most of my friends' parents slept together in one bed, I felt sad about my parents seeming lack of intimacy. At the same time, I remember admiring my parents' beds that had handsome head and foot boards, with polished Mahogany veneer finish matching their night table and their His and Hers dressers. The bedroom was very crowded. Our living room was a bit larger, accommodating a couch, two chairs, a coffee table, fake fireplace, big old radio, and beginning in the fall of 1948, when my sister and I lay facing each other on the couch sick with the measles, a black and white 15 inch television. There was no dining room. We ate all our meals in the small kitchen on a wooden gate leg table which stood against the windows that looked out across the river to New York City. My parents talked frequently about money and about saving for this or that. I knew we weren't really poor but I was aware that money was always very tight. Dad regularly worked two jobs and my parents struggled a lot to make ends meet.

Looking back, a big difference between the 1950s and 2014 is that back then the American dream seemed achievable. Today for many American families faced with stagnant wages and growing inequalities, no matter how hard they work, the dream seems out of reach.[1]

My memories of life in this apartment are positive. My parents were friends with other couples with children who also lived in our building. The women often wheeled baby carriages or walked us in the park along the boulevard overlooking the river, and with the view of Manhattan. I particularly remember Mary and Frank Dibella, an Italian couple with two daughters, Paula, a year older than me, and Rita, a few years younger. I always looked forward to visiting the Dibellas because Mary made the most wonderful layered dish, called lasagna with meatballs that she served in various shaped casserole dishes. Until I was ten or eleven, I thought only Mary could make lasagna. I think "Italian Mary's Lasagna" was the start of my liking foods from different countries and cultures.

On New Year's Eve my parents didn't go out dancing in New York City the way they did before Judy and I were born. Going out was too expensive, but for a few years they did join other couples who lived in our building in a progressive party that moved from appetizers and drinks in one apartment to a main course and dessert with more drinks in succeeding apartments, and ended in yet another apartment at 4 or 5 o'clock the next morning, with breakfast and cheap Champagne.

---

1. Meacham, "History of the American Dream," 35–39.

My sister and I remember Christmas times in our apartment as almost magical. When we went to bed on Christmas Eve, there was no evidence at all of the holiday. Mom and dad would stay up most of the night decorating the living room and wrapping presents. Dad and his friends would go to each other's apartments to help assemble bicycles, baby carriages and other toys. With the drinking I assume they did, it's amazing that the toys actually got assembled. When we woke up early on Christmas morning there was a fully decorated, lighted tree, an elaborate electric train and winter village scene around the tree's base, and, miraculously, all of the presents my sister and I had asked for in our letter to Santa Claus.

Growing up in West New York, most of my childhood friends were Italian and German. Two of my boyhood friends were Jewish. My first experience with prejudice occurred when I was seven and involved my best friend, Michael. Returning from a birthday party for Carmen, one of my Italian friends, I told my mother that I was sad that Michael wasn't at the party. She said, "Maybe he wasn't invited." I asked her why that would be and she explained that "it might be because Michael is Jewish." While she made it clear that she didn't think this was right, she explained to me about prejudice against Jews. I still remember the hurt I felt. I absorbed and remembered what my mother told me, but I didn't really understand.

My friends and I sometimes played stickball on 63rd Street, tagging parked cars as the bases. Sometimes we played "Cowboys and Indians." I can't remember if any of my friends ever pretended to be Indians, but I always imagined myself as a cowboy or a soldier in the US Cavalry. We also played "War," digging shallow pretend fox holes in the empty dirt lot half way up 63rd Street, shooting repeating cap rifles, and throwing dirt bomb grenades at imaginary enemy machine gun positions. We pretended that we were American soldiers fighting the Japanese in the Philippines or the Chinese in Korea. Thinking back, I suspected the fact that we never imagined ourselves fighting white Germans probably reflected the early, pervasive effects of racism.

I pushed myself and my friends to make pretending as realistic as possible and I always played very hard, sometimes with a sense of reckless abandon. In one of our war games, I was pretending that a neighbor lady's porch was the bridge of a Navy ship that I was commanding in the Pacific. Imagining the ship being tossed in rough seas, I reached up and hung onto a heavy cement urn filled with flowers and dirt. The urn tumbled off its pedestal toward me. When I tried to catch it to keep it from breaking, my left hand was crushed as the urn hit the cement porch floor. A two-inch square of skin was scraped off the back of my left hand, my fourth finger was gashed to the bone, and the tip of my pinky was hanging off, held on by one thin piece of flesh. I ran home bleeding and holding the tip of my finger so it wouldn't fall off. A doctor managed somehow to stitch the tip of my pinky back on, but my left hand still bears visible scars from this pretend war game.

In the summer of 1949, my enthusiasm for playing hard turned to sports. I got my start in Little League Baseball in West New York. "Pep" Evers, a handsome, tall, blond, crew cut coach taught me how to hit and how being tall and left handed gave me an advantage for playing first base. Our team was sponsored by Lou's Bar and Grill, the name we wore proudly in red letters on the backs of our gray baseball jerseys. After every winning game, our entire team was invited into Lou's Bar for pizza and soda and Lou personally gave each of us a dollar. I was sure a friend of mine who played on a rival team, Armelino's Construction Company, wasn't so lucky. In my second Little League season, our team advanced to the playoffs and we got to play against a team from Weehawken, just south of West New York. The big thrill was that we played the game at night under the lights on a field in the stadium that was built over the entrance to the Lincoln Tunnel. Even though we lost, playing there that night, I felt really grown up.

When I was in second and third grades at No. 6 Public School in West New York, I experienced my first love, other than my mother. Joan was a very smart, pretty girl with blue eyes and blond hair. I remember how really good and grown up I felt when a few times I actually walked Joan home from school.

Our Move to Packanack Lake

In 1951, my parents bought their first home for $7,000 at Packanack Lake, a club community about 15 minutes west of Paterson. Buying a home was a major mark of accomplishment for my dad and mom, as it was for many American working families in the fifties. We were really excited about moving from the apartment in the city to our new home in what seemed almost like the country. The lake was just down the hill six blocks away. My friends and I played in other people's row boats that were tied up at the shore. Our house was a very small, three room converted summer cabin with painted red imitation half-log siding on the outside, imitation knotty pine walls inside, and a screened in L-shaped porch on the front and side that in summer doubled the size of our house. For the first time, I had my own small bedroom with a door. My sister slept in a room divided by a curtain from the living room, where every night for five years, our parents slept together on a very uncomfortable convertible sofa. In summers when my grandparents visited, they slept on a convertible swing couch on the porch. When I was ten and my sister six, we got a puppy we named Rex. I remember going to pick him up from his litter at a friend's house and wheeling him home in our red wagon

When I was fourteen, we moved up the street to another converted summer home with imitation brown half-log exterior siding, plywood interior, and a two story stone fireplace in the living room. The bedrooms were upstairs off an open balcony which had a lacquered cedar log railing. My parents finally had their own bedroom where they could sleep again in their separate beds with the polished Mahogany veneer. Both our houses were definitely low end compared with most homes at Packanack Lake. We lived in the older, funky southeast corner of the lake community, where the streets were named after Indian tribes: Cayuga, Oneida, Seneca, and Mohawk. On the more upscale west side of the lake, where fewer of the homes were converted summer cabins, the streets were named after stately trees: Beechwood, Elm, Chestnut, and Oakwood. The combination of living on Cayuga Trail, and our home's half-log siding and cedar stair railing led some of my friends to call it "Ron's cowboy house," a reference that I remember embarrassed me as a teenager.

In many ways growing up in this lovely lake community from 1951 until I went off to college in 1960 was idyllic. While my mom and dad never reminded me of Ozzie and Harriet, life at Packanack Lake did seem to fit the prevailing idealized, fifties image of the safe and, for the most part, happy life of white, middle class, suburban American families. I experienced the way we lived as both normal and normative. I knew very little about how richer or poorer people lived. I was active in Cub Scouts and Boy Scouts, achieving my Eagle Scout, and God and Country awards by the time I was sixteen. I played hard at recreation league seasonal team sports, and for a few summers was a member of the Lake's youth tennis and swimming teams. My first tennis partner and main competitor at the Tennis Club was Diane, a very athletic tomboy who lived close by on Seneca Trail. In our friendly, but serious competition, as I recall, she won more matches than I did.

From the time I was eleven until fourteen, I earned money delivering the *Paterson Evening News* on my bicycle to thirty houses on the east side of the lake, and I occasionally baby sat for nearby neighbors, earning seventy-five cents an hour. I often rode my bike the mile and a half to Packanack Lake Elementary School. In both fifth and sixth grades my teacher was Mr. William Knolls, a rough and ready young Korean War veteran, who also was very warm, inquisitive and open minded. As we studied history and world affairs, Mr. Knolls organized classroom exercises that pushed us to imagine ourselves into the lives and experiences of others, including people with very different life experiences than ours. As an example, rather than simply having us read about life among ancient cave dwellers, one day Mr. Knolls had our class move all our desks and chairs back against the walls. Then we all got down on the floor on plastic tablecloths to eat raw vegetables and meat, with the biggest boys, including myself, getting to eat ahead of the others. While most students liked him a lot, some parents were uncomfortable and critical over his untraditional teaching methods. Mr. Knolls also loved theatre. In sixth grade, we produced the Gilbert and Sullivan operetta, *H.M.S. Pinafore*, for which Mr. Knolls helped us construct magnificent sets. I was one of the stars in the performance as Admiral of the Queen's Navy.

I attended Sunday school at Packanack Lake Community Church, where for two years my mother was the volunteer Sunday School Superintendent and where I was mentored by Mason Ellison, an enthusiastic, young Youth Minister. On Youth Sunday when I was 14, I preached a sermon about Christian vocation that I titled "Consider Your Call." The text was from Paul's *Letter to the Romans*, Chapter 12 that speaks about different vocations to which persons are called, including minister, teacher, etc.

and emphasizes loving others and overcoming evil with good. Prefiguring the role of older male mentors in my life, I remember a line from my sermon when I told about a confused youth responding to his older mentor's inspiration, saying, "If that's the man you see, Sir, then that's the man I'll be." I was enthusiastic, if also rather naïve, about being Christian. I talked a lot about my faith with my mother who encouraged me, my grandmother who seemed interested, and a few of my close friends who seemed indifferent but were kind enough to put up with my enthusiasm.

The same year that I preached on Youth Sunday, my enthusiasm over being Christian was given a big boost. None of my teenage friends being interested, I took a bus by myself into New York City to attend the Billy Graham Crusade for Christ at Madison Square Garden. My dad had taken me to the Garden a few times to the Barnum Bailey Circus and New York Knicks basketball games. On this occasion, the Garden setting resembled a combination of a giant church service and a mass rally. Emotionally inspired by George Beverly Shea's singing "How Great Thou Art" and by Billy Graham's preaching, I responded to his Call to Christ. Making my way down from the balcony alone, I went forward to publicly accept Christ as my savior. I felt a wonderful new sense of assurance and excitement about my faith. While I was aware there were many unanswered, even so far unimagined, questions about my life in the future, the most important question about my relationship with God seemed re-solved, as expressed in that favorite evangelical hymn, "Blessed Assurance, Jesus Is Mine." Later when I saw pictures of Graham with one American president or another, I remembered how at the time, like Billy Graham, my Christian faith and my faith in America were intertwined and very comfortably compatible.

Billy Graham referred people who came forward to their home churches—a practice which frustrated fundamentalists who wanted people referred only to "born again" churches. Thanks to Graham's practice, I remained active at Packanack Com-munity Church, continuing to have regular conversations with the Youth Minister and the Senior Pastor. As a junior in high school, I was elected president of our Youth Fellowship. That same summer when most mornings I ran three miles around the Lake to prepare for fall football, I developed the practice of stopping half way in a wooded area on the peninsula to pray. Growing in my understanding of Christian faith and aware of my abilities as a speaker, I began to think that, after college, I might want to go on to seminary and become a minister. Mom encouraged that idea. Dad kept pushing me to go to West Point, but that path was losing its appeal.

While in many ways I was outgoing and self-confident, I also experienced my-self as shy and awkward, particularly about girls and sex. By the time I was twelve, I discovered that I was attracted to boys as well as to girls, and at the time that troubled me. While sometimes it seemed that this simply was the way I was, given my own ignorance and prevailing public prejudices at the time, as a teenager, I kept this secret and hoped these feelings somehow would go away.

Recently at a college reunion, I was reminded that during my years there, one classmate was expelled for a year for being gay and another, who was presumed to be gay and was harassed by fellow students, committed suicide. Twenty-four years later, while there still is a long way to go, more informed, less judgmental public attitudes, especially among younger people, are a welcome change for persons who are gay, lesbian, bisexual or transgendered. Tragically, a whole lot of pain was caused and still is caused by people's ignorance and prejudice about human sexuality.

My parents weren't much help when it came to educating me about sex. Sharing my parents' bedroom for my first nine years and noticing that for so many years they slept in separate beds, despite the evidence of my sister's and my existence, I suspected that they never "did it." My mother, who talked with me a lot about just about everything, never talked about sex. My dad was always working two jobs, so he and I hardly ever talked about anything. As an example of my naiveté, when I was 12 and looking in the top drawer of dad's dresser for a tie to wear, I found several condoms. I remember feeling anxious and confused. For some reason, I associated condoms exclusively with illicit sex and prostitutes. I wondered and worried if dad was having sex with a woman who wasn't mom.

To her credit, at least mom made an effort at educating me. One evening, just after I had gone to bed, mom knocked on my bedroom door. Without looking at me – I guess she was embarrassed – she handed me a book through the partially open door and said, "I think you should read this." It was the *Red Cross Manual on Sex for Teenagers*. The booklet was so scientific and medical, and the diagrams so mechanical and boring that reading it could almost make one lose interest in sex. Not surprisingly, despite the dull *Red Cross Manual*, my interest in sex didn't diminish and, thankfully, some boys my age also helped to educate me. When I was thirteen, my friend John taught me the mechanics, if not the art of satisfying my sexual urge myself.

College High School

I was a good student through the elementary grades, and in summer 1954, I was accepted at College High School (CHS), a demonstration or lab school on the campus of Montclair State Teachers College. Getting there involved a 30 minute commute by car from Packanack Lake. Fortunately, my friend John was also accepted there, and his father could drop us off each morning on his way to work in Newark. Coming home after school, we could take a local train from Montclair to Mountain View where one of our moms picked us up. Given their modest income, my parents never imagined sending me to a private school. At the time, dad taught science at the local junior high school and worked evenings at Liggett's Drug Store, while mom had recently gone to work as secretary in a local elementary school. College High School tuition was less than $100 a year, so both mom and dad recognized this as a wonderful, and affordable opportunity to advance my chances of going to a good college, a high priority for both of them. I took a test for admission, but I think basically it was my straight A's in elementary school and my leadership qualities that got me admitted.

I realized later that going to College High, instead of the local public high school, was an important and formative early boundary crossing in my life. With only fifteen boys and fifteen girls in each grade, all of whom planned to go on to college, I had a very rich experience from seventh through twelfth grades. In contrast with the largely white, Anglo-Saxon Protestant community at Packanack Lake, there were several Jewish and Italian students in my class at CHS. For a while, there was one black student a grade or two above mine, but he left to return to public school, maybe because he was the only black in our school.

At the start of seventh grade at College High, our class went on a three-day overnight retreat to Stokes State Forest in northwest New Jersey. Staying in cabins and enjoying swimming, hiking and other outdoor activities, the class retreat was focused on our getting to know each other and on discussing values. The retreat was led by Dr. Fincher, a Quaker, and Miss Pennington, who team-taught Social Studies and English to the seventh and eighth grades. Our class spent one third of that school year studying different world religions, one third studying race and race relations, and one third studying the United Nations. While, at the time, I was confident, maybe even a bit arrogantly so, that Christianity was the best religion, learning about other religions was the beginning of appreciating them in ways that would become much deeper and more important later in my life. I assume the selection of race as a topic for our seventh grade studies was inspired by the May 1954, "Brown vs. Board of Education" Supreme Court decision that declared segregated schools to be inherently unequal. The selection of the United Nations as a topic for study came a year after President Eisenhower's December 1953 "Atoms for Peace" speech, at the UN where he projected a vision of worldwide use of nuclear power for peaceful purposes, a very different vision from the Cold War nuclear balance of terror that soon came to dominate world affairs. Even at the time, these three topics seemed timely, challenging, and forward-looking.

At CHS, all my teachers were college professors. College students who were studying to become teachers attended our classes as observers. Most classes were of high quality and challenging. In tenth grade, our English teacher, Professor Petegrove, provided a provocative and intense introduction to writings of Dostoyevsky and Shakespeare. That same year, a small group of students in our class began hanging out on a rarely used small staircase where we often discussed big issues, including religion, politics and world affairs. During the 1956 presidential election, a rematch between President Eisenhower and Adlai Stevenson, my friend John supported the liberal Stevenson and made fun of me for wearing a big I LIKE IKE button. Four years earlier in 1952, I had wanted General Douglas MacArthur to be president. I remember having doubts about my choice later when I learned that, if Truman had not recalled him from Korea, MacArthur might have led our country into all-out war with China.

I was given numerous leadership opportunities at College High. With the small number of students, everyone who was at all athletic got to play team sports. My senior year, I was co-captain of our football team and captain of our basketball team. There were many other extracurricular opportunities, including student government, drama, the yearbook, and the school newspaper. As a high school junior I was elected editor of the school newspaper, the *CHS Crier*. I remember writing an editorial on some issue that got me called into the office of the Principal who told me in no uncertain terms: "students have no business addressing that issue." By our junior year, several of my classmates had tagged me with the nickname Monk, both because of my active interest and enthusiasm for religion, as well as my positive attitude and can do spirit. I have little doubt that attending CHS was the bridge experience that enabled me to go to a very good college and helped prepare me to accept other unusual opportunities that would come my way in the future.

As a young boy in West New York and later at College High School, I had several Italian and Jewish friends but that was not the case living at Packanack Lake. As a teenager, I became aware that Italians, Jews, Blacks and Hispanics were not allowed to live at the Lake. The restrictive covenants governing who was allowed to buy property at Packanack were never mentioned to my white Anglo-Saxon parents when they bought our house. I found out about them in the summer of 1958 when I was fifteen and controversy erupted during our church's Vacation Bible School.

It was two years after the Montgomery Bus Boycott led by Dr. Martin Luther King Jr. As teenage volunteers in the Vacation Bible School, we planned for the children, some of whom were Blacks and Puerto Ricans from the nearby city of Paterson, to have a swim party at the Lake's public beach. But swimming at Packanack's beaches was governed by the same restrictive ethnic and racial covenants that limited who could buy property there. The church was informed by the Lake's manager that the Black and Puerto Rican children would not be allowed to swim at the Club's beaches.

Coincidentally, later that summer Packanack was planning a parade to celebrate a special anniversary. In response to the decision about the Bible School kids, our Church Youth Fellowship began to discuss a plan to enter a float in the parade shaped like Packanack Lake, with coiled barbed wire around the edge of the float. As it turned out, we didn't actually have to build the float. Just talking about our plan provoked a crisis among parents and Club officials. Embarrassed by the controversy and not wanting things to get out of control, the Lake's Governing Board and our Church Council agreed on a compromise. They decided that the swim party could be held at a private lakefront home of a church member.

My mom, sister and I hated the covenants. I never was sure about my dad's opinion. At the time, however, we didn't think about trying to do anything to get them eliminated. Despite the conflict over the Bible School kids, in the late 1950s, racism and segregation seemed to be problems somewhere else. The civil rights movement and crisis in race relations were primarily developments we read about in newspapers or saw on television. Experiencing the conflict over the swim party, I began to understand that attitudes and practices related to race and segregation were problems right where I lived in New Jersey, although I still didn't think there was much I could do about them. A few years later, in part because of threats of lawsuits, Packanack Lake did away with its restrictive covenants. Thinking back to the Vacation Bible School controversy, I realized later that this also was the first time I learned that sometimes you have to cause trouble to accomplish positive change.

Family Trip to California

In the summer of 1959, between my Junior and Senior years at College High School, I had another important boundary crossing experience. My dad was accepted to participate in a National Science Foundation (NSF) Summer Study Program at San Jose State College in California. Mom and dad announced that we all would be going to California. At first the idea of driving across the country didn't seem real. Until 1959, my only association with going to California was a circle game we sometimes played as kids. One kid would say, "I'm going on a trip to California, and I'm taking _____ (e.g., my bicycle, my radio, my dog) with me." Going around the circle, each person would have to remember and repeat what every previous person was taking and add something. The more people in the circle, the more confused and funnier the game became as each person tried to remember what everybody else planned to take on the trip.

I was proud of dad for being selected for the NSF program. He won a second grant the following summer to study at Arizona State University in Tempe. These summer grants led him to explore getting a teaching position in a foreign country. After coming close to taking a job in Saudi Arabia, in 1964 dad was offered and accepted a teaching position at the American School in Sao Paulo, Brazil. It was not until a few years later that I fully appreciated how big a break these opportunities were for him and even more years later that I realized how they affected my own interests and my enthusiasm for traveling and living abroad.

While neither he nor my mom talked about it much, dad's younger life had been marked by a lot of emotional turmoil and hardship. His mother took off with another man when he was eight. Then, when he was twelve, his father left with another woman. Dad was left to live with his grandmother who, according to mom, was a very good and caring woman. After his grandmother died, dad went to live with the DeMotts, a family with twin sons who were his boyhood friends. Dad worked at various jobs while he was in high school and then worked two jobs to get through Fordham University. It wasn't surprising that his primary goal for me was getting a college degree.

After he became a science teacher, first in Cliffside Park, then in Wayne Township, New Jersey, for most of the years when I was growing up, dad worked a second job every weekday evening and all day Saturday. Teachers' pay in the 1950s was even worse relative to living costs than it is today. Dad signed up to help organize a teachers union. I remember, one night after I had gone to bed, overhearing mom speaking anxiously with him about how she supported his getting involved, but she was worried that he risked losing his public school job. The two NSF Summer Study Grants gave dad points beyond his Master's Degree. Coupled with pressure from the newly formed teachers' union, dad was able to get a higher salary. With mom working as a school secretary, dad finally shed his second job, giving him a new sense of freedom. Even though I missed spending more time with him, I admired how hard dad worked to support our family. I think I inherited my ability to work hard, as well as play hard, from dad.

As soon as school was out in June 1959, the plan was for dad to take a train across the country to San Jose and for mom, my sister Judy and I, plus our dog, Rex, to take three weeks to drive across the country in our new Ford Station Wagon. Until that summer, dad had done all the driving on family trips. Since neither I nor my sister was old enough to get a driver's license, mom would have to do all the driving on our 3,000+ mile trip to California. On reflection, it seems quite extraordinary that mom was not only willing to do all the driving; and, even though she had never been camping, she also was willing to sleep on the ground in a tent every night to save on expenses.

In the days before we were to leave for California, I loaded our station wagon, including positioning and packing a 36" x 36" x 6" plywood pantry that I had proudly constructed to carry canned and dried foods for camping. With dad away, I felt like the man of the house, an image that my mother all too often reinforced. Mom idolized me in ways that both made me feel good and also put a whole lot of pressure on me. Only later did I understand how the pressures I felt from mom's idolizing me and often talking with me like I was her grown up man caused me to miss out on some more normal teenage boy adventures and misadventures. It also took me several years before I understood how mom's favoritism toward me was really hurtful to my sister Judy.

Mom was an idealist, in both the good sense of wanting the best for everyone and the problematic sense of sometimes being certain she knew exactly what was best for others. Both my sister and I inherited mom's idealism, but we are also different. While Judy feels disappointed, and sometimes bitterly so, at the ways ideals are so often betrayed, I tend sometimes unrealistically to believe that ideals can be fulfilled. I also sometimes exhibit my mother's tendency to act as if I know what would be best for someone, a quality that can get on my family's nerves. Coming from modest circumstances ourselves and inheriting a strong sense of idealism and compassion from mom and the habits of hard work from dad, both my sister and I identify with peoples' hopes and struggles for a better life for themselves and their children. We both also empathize with the frustration and pain many people experience over the barriers they have to struggle against and how often these barriers prevent them from achieving a better life.

Looking at a map, one would assume that going to California from northern New Jersey we would start by driving west into Pennsylvania, but we wanted to see as much of the country as possible. So, we decided to start by heading north to Niagara Falls, where my parents had gone on their honeymoon. As we added our unique zigs and zags to the orange-inked route mapped out for us by the ESSO Standard Oil Company on a series of state maps, it seemed that whenever two roads diverged, we somehow managed to travel both of them.

The first night on our cross country road trip definitely didn't turn out as we hoped. We stopped in the late afternoon and set up camp in a park in the Finger Lakes District of New York, about an hour south of Niagara Falls. During the night it poured down rain. Our heavy canvas tent, borrowed from the Boy Scouts leaked and at about 3 a.m. the wooden poles and tent collapsed on top of us. The rain stopped early the next morning. We recovered enough to get a fire going, cook a breakfast of blueberry pancakes and hot chocolate, and dry our sleeping bags and tent sufficiently to pack them. As we ate our breakfast, all three of us joked and laughed about our experience. I'm sure mom must have felt some ambivalence and anxiety over what she had gotten herself into, but to her credit, she never let on. She seemed quite resilient and laughed as hard as my sister and I did at this inauspicious, water-logged start to our expedition.

Knowing my mother's parents helped me to understand mom's resilience and her ready sense of humor, two other qualities that I believe my sister and I inherited. Mom's father, John Hofer, grew up in Hell's Kitchen, a tough neighborhood along Ninth Avenue on the west side of Midtown Manhattan. A short, light-framed man, in his teens and early twenties, John did some street fighting and even participated in some amateur boxing related to the local Golden Gloves. In winter, he worked alone delivering heavy baskets of coal to tenements and businesses. In summer, he delivered block ice. Initially, he made the deliveries by horse and wagon, then later, by truck. For several years, grandpa worked as a driver for Consolidated Laundry, collecting and delivering heavy loads of bedding and towels for Manhattan hotels. He had muscles the size of tennis balls on his thin upper arms.

Even in his seventies, grandpa was still a fighter. I remember hearing about the day when he was working as an unarmed auxiliary policeman in their neighborhood park in West New York. He was confronted by three teenage toughs, whom he had ordered out of the park for some violation of park rules. As they were leaving, one of the young men turned on my grandpa and said, "Old Man, if you weren't wearing that cap and badge, we'd show you who is boss in this park." My grandfather removed his cap and badge, placed them on a park bench and said, "And now, what are you going to do?" Luckily, the boys backed down, turned and left, muttering curses. Hearing the story, the very next day, my grandmother insisted that he quit his job as park policeman. I remember going with my grandpa to a N.Y. Giants baseball game at the

Polo Grounds. A much younger and bigger guy tried to cut ahead of us in the ticket line. Grandpa blocked him physically and, pointing with his finger, said, "I think your place in line is back there." The guy muttered something, but went back to his place in line. In the summer of 1965, when I returned from Selma, my grandfather showed me newspaper stories and photos he had clipped and saved, keeping track of two of our favorite fighters, Antonio Rocca, the professional good guy wrestler, and Martin Luther King Jr.

When I knew mom's mother, Mae (Schepp) Hofer, she was no longer working. After she died and I had worked with Martin Luther King Jr., I learned from mom that in her twenties and thirties grandma worked as a union organizer in the Paterson, New Jersey silk mills. I learned that she was the first woman Truant Officer in West New York, and the first woman elected as a member of the Hudson County Democratic Council. Like her two sisters and my great aunt Ethel, who kept going strong into her nineties, grandma also had a lively and bawdy sense of humor. Remembering these qualities and experiences of my grandparents made me suspect that family DNA may have contributed to the choices and commitments I made later in life.

On the second day of our trip to California, after viewing Niagara Falls from the Canadian side, we drove deeper into Canada and camped under a clear, star-filled sky on the north shore of Lake Ontario.

On visits to Canada in recent years from our home near Seattle, I've often thought about that first family trip into Canada in 1959, and how years later during the Vietnam War, I counseled young men who decided to seek refuge in Canada to avoid the choice of going to Vietnam or going to jail. I especially remember one young man who, after having his application for Conscientious Objector turned down, was ordered for induction into the military. A woman draft counselor friend of mine carried him illegally but safely in her car's trunk across the border from New York State into Canada.

Mom, Judy and I crossed back from Canada into the USA at Windsor. Driving through Detroit, we were struck by starkly contrasting images of the city. On the one hand, there were gleaming tall glass, metal and concrete corporate headquarters of the American auto giants and, on the other hand, we drove through dilapidated, poor, primarily black neighborhoods that a decade later erupted in urban racial riots. Driving through these neighborhoods, I wondered aloud with my mom and sister, how and why is it that as white people we seem so unaware of these awful conditions?

A decade later, in 1968, responding to riots in Detroit and other cities following the murder of Martin Luther King Jr., the Kerner Commission concluded that, "The media report and write from the standpoint of a white man's world. The ills of the ghetto, the difficulties of life there, the Negro's burning sense of grievance, are seldom conveyed."[2] The Commission's Report warned, "Our nation is moving toward two societies, one black, one white —separate and unequal."[3]

From Detroit, our trip that summer took us to South Bend, Indiana and a visit to Notre Dame University. The 1940 film, *Knute Rockne, All American,* about the famous football player and coach, starring Pat O'Brien and Ronald Reagan, was a favorite of mine. I remember a part of the movie where Father John Callahan, Notre Dame's president, talks about God's will for Rockne's life. The film caused me to wonder what God meant for me to be and to do. As a sixteen-year- old, I was beginning to ask myself how I would find my right place in the world.

Passing through Chicago, I remember being impressed that this was the first city whose size and skyline seemed to rival New York's. Continuing north and west through Wisconsin and Minnesota, we crossed the Mississippi River. In South Dakota we visited the Corn Palace, with its onion-shaped Moorish domes and Wall Drug Store, the Great Depression era souvenir shop featuring faked frontier mementos. We had been seeing signs posted along the highway for several hundred miles announcing, " ___ miles to Wall Drug." I remember thinking that the Corn Palace and Wall Drug Store were both rather bizarre, but also in some ways I didn't understand uniquely American landmarks. Driving west along the southern tier of Montana toward Billings, we stopped to visit the site of Custer's Last Stand, at the time named the Custer Battlefield National Monument.

In the 1990s, remembering our family trip in 1959, I followed the evolving historical understanding of the battle during two Presidencies. In 1991, President George H.W. Bush signed a law that renamed the site more inclusively the Little Bighorn Battlefield National Monument. On a 1995 visit I made to the Monument with my wife and two sons, we read the un-romanticized details of the Battle of Little Big Horn, including the Lakota/Northern Cheyenne's side of the story. Thanks to these revisions, we were forced to think about the battle from the perspectives of both sides. On Memorial Day 1999, by order of President Clinton, red granite markers honoring the Indians who fought and died at Little Big Horn were added to those honoring the American troopers who died there. These changes are a tangible example of how the "truth" about historical events depends in part on one's point of view, the times and context in which the history of particular events gets recorded, and who records them. Personally, I learned and relearned that lesson many times, as a white living in the black community in Memphis, as a Yankee traveling in Latin America, as an American visiting South and North Vietnam during the war, and on assignment for Quakers listening to Arabs and Israelis about the Middle East conflict.

Arriving in Yellowstone National Park late one afternoon in July 1959, mom, Judy and I were surprised by a summer snowstorm. We finally found space in a campground inhabited mainly by local fishermen families. With temperatures down in

2. Report of the National Advisory Commission on Civil Disorders, 366.

3. Ibid., 1.

the low 30s that night, we didn't pitch our tent; instead, all three of us and the dog slept in our station wagon. The next morning, as we were packing up to leave, a large brown bear wandered down the dirt road through the middle of the campground. Our dog Rex wanted to attack him. The three of us scrambled rather hysterically to get ourselves and Rex safely into the car. Most of the local campers calmly continued doing whatever they were doing and one banged on a pot, shooing the bear on its way. For us, encountering a wild bear up close was a unique and dramatic experience; for the locals, the encounter seemed relatively routine. As with reflections on historical events, I understood that our very different reactions reflected our very different experiences.

Our next major stop was in Glacier National Park where, having gained confidence from almost two weeks of camping every night, we chose to camp in a beautiful, isolated primitive campsite on the shore of St. Mary Lake. We had a campfire each night, and marveled at hearing, for the first time, the sounds of loons on the lake. All three of us remembered this time as the finest and most inspiring camping experience on our trip. The day we left our campsite was beautifully clear as we drove from East to West across the mountains on Glacier Park's famous Going to the Sun Highway.

Over the next couple of days, we crossed the narrow neck of Idaho and entered Washington State. We stopped one evening in Spokane for supper at a Chinese Restaurant. When we came out of the restaurant we discovered that our dog Rex had crawled over our camping gear and gotten out of the car through the partially open back window. He was gone. The three of us walked the neighborhoods around the restaurant for hours; we got enthusiastic volunteer help from neighborhood kids on bicycles and from a local policeman on patrol. We arranged for an announcement to be aired on the local radio station's Lost Pet Program. When the Chinese Restaurant closed at about 1 a.m., the owners brought us sandwiches and sodas. At about 4 a.m., Rex returned. He seemed as glad to see us as we were to see him. While appreciating that we tended to sentimentalize the incident, mom, Judy and I, always remembered this experience as an example of how ordinary people are often willing to welcome and offer help to strangers in trouble. It doesn't always work this way, but it does more often and in more different countries and cultures than we might imagine.

After crossing the Cascades and driving around Seattle we camped for a night in Mt. Rainier National Park, where we woke to see the mountain's snow-covered dome colored pink by the rising sun. We crossed into Oregon. Then we drove out to the Coast along the Columbia River and got our first view of the Pacific where this great river pours into the ocean, creating the treacherous Columbia Bar. We visited Fort Clatsop where the Lewis and Clark expedition wintered in 1805. Feeling pleased and proud about completing our own expedition across the continent, we were eager now to get to San Jose to be reunited with dad.

After a week in northern California, we packed everything into the station wagon, and began our trip home, with dad now doing the driving. We still wanted to see more of the country and more new places, so instead of heading east toward New Jersey, we started off from San Jose going south toward Los Angeles, where we visited Disneyland, Knott's Berry Farm and Hollywood. From there we headed east to Las Vegas, southeast for a night of camping on the South Rim of the Grand Canyon, and then across New Mexico and Texas to New Orleans. Reminiscent of times that our family had gone to the Hotel Astor in New York City, as a special treat in New Orleans, dad took us to have dinner at Broussard's, a famous and very expensive restaurant in the French Quarter. Heading northeast from New Orleans, on several days we simply travelled and camped or stayed in a motel, and didn't stop to see any sites. Time was growing short for us to get home but also I think all of us, including Rex, were tired of being squeezed in our station wagon and tired of travelling.

We were enthusiastic about having travelled so far and visited so many different places. Just as later travels to other countries would expand our love of the world, our love for our country was larger and richer for having made this more than 7,000 mile cross country trip. Now, we were glad to be coming home. We all cheered when we crossed the Delaware River and reentered New Jersey. It was August 1959.

September 1959 I entered my senior year at College High School. It was a busy and good last year, keeping on top of classes, participating in three seasonal team sports, working on our yearbook, and sending off applications to colleges. Having decided to go for a liberal arts school over the Military Academy, I applied for early admission at Wesleyan University, Williams College and Princeton. I was accepted and offered generous scholarships at all three. I chose Wesleyan because it was small and because, on visits to all three schools, I felt more comfortable at Wesleyan. I felt there were fewer preppy upper class social pressures there than at the other two schools. I've always believed that I made the right choice.

In June 1960, after I graduated from College High School, my dad, our dog, and I drove across the country a second time. This time our destination was Tempe, Arizona, where dad had accepted a second National Science Foundation summer grant to study at Arizona State University. Mom and my sister followed by train a couple of weeks later. I was glad for the chance to travel alone with dad, although we still didn't talk a lot or deeply about anything very important. Having gotten my driver's license several months earlier, I was able to do my share of the driving. We had only five days to get to Arizona, so we drove several hundred miles a day, stopping only to eat and walk our dog. We stayed in motels every night. On the evening we were passing through Kansas City, dad decided that we should take a break to go to a baseball game. I think Kansas City was playing our favorite team, the New York Yankees.

My parents had rented a small house for us in Tempe for the summer. Dad and I arrived the day before his NSF program was scheduled to begin. While he started classes, I spent the next few days looking for a summer job. It was very hot in Phoenix, with daytime temperatures over 100 degrees and sometimes reaching 115. I remember how we had to coax Rex to come out from the air conditioned house to go for a walk. I found the perfect job working from 3 to 11 pm as a life guard at the fancy Mountain Shadows Resort Hotel. I was able to arrange permission for my family to swim there during the day. One day at the pool, I met a girl named Kathy who became my first girlfriend for the summer. In July, we made a two-day trip across the border to Nogales, Mexico. This was only my second time out of the United States, the first being a year earlier when we camped for a night in Ontario, Canada. After dad's program ended, our family drove together back across the country, camping a few nights, but also staying in motels. Ironically, when we were only an hour away from home, because our house at Packanack Lake was still rented, our family had to camp for several days in Stokes State Forest, where six years earlier as a new seventh grader I had gone on my College High School retreat.

It was late August 1960. A week after we got home, I packed up my clothes to go off to Middletown, Connecticut to begin my freshman year at Wesleyan University. I was the first person in my family to go away to college, and that was a big deal. It was Saturday and, as usual, dad was working at the Post Office. Mom, my sister, grandma and grandpa, our dog Rex, and I piled into our station wagon to drive me to Wesleyan. Several of my classmates arrived at college that day driving their own cars. As we carried my things from the parking lot up to my room on the fourth floor of Clark Hall, Wesleyan's oldest, funkiest dormitory, I didn't see another freshman arriving with an entourage quite like mine.

Starting my freshman year at Wesleyan was my biggest border crossing that year. My studies and the relationships I developed there would open up new challenges and opportunities for learning and for engaging the world. At the time, I could not have imagined that I would drop out of college for a year or that I would not graduate from Wesleyan University until twenty-six years later.

2

Going South: "Hey Boy, Are You One of Them Civil Rights Workers?"

Loving Wesleyan and leaving for a year; going to Memphis to work with Rev. Jim Lawson in a black Methodist church; discovering I'm a white boy and have a lot to learn about racism and what's wrong in America; learning from Rev. Lawson about what following Jesus might really mean; meeting Martin Luther King Jr.; bringing my learnings back north to Wesleyan; leaving college again to go to Selma; encountering the amazing courage of the kids; meeting a Selma policeman who was becoming a new person; making history in a small Alabama city.

IN SEPTEMBER 1962, AS a college junior, I decided to leave Wesleyan University for a year and, at the suggestion of a religion professor, move to Memphis, Tennessee to work in a Black Methodist congregation with Reverend J.M. Lawson Jr., a close colleague and friend of Martin Luther King Jr., major leader in the Freedom Movement, and dedicated disciple and teacher of nonviolence. This boundary crossing experience had such a profound influence on the rest of my life that I came to think of it as my second baptism. My original baptism was performed when I was an infant with a sprinkle of water on my forehead. Combined with the influences of my mother's religious belief and mentoring by church pastors, I grew up as a committed, enthusiastic, if somewhat naïve, young American Christian. In comparison, living in the black community in Memphis, working with Reverend Lawson felt like a baptism by full immersion, including coming to understand the radical social implications of being a follower of Jesus, and experiencing new troubling tensions between teachings of my Christian faith and existing conditions of injustice and violence in my country and the world.

When I arrived at Wesleyan as a freshman in September 1960, I certainly didn't imagine taking off a year from college. I assumed I would go through college in four years and graduate in 1964. I loved Wesleyan with its commitment to liberal arts education, relatively small size student body with about 1,200 undergraduates (unfortunately, in the early 1960s, all males), its low student to faculty ratio, easy access to professors, and its emphasis on critical thinking and civic engagement. As an example of why I loved Wesleyan, in my first week as a freshman, I was able to speak personally with Vic Butterfield, Wesleyan's president, in one of several small groups he and his wife invited into their home as part of freshmen orientation. During the time I was at Wesleyan, I got to know Mark Barlow, the Dean of Students, even better, as he was an occasional mealtime guest at Eclectic, the eating club I joined my freshman year. From the start, I experienced attending Wesleyan University as an important blessed boundary crossing on my life's journey. A college reunion I attended in 2014 confirmed my high regard for Wesleyan's unique qualities.

As a freshman, I plunged enthusiastically into my courses, including especially History of Western Civilization. While some sections of this course were taught by one professor for the entire year, I had a different professor each semester. In fall semester, my professor was Michael Cherniavsky and then in spring, Kenneth Underwood. Both men significantly, if indirectly influenced my life's path. The text for the course was R.R. Palmer's *A History of the Modern World*. Thirty years later Palmer heard me lecture at Princeton on the Arab-Israeli-Palestinian conflict and became a regular contributor to my interfaith work for peace in the Middle East.

I admired and liked both my Western Civilization professors, learned a lot from them and appreciated personally getting to know each of them. Michael Cherniavsky's primary academic interests were in Medieval European, British and Russian history. I remember being struck by how, while he challenged us to discover the lessons from the past for the present, he approached history objectively, with broad interests and sensitivity. I think it was from Cherniavsky that I first learned the difference between being objective and being cold or uncaring, and how a person can have a passionate, personal point of view on issues and still be objective. Ken Underwood had authored the book, *Protestant and Catholic*, a study of the social policy interactions and influences of the two religious communities in New Haven, Connecticut. While it wasn't on the course reading list, I read his book during the semester I had him as my professor. Later, Underwood managed the Danforth Foundation's study of campus ministries, and was highly respected for his research on the relation between moral and ethical visions, and political power and public policy. Looking back, I'm grateful to professors Michael Cherniavsky and Ken Underwood for inspiring my love of history, my critical attention to social issues, and my interest in the interaction between religion and politics. I think each in his own way indirectly influenced personal and vocational choices I made later in my life.

In 1959 Wesleyan launched three European-style colleges with even smaller seminar classes, no grades, and a lot of independent study. In September 1961, I entered the College of Social Studies, which featured colloquia and seminars in government, economics, history, sociology and philosophy; and required students to write a ten page paper every week. CSS hosted weekly luncheons and monthly dinners with interesting, sometimes famous speakers, including during my sophomore year, Dr. Martin Luther King Jr. I also audited a very popular course taught by Dr. John Maguire entitled "Religious Currents in Contemporary Literature." We listened to engaging lectures by Maguire, and discussed novels by Albert Camus, J.D. Salinger, D.H. Lawrence, James Joyce, Ernest Hemingway, Robert Penn Warren, William Faulkner, and others. I got to know John Maguire, not only as a student in his course but also as babysitter for his young daughters on evenings when John and his wife, Billie, would go out. They became lifelong, personal friends.

At the end of my freshman year, I joined Eclectic, a local fraternity with a fine reputation. Unique among fraternities, Eclectic expected its members to make two literary presentations at weekly house meetings in our junior and senior years. As juniors, each of us was expected to do a reading from any author and then as seniors, each had to read a substantial piece of fiction or non-fiction we ourselves had written. In my junior year, I recited a lengthy excerpt from the play, *Zoo Story*, by Edward Albee and in my senior year, I read a fictionalized account of real experiences I had living and working in the black community in Memphis, but that's getting ahead of my story.

Home for the summer in 1962, between my sophomore and junior years at Wesleyan, I worked two jobs and did a lot of reading and reflecting. I was preoccupied primarily with questions about personal identity and what I would do in the future, but these issues were becoming entangled with questions about religion, society and social change that were being forcefully raised by dramatic events in the civil rights movement. In the mornings, I worked at the beach soda and sandwich shop my mother leased at the lake; and most evenings, from 5 p.m. until 1 a.m., I worked as a busboy at the old, elegant Meadowbrook Dinner Theatre in Cedar Grove, New Jersey. During breaks backstage, I read books, including Martin Luther King Jr.'s *Stride Toward Freedom* and a thick collection of Reinhold Niebuhr's writings, *On Politics, Religion and Christian Faith.* My soul searching was most intensely engaged that summer by writings of the Danish existential philosopher and theologian, Soren Kierkegaard, including especially *Fear and Trembling*, his critical treatment of the Abraham and Isaac story; *Either/Or*, his two volume treatise on the aesthetic versus the ethical life; and *The Present Age*, his searing critique of society, culture and religion, echoes of which remain very relevant today.

No doubt reinforced by reading so much Kierkegaard, my mood that summer was often melancholy. I was focused personally, in admittedly a rather self-absorbed way, on existential questions about myself and my future. Who am I? What was I meant to be? What did my Christian faith really mean to me? Was there something wrong with me that, except for dating a girl for a few weeks during the summer when our family lived in Arizona, I didn't have a girlfriend? Though I hadn't acted on my feelings, I was anxious at times about being attracted to guys as well as girls, and I didn't know anyone I could talk with about these issues. It would be several more years before I would feel relatively resolved and comfortable about my bisexual orientation. While I didn't yet imagine leaving school, I was asking myself, why was I in college anyway? Reading was both a way of distracting myself from being anxious and a way of helping me think about all these questions. Even though it felt sort of weird and a bit pretentious to be reading Niebuhr, King or Kierkegaard backstage at the Dinner Theater, it was my only free time, so I did it.

The closest I came to a sexual experience that summer happened one evening at the Dinner Theatre. I came around a corner backstage carrying a large tray loaded with fifty dirty dinner plates and almost bumped into that month's star, Mamie Van Doren, who stood just outside the door to the kitchen powdering her generous, mostly bare breasts. The crash of dishes resounded through the theatre. Every night after the incident, whenever we passed each other, Ms. Van Doren would smile and give me a "come hither" wink.

Despite all my reading and soul searching, as the summer came to an end, returning to Wesleyan in the fall of 1962 seemed the right thing to do. I eagerly bought books for my courses that fall and worked with my new roommate to round-up furniture for our two rooms in the Eclectic house. I felt proud to be in Eclectic and to participate in the process of recruiting freshmen as potential pledges. In August, as part of Eclectic's process of looking over the incoming class, my family and I hosted a dozen new Wesleyan students from northern New Jersey at my cowboy house at Packanack Lake. It was not really surprising in 1962 that all of the new Wesleyan freshmen who came to our house were white, so when we went swimming, there were no complications with the lake's racial restrictions.

Having worked with my roommate to fix up our rooms in Eclectic and with classes starting that week, one night I came to the rather awkwardly-timed decision that I wanted to leave college and do something different for at least a year. It hardly felt as elevated as a calling, but it did feel like what I had to do. While the courses I would have taken that year seemed interesting and relevant, I knew that I wasn't going to be able to focus the way I would need to in order to do well. I didn't have any idea what I wanted to do for a year. I just knew I needed to get away from school.

I went to see John Maguire, my religion professor and friend, to ask if he had any ideas. Maguire grew up in the South and along with Rev. William Sloane Coffin Jr., then Chaplain down the road at Yale, he had been arrested in a 1961 interracial Freedom Ride. Maguire had just returned that fall from attending the national convention of Dr. Martin Luther King Jr.'s Southern Christian Leadership Conference (SCLC). Aware that I was considering the idea of becoming a Christian minister, Maguire asked me if I would be interested in working in a black church in Memphis, Tennessee. I was totally surprised by the idea. When I couldn't think of a reason why I shouldn't be interested, I said, "I guess so." My response sounded as tentative as I felt, so Maguire suggested that I think about it and get back to him in a day or two.

At the time, there were only a few student activists at Wesleyan, and I wasn't one of them. On the contrary, discussing freedom rides during my sophomore year, I remember arguing rather strenuously and self-righteously with one of the activists that "I agree with Martin Luther King's goals, but I don't agree with his methods, particularly his breaking the law." I definitely was not yet an activist.

John Maguire's suggestion was inspired by a brief conversation he had at the SCLC Convention with the Rev. Jim Lawson, Minister of Centenary Methodist Church in Memphis. Lawson mentioned being interested in bringing on a white associate minister at some point and Maguire thought Lawson might be interested in having me come to work with him as an intern, as a step in that direction. I called Maguire the next day to say I was interested, although I was aware that my reasoning wasn't much deeper than the day before. I really didn't know what I was getting myself into, but it seemed like an opportunity I shouldn't turn down. Maguire telephoned Lawson and told him about me. Rev. Lawson responded positively and told Maguire to send me down. I told Maguire I would go to Memphis.

Leaving Wesleyan – Going Off to Memphis

Calling my parents to tell them that I had decided to leave Wesleyan and go to Memphis to work in a black church wasn't easy. My decision was especially hard on my dad for whom getting a college degree was all-important. Dad had worked fulltime when he was in high school and worked two jobs to get through Fordham University. During all the years I was growing up, in addition to teaching, dad worked a second job on weekday evenings and often a third job on Saturdays. During the summers when school was out, he had various fulltime jobs, including a bakery delivery route, clerk in the Post Office, and head life guard at the lake where we lived. Dad simply couldn't understand why I would want to drop out of college and risk losing my nearly full scholarship.

Dad was proud that I was at Wesleyan, although I think he would have preferred my going to Princeton or West Point for their greater prestige. Even after I was clear that I preferred a liberal arts school and I might want to become a Christian minister, dad still pushed the idea of my going to West Point. "Ronnie," he said to me one day when I was sixteen, "you can get a good education for free at West Point, serve in the Army for just twenty years, retire at half pay, and then still become a minister or whatever you want to be." I understood how that seemed like a pretty good deal to my dad, but by the time I was sixteen, I knew that going to West Point and serving twenty years in the army was not the path for me.

Even years later, my dad didn't seem to understand, let alone appreciate, how I felt I needed to drop out of college. He hardly talked with me at all about what I did during the year I took off or what I did later. In part because he worked several jobs while I was growing up and then because my parents lived out of the country

1964–68, most of the time, dad was more absent than present. After I dropped out of college and during the two decades before I finally graduated, dad would occasionally prod me about the importance of getting my college degree. Much to my relief and joy, he was genuinely pleased and proud when, in 1986 at forty-four years old, I submitted the book I wrote on the Middle East as my senior thesis for the College of Social Studies and received my Bachelor of Arts degree from Wesleyan University. My parents, my sister and her husband, and my five year old son Jonah came to my graduation ceremony. Carol was working at a hospital in Seattle as part of her seminary education and couldn't come. After the ceremony, I remember dad reaching up to adjust the tassel on my graduation cap, explaining how it had to be switched from one side to the other to signify that I had graduated.

My mom, who, as I already wrote, tended to idolize me, was anxious about what my decision to leave college meant and about whether I would return to finish in the future. Without knowing all the details, she was aware that I had been doing a lot of soul searching that summer. Initially, when I decided to leave school, she was worried about what I would do for the year off and, like my dad, also worried about my losing my scholarship. When I told her about the idea of my working in a black church in Memphis, this fit with her commitment to church and appealed to her sense of idealism. She appreciated that the work sounded worthwhile. However, given news stories at the time about violence by whites against civil rights workers, she was also understandably scared. To her credit, she didn't give voice to her worries and basically supported my decision.

At home for a few days before leaving for Memphis, we didn't talk much about what I was going to do, partly because of dad's strong negative feeling about my leaving college and partly because what I was going to do still seemed unclear and a bit unreal to me. Frankly, I didn't know much myself. Leaving school was a big decision, but it felt to me as if I had to do it, even though I was uncertain about the year ahead and how it would affect my future. The flight from New York to Memphis was my first time on an airplane. It was a Saturday and, like the Saturday when I went off to college, Dad was working at the Post Office. My mother and sister drove me to Long Island to see me off on the American Airlines flight from Idlewild Airport (later named John F. Kennedy International Airport).

Rev. Lawson told me in a telephone call the day before that when I arrived at the Memphis Airport, I should take a taxi to the YMCA since the Y was within easy walking distance of the church. He sounded warm over the phone and said he looked forward to seeing me in church on Sunday. After I got settled in what turned out to be the downtown YMCA, I called Rev. Lawson and told him that when I looked at the city map, I was confused about the church's location in relation to the Y. When I told Lawson the address where I was staying, he laughed and said, "Aha, Ron, you're at the 'white Y,' aren't you?" In 1962 in Memphis and in a lot of other cities in the South there was both a Young (white) Men's Christian Association and a Young (black) Men's

Christian Association. Since I was white, it was natural for the taxi driver, who also was white, to take me to the white Y. Given my ignorance about segregation, I guess it was also understandable that Rev. Lawson had to help me figure this out. There were many times during that year in Memphis, when he needed to orient me to where I was and what was going on. Rev. Lawson gave me directions to get to his church the next morning by city bus, and then suggested since I had already checked in and for the convenience of being downtown, I might as well stay there temporarily. He said again that he looked forward to meeting me and invited me to come to the Parsonage next door after church to have Sunday dinner with him and his wife, Dorothy.

I remember going to bed that first night in Memphis feeling alone, and ambivalent and anxious about my decision, but I was really tired and slept soundly. I arrived the next morning at Centenary Methodist Church, a modest-sized white wood and brick building south of downtown at the corner of Alston Avenue and Mississippi Boulevard. I was warmly welcomed by elderly ushers at the door and found a seat near the middle of the sanctuary. The Methodist service felt familiar, although both Rev. Lawson's preaching and the choir's and congregation's singing were more spirited than what I was used to back home at Packanack Lake Community Church. I was the only white person at the service, as earlier that morning I had been the only white person riding on the bus from downtown. This was a totally new experience for me. Up until that day, I had never been with any black persons, except in passing on the street or in a store in New York City or Paterson. My experience that Sunday made me think, for the first time in my life, how it must feel to be the only black person among all whites, and how that's different from my experience because in most situations whites hold most of the power. Rev. Lawson made no special introduction of me during announcements to the congregation, but after the service in the greeting line, he repeated his invitation for me to come next door for Sunday dinner.

At the Parsonage, Rev. Lawson's lovely wife, Dorothy, greeted me warmly and I met their four year old son, John, for whom I became the primary babysitter that year on the rare occasions when Jim and Dorothy went out together. After a great meal that Dorothy had prepared, Rev. Lawson invited me to sit with him in the living room. He explained the background to his invitation for me to come to work at Centenary. It became clear that, prompted by the call from Professor Maguire, his decision to invite me was quite spontaneous and that the church lay leadership had not yet made any decision about this project. He explained that he had work to do with the church council before my internship would become official and public. At the recent SCLC Convention, in a brief conversation with Maguire, Lawson had shared his vision of wanting to create an interracial ministry at the church as a step toward building an interracial congregation. He had not yet shared his vision with the congregation and he acknowledged, given the realities of conservative, segregated Memphis, bringing on a young white staff associate might make some members of the congregation nervous. Adding to the challenge, he had only been Pastor at Centenary for a year and his leadership of the nonviolent sit-ins campaign in Nashville may already have made some members nervous.

Rev. Lawson confessed to me that he had eagerly and enthusiastically jumped at Maguire's description of me and at my willingness to come to Memphis. He said he was pretty confident that the Council would approve the project, but it might take a few weeks. If it didn't work out, he told me that he would arrange for me to go to work with Dr. King at Ebenezer Baptist Church in Atlanta. The idea of working with Martin Luther King Jr. was exciting, but as it turned out, I am really glad I got to work with Rev. Lawson. He traveled less than King so I got to spend more time with him, and I came to appreciate that his understanding of nonviolence and of international issues at that time probably was deeper and more sophisticated than King's. When Lawson told me that he had not yet talked with the church leadership, of course I was surprised, but in the context of my rather sudden decision to leave school and the uniqueness of this situation, the uncertainty didn't seem unreasonable. In talking by phone that night with my mother, I downplayed the uncertainties, told her about how warmly I had been greeted at church and by the Lawson family at their home, and reassured her that "things are going well." That seemed to be what she needed to hear and, in reassuring her, I helped to reassure myself.

In the weeks that followed, I attended worship at Centenary Methodist Church each Sunday morning. I'm sure some members of the congregation wondered why this white boy was coming every Sunday. Perhaps some members were even nervous, but no one asked me anything and everyone was very friendly. The consultation process went on slowly for several weeks, in part because of Lawson's frequent trips to preach and lead workshops on nonviolence in other cities around the South. During these weeks, I did a lot of reading, including *Black Like Me*, by John Howard Griffin.[1] Griffin was a white Texas journalist who colored himself with shoe polish and chemicals to pass for being black and wrote about his experiences travelling by public transportation through Alabama, Georgia, Louisiana and Mississippi. Although he wrote about the two worlds, one white and one black, that I was getting to know and about many of the same realities of segregation I was experiencing in Memphis, my experience was different from Griffin's. While actually white, he wrote about experiencing racism and segregation as a black person. I wasn't pretending to be black. I was white and was at the beginning of a baptismal process as a twenty year old white person becoming immersed in Memphis' black community.

While waiting on the church's decision about my internship, I met a couple of times a week with Rev. Lawson who suggested books for me to read and engaged me in challenging discussions. I realized that I was being treated to a unique and invaluable private tutorial. Not only was I fortunate to have Jim Lawson as an extraordinary teacher and role model, but my being white living in a Southern black community was a unique context in which to learn about race relations and social change.

1. Griffin, *Black Like Me*.

With Jim Lawson as my teacher, I did a lot of rethinking about the implications of my Christian faith.

Books I read during that first year in Memphis that had significant impact on my thinking included: *Race and the Renewal of the Church* by Will D. Campbell, a southern white Christian with whom Dorothy Lawson had worked in Nashville; *An American Dilemma*, Gunner Myrdal's classic work on race relations; *Gandhi: An Autobiography*; G.H.C. Macgregor's, *The New Testament Basis of Pacifism*; Leo Tolstoy, *The Kingdom of God is Within You*; Richard B. Gregg's, *The Power of Nonviolence*; *Of Holy Disobedience*, a classic pamphlet on nonviolence by A.J. Muste; and *Peace Agitator: The Story of A.J. Muste* by Nat Hentoff. As important and shaping as these books have been for my faith and life, if I had not come to Memphis and worked with Jim Lawson, I suspect I would never have read any of them. Frankly, I might not have even known about several of them.

Reflecting over the years on my relationship with Jim Lawson, obviously, his being black and my being white meant there were huge differences in our life experiences. Still, in some important ways, I came to realize that my life commitments imitated his. As a student at Baldwin-Wallace College in Ohio in the early 1950s, Jim joined the Fellowship of Reconciliation (FOR), led at that time by A.J. Muste. In 1962 at twenty years old, I left college to go to Memphis to work for Lawson and, with his encouragement, I joined the FOR. In the mid-1950s, Jim refused cooperation with the draft, did time in prison, and served as Southern Field Secretary of the FOR. In the mid-1960s, I refused cooperation with the draft, served as FOR's National Director of Youth Work and worked with A.J. Muste in the formation of the anti-Vietnam War movement. Lawson deepened his understanding of and commitment to nonviolence as a short term missionary in India. I developed my commitment to nonviolence working with Lawson in Memphis. Clearly, in leading the successful Nashville nonviolent sit-in campaign and in his role shaping the vision and strategies for the Southern Christian Leadership Conference (SCLC) and the Student Nonviolent Coordinating Committee (SNCC), Jim Lawson was a major leader of the civil rights movement. While I did not play nearly as central a role in the anti-Vietnam War movement, I did play a leadership role in several national projects, including as a leader of the national draft resistance movement and as coordinator of the November 15, 1969 and May 9, 1970 marches on Washington for Peace in Vietnam. While my commitments were not nearly as radical, consistent or courageous as Jim Lawson's, it is clear that his life became model for mine.

Several weeks into the fall, Rev. Lawson encouraged me to drop the "Reverend" and "Mrs." Lawson and call them Jim and Dorothy. As his discussions with Church Council leaders about my possible internship continued, Jim kept me informed about developments. At one point, when it seemed the discussions were bogging down, Jim did call Dr. King about the possibility of my going to work with him at Ebenezer Baptist Church in Atlanta. Jim told me that King responded positively to the idea.

It wasn't surprising that the process of coming to a decision at Centenary took some time. There was a history of strong, sometimes violent, resistance to desegregation in Memphis, a city heavily influenced by the conservative culture and racial politics of Mississippi next door to the south. I imagined that at least some Centenary members, many of whom had grown up in Mississippi, may have been worried that taking on a white boy intern could cause serious trouble for the church. Their worries about possible trouble were compounded by their knowledge that only two years earlier in Nashville, Jim Lawson had trained hundreds of black college students in nonviolence and led mass, nonviolent demonstrations in a powerful campaign of civil disobedience to end segregation in public facilities. While to a person I'm sure all of the church's members supported the changes being accomplished by the Civil Rights Movement, some understandably may have been nervous about the potential violent reactions by whites.

The story of Rev. Lawson's unique leadership role in the Nashville nonviolent civil rights campaign was movingly portrayed in *A Force More Powerful (2000)*, the book and PBS film that tell the stories of several successful campaigns of nonviolent resistance. In 2008, the history of the campaign was also presented in a wonderful exhibit that my wife and I got to visit at the Nashville Public Library. In 1960 Jim Lawson was expelled from the seminary of Vanderbilt University because of his civil rights activity; in 2005 Vanderbilt invited Lawson to teach and named him a Distinguished University Alumnus.

After several weeks, I was invited to meet with the Church Council to be interviewed before they voted on the internship proposal. The interview proceeded positively. My responses to their questions were both honest and humble, closely reflecting the personal humility I certainly was feeling at the time. Jim Lawson told me later that evening that just before the vote, seventy-year-old Clarence Chapman, a member of the Council who grew up in Mississippi, stood up and made a brief speech. "Now, just like all of you," Chapman said, "I'm nervous about this project and I have many questions, including whether this young white man, Ronald, has skills or experience to make a real contribution to Centenary. But he's come down here to help us and wants to work with us." Then mirroring my own thinking in deciding to go to Memphis, Chapman said simply: "This is an opportunity God has given us that we just can't turn down." The Council voted unanimously to hire me. All during the time I worked at Centenary, Clarence Chapman, Myrtle Donoho and many older members of the congregation provided consistent, warm, strong support. To this day, I feel very grateful and blessed by my relationships with members of Centenary, and by the many ways they adopted, educated and encouraged me.

The Council decided that my duties at Centenary would include teaching senior high Sunday school, working with the Methodist Youth Fellowship and the Boy Scout troop, and organizing a church baseball team in conjunction with WDIA, the local Black radio station that provided all the equipment and uniforms. I would also do youth work in the neighborhood around the church, which included a large low income housing project named Lemoyne Gardens. The job description sounded very normal for a youth ministry position at any church. However, since I was white, the Minister and all the church members were black, and it was 1962 in Memphis Tennessee, objectively, this project was a part of the growing movement for change. Later, when I compared my experience with that of others my age who came south as civil rights activists, I was grateful to have had an ordinary church job during those extraordinary times. As I became a national activist and organizer myself during the Vietnam War, my initial experience working in a local church helped me to remain grounded in relation to the realities of people's daily lives and not to overestimate or overly romanticize the role of outside activists.

When Centenary decided to take me on as intern, there was no funding to support the project. Over the weeks and months, Jim managed it get bits and pieces of funding from different pockets in the church budget, but mostly I supported myself with money I had saved over the summer for college. In June 1963, nine months into my work at Centenary, I traveled by Greyhound bus from Memphis to Montreat, a Presbyterian retreat center in western North Carolina for a meeting of the Student Interracial Ministry (SIM), a program started in 1960 by a group of students at Union Theological Seminary in New York City. SIM placed black seminarians in white churches and white seminarians in black churches as summer interns. Thanks to Rev. Lawson's influence, my internship at Centenary was accepted as part of SIM, even though I was not a seminary student. As a result, Centenary was able to get some funding.

After several weeks living at the white Y and several months at the black Y, in the summer of 1963 and the next summer, Jim arranged for me to live in the small house of an elderly woman member of the church. To get to the church, I took a bus or borrowed the Lawsons' VW Beetle at night and returned it in the morning. I never had an apartment of my own where I could cook, so all during my time at Centenary, Jim and Dorothy and other members of the church provided me with most of my meals.

Living and working in Memphis' black community opened my eyes and mind about race relations in more ways, faster and more deeply than any books on race or courses in college could possibly have done. I became aware again how isolated and ignorant I was growing up white. In Memphis the lines of racial separation and segregation meant that basically there were two separate and profoundly unequal cities, one black and the other white. Just as there was a white YMCA and black YMCA, there were black neighborhoods and white neighborhoods, black schools and white schools, black churches and white churches. There were white hotels and restaurants, some quite elegant and expensive, like the famous, historic Hotel Peabody, and black motels and restaurants, mostly modest, like the Lorraine Motel where Dr. King was assassinated on April 4, 1968. There were a few black movie theatres but many white ones, some with shabby balconies reserved for blacks. There were predominantly black bus routes and predominantly white bus routes. Downtown stores and many other public businesses had "white only" restrooms and drinking fountains and some but not all also had restrooms and drinking fountains designated "colored." There were two cities, one white and one black, with very few places where they intersected, and wherever they did, it was very clear that whites held most of the power. I spent almost all my time in black Memphis.

From the viewpoint of the white Memphis police, I was out of place in the black community. During the initial months of my living and working there, I was stopped several times by police, searched every time, and one time physically poked and pushed around with their night sticks. The police warned me, "Boy, this neighborhood ain't safe and you don't belong here." Eventually I guess, like it or not, the police accepted that I was a regular in the black community. In a relatively short time, I felt very much at home there and, even though I was white, I felt nervous when occasionally I ventured into white parts of the city.

In addition to personally encountering the realities of segregation and two separate, unequal cities, I had much to learn about how vicious and violent whites' racism toward blacks could be. During the time I lived at the white YMCA downtown, I was befriended by J.W., a white man in his sixties. Once he discovered – given my accent it was easy – that I was from up North, J.W. took it as his personal mission to educate me about race relations in America, often while we showered or brushed our teeth in the bathroom we shared. He boasted about his active work with the White Citizens Council. After a while I suspected that J.W. might also be active in the Ku Klux Klan. He explained to me how, "Nigras are different from whites and definitely not as smart. They can laugh a lot, and be friendly, but they also can be violent and dangerous." He told me in a matter-of-fact tone: "Nigras are kinda like monkeys" and "you *gotta* understand, they really like being separate just as much as whites do." J.W. also explained how it was "them nigger-loving Kennedys" and "that smart 'Monkey Luther King'" who were stirring up all the trouble." He was very clear that "All these troubles are goin' lead to no good." He believed the troubles absolutely needed to be stopped, and he told me how he was working with men who knew for sure how to stop them, once and for all. J.W. also tried to convince me that the troubles were connected with what he believed the "*commonists*" (communists) were doing to take over America. Listening to him was both eerie and scary. He said all these things with a combination of what seemed like genuine personal warmth toward me and venomous, violent hatred toward blacks.

Growing up in New Jersey, I had known several political conservatives. I had many friendly arguments with a favorite conservative neighbor at Packanack Lake, who was a big fan of the book *Atlas Shrugged* by Ayn Rand and a strong supporter of Senator Barry Goldwater. But I never had met someone who had ideas like J.W. Sometimes it seemed clear that he believed there were only two alternatives, as he actually said to me at one point, "Either the nigras stay in their place or we're goin' kill 'em."

Given my tendency to be outgoing and friendly, even with someone like J.W., my initial inclination was to listen patiently and engage him in more conversation. He was my first experience with violent rhetoric that might lead to actual, physical violence. Fortunately, for my own personal safety and that of the church, and thanks to cautionary advice from Jim Lawson, I managed not to share any details with J.W. about what I was doing in Memphis or where I went during the day. J.W. seemed much more interested in spreading his venomous ideas than in learning anything about me, so that worked out okay.

Writing my memoir in 2011 and recalling J.W.'s extreme views and violent rhetoric, I was struck by the similarities with some of the gross lies and hateful, often overtly racist rhetoric that was directed at Barack Obama after he became president. As I later also learned about anti-Semitism working on Middle East issues, racism is a persistent, deep disease in persons and in society. While we have made progress, thinking we have eliminated racism or anti-Semitism is a dangerous delusion.

The month I arrived in Memphis was marked by an event that represented historic progress in the civil rights movement. On September 10, 1962 the Fifth Circuit Federal Court ordered the University of Mississippi, known as Ole Miss, to admit James H. Meredith as the first black student to enroll in the University Law School. In response to the court's decision, on September 29 at a football game, Ole Miss students sang, "Never, No Never." The next day, accompanied by US Assistant Attorney General John Doar and U.S. Marshalls, James Meredith arrived on campus. Encouraged by Governor Ross Barnett's defiant rhetoric and calls for resistance, a riot erupted on campus and spread through the town of Oxford, about an hour's drive south of Memphis. Two people were killed by gunfire, scores of marshals and protestors were injured and more than 300 persons were arrested. Reports of the events surrounding James Meredith's enrolling in Ole Miss continued to be the focus of major news stories in the press and on TV. As I spoke with members of Centenary Church about these events I learned that they all supported the court decision, but many naturally also were upset by the eruption of violence and anxious about possible racial repercussions in Memphis.

Shortly after the events at Ole Miss, I met the only other white person that I got to know in Memphis. One Sunday morning, a nicely dressed, middle-aged white man came to worship at Centenary. I spoke with him briefly after the service and learned that his name was Peter. He was a native of Mississippi who lived most of the time in Greenwich Village, New York. When Peter returned to church the next Sunday, I accepted his invitation to go out for dinner. From his effeminate accent and manners, I guessed that Peter was homosexual. Now in his fifties, Peter had grown up in Columbus, Mississippi, near the Alabama state line. His mother worked at Mississippi State College for Women (MSCW) which was founded in 1884 as the nation's first public women's college.

Peter grew up immersed in the racially segregated but somewhat progressive atmosphere of the women's college. Author and photographer Eudora Welty was MSCW's most famous alumna, and Peter was proud that he possessed one of her works in the small art and bookstore he owned in New York City's Greenwich Village. When I met him, Peter was making occasional trips down from New York to Mississippi to visit his elderly mother. While he was there, he came up to Memphis some weekends, confessing that he needed to escape from Columbus' rather claustrophobic atmosphere.

Over a few dinners we had together that fall, Peter and I talked a lot about the conflict over James Meredith's enrolling in the University of Mississippi. I learned that Peter knew James Silver, a retired 'Ole Miss' History Professor who became a friend and advisor to Meredith, and in 1964 authored the book, *Mississippi, The Closed Society*. Peter's stories and insights about the South, white Southerners, and the complex relationships with blacks provided me with a very different perspective from J.W.'s. Peter also offered important personal commentaries on what I had learned about race relations from reading William Faulkner's novels and listening to Maguire's lectures on Faulkner at Wesleyan. Despite the crippling effects of prejudice and racism on all of us, a big difference between the North and the South in our country is that whereas many northern whites, including myself, could grow up and live our entire lives without ever relating personally to any black persons, most southern whites had personal relationships with blacks, even if the relationships were stunted and corrupted by racism, the system of segregation, and radical inequalities of power. Peter and I became good friends. Neither of us expressed any romantic interest in the other and I never talked with Peter about my own bisexual orientation. Sadly, I lost contact with him in 1965.

A couple of months after I arrived in Memphis, Dr. Martin Luther King Jr. came to preach at Centenary and meet with Rev. Lawson to discuss strategies for SCLC. It was clear that there was a very strong bond of affection and respect between the two men. After church, King came for Sunday dinner at the Lawsons' home. I had met King briefly when he lectured at the College of Social Studies during my sophomore year at Wesleyan, but this was the first time I met and spoke personally with him. I really appreciated meeting King, the man. What struck me most about him that day and on a few other occasions when I met him was how warm, relaxed and personable he was. Sitting together with him in the Lawsons' living room, Dr. King asked me questions about my life, my family, and my future plans. We talked about football. We laughed a lot and I learned that King had a very lively, warm sense of humor.

In addition to witnessing Dr. King's extraordinary qualities as preacher and prophet, I was privileged to meet him at the Lawsons' home several more times, and to know Martin King, the man, at least a little bit in this more personal way. In a 2008 visit to the memorial museum at the Lorraine Motel, my wife and I learned that the last thing King did before walking out onto the motel balcony where he was shot and killed was to provoke a pillow-fight with two of his SCLC staff colleagues. I've often shared that story with children and adults to remind us of Martin King's humanity and sense of humor and to remind us that, rather than an historical icon, he was a person like each of us.

King had an amazing capacity to remember and care about people he met. As an example, my sister Judy met Dr. King only one time. After one of several times King spoke at Wesleyan University, Judy and I drove him, his wife Coretta, and Wyatt T. Walker to New York City, where he was scheduled to speak and receive an honorary degree at the Jewish Theological Seminary, at the invitation of Rabbi Abraham Joshua Heschel. Several months later, I encountered Dr. King in Lincoln, Nebraska, as he entered a huge auditorium to address the Methodist Student Movement National Convention. Greeting me, King asked, "How are you Ron, and how is your sister, Judy?"

What was profoundly true about both Martin Luther King Jr. and Jim Lawson, and a basic reason they inspired so many people is that both of them projected a hopeful, positive vision of the future, even as they struggled against stubborn conditions of injustice, oppression and violence. Beyond the goal of justice, both spoke often and movingly about seeking the beloved community and expressed confidence in the human potential to transform our lives for the good.

Both men preached that message. Even more amazingly, in the face of very difficult conditions and challenges they faced, both men lived as if they really believed it. They shared a profound sense of the connections between the Christian vision of a New Jerusalem and the best of American ideals, and they believed deeply in the importance of bringing very different people together to work for justice and peace.

In 2003, I was privileged to meet and become a friend of Imam Feisal Abdul Rauf, founder of the Cordoba Initiative and leader of the project to build an Interfaith Center near the site where the World Trade Towers stood. Feisal's book, *What's Right with Islam: A New Vision for Muslims and the West,* presents a hopeful Islamic vision closely analogous to King's and Lawson's for a better American and world future. Mirroring their sense of connections between Christian and American ideals, including a principled preference for nonviolence, Feisal's book explores parallels between Islamic and American ideals.

For King and Lawson, and for Imam Feisal, though not a pacifist, rejecting violence, making a principled commitment to nonviolence, is essential to realizing their vision of a better future. At the same time, I observed personally how the tension was always there between believing and pursuing the dream and confronting the daunting, often death-delivering realities of injustice, oppression and violence. A stark example of this tension was that less than a month after his historic, inspiring, "I Have a Dream" speech at the March on Washington in August 1963, King had to travel to Birmingham, Alabama to deliver the "Eulogy for the Martyred Children," honoring the four young black children murdered by a terrorist bomb blast as they attended Sunday School at the 16th Street Baptist Church. While King's and Lawson's vision of a better future and their commitment to nonviolence inspired me, living in the black community, and experiencing the grinding realities of racism and poverty provided powerful daily reminders of the challenges we face working to fulfill their vision.

King is gone, Romero is gone, Mandela is gone, but their visions, the examples and inspiration of their lives are still very much with us. We live, as they did, in the tension of the in-between time, between the hopes and vision for America—and the world—that can be, but is not yet. And we live and move toward that possible better future in a great company of contemporary witnesses, in the company of a "cloud of witnesses" who have gone before us, and in the blessed hopeful company of younger people who are coming after us.

A few months after I arrived in Memphis, a terrible incident occurred that reflected the harsh realities of racism and segregation. A white Memphis police officer drove his police cruiser very fast through a stop sign at the edge of the Lemoyne Gardens housing project, with neither his siren nor his flasher turned on. He hit and killed a six-year-old black boy named James Wicks. It was commonplace for white police officers to come through the black projects with little regard for the people who lived there. James was the younger brother of Edward Wicks, whom I knew as a funny, awkward twelve- year-old member of the church's Boy Scout troop and baseball team. I had been to the Wicks' apartment in the projects several times. With my encouragement, Edward's mother, who worked six days a week cleaning houses for white families and didn't regularly attend church, arranged with Rev. Lawson to hold a memorial service for James at Centenary. She asked me to give the eulogy. As the day approached for the memorial, people's feelings in the neighborhood became all the more bitter as a result of rumors that the white police officer who killed James apparently wasn't experiencing any serious negative consequences in the Memphis Police Department.

I struggled with what I could conceivably say at the memorial service. Some people tried to console themselves and the family by saying, "the boy's death was God's will." That response made me sick. There was no way I could accept that. Jim Lawson encouraged me to look at Paul's Letter to the Romans, Chapter 8, verses 38 and 39 that read, "There is nothing—absolutely nothing—that can separate us from the love of God." Strengthened and guided by this text, I read it aloud at the service and was able to offer a eulogy that day with tears and rage swelling up in me. I said, "James death was not God's will. Indeed, God cries out with us over James' death, but God's love for James and for us is strong and enduring. God's incredible love for us and our love for one another will somehow get us through this." After the service, James' mother embraced me and, through her tears, thanked me for my words.

That text from Romans never again seemed abstract or theoretical to me, and I could never hear it read without thinking of James and Edward and their mother. I felt blessed to know the Wicks family and, as happened many other times, I experienced the irony that this family in their grief gave inspiration to me; people who are suffering much so often give much to those of us who are suffering less.

I especially remember two other black families in Memphis who faced harsh conditions and yet embodied a spirit that inspired me. The families lived in North Memphis where Centenary supported a small church mission in a rundown house out of which I worked with young teenagers in the neighborhood. The first family included an elderly widowed grandmother who was 80 percent blind and her twelve-year-old grandson, Joe. Joe was a bright, feisty kid with more than a chip on his shoulder, but also with real leadership potential. From the time I first met him, I thought Joe's chances of his potential being tapped for good seemed small. Already he had been picked up a few times by police for stealing, mostly food and sundry from local grocery stores. He frequently skipped school and got into fights in the neighborhood. I thought of my grandfather growing up in Hell's Kitchen and how simply because my grandfather was white and lived in New York, his chances of surviving and thriving had been a lot better than Joe's as a young black kid growing up in Memphis in 1963.

I remember visiting Joe and his grandmother in their small apartment one day. Joe's grandmother offered me a glass of milk. When she opened the refrigerator, I saw that it was basically empty, except for a quart of milk and a loaf of Wonder Bread. I thanked her for the glass of milk and drank it. Later that day, I bought a quart of milk and gave it to Joe to take home, telling him to thank his grandmother. She was very grateful for my friendship with Joe, including my getting him involved in Boy Scouts and taking him and a dozen other boys on a weekend camping trip. But after a few months, Joe dropped out of Scouts, and, basically, out of sight. When I went to their apartment, it was empty. Joe and his grandmother were gone, and neighbors didn't know what had happened to them, although one thought Joe might have been arrested. I checked with the police but found no record. I felt badly to lose contact with Joe and his grandmother. I never saw them again.

Another family, the Winfrey's, included the dad, Clarence, who drove a long distance truck, the mom, Sarah, who, like Mrs. Wicks, cleaned houses for white families, and their four children. Although both parents worked full time, the Winfreys lived in a very poor housing project and hardly made ends meet. I worked mainly with their older son, Clarence, Jr. who was outgoing, warm, strong, fourteen-year-old, and quite a good baseball player. The Winfreys invited me to come to their house one evening for dinner. Climbing the stairs to their second floor apartment in a rundown building, I was aware of the strong smell of urine. Their apartment was small. The living room had a couch and two tattered, stuffed chairs. We ate on a plywood table top over a card table with six folding chairs and an old stool. Mrs. Winfrey served fried chicken, mashed potatoes, collard greens and Kool Aid. Participating in this meal made me feel the way I often feel in our congregation receiving Holy Communion, profoundly humbled and thankful for God's generous love and the experience of diverse community

Most of my experiences working in Memphis were not at all dramatic, but many of them contributed to my ongoing learning process about racism, segregation, and poverty. Several times in my first months at Centenary I naively suggested an activity for the church's Youth Fellowship only to be reminded by the youth that because of segregation, "we can't do that" or "we can't go there." While separation and segregation was still the common practice, as some public places became open to all, a few times black teenagers from the church and I decided to ride on a bus or go to some public facility, i.e., to "do that" or "go there" together. Fortunately, while our racially mixed group generated quite a few puzzled looks from blacks and dismayed and even hostile stares from whites, we did not experience any violence. Those times when the black teenagers and one white guy did something new together, we recognized that in a modest way we were participating in changes taking place in Memphis and in our country.

Another learning experience for me about race relations was when I realized I was no longer having trouble distinguishing different faces of black people who were members of the congregation or who lived in the neighborhood. Conscious that my reaction was a stereotype many whites believed to be true, I felt ashamed during my first few months in the black community confusing several people, thinking, "They look alike." Later in my time in Memphis, having gotten to know people personally, I wondered how I ever could have been so blind and stupid. It was wonderfully humorous when, one Sunday evening, sitting around together after a Youth Fellowship meeting, several black teenagers shared funny stories about how when I first came into the neighborhood, blacks saw me simply as "that white guy," and often confused me with other white guys, e.g. a mailman, delivery man or even a policeman who occasionally came into the neighborhood. Then over time people's perceptions of me changed as they came to know my name and what I was doing in their neighborhood. I was relieved when the teenagers told me that for many blacks relating to me, in the beginning, they thought, "all whites look alike."

Another important personal breakthrough occurred when, about three months into my internship, the Church Council rejected a proposal I brought regarding a Youth Fellowship program. After the meeting, seeing that I was disappointed, Rev. Lawson gently pointed out that, despite my lack of experience, up until that meeting, the Council had consistently given almost automatic approval to every idea I presented. "Well, of course," Jim said smiling, "after all, Ron, you are white, so your ideas must be right." I joined Lawson in a few minutes of embarrassed laughter, celebrating this instance of progress and recognizing how slow I was to perceive what had been happening earlier. Part of me was tempted to want to keep things as they were, so that my ideas would always get positive responses, but more of me welcomed this breakthrough to real, even if less predictable, relationships.

Occasionally, I went somewhere or did something that blacks in Memphis could legally do, but still, either from fear or habit or both, most blacks still avoided. One

Saturday in November 1962, I wanted to go to a Memphis State University football game. I asked Jim if he thought it was okay for me to go to the game and if he wanted to go with me. He said he wasn't interested, but it was fine for me to go. Lawson, who had been a college athlete and a member of the Fellowship of Christian Athletes, was generally quite critical of southern college sports, not just because he opposed segregation, but also because, as he rightly pointed out, the Southern teams were not nearly as good as they could have been if they had included black athletes. Given my almost total immersion in the black community in Memphis, I felt somewhat out of place going to the game. When I entered the stadium that Saturday with the 99 percent white crowd, I felt as if I was undercover, pretending to be a regular white guy. Once at the game, given my love of football, it felt pretty natural. It all worked fine and I felt comfortable up until halftime when a small plane flew low over the stadium and dropped thousands of tiny leaflets, the size of fortune cookie papers, with the ugly message: "Take a Nigger to lunch!" I felt sick to my stomach and, for a moment, I was tempted to stand up and protest, but instead I simply got up and quietly left the stadium. Except for mentioning the incident to Jim Lawson, who shook his head but didn't seem surprised, I didn't speak about it with any of the black teenagers or adult members of the church. I felt ashamed and guilty about the incident. Even though I was disgusted by the leaflet, I was very aware that, regardless of my views, I was still and always would be a white guy, even if not a regular white guy.

Several months into my time in Memphis, a white friend of mine from back in New Jersey asked me in a letter if I ever felt afraid living in the black community. I wrote him that while occasionally I was aware of blacks looking at me suspiciously, with what seemed like some hostility lurking below the surface, most of the time around the church's neighborhood, I felt very comfortable and welcomed. There was only one occasion when I felt frightened. The incident occurred in January 1963, after I had moved from the downtown white Y to the black Y much nearer to the church. I was walking back to the Y from the church at about 10 o'clock at night. At one point Mississippi Boulevard passes through a twenty-foot-long tunnel under a railroad bridge. Lights in the tunnel were often broken and at night the passage was usually very dark. As I entered the tunnel, I was aware of three young black men walking behind me. One of them was swinging a tire chain rather menacingly and, while I couldn't hear what they were saying, they were joking and laughing with each other. As we passed through the tunnel, I could hear them walking faster until they were within eight or ten feet behind me. Thinking of Rev. Lawson and what I had learned from him about nonviolence, as we emerged from the tunnel, I stopped, turned around and faced the three guys. I took a step toward them and held out my hand saying "Hey, I'm Ron, I work at Centenary Methodist Church at Mississippi and Alston. What are your names? We're heading the same way, why don't we walk together." They seemed totally surprised, then relaxed and each of them said his name.

I don't know what their intentions had been, but we now walked on together, with each of us introducing himself a bit more fully. I explained that I lived at the YMCA. One of them said he was still in high school, the other two said they were out of school and looking for jobs. We parted a few blocks from the Y. I felt good about how I had responded and also lucky at how this encounter had turned out. I recognized that another situation like this might end differently. In this case, whatever tension and danger may have existed seemed to have melted.

One of my most memorable learning experiences was a trip I took with Jim Lawson down into Mississippi. In 1962–63, Jim made frequent solo car trips from Memphis to small towns in the Delta of Mississippi for meetings and training sessions with local blacks about registering to vote and the practice of nonviolence. I asked him if I could go with him on one of these trips. Initially, he said it was too dangerous. Jokingly he said, "even if you rode in the back seat and I pretended to be your chauffer Ron, we would not fool anyone in my VW Beetle convertible." Respecting Jim's judgment about the dangers, I didn't ask him again. Then, a few months later, he asked me if I was still interested in going with him. I said yes, and the next night we drove to Ruleville, Mississippi, about an hour south of Memphis. Before leaving Memphis, Jim made sure we had enough gas for the round trip since it was smarter and definitely safer for blacks, and even more so for a black and white traveling together, to not make any stops along the way.

The meeting in Ruleville included about twenty, mostly older, local black people and took place in a small wood-framed church. Jim spoke briefly about what was happening in other places, including people's commitment to nonviolence and their willingness to risk their lives. He put everything he said, including the risks involved, into a biblical framework, drawing on lessons from the Hebrew prophets and the life of Jesus. People were silent for a few minutes after Jim's talk. Then, an elderly man who I guessed was in his seventies, stood up to speak, or more accurately, to give a personal testimony in the style of a religious revival, about how he had come to decide that it was time to act. One after another, several people spoke about how they knew they might be beaten or jailed or maybe even killed, but they knew, as several of them said, "it's our time now," and "we're ready now" to go down to the County Courthouse to try to register to vote. This was a lesson about Christian faith, extraordinary courage, democracy and the importance of voting that I would never have learned in school. The courage in those commitments and the power in those personal testimonies, the ways they paralleled religious testimonies, go a long way in explaining the strength and resilience of the freedom movement. The meeting ended about 9 o'clock, with most participants pledging to try to register to vote. Jim and I drove back to Memphis that night, without stopping for gas or coffee or to use a restroom. We did have one brief scary experience, when for several minutes we thought a pickup truck with three white men in it might be following us. But the truck turned off the main road and we didn't see it again. I was really glad to have this experience with Jim, and very thankful that night when we got back home to Memphis.

In August 1963, Jim and Dorothy Lawson flew to Washington, D.C. to be on the platform with Martin Luther King Jr. at the historic March for Jobs and Freedom. I stayed at the church parsonage over the weekend taking care of their four-year-old son John. With little John sitting next to me in the living room, we heard Dr. King's famous "I Have a Dream" speech on the family's black and white television.

Following the historic march, when Jim and Dorothy returned, I packed up my things and headed back to Connecticut for my junior year of Wesleyan. On Friday, November 22, 1963, driving home from Wesleyan for Thanksgiving, I heard the news that President Kennedy had been assassinated in Dallas. This was just five months after he had given a speech declaring civil rights "a moral issue" and calling for a Civil Rights Act giving all Americans the right to be served in facilities which are open to the public. The Act became law a year later when it was signed by President Lyndon B. Johnson. Despite this sign of progress, the struggle was far from over. While I managed through that year to keep up with required course work in the College of Social Studies, I also got involved in civil rights activities on campus and in Connecticut in towns around Middletown. I accepted invitations from several churches and schools in Connecticut to speak about my experiences in Memphis. On these occasions, I frequently encountered challenging questions and arguments from whites who were critical of King's methods, as I had been earlier. During my year in Memphis, I had become a strong supporter and articulate advocate for both King's goals and his methods of nonviolence, including occasionally acts of civil disobedience. Recalling the controversy about black and Puerto Rican Vacation Bible School kids swimming at the lake where I lived in New Jersey, in my talks at churches, I would often quote Jim Lawson quoting Frederick Douglass who said, "Those who want change without causing trouble are like those who want a harvest without plowing up the fields." I realized and friends at Wesleyan realized I was becoming an activist.

My experiences in Memphis, including my private tutorial sessions with Jim Lawson challenged and changed many of my views, not only about race relations, but also about violence and nonviolence, and about war and peace. The basic contextual question for Jim always was, "What does it mean to be a follower of Jesus?" As a young teenager, I had been an enthusiastic believer in how Jesus revealed God's extraordinary love for the world through what he taught, the way he lived and died, and especially how he modeled the power of love. Unlike some evangelicals, even as a youth, my Christian faith had more to do with how to live here and now in the world than it did with "feeling saved" or secure about my fate after I died. In 1963, as a twenty-one-year-old, the combination of my experience living for a year in the black community, my reading, and, most importantly, my relationship with Jim Lawson forced me to think much more deeply about the radical implications of what it meant to be a follower of Jesus and how Jesus' teaching applied to race, poverty, violence, and struggles to change the social order. I was developing a new critical mental toughness about what it meant to live as a faithful Christian amidst the complex and harsh realities of injustice and violence in my country and the world. I no longer equated my Christian faith simplistically with faith in America. I continued to have deep love for my country, including profound respect and appreciation for its many positive values and accomplishments. But I began to identify more with a phrase that Rev. William Sloane Coffin often used, describing the life of a committed American Christian as "a lover's quarrel with America and the world." When I got to know Coffin personally a few years later, he explained that he had adapted the phrase from the poet Robert Frost's self-chosen epitaph.

In the summer of 1964 I returned to Memphis to work again at Centenary Methodist Church. Centenary and nearby Le Moyne College provided hospitality for the student volunteers who came from colleges around the country to work on a voting rights campaign called Mississippi Freedom Summer. On June 21, just three weeks into the campaign, three of the college volunteers: James Chaney, a black from Meridian, Mississippi, and Michael Schwerner and Andrew Goodman, white, Jewish volunteers from New York, disappeared and were presumed dead. Despite resistance from J. Edgar Hoover, President Johnson forced the F.B.I. to join the investigation. Two months later we learned that the three students had been brutally murdered and their bodies buried in a crude earthen dam. Members of the church where I worked were inspired and encouraged by the black and white college volunteers coming to Mississippi to help in the voter registration drive. At the same time, the brutal murders of the three young men reminded us all of how determined and violent white resistance could be to efforts to challenge segregation and the power relationship between whites and blacks.

All the dramatic changes that were happening, including the changes in me, also affected my family. In July 1964, in the middle of Freedom Summer, my mother and seventeen year-old sister drove down to Tennessee to attend a Methodist church camp near Nashville with black teenagers from Centenary Church. Given my mother's tendency to avoid any discussion about sex, it was ironic that the focus for that summer session was a new Methodist church pamphlet entitled, "Sex and the Whole Person." To her credit, my mother did fine as a camp counselor while Judy got along great with the black senior high students. After the week at camp, one evening back in Memphis, Judy went out with a few of the black teenagers to a popular downtown Memphis restaurant that was technically no longer for whites only, although very few blacks went there. The teenagers took a booth in a window to make their point publicly to everyone walking by.

Several years later, my mother became active in the League of Women Voters in Florida on issues of equal rights. Among other activities, in 1968 my sister slept in the mud on the Mall in Washington, D.C. as a participant in the SCLC Poor Peoples

Campaign. I felt good about the ripple effects of my experience and proud of my mother's and my sister's involvement.

As a white college student from the North working in a black congregation in Memphis in the early 1960s, objectively, I guess I played a small role in the civil rights movement. I am certain that my experience benefitted and changed me more than any external impact that I may have had. One personal experience in August 1964, just before returning to Wesleyan for my senior year, helped me to keep appropriately humble about my contribution. Given the quite conservative nature of Memphis, including its black community, there hadn't been many demonstrations in the city while I lived there. In August, the NAACP made plans for a large march to demand desegregation of schools. A.W. Willis, the prominent lead attorney for the Memphis NAACP, was a member of Centenary Church and a close friend of Rev. Lawson. Naturally, both Lawson and Attorney Willis were leaders of the march. I decided to participate. It seemed a fitting final act to my time in Memphis. While somehow I didn't anticipate it, not surprisingly, I was one of only a half dozen white persons in the march, along with more than 2,000 blacks. A few weeks earlier, I had grown my first beard, which as I recall had something to do with feeling radical. Frankly, my beard was rather scraggily and ugly. You could almost count the hairs in it. The day after the NAACP march, the *Commercial Appeal*, Memphis' major conservative daily newspaper, published a news story about the march, with a photograph that prominently featured me. The caption read, "Young white, bearded college student from Connecticut joins NAACP march for school integration." To the newspaper, I represented the perfect negative caricature of a white ally for the black march. I remember Jim and A.W. Willis chuckling over the photo and caption. All three of us agreed that, while it may not have set the civil rights movement back, the newspaper photo and caption probably didn't help to advance the movement's goals or win over the sympathy of any white Memphians.

Many years later, I am still very much aware how my second baptism by immersion, living in the black community in Memphis and working with Jim Lawson, profoundly affected my thinking and what I've done during the rest of my life. I've always been much less aware of what impacts my living and working there might have had on others. On a visit to Memphis with my wife in 2008, we went to worship at Centenary Methodist Church and were very warmly greeted by members of the congregation and by the pastor who succeeded Jim Lawson. In welcoming us, the pastor said that when he came to Centenary he heard about me from people who lived in the neighborhood. "People told me," he said in welcoming us, "Ron was the only white guy who came into the Lemoyne Gardens housing project who people trusted." I also was surprised and deeply moved to learn from several of the now-sixty-year-old black men and women who had been teenagers when I worked as a twenty year old with the church's Youth Fellowship, how much knowing me and my working with them had meant to them at the time and how often over the years they remembered and appreciated this experience.

In September 1964, I returned to Connecticut for my senior year at Wesleyan. Clearly, my consciousness and commitments about race and civil rights were quite changed from what they were when I left school in 1962. During both my junior and senior years at Wesleyan I was quite active in civil right efforts on campus and in Middletown and surrounding communities. On weekends I worked as Youth Minister at the First Congregational Church in East Hampton, Connecticut. In my monthly sermons and in weekly youth fellowship programs, I think members of the church who, except for one family, were all white, heard more from me about race relations and the civil rights movement than they probably wanted to hear. I was dating a twenty-year-old black nurse at the time and I had met a black nonviolent organizer my age to whom I was attracted, as he was to me. On one Sunday, I brought the nurse and on another, the activist to morning worship and to the evening meeting of the youth group. I invited an older radical Jewish speaker from the Committee for Nonviolent Action (CNVA) to come one Sunday evening to speak to the youth group about nonviolence. I took fifteen of the church youth on a weekend retreat at the Fellowship of Reconciliation headquarters in Nyack, New York, where they got to hear Glenn Smiley talk about his work with Martin Luther King Jr. during the Montgomery Bus Boycott. I organized teenagers from the church to pass out flyers and hold a vigil in East Hampton's Town Square in support of the 1965 Voting Rights Act. Youth at the East Hampton church generally seemed to appreciate that they could participate in the historic changes that were taking place in our country. In discussions over Sunday dinners at their homes, I learned that some of their parents were less enthusiastic, but they seemed to tolerate my zeal.

At Wesleyan I arranged for Rev. Jim Lawson to speak at a Sunday Chapel Service and, on a separate occasion, I was invited to give a brief talk and introduce Dr. King at the College Field House before a packed audience. I'll never forget that when King got up to speak, he said, "After Ron's good talk, I hardly need to speak at all." I took a leadership role with other students and several members of the faculty in pressing the Wesleyan Admissions Department to develop a new recruiting program to reach out to prospective black students, including students at predominantly black high schools, which until then Wesleyan admissions staff hardly ever visited. Given the times, King's popularity on campus, and a liberal, sympathetic university administration, making progress on these issues was relatively easy. However my experience demonstrated that without active pressure and at least the potential for more disruptive action, even these modest positive changes probably would not have happened. Our experience also revealed the high degree of indifference and complacency among many white students and faculty. Several times, I heard echoes of my own earlier view, "I may agree with King's goals, but not with his methods." By this time, I understood that it wasn't just King's methods that people questioned; I came to believe that some students and faculty really did disagree with King's goals for radical social transformation.

I knew that admitting more black students to Wesleyan would make a significant difference in the school's social and political dynamics. Over Christmas break in 1964, the admissions department paid for several students, including me, to make recruiting trips to black high schools around the country. Naturally, I flew down to Memphis, where I knew several students. One concrete outcome was that Edwin Sanders, who had been president of the Methodist Youth Fellowship at Centenary when I worked there, came to Wesleyan. During his student years, Edwin agitated for change and organized the Wesleyan Black Students Organization; after graduating, he became an ordained minister and then a leader in the international struggle against HIV and AIDs. Several years after he graduated, I had the privilege of voting for Edwin in his successful bid to become a member of the Wesleyan University Board of Trustees. In 2014, back on campus for a college reunion, I attended a service where Wesleyan honored Edwin by presenting him with a Distinguished Alumnus Award.

Selma, Alabama March 1965

In spring 1965, I was a senior in the College of Social Studies at Wesleyan and assumed I would graduate in June, just a year behind schedule. In addition to doing ongoing course work and preparing for my CSS final exams, I was working on a thesis of 100 to150 pages required for graduation. Based on my experiences and what I had learned from Jim Lawson and the nonviolent struggle for social change, I was working with concepts of power, political action, violence and nonviolence. Inspired by my personal experience with Lawson and by my exposure to Hannah Arendt's writings, I planned to address ideas she developed in, *The Human Condition* and *On Revolution*. I had been very fortunate to participate in a small seminar that Dr. Arendt taught during the year she spent doing research and writing at Wesleyan's Honors College. A specific focus of my thesis was the issue or role of forgiveness in the process of social change. In *The Human Condition* Arendt wrote,

> The discoverer of the role of forgiveness in the realm of human affairs was Jesus of Nazareth. The fact that he made this discovery in a religious context and articulated it in religious language is no reason to take it any less seriously in a strictly secular sense. . . . Forgiving, in other words, is the only reaction which does not merely re-act but acts anew and unexpectedly, unconditioned by the act which provoked it and therefore freeing from its consequences both the one who forgives and the one who is forgiven.[2]

I was particularly interested in the role of forgiveness as one element or perhaps the primary characteristic of a radical, nonviolent style of political action. Unfortunately, I didn't get very far in work on this ambitious senior year project.

---

2. Arendt, *The Human Condition*, 214–215.

On Sunday, March 7, I was working on my thesis when TV flashed news from Selma, Alabama that civil rights marchers, including John Lewis, Chairman of the Student Nonviolent Coordinating Committee (SNCC), had been attacked and beaten by police. The media labeled the events "Bloody Sunday." Dr. King issued a call for people to come to Selma to help. A second march was planned for Tuesday, March 9. Feeling an urgent personal impulse to respond, I found four other Wesleyan students who wanted to go to Selma. I had only one scheduled class and when I notified my professor of my plans, he was supportive. On Sunday evening, five of us piled into a VW Beetle and took off from Middletown. Wanting to get to Selma in time for Tuesday's march, we didn't stop along the way, except to get gas and pick up food that we ate in the car as we took turns driving. We arrived in Selma early on Monday evening, March 8.

Beginning in 1962, the small city of Selma, county seat of Dallas County, Alabama, became an important focus for the civil rights movement. That summer, Bernard Lafayette of SNCC, along with black clergy and community leaders, organized a local voter registration drive. Along with John Lewis and Diane Nash, Bernard Lafayette was one of scores of student leaders who were trained in nonviolence by Jim Lawson in Nashville in 1960. Their story is told movingly in David Halberstam's book, *The Children*. Five years after the events in Selma, in July 1970, Bernard Lafayette participated with other religious and student leaders in an interfaith, interracial fact-finding mission I organized and led to Saigon that focused on repression in South Vietnam. In 2014, at seventy-three, Bernard was an active leader in resisting efforts in several states to roll back voting rights.

In 1965 more than 50 percent of Selma's population was black, but only one percent were registered to vote. City and County officials, including Sheriff Jim Clark, aggressively resisted any civil rights activities. Many blacks who attempted to register to vote or tried to desegregate public facilities were arrested, beaten and/or fired from their jobs. As tensions and dangers increased, there were disagreements between SNCC, headed by John Lewis, and SCLC, Dr. King's organization, about the priority for work in Selma and about how hard to push. Dr. King and SCLC were reluctant to focus on one town in one county, especially a town as resistant to change as Selma. SNCC, led by John Lewis, was determined to push harder, believing that Selma represented a crucial testing ground and a possible "tipping point" for the national voting rights campaign.

In January 1965 SNCC and SCLC reached an agreement to intensify the campaign in Selma, although SNCC continued to provide most of the outside support. After 3,000 people had been arrested and many beaten for trying to register to vote, and Jimmie Lee Jackson, a local young black civil rights worker, had been murdered, leaders decided to organize a march to Montgomery, the State Capitol, beginning on Sunday, March 7. The march got only as far as the east end of the Edmund Pettus Bridge across the Alabama River, when a combination of local and state police, some on horseback, attacked the marchers with tear gas and beat people with Billy clubs. John Lewis of SNCC, who was leading the March, was beaten severely and his skull was fractured. That beating headlined the news story that motivated us to come down from Wesleyan, and it forced Dr. King to make Selma an even higher priority.

Driving practically nonstop, we arrived in time to participate in a mass rally on Monday night at Brown's Chapel, where Dr. King preached and where we joined in spirited singing of the song, "Ain't Gonna Let Nobody Turn Me Round," led by local black teenagers. The next day we participated in a second, largely symbolic march led by Dr. King and many prominent clergy, including Rabbi Abraham Joshua Heschel. Rather than force a confrontation, with the highway ahead blocked by police, Dr. King and leaders of the March decided to turn back into town after crossing the Edmund Pettus Bridge. Civil rights lawyers then took the issue of the right to march to the Federal District Court of Southern Alabama.

We five Wesleyan students were together for a week in Selma, hosted by a local black family in a small apartment, three of us sleeping on a pullout couch and two on the floor. During the course of the week, we learned that many black parents in Selma were understandably very fearful about their teenagers getting involved in the civil rights activities, and some urged their sons and daughters not to participate. But Selma's youth were determined. As in many places across the South, young people composed the majority of participants in the demonstrations. Despite the dangers, their youthful sense of hope and their belief that change was going to happen fueled their determination. The courage of these kids was amazing. During our days in Selma, we attended mass meetings and training sessions about nonviolence in the two local, large black churches. We participated in two more test marches that also were turned back by police. Among the most inspiring of our experiences was singing at the mass meetings, led by Selma teenagers who improvised verse after verse for various freedom songs, inserting their own local and personal lyrics. For Selma's teenagers, the civil rights movement was very personal, evoking their deepest youthful hopes and aspirations. To the tune of *Joshua Fit the Battle of Jericho*, at one night's mass meeting, the youth led us all in singing their localized lyrics, the key line of which was "Segregation's wall is goin to fall." Another night, to the tune of, *Oh Freedom*, the teenagers led us singing, "No more Wallace over me," referring to Alabama's staunchly segregationist governor, George Wallace.

At one mass meeting, responding to people's frustration and anger at being blocked from marching, James Bevel, a charismatic and eccentric—some said crazy— SCLC worker, led several hundred people in an amazing, spontaneous, unscripted debate about what to do next. Initially, Bevel sounded sympathetic to the angry mood of several of the most vocal men and seemed ready to endorse the use of violence. Then he shouted out a series of questions to the crowd to help us anticipate what might happen. "What will we do next, he shouted?" And then "What will the police do next?" In the style of a revivalist preacher, Bevel led the mass meeting in imagining a scenario, eventually evoking a consensus that nonviolence was a smarter, more effective strategy. He didn't ask the crowd to love Sheriff Clark and the other white policemen. Instead, using a brilliant double *entendre*, Bevel shouted that nonviolence was "the way we can win and, while we're winning, we'll love the hell out of them." Participants at the mass meeting responded with a combination of laughter and recognition that Bevel had succeeded in making the practical, if not the moral or philosophical, case for nonviolence. All of these meetings and preparations were to get ready for the big march to the State Capitol at Montgomery, the legal fate of which was being argued in the Federal District Court.

After about a week, the other four Wesleyan students drove back to Connecticut My experiences living in Memphis and my connections with King led me to decide to stay in Selma as a volunteer. I feared that this might mean I would not complete my senior thesis on time and possibly not graduate again that year from Wesleyan, but I decided to stay anyway.

Having met him several times at Jim Lawson's home in Memphis and twice at Wesleyan, when I decided to stay in Selma, I went to Dr. King and asked if there was anything I could do to help. He asked if I would be willing to travel by car with a few of his black staff to attend night meetings in two or three small towns in the area. King explained that events in Selma were inspiring blacks in smaller communities to get organized to register to vote. I agreed to go. Since I had no specific role in the meetings, I assumed that my presence might be to offer a little "protection" from attacks and some assurance if there was an attack that it would be covered in the news. Everyone was aware, if something bad were to happen, the media would likely pay more attention if a white guy got hurt or killed rather than only blacks. Just as when I travelled with Rev. Lawson to Mississippi, I could feel the tension in the car as we drove together from Selma to Peachtree, Alabama.

Like the meeting in Ruleville, Mississippi, the meeting in Peachtree was held in a small, rickety wood-framed church, which had several visible air spaces between boards in the walls and floors. Shortly after the meeting began we all were startled by the sound of a car screeching to a halt outside. Bright car headlights suddenly shone through the cracks in the wall causing a wave of fear-filled outbursts, including several people crying, "O Lord" and "O My Jesus," as if they were preparing to meet their maker. Fortunately, the car belonged to a local black minister arriving late for the meeting. As he entered the church and apologized for being late, everyone breathed a sigh of relief and laughed out loud. About twenty-five local people attended the meeting and, as had happened in Mississippi, after brief talks by two of Dr. King's staff, one by one older people stood up and gave testimonies that, even though they knew they might be killed, "it was time to act." They were ready to go down to the courthouse to register to vote.

On another night in Selma, as on most nights, I walked alone from a mass meeting at Brown's Chapel back to the house where I was staying with a black family. It was about nine o'clock and not having had dinner, I paused momentarily outside a café, near where a week earlier James Reeb, a Unitarian Minister, had been savagely beaten by a mob of angry whites. Reeb died two days later in a Birmingham hospital. Seeing the closed sign on the door, I turned to walk on. As I did, a black sedan pulled up next to me at the curb. The white driver leaned toward me, rolled the window down on the passenger side, and called out, "Hey boy, are you one of them civil rights workers?" I pretended not to hear him and walked on. Pulling alongside me again, the man added, "I'm a policeman. I don't want to hurt you. I just want to talk with you." I walked on a bit faster, still trying to ignore him. He drove his car up onto the sidewalk ahead of me, reached over and opened the passenger side door of his car right in front of me. This time, in a more pleading voice, he said, "You don't need to be afraid, really, I just want to talk with you." I stood at the open car door trembling and wanting to get away. But after he showed me his police badge, I was not sure what to do. "By the way," he said, "my name is Charlie."

As I stood next to the open car door, Charlie explained how "them marches and specially the singing by them nigra kids was getting to me." He told me how a couple of times, much to the disbelief and frustration of his policemen buddies, he found himself humming "We Shall Overcome" in the Selma police station. My trembling eased off, but now I was wondering if what was happening was some sort of dream. After a few more minutes of his pleading, I became nervously convinced that Charlie was sincere. I introduced myself, got into his car and agreed to let him drive me to near where I was staying, though not to the exact house since I still was unsure and scared. I also kept my hand on the car door handle just in case I had to jump out. We talked in his car for at least a half an hour during which he confessed that he had come to believe that "Nigras should be able to vote and have the same rights as we whites do." Then he said, "But I'm also kinda nervous. If this happens," Charlie said, "then one day when she grows up, my young daughter might marry a nigra." I decided not to pursue that topic that I had learned permeated so many issues in race relations, but instead said how pleased I was to meet him. I wished him a good night and good future. A few weeks later I saw a picture in a magazine of a policeman in Selma who sort of reminded me of Charlie. He was dressed in full police gear and a helmet, with a visor pulled down so I couldn't see his face. The photograph made him appear as a fierce, determined defender of segregation. If, in fact, the photo was Charlie, I had met him and I knew that his views were changing.

On Sunday, March 21, two weeks after Bloody Sunday, with support from a positive Federal Court decision about the right of people to march and some protection provided by the Justice Department, more than 3,000 people set out from Selma across the Edmund Pettus Bridge to march to the State Capitol at Montgomery. The plan was to walk ten to twelve miles a day and to sleep at the side of the highway at night. I wanted to participate in the march, but I was worried about preparing for my final senior exams. I flew back to Connecticut and returned to Wesleyan. On

Thursday the march, now with 25,000 participants, reached the capitol where Dr. King spoke and Harry Belafonte sang. Five months from when President Lyndon Johnson spoke to the Congress, invoking the scene of bloody Sunday in Selma and echoing the words, "We Shall Overcome," on August 6, 1965, Johnson signed the historic Voting Rights Act which outlawed discriminatory practices that had prevented blacks from registering to vote.

Back at Wesleyan in late March, 1965, I crammed for and passed my senior College of Social Studies exams but, with limited time, decided to postpone work on my senior thesis. Having started in 1960, if I had gone straight through college in four years, I would have graduated with the class of 1964, but didn't because of my year in Memphis. Now, as a result of participating in events in Selma and postponing my senior thesis, I also didn't graduate in 1965. This was upsetting to my family, especially to my dad. Frankly, at the time, I felt uncertain about whether I would ever actually graduate and, at a deeper level, I had some doubts about how important graduating was. I planned to go to work on the national staff of an old, established religious pacifist organization. The "push" of my experience working with Jim Lawson in the black community in Memphis and the "pull" of the growing debate over the American military build-up in Vietnam, gave me confidence that the path I was pursuing was right for me, even though it certainly was not a path I could have imagined when I started college.

In January 1965, even before going to Selma, on the recommendation of Jim Lawson, I had been offered and accepted a position as National Director of Youth Work for the Fellowship of Reconciliation (FOR), a fifty-year-old religious pacifist organization. In June 1965 I moved from Middletown, Connecticut to Nyack, New York, a small city 25 miles north of Manhattan on the west bank of the Hudson River, to take up my new job. The FOR provided me with a room to sleep in and access to a kitchen in the national headquarters which was located in an aging three-story mansion in Upper Nyack, with a view across the Hudson to Tarrytown. At the time, expanding U.S. military involvement in Vietnam was becoming increasingly controversial. While I had a lot to learn about Vietnam and my opposition to U.S. policy was still very much in formation, as events developed, working to end the Vietnam War would soon become the new consuming focus of my still young, American activist life.

Before recounting the ten years I worked opposing the Vietnam War, I want to describe my personal encounters with US involvement in Latin America, including living through the Cuban missile crisis in Fall 1962, my experiences in the Dominican Republic in 1965 during the US military occupation, my visits in Brazil and in Haiti where my parents lived and taught for four years, and my meeting Archbishop Oscar Romero of El Salvador in March 1980, one day before he was assassinated.

3

Visiting Latin America: A Yankee in Haiti, Dominican Republic and El Salvador

Living through the Cuban Missile Crisis in Memphis; being challenged by Rev. Lawson's questions and alternative views about Cuba, nuclear war and non-violence; visiting my parents in Haiti and learning the history of US involvement; traveling to Santo Domingo during the US occupation and meeting President Juan Bosch; attending an international conference in Uruguay on nonviolence and social change; visiting my parents in Brazil during the military dictatorship; and meeting Archbishop Oscar Romero in El Salvador one day before he was assassinated.

IN 2010, WHILE I was writing about my personal experiences related to American policies in Latin America, the catastrophic earthquake struck Port-au-Prince, Haiti, a city where my parents lived and taught school for a year. Witnessing the intense media attention and the outpouring of American goodwill and generosity, I remembered how ashamed I felt when I first read the history of US relations with Haiti. The US occupied Haiti for two decades 1915–34 and supported dictatorship for most of rest of that century. I first read Haiti's history during Christmas week in 1967 when my sister and I visited my parents, staying at the modest but comfortable hotel where they lived in Port-au-Prince. During the time that my father taught at the American school, they had several firsthand experiences with Haiti's dictatorship. One evening during dinner at their hotel, my parents watched helplessly as four of "Papa Doc" Duvalier's *TonTon Macoute* security men burst into the dining room, beat and dragged out a Haitian patron at gunpoint. I was dismayed to discover that most Americans either never knew the history of our relations with Haiti or forgot it. I worry that, despite all the American goodwill and good intentions in response to the earthquake, Haiti will remain extremely impoverished and without a government committed to or capable of working for democratic and social progress.

And I worry that American corporate interests and government policies may hinder rather than help Haiti to resolve its problems.

During that Christmas week visit in 1967, I was surprised to learn that Haiti was the second country in this hemisphere to declare independence from European colonial rule. Just as the American colonies rebelled against the British in 1776, Haitians staged successful uprisings against French and British rule, gaining independence in 1804. While the US war of independence was led by whites, Haiti's struggle was led by blacks. The example of the successful black Haitian struggle for independence provided powerful inspiration for African American slaves in the United States and, not surprisingly, frightened Southern white slaveholders and politicians. As a result, the US withheld diplomatic recognition of Haiti for more than five decades until 1862. Powerful US economic interests were also involved. From 1915 to 1934, during the American military occupation, the US controlled Haiti's national bank and legislature largely for the benefit of North American banking and corporate interests. Then, throughout the years of the Cold War, our nation supported or was indifferent to the brutal anti-communist dictatorships of "Papa Doc" Duvalier and his son, "Baby Doc." While my experience in Haiti was eye-opening, it wasn't my earliest encounter with US policy toward a Latin American country.

Living Through the Cuba Missile Crisis

The first time I remember paying attention to US policies in Latin America was in the fall of 1962 during the Cuban missile crisis when I was living in Memphis, working at Centenary Methodist Church. With his radical Christian commitment to justice, peace and nonviolence, Jim Lawson's response to the Cuban missile crisis went against the grain of prevailing, mainstream public thinking. He raised well-reasoned and challenging questions that made me think about Cuba, our policies in Latin America, and the prospect of nuclear war in ways that were new and very different from my previous, limited ideas.

In October 1962, just a month after I arrived in Memphis, a confrontation between the Soviet Union and the United States brought the world to the brink of nuclear war. In the context of the failed Bay of Pigs invasion of Cuba in 1961 and subsequent US plots to get rid of Cuba's Communist president, Fidel Castro, Soviet Premier Nikita Khrushchev decided to provide long range missiles to the Cuban government. In response, President Kennedy ordered a naval blockade of Cuba and demanded that Soviet missiles be withdrawn. There was much talk about the possibility of nuclear war. For the first time, I read *Hiroshima*, John Hershey's extraordinary account of six survivors of the atomic bomb attack on Japan. In August 1946, *The New Yorker* magazine devoted an entire issue to Hershey's article; then, two months later it was published as a book by Alfred A. Knopf.[1]

1. Hershey, *Hiroshima*.

Years later, I read two other accounts of the bombing and its aftermath, including Gar Alperovitz' controversial, critical analysis, *The Decision to Use the Atomic Bomb and the Architecture of an American Myth;* and *Hiroshima in America: Fifty Years of Denial,* by Robert Jay Lifton and Greg Mitchell, which examines the impact on American political culture of the government's dropping the bomb and then suppressing public debate about it.

By 1962, the year of the Cuba Missile Crisis, both the United States and the Soviet Union possessed much more powerful nuclear weapons than those our nation had used against Japan; and the analyses I read agreed that nuclear war between the two superpowers would result in death and devastation on an unimaginable scale. I felt anxious about the Cuba crisis and the threat of nuclear war, but I was ignorant about alternatives; and, frankly, I felt there wasn't anything I could do about it.

In the midst of talk about nuclear war that fall, I remembered how in grade school in New Jersey, I participated in mock air raid drills in which we were instructed to pull the shades down in our classroom and crouch under our desks to practice protecting ourselves in the event of an nuclear attack on New York City. Living initially a mile, then twenty miles from New York, I came to realize that those exercises were futile and foolish. In 1962 in Memphis, I read news stories about how some Americans were gathering supplies of water and emergency food to store in their basements or in new family fallout shelters. My sense of the irrationality of most civilian preparations for nuclear war was reinforced when I learned that during this same period in the 1960s in the event of a nuclear attack on Great Britain, the BBC planned to play tunes from Rogers and Hammerstein's *The Sound of Music* as a way of reassuring people and keeping up public morale.[2] Jim Lawson taught me that there were activists who protested preparations for nuclear war, including some who committed civil disobedience by refusing to participate in government sponsored public Civil Defense exercises. At the time, however, there wasn't much news coverage of these protests and, though I was sympathetic, I certainly didn't yet imagine myself participating in such a protest.

Helping me to break free from a disempowering combination of ignorance, fear, helplessness and cynicism, Jim not only challenged popular perceptions of the missile crisis, but also raised challenging ideas about possible alternative US policies toward Cuba and the nuclear arms race. During the crisis, even as people recognized that the confrontation could lead to nuclear war, American public opinion overwhelmingly supported President Kennedy's tough resolve in imposing a naval blockade of Cuba and demanding that Soviet missiles be withdrawn. In contrast, Jim posed the question to me one day, "If nuclear war would very likely destroy the world as we know it, isn't pursuing policies that could lead to nuclear war morally wrong and really a type of insanity?"

2. "Programs for Broadcast."

In stark contrast to Jim Lawson's thinking, I read *On Thermonuclear War*, by Herman Kahn, a mathematician and war strategist at the Rand Corporation.[3] Kahn argued that our having a policy for fighting nuclear war was rational and that nuclear war was not only survivable, but winnable. His theory, labeled "thinking the unthinkable," projected a scenario for winning nuclear war. I was impressed by Kahn's seeming rationality and logic, but I began to believe that there was something basically irrational and immoral about the whole enterprise of preparing for nuclear war.

As the crisis developed, Jim Lawson forced me to think about several other issues that hardly got any attention in most American media. Jim introduced me to *I.F. Stone's Weekly*, a four-page newsletter, written and published by Isidor (Izzy) Stone that consistently offered important and challenging alternative news, analyses, and commentary on current events. In the 1960s *I.F. Stone's Weekly* had only about 70,000 subscribers, but it was frequently passed along by hand to many more people. A 1999 survey sponsored by New York University's School of Journalism ranked Stone's Weekly sixteenth in the list of "the greatest US journalistic achievements in the twentieth century."[4]

A combination of personal discussions with Jim Lawson and my reading got me thinking about new questions. What did the Cuban people think about the revolution and about Fidel Castro? Was Cuba, even with Soviet missiles, really a threat to us? What were Khrushchev's and the USSR's perspective on the crisis? Could the United States have pursued alternative policies, other than confronting the Soviet Union and threatening nuclear war?

I read about life in Cuba and America's policy toward Cuba before the revolution that brought Castro to power. During these years, largely motivated by the Cold War, corporate sugar interests, and American mafia investments in Havana's casinos, our government supported the right wing military dictatorship of Fulgencio Batista. While Castro's government clearly was authoritarian, I learned that the new government was popular among a majority of Cubans for its commitments to eliminate extreme poverty, radically reduce illiteracy, and provide basic healthcare for all Cubans. It seemed to me that you didn't need to be a communist or think that Castro's government got everything right to appreciate that these were real and important improvements for the vast majority of Cubans. For most Americans, including most American politicians and news media, Cold War anti-communist ideology didn't allow for such a nuanced view.

Rejecting Herman Kahn's logic about winning, Jim Lawson also offered an alternative view about what the United States could do related to the nuclear arms race. He asked, "What if one started from the assumption that, since nuclear war would pose a threat to civilization itself, all nuclear weapons—ours as well as the Soviet Union's—need to be eliminated?" The USSR had justified sending missiles into Cuba in part

3. Kahn, *On Thermonuclear War*.
4. "The Top 100 Works of Journalism in the United States in the 20th Century."

because our country had recently installed missiles in Turkey aimed at the USSR. As an alternative, Jim posed several challenging questions that forced me to think:

> What if Kennedy turned Khrushchev's decision into an opportunity to reverse the nuclear arms race, rather than simply viewing it as a provocation which deserved an equally provocative response? What if Kennedy promised to take US missiles out of Turkey in exchange for Khrushchev's withdrawing Soviet missiles from Cuba, and then challenged the Soviet Union to join the United States in reducing both countries' nuclear arsenals toward the goal of zero nuclear weapons worldwide?

If President Kennedy had successfully mobilized public and congressional support for this approach, the world situation today regarding nuclear weapons and nuclear proliferation might be very different.

In 1962, the Cold War was the controlling framework for US policies, news media coverage, and popular attitudes. In conversations with Jim Lawson, I realized how much the Cold War controlled my own thinking. The Cold War divided the world simplistically and rigidly into good anti-communist versus evil communist countries and political movements, often lumping any left-leaning political leader or movement together with evil communism. I understood that Jim's questions and views were outside of mainstream thinking and were considered radical, but the more I thought about them, the more they seemed to make moral and practical sense. In addition to learning from Jim Lawson, I learned a lot from reading C. Wright Mills, the most important liberal American sociologist in the 1960s. Mills offered a radical critique of the nuclear arms race and US policy toward Cuba. Mills was critical of Castro's authoritarian rule; but, at the same time, sympathetic to the Cuban revolution. As a twenty year old living through the Cuban Missile Crisis, two of Mills's books that I found especially helpful were *The Causes of World War III* and *Listen, Yankee: The Revolution in Cuba*.

The Cuban Missile Crisis ended a month after it started, when the USSR withdrew its missiles from Cuba, the United States relaxed its naval blockade, and the world escaped the threat of nuclear war. Unfortunately, most Americans believed that Kennedy's tough, confrontational stance forced Khrushchev to back down, leaving an impression that possessing nuclear weapons added positively to American power and that threatening their use could help achieve our nation's objectives. What Americans didn't know was that President Kennedy had actually struck a secret deal with Premier Khrushchev. A short while after Khrushchev withdrew Soviet missiles from Cuba, Kennedy quietly withdrew U.S. missiles from Turkey. The fact that the Cuban Missile Crisis had actually been resolved by a negotiated, albeit secret, compromise should have led to a lot more critical thinking about possible alternative policies, but it did not. Instead, the outcome of the crisis reinforced public support for the theory of Mutual Assured Destruction (MAD). A short time later, fear of the dangers of radioactive fallout from nuclear testing did lead Kennedy and Krushchev to work together for a Nuclear Test Ban Treaty. Some close supporters of Kennedy believed that he did learn important, alternative lessons from the Cuban Missile Crisis and that in a second term as president, he might have pursued serious steps toward nuclear disarmament. Tragically, just a year later, only half way through his first term, President Kennedy was assassinated.

According to the theory of mutual assured destruction, since the USA and USSR each had the capacity to destroy the other, the balance of terror reduced the chances of nuclear war. Based on this logic, it was inevitable that in any regional conflict, if one side possessed nuclear weapons, the other side would want to acquire them. In the years following the Cuban missile crisis, despite public support for limiting the spread of nuclear weapons, it became clear to me that the appeal and logic of the theory of mutual assured destruction would continue to fuel the dangerous dynamic of nuclear proliferation. The Soviet Union's nuclear arms stockpile continued to compete with the American stockpile. India and Pakistan that were contesting control over Kashmir both eventually acquired nuclear weapons. North Korea sought them to counter the American nuclear umbrella over South Korea. Although the Israelis never confirmed having them, it was widely known that Israel possessed some 200 nuclear weapons. In recent years, the dangers of the MAD logic have been compounded by the threat that Iran, then Saudi Arabia, and possibly a non-state terrorist group might acquire nuclear weapons. Unless the US leads with a sense of urgency toward the goal of zero nuclear weapons, the chances that some country or party will use nuclear weapons are likely to increase.

The alternative approaches to international conflicts that Jim Lawson raised during the Cuban missile crisis stayed with me and helped me think differently about many other situations. At a more basic level, like Jim Lawson and Martin Luther King Jr., I came to believe that if we approach conflict situations with the assumption that violence and war are necessary, we will all too easily justify the use of violence when it takes place. In contrast, by making a principled commitment to nonviolence and refusing to accept the idea that violence is inevitable, we force ourselves to consider a much wider range of alternative policies. I recognized that saying a principled "no" to violence doesn't answer all the questions and it doesn't necessarily rule out the use of violence in all circumstances, but it does push us to ask more and different questions. I brought these new views with me in 1965 when I went to work as national director of youth work at the religious, pacifist Fellowship of Reconciliation (FOR).

Trips to the Dominican Republic during the US Occupation

My next personal encounter with US policy toward Latin America occurred in spring 1965. As I was preparing to start work at the FOR, President Lyndon Johnson ordered American military forces into the Dominican Republic. He justified the invasion and occupation by claiming that the country was turning into a second Cuba. Many knowledgeable observers rejected the analogy between Fidel Castro and Juan Bosch, the Dominican Republic's first freely elected president, arguing that the real US motive for invading was to protect American corporate sugar interests.

During three decades of rule by Rafael Trujillo's military dictatorship in the Dominican Republic, Juan Bosch, a popular, left-leaning, non-communist democrat, had been jailed and then exiled from his country. Following Trujillo's assassination in 1961, Bosch returned home; and, in the country's first free elections, Bosch won a big electoral victory to become president. Seven months later, his government was overthrown in a rightwing military coup. In April 1965, a popular, counter-military coup was on the verge of returning Bosch to the Presidency when the United States invaded.

During the 1940s and 1950s, Democrat and Republican presidents, as well as majorities in Congress, supported rightwing military dictatorships in Cuba, the Dominican Republic, Haiti, and elsewhere in Latin America, as well as in countries in Africa and the Middle East. Based on the Cold War theory of containment, America's support for military dictatorships was commonly justified to prevent the spread of communism. However, economic interests, including oil in the Middle East, mining in Africa, and mining and sugar in Latin America, as well as the specific interests of the United Fruit Company in Central America, played important and sometimes decisive roles in determining US policies. In implementing these policies, US government officials frequently fabricated facts, and at times acted directly in violation of US laws.

Following the 9/11 terrorist attacks on New York and Washington, the Bush/Cheney administration echoed these earlier Cold War rationalizations to justify extraordinary rendition, water boarding and other forms of torture, now under the rubric of the War on Terrorism. Terrorists are evil people who will use any means to attack us, so we're justified in using immoral and illegal means against them. In addition to the issues of the morality and legality of the practices, there are two big problems with this reasoning: first, justifying actions based on the means used by opponents isn't necessarily the most effective response and may compromise or cancel out whatever good ends the United States claims to be seeking; and second, viewing other countries or political movements primarily through these rigid frameworks, doesn't address what motivates opponents and fails to explore possible responses that could lead to reduction of conflict.

The April 1965 US military invasion and occupation of the Dominican Republic, rationalized by the Cold War, prevented Juan Bosch from being returned to his elected office. An interim government was installed and new elections were promised for June, 1966. Immediately after the US invasion and with the US occupation on the ground, news reports began to appear about increasing incidents of rightwing intimidation and violence against Bosch's campaign staff and supporters. In May 1965, at the urging of Sidney Lens, a union organizer and writer from Chicago, the FOR organized a three-person delegation composed of Sid Lens, Glenn Smiley, FOR national program director; and myself, soon to be installed as FOR's national director of youth work, to visit the Dominican Republic.

I was very glad to have this opportunity to travel and work with Sidney Lens. My thinking about the Cold War had been significantly influenced by his book, *The Futile Crusade: Anti-Communism as American Credo*[5] which I read when I worked in Memphis. At the time of its publication, Lens' book drew high praise from D.F. Fleming, Professor of International Relations at Vanderbilt University, whose own two-volume book, *The Cold War and Its Origins,* was a respected and comprehensive analysis of the Cold War.

Before 1965, I had made only two brief family vacation trips out of the country, in 1958 through Ontario, Canada and in 1960 to Nogales, Mexico. Thus, this trip to the Dominican Republic was my first real international experience. Our three-person delegation flew to Santo Domingo by way of Puerto Rico. As we travelled around meeting many young idealist Dominicans who opposed the invasion, it felt strange and disturbing to me to see thousands of Americans my age who were part of the occupation force, especially since only ten years earlier, with my dad's encouragement, I had considered going to West Point. If I had gone there, I probably would have graduated in 1964 and might have been one of those young American officers leading the occupation of the Dominican Republic.

Our delegation met twice with President Juan Bosch. I found him to be very personable, compassionate and inspiring. I was deeply moved by his commitments to restoring democratic rule and to bettering the lives of his people, particularly the poorest and most marginalized. This would not be the only time when I met and was inspired by a popular political leader of another country whom the government of my country viewed with suspicion or labeled as an enemy. Even after only two meetings, it was easy to understand why Bosch was so popular with many poor Dominicans and why many wealthier Dominicans and many in the military feared him. It was also clear how his vision for democratic change, including his support of greater rights for sugar industry workers, challenged American companies' economic interests in preserving the status quo. With the help of an interpreter, Lens, Smiley, and I spent several days travelling in the countryside, interviewing people involved in supporting Juan Bosch. People feared that unless the harassment and threats against him and attacks on his supporters were somehow stopped soon, the election's outcome would be determined long before the election was held.

A month later, in June 1965, I made a second visit to the Dominican Republic, this time by myself. I was on my way to attend an International FOR Conference in Montevideo, Uruguay on nonviolence and social change, and to visit my parents in Brazil. I met again with Juan Bosch and once again toured in the countryside with

5. Lens, *The Futile Crusade.*

one of his young associates. Particularly in the rural areas, harassment and violence against Bosch's campaign workers and supporters was even worse than our FOR delegation had witnessed in May. I wrote an Op-Ed article along these lines that I submitted to *The New York Times*. During the next twelve months, the situation became even worse. U.S. military forces and forces of the Organization of American States (OAS), remained neutral, which meant they did nothing to stop the threats and violent attacks being against Bosch campaign staff and supporters. Juan Bosch lost the election and Joaquin Balaguer, a conservative politician, with strong ties to the former dictator and support from the United States, became president.

Tragically, two icons of the American left played an important and I believe seriously flawed role in relation to the elections in the Dominican Republic. Bayard Rustin, chief strategist for the 1963 March on Washington, and Norman Thomas, perennial Socialist Party candidate for president, came to Santo Domingo leading a small delegation of election observers sponsored by the AFL-CIO. They stayed only a few days and limited their mission to the capital city of Santo Domingo. They did not visit the countryside where the worse violence against Bosch supporters had been taking place for months. They ignored evidence that in the final months leading up to the elections, direct threats against Bosch's life were so common that he was rarely able to leave his house to campaign. Then, immediately after the official election results were announced, apparently on Rustin's advice, they declared that the elections had been free and fair. Particularly given their prior commitments to human rights and social justice, their methods and conclusions were very disappointing and disturbing. In retrospect, I concluded that their hurried and poorly implemented mission reflected the prevailing Cold War anti-communist politics of their AFL-CIO sponsor more than principled concern for human rights. In the weeks following Balaguer's inauguration, rightwing death squads assassinated several of Juan Bosch's key supporters. No one was ever arrested for the killings.

In June 1965, I flew from Santo Domingo to Montevideo, Uruguay to attend an International FOR Conference on nonviolence and social change in Latin America. It was a time of both hopeful and threatening ferment for change throughout the continent. I was personally inspired by meeting the keynote speaker, Reverend Emilio Castro (no relation to Fidel). Rev. Castro was a Uruguayan Methodist pastor, committed to nonviolence and social change. In 1965 he was head of the Latin American Council of Churches and a few years later General Secretary of the World Council of Churches. I was struck by the similarities between Emilio Castro's Christian views and those of Jim Lawson and Martin Luther King Jr. All three shared a deep identification with poor and marginalized people as well as a principled commitment to social justice and to nonviolence as the morally and practically soundest method of struggle for social change. Rev. Castro rejected the Cold War as the primary guide for viewing Latin American issues and conflicts.

Emilio Castro was critical of both communist and capitalist ideologies. He explained that while communism emphasized economic justice and promised that freedom would follow after the revolution, capitalism emphasized freedom and promised that economic justice would follow as a byproduct of free enterprise. It was becoming increasingly clear to me that neither of these views was born out by history. Rev. Castro believed Christians should not align ourselves with either ideology, but should instead work nonviolently for what he called a "just, participatory and sustainable society." While many Latin American pastors and priests were inspired by teachings of Emilio Castro and by advocates of liberation theology, these views were strongly opposed by the conservative hierarchy of the Roman Catholic Church and generated considerable debate among Catholic and mainline Protestant leaders in the United States.

An American Protestant theologian who interpreted Latin American "liberation theology" in our North American context and significantly influenced my own thinking was Robert MacAfee Brown, whom I met in the early 1970s when he was one of the national leaders of Clergy and Laity Concerned About Vietnam. A Presbyterian theologian who taught at Union Theological Seminary in New York and at Stanford University in California, Brown had wide influence through his books, including *Religion and Violence: A Primer for White Americans* and *Theology in a New Key: Responding to Liberation Themes*. A sign of significant change in the Catholic Church occurred in September 2013 when, after decades of official censure, Pope Francis welcomed a founder of liberation theology, the Rev. Gustavo Guterriez, to the Vatican.

After the Conference in Montevideo, I joined my sister Judy visiting our parents who were living in Sao Paulo, Brazil, where my father was teaching at the American school. While on the surface, Sao Paulo seemed calm and daily life seemed normal, in fact Brazil was being ruled by a military dictatorship. A year earlier, the Brazilian military, with tacit support from our country, had carried out a coup against the elected government of the popular leftist, Joao Goulart. At the conference in Uruguay, I was given the names of three activist Brazilian Christian student leaders to look up in Sao Paulo. I managed to meet two of them, but it was clear that they were very reluctant and fearful to talk with me or to voice any criticism of the ruling military junta. The language barrier between us was part of the problem, but I believe the students were afraid to trust me, and I didn't press them. This was my first personal experience of being in a context so repressive that even people who might have a lot in common didn't dare to speak openly with each other.

My travels led me to read more about Latin America and US policy. I would have liked to make Latin America more of a focus of my work, but when I joined the FOR staff in June 1965, public controversy about the Vietnam War and the draft were fast becoming the major issues for the American peace movement. A shift in focus seemed appropriate. From 1965 to 1975, initially at the FOR and then at the American Friends Service Committee (AFSC), working to end the Vietnam War was the primary focus of my work (see Chapters 4 and 5). After the Vietnam War ended in the spring of

1975, as AFSC national peace education secretary, I led a process to determine AFSC's nationwide peace education emphases. We decided to make US policy and human rights issues in Southern Africa and Latin America, along with disarmament and peace in the Middle East, high priorities for peace education and action.

Visit to El Salvador: Meeting Archbishop Romero

My next personal encounter with US policy in Latin American occurred in March 1980, when I was invited to participate in an ecumenical delegation to El Salvador. An intense struggle, verging on civil war, was taking place between the Salvadoran military and right-wing death squads on one side and opposing them, the Marxist Farabundo Marti National Liberation Front (FMLN) and independent religious and secular human rights activists. Based on an anti-communist, anti-leftist ideology, America was providing substantial aid to the Salvadoran military. There were numerous reports of human rights abuses and killings of human rights activists, including several Catholic priests. The purpose of our ecumenical delegation was to meet with a variety of people and learn as much as we could about human rights issues and the role of US policy. Our delegation was led by Thomas E. Quigley, the very knowledgeable and highly respected Latin America policy advisor at the United States Conference of Catholic Bishops.

Our first stop was in Guatemala, where we were met by Phillip and Angie Berryman who were serving as AFSC's Central America Representatives. Phil accompanied us to El Salvador, helped to arrange appointments in the capital, San Salvador, and, despite the dangers, also in the nearby countryside. Having been warned shortly before our visit that rightwing Salvadoran death squads might already have marked him as a target for assassination, Phil tried to maintain a low profile, going with our delegation on some parts of our schedule and not on others. We received a briefing from the newly appointed US Ambassador, Robert White, who supported a political solution to the conflict and was publically critical of the Salvadoran military's collaboration with violent right-wing civilian groups.

President Carter, who made human rights a high priority of his presidency, had given Robert White his first major foreign posting, appointing him ambassador to Paraguay in 1977. Paraguay was ruled from 1954 to 1989 by Alfredo Stroessner, who was described in the *Washington Post* obituary as "the Paraguayan despot whose 35-year reign marked an uninterrupted period of repression in his country, which became a haven for Nazi war criminals, deposed dictators and smugglers."[6] Ambassador White played an important role in helping to unsettle the Stroessner regime, specifically by supporting labor organizers and helping to reveal that the notorious Nazi war criminal, Joseph Mengele, the "Angel of Death, had been living comfortably

---

6. Bernstein, "Alfredo Stroessner: Paraguyan Dictator."

in Paraguay for years. Almost from the day the Whites arrived in El Salvador, Robert White's reputation for supporting human rights and his inquiries about human rights activists who had "disappeared," generated rightwing death threats against him and his wife, Mary Ann. He told us that he also experienced an increasingly cold reception from many representatives of the American business community in El Salvador.

Our ecumenical delegation especially looked forward to meeting Oscar Romero, who had been appointed archbishop of El Salvador in 1977. Romero was not a political activist; indeed, he was critical of some of the more activist, politically leftist priests. However, his deep pastoral commitment to the people led him to become increasingly involved in defending and advocating for the poor, opposing violence, and persisting in attempts to appeal to wealthy Salvadorans and members of the military. Between 1977 and 1980, Romero had performed funerals for six Salvadoran priests assassinated by right-wing death squads. A short time before our delegation arrived, he had taken the bold step of writing a letter to Carter urging him to cancel all military aid to El Salvador. Unfortunately, the Carter administration didn't act on Romero's appeal and the US continued to provide aid to the Salvadoran military. The movie, *Romero*, starring Raul Julia, is an excellent and moving portrayal of the life and death of Archbishop Romero.

On Sunday, March 23 our ecumenical delegation attended mass at the Basilica in San Salvador. At the invitation of the archbishop, we were seated in the chancel area facing the congregation, behind and off to the side of the pulpit from which Romero would deliver what turned out to be his most famous and final homily. After being shut down by the military for several weeks, the Basilica was filled to overflowing that Sunday morning, with most worshippers standing. I noticed one elderly man leaning on the front rail, demonstrably reading a copy of the FMLN political newspaper, *Liberation*. This also happened to be the first Sunday that the church's radio station was back on the air after having been blown up. When the archbishop rose to speak, a young Catholic seminarian stood beside him holding an old black telephone mounted on a big, heavy wooden box so that Romero's sermon could be broadcast live over the church's radio station to people listening all over the country. The old box and phone equipment was so heavy that several seminarians took turns holding it up. The most dramatic moment came when Romero made a personal appeal to Salvadoran soldiers to stop the repression and stop killing the people.

> I would like to make an appeal in a special way to the men of the army, to the police, to those in the barracks. Brothers, you are part of our own people. You kill your own campesino brothers and sisters. And before an order to kill that a man may give, the law of God must prevail that says, thou shalt not kill! No soldier is obliged to obey an order against the law of God. No one has to fulfill an immoral law. It is time to recover your consciences and to obey your consciences rather than the orders of sin. The church, defender of the rights of God, of the law of God, of human dignity, the dignity of the person, cannot

remain silent before such abomination. We want the government to take seriously that reforms are worth nothing when they come about stained with so much blood. In the name of God, and in the name of this suffering people whose laments rise to heaven each day more tumultuously, I beg you, I ask you, I order you in the name of God: Stop the repression![7]

The archbishop was certainly aware that we were a mixed ecumenical delegation, including a Quaker, a Methodist and a Unitarian, and he certainly knew the Catholic Church's teaching that only baptized Catholics are eligible to receive communion. Nevertheless, following his homily, Romero came to our delegation and offered each of us the communion bread. We all took the bread and ate it.

A few years later, I asked a rabbi who is a personal friend what he would have done if he had been with us in the Basilica that Sunday morning when Archbishop Romero offered each of us the bread of Holy Communion. Tears came to the rabbi's eyes and then to mine as he explained, "You know Ron, when Jews think of the Christian communion ritual, involving the body and blood of Christ, we are reminded of how Jews were blamed for the death of Christ and how that contributed to centuries of terrible persecution of our people." Then the rabbi continued and said, "However, in that context, I know that Archbishop Romero's offering the bread to everyone in the delegation was an invitation to join God's suffering with the poor and oppressed—an invitation to join in God's work of healing the world." The rabbi explained that the Torah teaches that we all are commanded to work for healing the world, *Tikkun Olam*. "So, yes," he concluded, "in that context, at that table, invited by Archbishop Romero, I, too, would have taken the bread and eaten it." I know that many rabbis would not answer the same way, but I hope we all can appreciate the spirit of this rabbi's response.

A day after Sunday's service in the Basilica, late in the afternoon, Archbishop Romero went to a hospital to visit an elderly woman parishioner who was ill. While he was offering Mass in the hospital chapel, he was assassinated. Hit in the chest by bullets, it was reported that Romero's blood spilled out onto the altar. It was later confirmed that the archbishop's assassination had been ordered by Major Roberto D'Aubuisson, who had organized right-wing groups most Salvadorans believed were responsible for many human rights abuses and for several politically motivated assassinations.

Hearing the news of Romero's assassination and fearing that chaos might erupt in the capital, our ecumenical delegation gathered at the American Embassy. Ambassador White invited us to come to his residence, where we spent most of the night gathered with Robert and Mary Ann in their living room, in somber, silent vigil, occasionally eased with sips of whiskey. Our silence was broken at times by Ambassador White or Mary Ann, or Phil Berryman or Tom Quigley, the four most knowledgeable among us, offering personal reflections about Romero, the escalating right-wing repression and violence, and the role and responsibility of our government. As an

7. Archbishop Romero, The Last Sermon.

American ecumenical religious delegation concerned with human rights, it was good to be with Ambassador White and his wife that night. They both shared our deep sadness and anger over Archbishop Romero's death and they, like us, were troubled by the role and responsibility of US policy related to events unfolding in El Salvador. This was one of several times in my life when I was impressed and inspired meeting an American Foreign Service officer, and wished with all my mind and heart that our country's policies more closely reflected the ambassador's views.

The following day we prepared a consensus report on our visit, including our support for the archbishop's plea for an end to US military aid to El Salvador. Our delegation returned to Washington, DC where we held a well-attended press conference and circulated our report to all members of Congress. Six days after the assassination, 250,000 Salvadorans attended Archbishop Oscar Romero's funeral.

In 1980 alone approximately 9,000 Salvadorans were killed, the vast majority by the Salvadoran military and rightwing death squads. In early December 1980, Ambassador White and his wife hosted Jean Donovan and Sister Dorothy Kazel, two Catholic women workers, for dinner and overnight in their residence. White was deeply moved by the women's personal moral commitment to the poor and by their sincerity and courage. He differed with them, however, about the best strategy for change, arguing for the possibility of altering US policy from the inside. The next day, the two women, plus Sister Ita Ford and Sister Maura Clarke, were kidnapped, raped, mutilated and murdered by a rightwing death squad. Robert and Mary Ann were sick with anger over the women's deaths, as they had been over Romero's assassination.

In early 1981, Alexander Haig, President Reagan's newly appointed secretary of state, unceremoniously dismissed Robert White from his ambassadorial post. Reagan and Haig strongly supported military aid to rightwing, anti-communist regimes. Robert White was a conscientious, committed, diplomat who believed deeply in the work he was doing. His life story provides very interesting critical perspectives on US policies in Latin America and worldwide. He later worked through non-governmental organizations, including the Center for International Policy, for reform of American policies around the world.

In 2001, in a very moving article in the Catholic magazine, *Commonweal*, "Death and Lies in El Salvador," Margaret Steinfels wrote that Ambassador White, "moved from being a Cold War liberal to become a liberal internationalist with an abiding commitment to diplomacy as a means of bringing change and deep skepticism about military power as a tool of foreign policy."[8] She then quoted White's own criticism of US foreign policy priorities as reflected in our nation's budget. "If you've got a Pentagon that's overfunded and you've got a CIA that's overfunded and the State Department is underfunded, and AID (the Agency for International Development) has practically no money, then you're going to get policies that emphasize the wrong things for a

---

8. Steinfels, "Death and Lies in El Salvador."

democracy to emphasize."[9] In 2011, Ambassador White's critical concern about how distorted priorities generate misguided policies was dramatically demonstrated in the Middle East when massive popular, democratic uprisings overthrew corrupt, dictatorial Arab regimes that had been supported for decades with large amounts of US military aid.

I am grateful for the opportunities I had to cross boundaries, making several trips to learn about our policies in Latin America. I wish I could have spent more time working on those but in 1965, the Vietnam War became the primary focus of my work. Moreover, I came to understand that US policies in other areas of the world followed similar patterns and presented similar problems. I've given hundreds of public talks about these problematic foreign policy patterns. In chapter six, I offer more thoughts about how these problematic tendencies have negatively affected American initiatives for peace in the Middle East.

On a speaking trip to Chicago in 1985, after returning from three years living in the Middle East, I stayed overnight at the home of Sidney and Shirley Lens. As I mentioned, my critical thinking about the negative effects of the Cold War on American foreign policy was initially shaped by reading Sid's book, *The Futile Crusade,* and I had gone with Sid on the FOR delegation to the Dominican Republic in 1965. Sid was very aware of the problematic patterns in American foreign policy worldwide. On his living room wall was a framed, signed photograph from Mohammad Mossadegh, the popularly elected president of Iran, who was overthrown in August, 1953 in a violent military coup financed and orchestrated by the CIA. This shameful chapter in relations with Iran is hardly remembered by most Americans, but has never been forgotten by most Iranians. The hand-written note from President Mossadegh read, "To Sidney Lens, who told the truth about what happened here."

Returning to the United States from El Salvador in spring 1980, I wanted to speak truthfully based on what I had experienced. While always trying to acknowledge complexities and respect different viewpoints, I wanted to speak about what I had seen, and in particular how aid to the Salvadoran military contributed to the suffering of the people of El Salvador and was clearly counterproductive to proclaimed US interests in fostering democracy. I wanted to tell the story of Archbishop Romero who, like Martin Luther King Jr., conscientiously opposed injustice while nonviolently walking a path of ministering to the poor and marginalized. In religious terms, Romero's response to the vertical axis of the cross—his experience of the extraordinary generosity and impartiality of God's love—led him to stretch his human love horizontally and nonviolently to both the oppressed and oppressors in ways that—as with Gandhi and King—led almost inexorably to his death.

In my public talks, I spoke about how our government's policies were blinded by Cold War anti-communism and corrupted idealism, and motivated by short term economic greed. They consistently overestimated the power of military means, and

9. Ibid.

underestimated the power of people's aspirations for justice, thus contributing to injustice, repression and death. What I experienced and learned on my brief visit to El Salvador in 1980 mirrored patterns of US policy I witnessed writ excruciatingly large over ten years in America's war against Vietnam. Much of my thinking about what was wrong with American foreign policy developed during 1965 to 1975, when I worked as a young leader in the American peace movement opposing the Vietnam War. It's now time to tell that part of my story.

4

Meeting the Vietnamese "Enemy:"
Resisting the Draft; Mass Marches in D.C.

Joining the national staff of the FOR; resisting the draft made the war personal for me; being indicted, but believing I am America; crying over King's assassination and celebrating my first intimate relationship and marriage; meeting Vietnamese in Bratislava who don't feel like "enemies" to me; coordinating national peace marches on Washington in November 1969 and May 1970; protesting and marching don't feel like enough.

THE FELLOWSHIP OF RECONCILIATION (FOR) is an international, religious pacifist organization started on the eve of World War I, by a British Quaker and a German Lutheran Pastor who vowed as followers of Jesus that they would not participate in war. The American FOR was organized a year later in 1915.

Joining the national FOR staff in June 1965, I became a participant/leader in the organization's unique and interesting history, a history that demonstrates the political relevance of nonviolence to movements for progressive social change. In the 1920s, the FOR was instrumental in the formation of the American Civil Liberties Union and the National Conference of Christians and Jews. In the 1940s, the Congress of Racial Equality (CORE) and the American Committee on Africa (ACOA) started as FOR committees, and then soon became independent organizations, led respectively by James Farmer and George Hauser, both of whom were former national FOR staff. CORE organized some of the earliest sit-ins for civil rights in Chicago in 1943, and in 1947 sponsored the first interracial freedom ride, called the "Journey of Reconciliation." For four decades, ACOA played a major role in efforts to end Apartheid in South Africa. During both world wars, the FOR supported the rights of conscientious objectors, like Alfred Hassler and Glenn Smiley, who refused cooperation with the draft and served time in federal prison. In 1956, Glenn Smiley played a major role advising Martin Luther King Jr. about nonviolence during the Montgomery Bus Boycott. When I joined the FOR staff in 1965, Glenn Smiley was FOR's national program director and Al Hassler was executive secretary.

In February, 1965, a month before I went to Selma and five months before I actually started my job at the FOR, Al Hassler invited me to what he described as a very important meeting in New York City. It turned out to be a gathering of several older leaders in the American peace movement, including Hassler representing FOR; Bayard Rustin, FOR youth director in the 1950s and chief strategist of the 1963 march on Washington; Robert Gilmore of Turn Toward Peace; Norman Thomas, perennial Socialist Party candidate for president; David Dellinger, editor of *Liberation* magazine; David McReynolds, executive secretary of the War Resisters League; and A. J. Muste, the octogenarian radical pacifist, former minister, former Trotskyite, and FOR's executive secretary in the 1950s. I was by far the youngest participant in the meeting and, when it came to peace movement politics I was a complete novice.

The meeting had been organized because Al Hassler and some of the others were worried about the first national march against the war in Vietnam being planned for April, 1965, sponsored by the Students for a Democratic Society (SDS). Several of the older leaders believed the SDS approach was naïve and too confrontational. They were worried about SDS' decision to invite speakers who might openly encourage young men to resist military service and by their willingness to allow marchers to carry whatever signs they wanted, rather than signs with a single approved slogan. They feared that some marchers would wave Vietcong flags. As it turned out, a few participants did carry flags, thus providing ammunition for some critics to label them as pro-communist or enemy sympathizers.

Hassler and several of these older leaders were critical of SDS for being soft on communism, which they believed should be taboo for the American peace movement. They believed that the peace movement should be explicitly and publicly anti-communist, both for reasons of principle—to oppose totalitarian rule in the Soviet Union—as well as for political and tactical reasons, given the tight grip that anti-communism had on American attitudes. As discussed in the previous chapter, from the late 1940s until the collapse of the Soviet Union forty years later, most American political leaders, both Republicans and Democrats, and most of the news media, viewed foreign policy choices through the lens of the Cold War that divided the world simplistically between good anti-communist countries and movements and bad communist countries and movements. The Cold War colored and controlled most discussions about foreign policy issues and even debates about many domestic policy issues.

I felt somewhat intimidated personally participating in this meeting, and assumed Al Hassler included me as part of my orientation to the peace movement. What I learned at the meeting was not exactly the lessons that I think Al wanted me to learn. While I never even heard of any of these leaders when I was growing up, I had come to admire several of them during my time working with Rev. Jim Lawson and from reading I had done. With no experience in the peace movement, I didn't yet have any developed opinions about the issues being discussed. At times I found myself rationally attracted to Al Hassler's critical concerns and arguments, but instinctively and emotionally I more often identified with the SDS perspective. Al Hassler's goal for the meeting was to craft a consensus and then issue a public statement to advise the younger SDS leaders. As I listened to the substance and even more to the tone of the discussion, the idea of such a statement seemed patronizing, and that bothered me. A.J. Muste, one of the oldest leaders in the room, spoke strongly against what at one point seemed to be an emerging consensus. In what I would learn was a characteristic Muste gesture, A.J. waved his long slender finger at the others and warned that issuing such a statement would likely have the opposite effect from what they wanted to accomplish. His views were strongly echoed by David McReynolds and David Dellinger. All three seemed to empathize with the growing outrage against the Vietnam War, especially among youth, and, as a matter of principle, they were against allowing anti-communism to control anti-war politics. After about two hours of discussion, the meeting broke up without agreement. Participating in that meeting introduced me to personalities, issues and conflicts with which I would be involved for the next ten years.

As I traveled back to Wesleyan, I worried about what this meeting signaled for my future relationship with my boss, Al Hassler. I came to believe that Hassler seemed stuck in a contradiction between being as strongly anti-communist as he was against war, and not understanding or appreciating the new youth activism. Thanks to A.J. Muste, David McReynolds, and David Dellinger, I learned that both sides had well-reasoned arguments and that the division was not simply between older, more experienced leaders and younger, less experienced ones.

Despite my appreciation that older people could be just as critical and radical as young people, a few months later at a conference in New York, I exhibited the impatient, angry temperament characteristic of many of my young 1960s activist peers. I was in a workshop where a middle-aged black woman angrily asked the mostly older, white, male participants how they would respond if one morning with their three kids waiting for breakfast, they opened the refrigerator and found it empty. A distinguished looking white-haired clergyman responded: "Remember, Jesus said, 'Man shall not live by bread alone.'" I was outraged and before he could say anything more, I interrupted him and loudly replied, "If that's your response, I would want to go join the Communist Party and burn a church down on the way." A short while later, my boss, Al Hassler introduced me to Dr. Howard Schomer, a major leader in the FOR, who had marched in Selma and helped to write the Universal Declaration of Human Rights. Recalling my outburst in the workshop, Dr. Schomer smiled and said quietly, "Yes, Ron and I already met." Going up to Schomer alone later, I apologized. He said he knew his initial response to the woman sounded awfully uncaring and cold. If I had not interrupted him, he assured me that what he intended to say next was much more responsive and sympathetic to the woman's question.

As the sixties wore on, the generational divide became wider and much more intense. Because of my close relationship with older nonviolent radicals like Jim Lawson, David McReynolds, David Dellinger and A.J. Muste, I never accepted the idea that age was the most important factor in shaping one's commitment to social change or one's willingness to act with courage to challenge the status quo in working for justice and peace.

I came to realize that several older men served as mentors and role models— indeed as surrogate father figures—for me in my teens and twenties. While my dad loved me and certainly taught me the value of hard work, given his pattern of regularly working two or three jobs, he was mostly absent from my life, and hardly seemed to care about the issues that increasingly concerned me. I never completely adopted the views of any one of these older mentors—and I assume at times I must have disappointed every one of them—but each man had qualities I admired and imitated, and they all had significant positive influence on my development.

Clearly, Reverend Jim Lawson had the most substantial influence, including guiding me to a radical, biblically-based personal and social understanding of what it means to be a follower of Jesus. Lawson also indirectly influenced many of my vocational and life choices. While his influence on my Christian faith was unique and transformative, I was aware that it also built on earlier influences in my life. As a young teenager I was influenced by my friendship with Mason Ellison, a humble, mild mannered, socially conscious youth pastor who mentored me at my home church at Packanack Lake. When I was fourteen, Rev. Ellison took me to visit a seminary in New York City, and encouraged me to think of becoming a minister. That was the same year that I went to the Billy Graham Crusade for Christ Rally at Madison Square Garden in New York and went forward in response to Graham's "Call to Christ."

As a freshman and sophomore at Wesleyan, I developed a close personal relationship with Dr. John Maguire, who arranged for me to work with Rev. Lawson in Memphis. Both Maguire's teaching, particularly his course, "Religious Currents in Contemporary Literature," and the example of his life led me to understand that a responsible Christian life involves projecting moral norms deeply into complex political realities. I came to believe that a Christian life is not to be lived privately, apart from the world, but needs to be lived publically in the world. As I learned from the lives of the Hebrew prophets and the life of Jesus, and from Martin Luther King Jr., Jim Lawson and Oscar Romero, with God's generous, impartial and unrelenting love for the world as a model, the Christian life is not basically about a better life after death, but needs to be lived fully engaged now for love of the world.

Despite these strong explicitly Christian influences and while I read a lot of theology, I never did pursue formal academic study of the Bible and never did go to seminary or become an ordained minister. For many years my sense of what being a follower of Jesus meant was informed by Dietrich Bonhoeffer's book, *The Cost of Discipleship*, and inspired by Bonhoeffer's phrase, "religionless Christianity" in his *Letters and Papers from Prison*.[1]

At the FOR, despite our differences on some issues, Al Hassler provided a model of professional responsibility and relative success in a peace movement field mostly populated by unpaid volunteers. His example and my paid position at the FOR helped me accept that I was now taking on this work for justice and peace as a profession, not simply as a matter of personal witness. Al's conscientious, liberal pacifist views on most issues were largely ones I admired and agreed with. At the same time, I experienced his strong, ideological anti-communist views and his critical instincts in relation to the developing youth culture of protest and resistance as too conservative and constraining. Furthermore, during my seven years at the FOR and subsequently, I did not always see a pacifist answer to every situation. It bothered me that Al Hassler never seemed to doubt his pacifism. On a personal level, while I often disagreed with him about advocacy positions and strategies for the anti-war movement, I always liked him. Indeed, during a year when I dated his daughter, Laura, I warmly imagined Al as my future father-in-law.

My views were more consistently aligned with the radical pacifism of A.J. Muste, Martin Luther King Jr. and Rev. Jim Lawson. I also admired and learned a lot from the non-pacifist perspectives of Yale's Chaplain, Rev. William Sloane Coffin Jr.; Presbyterian minister and theologian, Robert MacAfee Brown; and Rev. Richard Fernandez, all three of whom were leaders in Clergy and Laity (initially, Clergy and *Laymen*) Concerned About Vietnam (CALCAV or CALC). Bill Coffin and I participated together in several anti-war/anti-draft demonstrations. Bob Brown nurtured my thinking about liberation theology and policies in Latin America. I worked on many joint projects and became a close personal friend with Dick Fernandez, who played a major leadership role in the religious community during the Vietnam War years as the executive director of CALC.

As FOR's executive in the 1950s and for many years before then, A.J. Muste consistently identified clear connections between issues of class, race, war, and peace. On more than one occasion, he put his life on the line resisting injustice and war. Muste's 1952 essay, *Of Holy Disobedience*, remains a classic radical pacifist statement on nonviolence and civil disobedience. During 1965 and 1967 when I worked with him, A.J. demonstrated a political integrity and practical sense of strategy as he led the formation of a broad, inclusive, anti-war coalition of religious and secular activists, liberal and radical youth, and a variety of old leftists, most of whom shared some but certainly not all of Muste's radical pacifist views. While I never had his sharp analytic skills, charisma or courage, his ability to lead people of diverse views provided a very important model for me when, in 1969 and 1970, I served as coordinator of

---

1. Bonhoeffer, *Letters and Papers from Prison*, 161–166.

the National Mobilization Committee for Peace, the coalition that he had been instrumental in founding.

I also really admired Muste for the way his radical commitment to nonviolence led him to carry on respectful, serious, intellectual dialogues with a wide variety of political figures on the left, as well as in the center and on the right. It's a discipline and practice I've tried to emulate, especially during my years working for Arab-Israeli-Palestinian peace. Like Jim Lawson and Dr. King, Muste personally challenged me in ways that sometimes inspired me and other times left me feeling that I wasn't yet willing to risk enough for what I believed. I identified wholeheartedly with A.J.'s honesty and humility about pacifism. He once said to me, "Ron, most mornings I wake up believing I'm a pacifist, but after thinking objectively and trying to act responsibly on the complex evils of the world, by the end of the day, frankly, I am often surprised that I still am a pacifist!" There was nothing comfortable or self-satisfied about A.J.'s pacifism.

Glenn Smiley, who was national program director at FOR when I first joined the staff, was a steady source of personal encouragement and often served as a mediator in tensions I had with Al Hassler. Allan Brick, a humanist Quaker, followed Smiley and carried on as interlocutor and mediator for us. When I was being considered for the youth work position, Allan was chairman of the FOR personnel committee and I believe played a key role in FOR' decision to hire me. All during my tenure, Allan Brick was a role model and an important ally. He became a life-long friend and he introduced me to Trudi Schutz, whom I later married.

Allan Brick's radical analysis of society, while frequently convincing, was also sometimes difficult for me to act on, because I feared it could lead people to become frustrated and cynical. He seemed to underestimate people's capacity to change, and he wasn't always very strategic. But he consistently challenged my idealism and my sometimes simplistic optimism—a tendency I believe I inherited from my mother. Allan reminded me that without an adequate and realistic analysis of the depth of the problem, a strategy for change could be just scratching the surface and really not getting anywhere. I still live with all these influences and tensions.

A quotation from A.J. Muste best reflects what I most admired about all of these men and what, at the deepest level, continues to draw me to nonviolence.

> I've always tried to keep communication open between radicals and non-radicals, between pacifists and non-pacifists. It goes back to something very fundamental in the nonviolent approach to life. You always assume there is some element of truth in the position of the other person, and you respect your opponent for hanging on to an idea as long as he believes it to be true. On the other hand, you must try very hard to see what truth actually does exist in his idea, and seize on it to make him realize what you consider to be a larger truth.[2]

2. Hentoff, *Peace Agitator,* 251.

A. J. Muste's understanding of and commitment to nonviolence is a lot easier to describe than it is to practice. It requires conscientious commitment and disciplined patience to listen to the other, including political opponents and even enemies. This nonviolent approach is neither naïve nor passive. Rather, I believe it reflects a more profound realism about the power of love in action to press for deeper mutual understanding and worthwhile common ground that can help move all of us in the direction of justice, peace and reconciliation.

Going to work as national director of youth work at the FOR in 1965 involved changing my focus from race relations and the civil rights movement to the war in Vietnam and the draft. Objectively, this reflected what was happening in society as well as my own personal situation as a twenty-three-year-old facing the draft. This shift made sense at the time and, in retrospect, still makes sense to me today. However, one unintentional and unfortunate effect was that I almost entirely lost contact with black people, including the Memphis community where I had lived and worked for nearly two years and which had such a profound influence on me. I wish it hadn't happened, but it did. In 1965, the organized anti-war movement was almost entirely white. This was true despite the fact that compared to their percentage in the population, not only were blacks disproportionately participating in the war in Vietnam, but as it escalated, at least as high a percentage of black Americans as white Americans opposed the war. In part it was his recognition of this reality that led Dr. King to make his famous speech against the Vietnam War, "A Time to Break the Silence," at Riverside Church in New York City on April 4, 1967.

My separation from the black community was not absolute. At least some national organizers tried, usually with only partial and temporary success, to build a black-white coalition against the war in Vietnam and for social justice at home. Often these efforts were spearheaded at the national level by George Wiley, of the National Welfare Rights Organization (NWRO), which was composed of incredibly strong, courageous black women on welfare. Most of the women were from northern cities, but they reminded me of southern black women like Ella Baker, Fannie Lou Hamer, and Dorothy Cotton who played such important leadership roles in the southern Freedom Movement. There were times when I was involved in educational work or legal defense efforts trying to protect Black Panthers from persecution by police and the courts. Occasionally, I counseled young black men facing the draft or considering applying for C.O. status while serving in the military. Sometimes I got to meet with black students on college campuses where I spoke.

In 1966, at Jim Lawson's suggestion, Rev. Ed King invited me to speak at Tougaloo College in Mississippi. Ed King was the Mississippi-born white Methodist Chaplain at Tougaloo who had been severely beaten by whites for his political work with NAACP leaders Medgar Evans and Aaron Henry, and for his work bringing black Tougaloo students together with white students from nearby Millsaps College. Tougaloo students responded very positively to my talk, titled, "Selma, Saigon, Santo Domingo" that focused on the role of young people in pressing for radical social change in all three of those very different situations. The formal program was followed by hours of intense late-night discussion with the students. My visit to Tougaloo was an extraordinary, but all too brief and exceptional experience bridging my involvement in the civil rights and anti-war movements. I realized that by going to work at the FOR and becoming involved with other national peace organizations, I unintentionally had crossed back to the white side of the boundary I had crossed in the opposite direction three years earlier by going to work in Memphis. My personal experience and the failure to generate a serious interracial national coalition for justice and peace reflected the ongoing deep divide in 1965, even in liberal and progressive circles, between the vast majority of whites and blacks

Almost fifty years later, despite all the achievements of the civil rights movement, while there are some encouraging examples of new equalities and interracial cooperation, we are still a very long way from fulfilling Dr. King's vision of the American Dream and Rev. Jim Lawson's vision of the Beloved Community. Two books, as well as a highly regarded, widely quoted 2011 study by the Pew Research Center revealed how far we still have to go. When it comes to black-white relations, in schools, prisons, housing, work, and in worship on Sunday morning, as David Shipler titled his important, well-researched 1997 book, our nation is still mostly, *A Country of Strangers*.[3] In her 2010 book, *The New Jim Crow*, Michelle Alexander made a solid, statistically-based case that the way the war on drugs has been fought and the way our judicial and prison systems work have imposed a new form of Jim Crow on black Americans.[4] In July 2011, a Pew Research Center study revealed that incomes of white families are twenty times greater than those of African American families and eighteen times greater than Hispanic families, the largest gaps since the government started doing the survey.[5]

When I went to work at FOR in 1965, I did a lot of reading about Vietnam and US policy in Asia. I read *Vietnam: History, Documents and Opinion*, edited by Marvin E. Gettleman; *The Making of A Quagmire* by David Halberstam; *The Arrogance of Power* by Senator J. William Fulbright; and "The United States in Vietnam," a very important article by George McTurnan Kahin in the June, 1965 *Bulletin of Atomic Scientists*, that two years later was published as part of a book by the same title, co-authored with John W. Lewis. In the course of my reading and following the news, I became convinced that the US war in Vietnam was morally wrong. It would take me a few years to realize that, despite America's awesome military power, the war was also unwinnable.

During my first summer and fall at the FOR, I began travelling across the country to speak at churches, colleges, and, occasionally at high schools, explaining and

---

3. David Shipler, *Country of Strangers*.

4. Michelle Alexander, *The New Jim Crow*.

5. "Social and Demographic Trends."

advocating the principles of nonviolence, supporting the civil rights movement, and promoting the growing movement against the Vietnam War. I also began attending meetings of the newly formed Fifth Avenue Vietnam Peace Parade Committee in New York City, where I first met Norma Becker. Norma was an incredibly effective New York City school teacher, pacifist, and civil rights activist. Along with A.J. Muste and David Dellinger, she played a key role in organizing the Peace Parade Committee, which brought together a diverse coalition of women from Women's Strike for Peace and the Women's International League for Peace and Freedom, civil rights activists, students and youth, union organizers, particularly from the American Federation of State, County and Municipal Employees, old and new leftists, clergy and pacifists. Like Muste, and in contrast with my boss, Al Hassler, who opposed cooperation with communists, Trotskyites, and other old leftists, Norma Becker was committed to building a principled, inclusive anti-war coalition. It was a new experience for me to be at meetings with people who represented such a mixture of political views. I watched and listened closely to A.J. and Norma as they chaired the meetings. What united everyone was the shared conviction that the war in Vietnam was wrong and we needed to act together to stop it. The Peace Parade Committee mobilized thousands of people in New York and the Metropolitan area to participate in a series of anti-war marches. It became the model for similar inclusive, if sometimes also rather unwieldy, local coalitions in other cities and nationally for the Mobilization Committee to End the War in Vietnam.

On November 27, 1965, seven months after the anti-war march sponsored by the Students for Democratic Society, there was a second big national peace march in Washington. It was sponsored by the older, liberal, national Committee for a Sane Nuclear Policy (SANE), and involved many more adults than the SDS march, though I think it was a fact again that a majority of the marchers were young people. For many people, the most memorable speech was delivered by Carl Oglesby, president of SDS. Entitled "Let Us Shape the Future," it became very important and influential in shaping the anti-war movement. As I listened to Oglesby, the anxious concerns Al Hassler had expressed at that meeting of older peace movement leaders were very much on my mind. Interestingly, Oglesby himself had conservative roots and his speech that day represented a substantial evolution in his thinking. His family had moved from the South to live in Akron, Ohio, where his father worked in the rubber mills. As a high school senior in the early 1950s Carl Oglesby won a prize for a speech he wrote supporting the Cold War. Ten years later, after trying for a career as a playwright and novelist in New York City, Oglesby wrote an article in the University of Michigan campus magazine critical of US policy in Asia. Shortly after that, he joined the national leadership of SDS and soon was elected its president.

Carl Oglesby's speech on November 27 seemed almost a direct response to Al Hassler's concerns. He eloquently and passionately challenged the ideology of containing communism as the primary basis for American foreign policy. As a principled and strong advocate of participatory democracy, Oglesby opposed authoritarian rule. While acknowledging that the Vietnamese movement, the Viet Minh, and its leader, Ho Chi Minh, were Communists, as a matter of principle, Oglesby supported the Vietnamese struggle for independence. He condemned the US war and explicitly called for withdrawal from Vietnam, which became the benchmark position of the activist anti-war movement. In 1967, the ideas in his speech were incorporated into an important book entitled, *Containment and Change*,[6] coauthored by Oglesby, a secular radical, and Rev. Richard Shaull, a Presbyterian minister and theologian.

Protest and Resistance to the Draft

While the early anti-war marches were impressive, they were not the most compelling or dramatic form of protest in 1965. Growing opposition to the war that year was marked by extraordinary personal acts of resistance. Inspired by the self-immolation of a Vietnamese Buddhist monk, Thich (Venerable) Quang Duc in 1963, Alice Herz, an eighty-two-year-old grandmother in Detroit immolated herself on March 16, 1965 and died ten days later. On November 2, Norman Morrison, a Baltimore Quaker and personal friend of Allan Brick, carefully placed his infant daughter Emily a safe distance away, then set himself on fire and died on the lawn next to the Pentagon, just below the office window of Defense Secretary Robert McNamara. Four days later, defying a new federal law, David McReynolds and several young Roman Catholics associated with the Catholic Worker movement publicly burned their draft cards at a peace rally in New York City. On November 9, Roger LaPorte, a twenty-two-year-old former Catholic seminarian, seated himself in the posture of a Buddhist monk in front of the United Nations, and immolated himself. Though he died the next day, he was able quietly to declare: "I'm a Catholic Worker. I'm against war, all wars. I did this as a religious action." These self-immolations were terrifying, but they also profoundly challenged the moral consciences of many of us. We began to ask ourselves, "Are we doing enough to stop this war?" This question would trouble and motivate many of us again and again as the war continued for the next ten years.

From 1965 to 1975, protesting and resisting the Vietnam War and the draft, including deciding to burn my own draft card, organizing draft resistance, speaking publicly at hundreds of campus and community events across the country, and coordinating mass marches in Washington, became the consuming focus of my life. The potential implications and personal risks of acting on beliefs I had developed during my involvement with Jim Lawson in the black community in Memphis became a lot clearer to me during those years.

During 1965 and 1966, American military involvement in Vietnam steadily expanded and so did demonstrations against the war and the draft. Two dramatic

6. Oglesby and Shaull, *Containment and Change*.

cover stories in the mainstream *Life Magazine* reflected realities about the war and the draft. The first, on November 26, 1965, a day before the SANE March on Washington, portrayed a photo of a young "Vietcong" prisoner with his eyes and mouth covered with duct tape, and was entitled "The Blunt Reality of War in Vietnam."[7] A year later, the December 9, 1966 issue, was entitled "The Draft –Who Beats It and How."[8] On the cover were silhouettes of four young American men, wearing only undershorts and socks, about to be inducted into the military. Subtitles on the cover included: "What's wrong with the law; attitudes on the campus; dodging techniques, legal and otherwise; and pro football's magical immunity."

In my role as the FOR director of youth work, I became heavily involved in counseling young men about their choices related to the draft. While Vietnam initially seemed far away to many Americans, as a twenty-three-year-old who was no longer eligible for a student deferment, questions of what to do about the draft and the war had become very personal. I met with many young men who were approaching draft registration age, who were opposed to the war and interested in considering Conscientious Objector (C.O.) status. Counseling them, I was aware that I never even thought about that question of becoming a C.O. when I was their age. In 1960, at eighteen, when I registered for the draft, the process seemed as harmless and routine to me as registering a new mailing address at the Post Office.

Since my time in Memphis and Selma I had been wrestling with my views about violence and nonviolence. I still wasn't able to answer all the questions about what I would do in every imaginable circumstance but, like the founders of the FOR, I believed that the path of nonviolence came closest to the path of Jesus and was essential to finding better ways to deal with conflict. While I still wasn't sure what I might have done in World War II, I knew that I would not fight in Vietnam or any other war I could imagine. I decided to apply for C.O. status.

In 1965, legally qualifying as a C.O. required that I convince my local draft board, composed of four men and one woman all in their fifties, that "based on my religious beliefs, I was sincerely opposed to war in any form." I submitted an essay addressing these issues and then was called before the board in Paterson, New Jersey, to answer questions and further substantiate my claim. While I was fairly confident and articulate about my views, I was nervous and appreciated Glenn Smiley's offer to accompany me.

After what seemed a rather simplistic and boring discussion with the draft board members about my views on violence and war, Glenn and I left feeling good about my chances. A few weeks later the draft board granted my C.O. status and I received a classification exempting me from military service, but obligating me to perform two years of approved alternative civilian service. At the time, I believed this was a fair

7. "The Blunt Reality of War in Vietnam."
8. "The Draft—Who Beats It and How."

and acceptable outcome, but it turned out to be only the beginning of my personal struggle with the draft and the war.

As public opposition to the war in Vietnam grew, so did the numbers of young men with intense convictions against participating in the military. During World War II and the Korean War, most young men who applied for C.O. status came from religious groups with strong pacifist traditions, such as the Church of the Brethren, Mennonites and the Religious Society of Friends (Quakers). Beginning in 1965, I and other draft counselors around the country encountered growing numbers of young men who were scared and/or thought it was morally wrong to fight in Vietnam. Most of the young men I counseled seemed just as sincere and conscientious as the earlier more traditional C.O.'s. However, many of them did not qualify under the narrow Selective Service definition either because their opposition to going to war was not based on religious beliefs or because they were not opposed to war in any form.

In 1965, Dan Seeger, a humanist Quaker, was denied C.O. status because he didn't believe in a "supreme being." He refused induction, and later won a significant Supreme Court ruling that even beliefs that were not explicitly religious could be a legal basis for conscientious objection. Thus, if the local draft board turned them down, young men with humanist beliefs could pursue C.O. status through an appeals process and eventually in the courts. In practice most young men were unaware of this change and draft boards certainly didn't advertise it. In any case, the bigger obstacle was that selective conscientious objection—objection to a particular war—still was not recognized. A conscientious objector had to be opposed to war in any form.

As the war escalated, I counseled growing numbers of young men who clearly were opposed to fighting in Vietnam as an act of conscience. I began to question whether it was right for me to take advantage of the fact that my religious convictions qualified me for C.O. status, while their equally conscientious convictions did not. They were forced to face very hard personal choices between going into the military against their will, fleeing to Canada or possibly being convicted and serving time in prison for refusing induction. I became more and more troubled about my privileged position. I also felt the need to put more of my own life on the line against what our government was doing to Vietnam.

In 1966 and 1967 I coordinated a generously-funded project sponsored by the FOR that resulted in student body presidents at close to a hundred colleges signing a two-page ad in *The New York Times* declaring: "We believe the war in Vietnam is unjust and immoral, and we should not be forced to fight in it." 100,000 draft age students and youth from across the country signed FOR pledge cards making the same declaration. This project provided impressive evidence that public sentiment against the war, particularly among youth, was strong and growing, and might make it very difficult for the government to carry on the war. At the same time, it was clear to me that many of those young people—most of whom still had student deferments—might not actually be called up by the military or, if they were called up, might not actually refuse induction. An artist colleague on the national FOR staff who appreciated the moral ambiguity of the situation, drew a cartoon depicting me, with money hanging from my pockets, gathering signatures. The caption on the cartoon satirically labeled the pledge card protest as the, "We *May Not Go* Movement."

My own approach to organizing, for the most part supported by FOR, was to work with a broad range of young people with concerns about the war and the draft, appreciating their different personal backgrounds, social contexts, and thresholds for more courageous activism. Thus, during the same time that I was coordinating the pledge card campaign, I was also working with a much smaller but growing number of young men who were risking arrest by publicly calling for open resistance to the Vietnam War and the draft. Some formed local groups based on the declaration, "We Won't Go," while others tore up or burned their draft cards as public acts of non-violent civil disobedience. I worked in both arenas and authored a widely circulated FOR pamphlet entitled, "It's Your Choice," describing the realities of modern warfare in general, and the Vietnam War in particular. I contrasted the realities of war with religious teachings about "love thy neighbor" and ethical standards for a just war. I presented the options and possible consequences for young men facing the draft, with an emphasis on the moral imperative to "Say No to War!"

As my personal opposition to the war and the unfairness of the draft deepened, I became convinced that I could no longer conscientiously cooperate with the draft. In spring, 1967, I made a decision to join with fifty other young men in publicly burning our draft cards in New York's Central Park, hours before a large anti-war protest march to the United Nations, sponsored by the Spring Mobilization Committee. On Saturday, April 15, I dropped my burning draft card into a Maxwell House coffee can, in exchange for a bright yellow daffodil presented to me by a lovely young girl in a hippie dress. I felt a combination of an adrenaline rush and a wave of anxiety about what would happen next. The fifty of us who burned our cards that morning knew FBI agents were taking photographs. We feared that we might immediately be arrested and had agreed, if the police came for us, to lock arms and nonviolently re-fuse to cooperate. None of us were arrested that day, but I was aware that this action represented crossing a boundary for which I might go to prison for a couple of years, an experience for which I didn't feel prepared.

Many of the moderates and old leftists in the committee that sponsored the march to the UN that day were worried that burning draft cards would alienate more mainstream opponents of the war. A majority had voted not to associate the com-mittee with our action. I remember learning that Al Hassler, my boss at the FOR, didn't even participate in the march that day but observed it from a penthouse apart-ment overlooking Fifth Avenue. I was aware of the irony that some older political leftists and anti-communist pacifists who disagreed with each other about a lot of things, agreed on distancing themselves from the draft resisters. I knew that Hassler respected my conscientious position of noncooperation with the draft. He had taken a position of noncooperation in the 1940s, for which he was sentenced and served time in prison. In April 1967, however, he believed that draft card burning, the inclusion of old leftists in the anti-war coalition, and the decision by the Spring Mobilization Committee to invite Black Power advocate Stokely Carmichael to speak at the April 15 rally along with Martin Luther King Jr. were unnecessarily confrontational and politically counterproductive. By this time, I simply accepted that my positions on these issues and others were different from his. I believed he was out of touch with the depth and breadth of popular opposition to the war, especially among growing numbers of young people.

In contrast, I remember the last time I was with A.J. Muste in 1966, on a flight back to New York City from a national anti-war meeting in Cleveland. A.J. was chairman of the Spring Mobilization Committee planning the April 15, 1967 march in New York. On the plane trip back to New York, A.J. and I talked about plans for the demonstration and about the controversies surrounding speakers and the planned draft card burning. I explained my reasons for deciding to burn my draft card and discussed my role in the "We Won't Go" public draft resistance movement. A.J. could tell I was nervous about the prospect of going to prison, and he quietly reassured me in a pastoral manner. Next he talked about the important moral and political significance of organizing open, public resistance to the draft. He fully supported my role in this movement. His views and his calm, confident manner helped me to feel more at peace with myself and more convinced that I was on the right track. Sadly, A. J. Muste died on February 11, 1967, two months before the April 15 Spring Mobilization demonstration that he had played such a major role in organizing.

The mass march and rally on April 15 at the United Nations brought out tens of thousands of people, many of them for the first time, to publicly oppose the war. However, an event took place eleven days earlier that was much more momentous. At a gathering at Riverside Church organized by Dick Fernandez of Clergy and Laity Concerned, more than 1,000 people heard Martin Luther King Jr. deliver a powerful address, "A Time to Break Silence," linking opposition to the Vietnam War with the civil rights movement. Practically all of the media and many important civil rights leaders criticized King for making this link and for directly attacking the Johnson administration. Led by his conscience, King had declared,

> I knew I could never again raise my voice against the violence of the oppressed
> in the ghettos without first having spoken clearly to the greatest purveyor of
> violence in the world today—my own government.[9]

Exactly one year later, on April 4, 1968, Martin Luther King Jr. was assassinated in Memphis.

The day after I burned my draft card, I wrote a letter to my draft board explaining why I could no longer cooperate with the Selective Service System and requesting

9. Martin Luther King Jr., "A Time to Break Silence," 233.

an opportunity to meet with them. I never received a response. A few months later, I received an order to report for alternative service as a Conscientious Objector. In yet another letter to my draft board, I explained why my opposition to the war and my identification with other young men facing the draft had led me to refuse any further cooperation with the draft. Once again, I asked for an opportunity to explain my views, and once again, they did not respond.

Two months later, in early June 1967, America's attention temporarily and suddenly shifted from Vietnam to the war between Israel and the neighboring Arab nations of Egypt, Syria and Jordan. Egypt's decision to close the Straights of Tiran to Israeli shipping and order UN forces out of the Sinai buffer zone were the immediate provocations for Israel's preemptive attack. Syria and a reluctant Jordan joined Egypt in response. At first, Arab armies seemed to have the advantage; however, within a few days the tide turned. Israel's superior air force destroyed much of the Egyptian and Syrian air force, and Israel's army then drove into Arab territory. Six days after it started, the war was over and Israel had captured Gaza and the Sinai from Egypt, the Golan Heights from Syria, and the West Bank, with its 2,000,000 Palestinians and the prized Old City of Jerusalem, from Jordan. Jews were relieved and elated. While some on the left—including a small minority of Jews, some American Protestant leaders and some student activists—were critical of Israel, I think most Americans, including the vast majority of American Jews, admired Israel's speedy victory. In contrast with the Vietnam War quagmire, this was the kind of war most Americans liked: quick, decisive, and victorious.

Of course, the situation was more complicated. Israel's occupation of the West Bank and Gaza generated new recognition of the core conflict with the Palestinians. New tensions about the Israeli occupation arose on the American left that would continue to play out in years to come. In 1967, I had no idea that fifteen years later I would be living in the Middle East working for Quaker agencies crossing boundaries to meet with people and listen to their views on both sides of the Arab-Israeli divide.

In the meantime, the war in Vietnam continued to escalate, as did anti-war protests and resistance at home. Popular opposition to the war developed in two directions, from protest to political action and from protest to resistance. In the weeks following Dr. King's speech at Riverside Church and the massive April 15 march in New York, inspired by Freedom Summer in 1964, plans and substantial funding developed for what was called Vietnam Summer, a massive nationwide grassroots public education campaign, involving thousands of young people ringing doorbells and organizing community meetings against the war . In the fall, on October 21, 1967, 100,000 people came to Washington, D.C. to "Confront the Warmakers" at the Pentagon. The mass rally and civil disobedience that followed were memorialized in Norman Mailer's book, *Armies of the Night* that won a Pulitzer Prize and National Book Award. Just before the rally and march, 2,000 people gathered on the steps of the Justice Department, where I spoke along with Rev. Bill Coffin, Chaplain at Yale

University. Then a delegation went in to Attorney General Robert Kennedy's office to deliver pledges by hundreds of draft-age young men who planned to resist fighting in Vietnam.

In January 1968, I received a federal indictment in the mail that began: "THE UNITED STATES OF AMERICA VS. RONALD JAMES YOUNG." While I suppose I could have anticipated this heading; nevertheless, it came as quite a shock for a guy who only ten years earlier had earned the Boy Scouts' Eagle Scout and God and Country awards, had been president of my church Youth Fellowship, and had seriously considered applying to West Point. While I was shocked and nervous about the prospect of going to prison, I didn't feel any moral contradiction between my Scouts activities and my decision to resist the draft. I believed both were solidly based on core Christian and American values. As a teenager, I was inspired by love of my country and by my Christian faith, and those same values were still guiding me as a twenty-six-year-old. I expressed all of this in a poem I wrote, which I was invited to read in Washington, in February 1968, at the national gathering of Clergy and Laity Concerned about Vietnam. I titled the poem, "*We Are America.*" Here are excerpts:

We Are America

I was expecting it
But it's still hard to believe it happened.
I've been indicted,
And the indictment reads,

THE UNITED STATES OF AMERICA
Vs.
RONALD JAMES YOUNG

How can this be?
There must be some mistake.
Am I not America?

After working a year in a black church in Memphis,
The issue of black people and me
And America
Became a question of being,
Not merely of policy.
And the new being was the basis of a new politics,
Having less to do with parties, and polls, and candidates—
For now, for me—
And more to do with issues,
And relationships,
And risking something important for something good.

The year I lived in Memphis
Was the Cuban Missile crisis,
And the first time our government lied—
To me, anyway—
And almost led the nation to the final war.

The Vietnam War started like civil rights,
As a question in my mind.
But cut quickly and deeply into me,

The government of my country
Is destroying the Vietnamese people,
In the name of national security,
And in the name of saving Vietnam,
A salvation from which
Vietnamese are trying to save themselves.

The government needs more soldiers.
And continues to send them to the slaughter.
But we do not go willingly as before.
Because of the Atom Bomb,
And civil rights,
And wars in the cities that have begun,
And the Beattles and Alice's Restaurant,
And P-O-T and L-S-D.

And because the government
Doesn't always tell the truth.
And because we are learning the Truth
That people are more important
Than any idea or system.
And that people are power.

The government needs more soldiers
But we have something to say now,
"We won't go."
We want to build not burn."
And we're telling our friends.

And we earnestly believe we are right.
And no matter how the indictments may read,
We believe we are America,

And We Shall Overcome.

In 2011, reading Robin Wright's book, *Rock the Casbah*, about the Arab Spring, I was reminded of our strong belief as young Americans opposing the Vietnam War that, "we are America." I remember in several talks I gave during the Vietnam War rhetorically asking the question, "Will the real America please stand up?" In her book, Robin wrote about *Dark2Men*, a young, proud, defiant, anti-establishment, anti-extremist Arab Muslim Hip Hop group in Saudi Arabia. Clearly rejecting religious extremism and the pejorative labels put on them by conservative Arab leaders, the young Saudi musical group asserted that in caring for women and family, and neighbors and community, they believed that they are the true Muslims. [10]

My parents were living in Brazil when I burned my draft card in April 1967 and they were living in Haiti when I was indicted in 1968, so we never talked face-to-face about these developments. I know that my father viewed my decision as, at best, impractical and one more unnecessary and unwise postponement of getting my all-important college degree. For my mother, my indictment was another occasion, like when I went off to Memphis, which worried her, but she recognized that it reflected idealism I inherited from her and probably from my grandmother, the Silk Mills union organizer, and my street-fighting grandfather. The fact that later in 1968 I got married helped reassure my parents—as it did me—that I was still growing up in a relatively good and normal way.

From my experiences in Memphis, I was very angry about racism in our society, about the war against Vietnam, and about the unfairness of the draft. At the same time, I felt deeply disappointed and sad because I believed our country had so much that is positive to offer the world. While I identified more with young Americans refusing to fight in Vietnam, I also respected the young Americans who were in the military fighting in Vietnam. Unlike some anti-war activists—a very small minority in my experience—I didn't feel any anger toward American soldiers. I believed that leaders in government and all of us as citizens were much more responsible for betraying our country's ideals than the young Americans sent to fight.

Many years later I became acquainted with George Ratcliffe, a member of the congregation in Seattle that my wife served as Pastor. George had made a career in the Air Force and had flown transport planes in and out of Vietnam during the war. Knowing of my involvement in the anti-war movement, one day George told me about a disturbing incident he witnessed near a military base in California, where anti-war activists cursed and spat at returning veterans. George believed me when I told him I condemned such behavior and, didn't feel any personal hostility toward soldiers. We listened carefully to each other's stories and views. We became warm friends. In the lead up to the invasion of Iraq in 2003, invited by my Pastor wife, George, his wife

10. Wright, *Rock the Casbah*, 122–123.

Gloria, and I stood together with others after worship outside our church in a vigil for peace, opposing the invasion.

Marriage to Trudi

If my being indicted for resisting the draft was my hardest personal experience in 1968, clearly the best and most joyous experience was entering into a relationship with Trudi Schutz and our decision to get married in October. This was my first intimate relationship. While I hadn't talked about it with anyone, I was aware since my teens that there was a painful personal gap between my abilities as a speaker and outward sense of confidence and my shyness and self-doubts, especially about girls, sex and intimate relationships. While I later came to accept that I was viewed by some young women as "a good catch," my shyness and lack of confidence with women and my ambivalence and anxiousness about my bi-sexuality caused me to resist initial signs that Trudi was attracted to me.

The first time we met was at a Peace Parade Committee meeting in New York City, where I spoke briefly about draft resistance. Trudi had come to the meeting with Allan Brick, with whom she worked at the AFSC in Baltimore. I later learned that after my talk that day, Trudi whispered to Allan, "That's the man I'm going to marry." We met again at a summer youth conference where Trudi had arranged for me to speak. One evening she came to my cabin and volunteered that she was attracted to me. Though I also was attracted to her, I was too nervous and unsure of myself to respond and rebuffed her. That fall, Trudi invited me to come to Baltimore to have dinner and stay overnight. I accepted her invitation, but then totally forgot about our date. Instead, I went into New York City with my sister, Judy, that evening to see Pele, the famous Brazilian soccer star, play in an exhibition game. Judy and I felt a connection with Pele because our parents lived in Brazil 1964–67, and they had seen him play several times. When I didn't show up at her apartment for dinner, Trudi was very angry. The next day she claimed over the phone that she dumped an entire wonderful paella dinner into the garbage. I believed her. I apologized profusely and asked her to give me a second chance. Some weeks later, I went to Baltimore to visit Trudi at her apartment, had dinner (not elaborate paella this time), and stayed overnight. I volunteered that I would sleep on a mattress on the floor in the living room, hoping she would interpret my reluctance to share her bed as a lack of nerve, not lack of interest. I saw Trudi a few more times in Baltimore and then in Philadelphia where she moved to work on the national staff of the Central Committee for Conscientious Objectors (CCCO). Our attraction for each other grew.

Trudi was a Quaker whose mostly unspoken religious beliefs paralleled my own sensibilities at the time. We shared strong convictions about race, civil rights, the Vietnam War, the draft, and nonviolence; and we both enjoyed working with high school and college age young people. We were drawn to some of the same music, including

Donovan, the Beatles, Pete Seeger, Judy Collins, Joan Baez, Phil Ochs, and Peter, Paul and Mary. Trudi loved to laugh, as did I. We both loved good food, and preparing it. Trudi had earlier experience with intimacy and gradually helped me to overcome my awkwardness, without ever seeming to be teaching.

After sharing several good times together, I invited Trudi to stay with me for a weekend in Stony Point, New York, where I was living in my parents' small mobile home while they were living in Haiti. It was Easter weekend. Trudi and I didn't go to church, but we did go out for two dinners and for a long walk in nearby Harriman State Park. It was the longest time we had spent together and the first time we shared a bed. Reflecting on my earlier limited experience while I was still at Wesleyan—dating a young woman while at the same time being attracted to a guy my age, as well as my more recent experience dating my boss' daughter—I knew that what was happening with Trudi was different and deeper. While for increasing numbers of my generation, sexual intimacy and marriage no longer necessarily went together "like a horse and carriage," in a simple way, for me they still mostly did. By the end of the weekend, I felt sure that I wanted us to marry and I believed Trudi felt that way too. I remember going into work at FOR on Monday morning, feeling a wonderful new sense of confidence and joy. My secretary, Val Green—a beautiful, blond middle-aged woman, veteran nonviolent activist, and mother of two sons my age—smiled knowingly and said, "Ron you're glowing, I've never seen you look so happy." She sure read me right.

It says a lot about the delicious personal highs and devastating lows that often followed closely on each other in the 1960s that my wonderful April Easter weekend with Trudi came just ten days after Martin Luther King Jr. was murdered in Memphis. I remember hearing the news of his assassination on my car radio while I was driving in Queens, New York. I pulled over to the side of the highway and sat there for a while stunned and sobbing with tears streaming down my face. Two months later, on the night he won the primary in California, becoming the presumptive Democratic Party candidate for president, Robert Kennedy was murdered. To lose both Martin Luther King and Bobby Kennedy within a period of two months—and less than five years after the assassination of President John Kennedy—was an incredible loss for our country and the world. It was also a profoundly disturbing revelation about the pervasive violence in our society.

Following our first wonderful weekend, Trudi and I spent several more weekends together. With blessings of both sets of parents, we decided to take a week's vacation in August in Bar Harbor, Maine. Trudi's father offered to pay for the small cabin where we would have a pre-wedding honeymoon. We were married in October 1968 at the old FOR headquarters mansion overlooking the Hudson River in Nyack, New York. Fr. Tom Hayes, an Episcopal priest and close friend, who later moved to Sweden to minister to American war resisters, performed our wedding ceremony. As soon as Fr. Tom began to speak, it was clear that he had already drunk too much wine. At the end of the ceremony, as 100 brightly colored (environmentally unsound) helium-filled balloons urging "Amnesty for Vietnam War Resisters" floated skyward up over the Hudson River, Fr. Tom, inspired by wine as much as by our ceremony, pronounced our marriage partnership to be "a cadre of resistance." I am certain that neither Trudi's parents nor mine understood the image. I'm not sure Trudi and I understood it either, but we liked it. Before the wedding, Trudi's mother, Adele, who had fled Austria to America on the eve of the German invasion, expressed her nervousness about our non-traditional plans. She asked, "Is it going to be a hippie wedding?" Trudi asked in response, "What's a hippie wedding?" Her mom replied, "I don't know but I'm scared."

Having a committed, intimate relationship and deciding to marry was a major boundary crossing for me. Though she was four months younger, Trudi's greater maturity, particularly her earlier experience with intimacy, was very important to our getting through the initial stages of our relationship and making our marriage work for six years. While I was sufficiently liberated to understand that cooking and house cleaning duties were to be shared, I was still traditional in many ways and Trudi was less liberated than she may have thought. For example, I simply assumed and Trudi readily agreed that she would take my last name, give up her very good job at CCCO, and move from Philadelphia to live with me near the FOR in Nyack. We never really discussed these decisions. A few months later, Trudi acknowledged feeling depressed and we recognized that, in fact, these were important and sensitive issues that we needed to responsibly address. A deeper and more problematic issue was the way I experienced our relationship emotionally and psychologically. In marrying Trudi, I felt as if I had entered into a safe harbor that would protect me till death do us part. This very comforting, if unrealistic, image had come to me one night in a dream. Even while I recognized that the image of a safe harbor was more appropriate to a child's relationship with his mother than to an intimate adult relationship, I continued to lean on the illusion.

In fact, Trudi did help me to deal with my anxiety over the prospect of prison and my growing leadership responsibilities in the anti-war movement. But there was no way that our relationship could shield me from the emotional, psychological and physical risks involved in the tumultuous events of the 1960s. As an example, in August 1968, two months before we married, I participated in the demonstrations at the Democratic National Convention in Chicago. While I had no significant leadership role in the demonstrations, I was close to several of the leaders. Months later, recalling the violent attack by the Chicago police outside the Hilton Hotel, I remained confused and troubled by my lack of courage, and my uncertainty during the intense debates over movement strategy and tactics, including arguments about the efficacy of nonviolence. Our relationship could not shield me from these pressures. Indeed, the times took a toll on each of us and on our relationship. As in the popular Simon and Garfunkel song of 1969, I was still learning that friends and especially a lover could help calm my fears and dry my tears, but sometimes there is no bridge over troubled waters. Some troubled waters, I would learn, you have to face alone, and somehow just wade through them.

Trudi and I enjoyed a honeymoon in December 1968 when I was invited to speak at an anti-war conference at the Church of the Crossroads in Honolulu. It wasn't the first or the last time that I managed to combine personal pleasure with a work trip. We had a wonderful time on Kauai, enveloped by the peaceful, natural beauty of the island. Our time in Honolulu was emotionally much more complicated. The presence of known FBI agents at the conference recording my talk openly advocating draft resistance caused me a renewed rush of anxiety about the prospect of going to prison. The situation became even more complicated when two young men who were AWOL from Kaneohe Air Force Base showed up seeking sanctuary at the church. After a lot of intense discussion, conference participants including Trudi and I, offered to hike with the young men back to their base, where they planned to turn themselves in and apply for conscientious objector status. We all knew that, while it was not impossible, seeking recognition as C.O.s from inside the military, was a very difficult and often unsuccessful process.

Our time together in Honolulu was further complicated by an incident during our visit to the home of the poet Paul Goodman and his wife. Before dinner, a few of us, including a twenty-year-old Asian American boy who was living with the Goodmans, went swimming. It was pretty clear that Paul and the boy had a close personal relationship, but that didn't stop me from admiring his beauty as we swam and played together in the surf. Our honeymoon nights in Honolulu turned into quite an emotional mess involving very little romance and a lot of painful tension related to my anxiety about prison and my physical attraction for Paul Goodman's friend. At twenty-six years old, intellectually, if not always emotionally, I accepted the fact that I was bisexual. Trudi also accepted that about me. Still, there were times, like this one, when my attraction for guys caused trouble in our marriage.

Trudi and I got over this episode and later that month enjoyed a wonderful family Christmas in Baltimore at her parents' home. We had ordered orchid leis sent from Hawaii for our mothers and sisters, and for Trudi's dear Tante (Aunt) Mitsi. Thanks to the deep love and respect we had for each other, our strong common commitments on the issues of the day, our ability to laugh at ourselves, good friends, and some good luck, Trudi and I were able to get through several tough times together.

In 1970, I came up for trial in Newark, New Jersey, fully expecting that I would be found guilty and sentenced to prison. On the day my trial was scheduled to begin, 200 people, including Trudi, my mother, and several FOR colleagues gathered at an Episcopal church near the courthouse for a Celebration of Conscience. Al Hassler, Rev. William Sloan Coffin and Thich Nhat Hanh, a Vietnamese Buddhist monk and author of the book, *Vietnam: Lotus in a Sea of Fire*, spoke in support of my decision and for peace in Vietnam. They all marched with me to the federal courthouse, behind a banner that Trudi carried which read, "Trudi Says YES to Ron Who Says NO!"

When we arrived at the courthouse, my lawyer came out and whispered to me that the trial was postponed. Later over lunch, I commented to Bill Coffin, whose love of playing piano was legend, that obviously this was an occasion with a hell of a lot of pomp, but practically no circumstances.

My trial was rescheduled a few months later and this time the celebration of conscience happened inside the courtroom. I was found guilty, but instead of sentencing me to prison, Judge Lawrence A. Whipple released me to probation on the condition that I would continue to work for the FOR. He assigned me to a black probation officer who told Trudi and me privately that as a younger man he had been a member of CORE, which was started by the FOR in the 1940s. Whatever his personal beliefs about the war, fortunately for me, by the time I came before him, apparently Judge Whipple, had become tired of sending guys with convictions like mine to prison. I couldn't help wondering, if I were black, would Judge Whipple have handed down the same decision? With an almost giddy sense of relief and joy, Trudi and I went out for a celebratory dinner at the 1776 House, an expensive restaurant near our home.

Trip to Bratislava, Czechoslovakia

During the summer of 1967, a new conflict arose between Al Hassler and me. I was invited by David Dellinger, the editor of *Liberation* magazine, and Tom Hayden, former president of SDS, to represent religious pacifists in a delegation of forty American anti-war activists who were going to travel to Bratislava, Czechoslovakia in September to meet with forty Vietnamese from North Vietnam and the National Liberation Front (NLF) of South Vietnam—known in the media as the "Vietcong" (Viet Communists). I understood that this would be another boundary crossing, in the sense that Americans who participated would be meeting with people representing a government and a liberation movement that our government had declared to be our enemies. I didn't believe that any Vietnamese were my enemies. Indeed, I fully sympathized with Muhammad Ali and young black activists who had adopted and promoted the saying, "No Vietcong ever called me 'nigger.'"

I was excited by the diverse group of American peace activists who had agreed to participate in the Bratislava Conference. Several staff colleagues and members of the FOR executive committee supported my participation, but Al Hassler adamantly opposed my going to meet with communists. He told me that I could not represent FOR at the conference and could not use FOR funds to get there. Rather than intensify this conflict, I offered to take personal vacation time and to pay for my travel with my own money.

Our delegation flew from New York to Prague and then to Bratislava, the capital of Slovakia, which is a very beautiful, several-hundred-year-old city with three universities and a rich, complex, cultural history, located on the Danube River only thirty-seven miles from Vienna. Unfortunately, except for an evening cruise on the

Danube marked by good food and too much vodka, we didn't get to see much of Bratislava and hardly saw Prague at all..

Around the edges of our conference with the Vietnamese, some of us learned that Bratislava was an active center of the growing underground opposition to Soviet control of Czechoslovakia. This was just months before the liberalization period known as Prague Spring in 1968. One night a small group of us who were resisting the draft in America met secretly in a basement with young Czechs who were hiding to escape obligatory service in the Soviet military. These young men faced much more severe and dangerous circumstances than we did, but we all drew inspiration and courage from meeting one another. I noted that particular historical circumstances—in their case, Soviet domination, and in ours, the Vietnam War—were the immediate causes generating increased resistance to military service. However, I was encouraged that, especially among youth, there also were more public expressions of fundamental resistance to militarism and violence. The title and lyrics of Phil Ochs's popular 1965 song, "I Ain't Marchin' Anymore," reflected this defiantly hopeful spirit that was rising among young people worldwide.

In our meetings with North Vietnamese and members of the NLF, both we and they learned new things about each other's country, and our respective social and political movements. Although the brief presentations by participants from both delegations tended to be too optimistic and uncritical, by the end of the week I believe most of us had more accurate and complex understandings of each other's society than when we first arrived. Most of the Americans gravitated toward those Vietnamese who were willing to talk about their personal lives and convictions. While most members of North Vietnam's delegation seemed more ideologically rigid than the Southerners, Do Xuan Oanh, a brilliant, very personable North Vietnamese in his forties who had worked with Tom Hayden to arrange the meeting, was a very special exception. Born of a poor Vietnamese mining family, Oanh was a poet who also wrote folk songs. He spoke fluent English and had translated several American novels into Vietnamese, including Mark Twain's *Huckleberry Finn*. His understanding of American history and culture far surpassed the understanding any of us had of Vietnam. Our experience was a powerful example of how victims of colonialist or other forms of oppression often understand their oppressors much better than people from the oppressing country understand their victims.

While most of the conference dialogue focused relatively clearly and exclusively on politics, one incident comically revealed a cultural gap between our delegations' views of sexuality. John (Jock) Pairman Brown, a radical Protestant theologian from Berkeley, was explaining different responses by American religious leaders to the Vietnam War. At one point, Jock criticized the stance of some mainstream American religious leaders as representing a kind of "religious masturbation." The translation process abruptly stopped. Tom Hayden, who was assisting the Vietnamese translator, appealed to Jock to substitute some other phrase, but Jock refused, insisting that this was the only appropriate phrase to make his point. American participants laughed. Some of the Vietnamese participants smiled embarrassedly. A red-faced Hayden fumbled with an explanation to the Vietnamese translator and the discussion moved awkwardly forward.

The most prominent Vietnamese in the Bratislava meetings was Madame Nguyen Thi Binh, one of the leaders of the NLF delegation. She was a former school teacher who had been active in the Vietnamese anti-colonialist rebellion against the French in the late 1940s and early 1950s. She was jailed by the French from 1951 to 1953. Two years after our meeting in Bratislava, Madame Binh emerged as foreign minister of the Provisional Revolutionary Government of South Vietnam, and was a key participant in most negotiations with the United States. After the war, she served as vice president of newly reunited Vietnam.

For me and most of the Americans, meeting Vietnamese in Bratislava deepened our convictions that the war was immoral, unjust, and unwinnable. In contrast with the call for "Negotiations Now," by Al Hassler and some other older, more anti-communist peace movement leaders, this experience reinforced my commitment to the more activist call for "US withdrawal now" or simply "Out Now." Howard Zinn, a historian and social activist made the argument eloquently and succinctly in his 1967 book, *Vietnam: The Logic of Withdrawal*[11]. Howard Zinn's classic 1980 work, *A People's History of the United States* has had an enduring influence on American social activism and on the study of grassroots social and political protest movements in American history.

My personal goal in Bratislava was to get to know at least one Vietnamese on a deeper, more personal level, to learn all I could about his life and to share my life story with him. I imagined telling his personal story in talks that I would give on college campuses when I returned home and using it as a way of breaking through the abstract Cold War, anti-communist lock that still controlled much public discussion. Nguyen Hoc Lo (a pseudonym) was my age, 25. He came from a village in the Mekong Delta in South Vietnam. At seventeen he enrolled in Saigon University hoping to become a journalist. One year later, he became active in the South Vietnamese nationalist student movement and joined demonstrations against the dictatorial rule of Ngo Dinh Diem, the anti-communist president of South Vietnam who was supported by our government. After being arrested twice and tortured by the police, and being warned by friends that he might be killed, Nguyen dropped out of University, left Saigon and went to live near Quang Ngai, where he was recruited by the NLF. Nguyen told me that, like most Vietnamese, he admired Ho Chi Minh for having led the successful struggles to defeat the Japanese occupation and the attempt by France to re-impose colonial rule. Although he was a member of the NLF, Nguyen said that he was not a communist. While I had no way of confirming that, I liked him and sensed he was speaking truthfully. Moreover, by 1967, I had read enough about Vietnam's history to

11. Zinn, *Vietnam: The Logic of Withdrawal*.

know that whether or not he was a communist was less important than other pieces of his personal story. As planned, I did tell Nguyen Hoc Lo's story in dozens of talks on college campuses that fall, including at a packed convocation in the chapel at Wooster College in Ohio. While no doubt some who heard me speak were critical of my having met with the enemy, the mood of most students on many campuses by then was much more open and receptive to what I was saying than it had been even a couple of years earlier. As Bob Dylan declared in song, "The times, they are a-changin.'"

On our last day in Bratislava, David Dellinger called me aside and invited me to accompany him and two other Americans who were going on to Hanoi. He told me that this small American anti-war activist delegation would likely meet with Ho Chi Minh, North Vietnam's famed president. As it turned out, the Americans did have a meeting with President Ho. I was tempted to go, but felt that I had already stretched Al Hassler's patience enough. So, even though I was pleased to be asked and I was very interested in going to Hanoi, I decided not to go. Crossing that boundary would happen three years later.

March on Washington for Peace in Vietnam, November 1969

In June 1969 I was chosen to be the coordinator of the National Mobilization Committee to End the War in Vietnam (known as the Mobilization or 'Mobe'), a broad coalition of organizations that were planning anti-war marches in Washington and San Francisco on November 15. Despite Al Hassler's reservations about the inclusive nature of the coalition and its call for "Withdrawal Now," FOR agreed to release me with pay to take on this responsibility. During the summer and early fall, Rev. Dick Fernandez of CALC, Stewart Meacham of the AFSC, and I organized small representative teams of national anti-war activists and leaders, including representatives of clergy, secular political groups, women's peace organizations, and students, to travel to more than forty cities nationwide to encourage participation in a variety of protest activities that fall, including the November 15 mass marches and rallies. I participated in a team that visited ten cities in five days, meeting with local anti-war activists in two cities each day.

As plans for the march on Washington developed, I also began meeting every two weeks in Philadelphia with representatives of several religious groups, including AFSC, CALC, FOR, and A Quaker Action Group to discuss the idea of adding a morally compelling, symbolic action component to the November protest plans. By this time, there already had been many local demonstrations in which people gathered publicly, often outside of draft boards or military recruiting stations, to read the names of Americans who had been killed in Vietnam. The discussions in Philadelphia came up with an idea that we decided to call the "March Against Death." We developed an ambitious plan to recruit Americans from each state equal to the number of soldiers from that state who already had been killed in Vietnam. The delegations would gather at Arlington Cemetery in alphabetical order by state and walk slowly in single file from there to the Capitol, each person carrying a placard with the name of a soldier from their state who had been killed. As they passed by the White House, each marcher would turn and call out the name he or she was carrying. When they reached the Capitol, participants would place their placards in a large wooden coffin on the Capitol steps.

As preparations continued, we realized that we could never have the names of hundreds of thousands of Vietnamese who had been killed, so we decided to add placards with the names of Vietnamese villages that had been destroyed. This idea was inspired by a news story filed by Peter Arnett of the Associated Press on February 7 1968, quoting an anonymous American army major commenting on the destruction of Ben Tre, a South Vietnamese provincial capital. The Army major told Arnett that to prevent Ben Tre from falling to the communists, "It became necessary to destroy the town in order to save it."[12]

While I focused most of my energy on mobilizing support for the mass march and rally, Trudi worked with Dick Fernandez and others organizing the logistics and recruiting state delegations for the March Against Death. We estimated that with participants walking slowly from Arlington Cemetery to the Capitol in single file, six feet apart, carrying the names of more than 38,000 American servicemen, interspersed with names of destroyed Vietnamese villages, the March Against Death would continue for approximately thirty-six hours. Since Saturday's mass march and rally was scheduled to begin at 11 a.m., counting backwards, the Alabama delegation would have to step off from Arlington Cemetery at approximately 11 pm on Thursday night, November 13. The March Against Death worked as planned, with delegations arriving at Arlington near their scheduled times. Participants were provided housing and food at a dozen downtown churches.

Inspired by the theme of the march, Pablo Picasso donated an image for a special commemorative poster. Reminiscent of *Guernica*, the poster showed a smiling tank crushing and chewing up human figures. I believe many people who participated in the March Against Death have never forgotten the name they carried during the long walk from Arlington Cemetery to the Capitol.

The March Against Death represented a high standard of protest that uniquely and movingly honored Americans who gave their lives in Vietnam and, at the same time, made a very strong statement against the war. It combined a clear moral message with the capacity to communicate to diverse publics. I wish that high standard had guided all anti-war protests.

Arranging the logistics, including transportation, parking, communication equipment, sanitary facilities, and security, for the two events in Washington was complex and challenging. The Nixon administration, which not surprisingly opposed the protests, put up numerous administrative, political and legal obstacles to inhibit

12. Quoted by Peter Arnett, AP.

us. I participated in Mobilization delegations that met regularly with Deputy Attorney General Richard Kleindeinst and his assistant John Dean. Our negotiating sessions were frequently followed by pressurized press conferences, including one that I chaired with Coretta Scott King and Dr. Benjamin Spock as spokespersons for the march. Provoked by rumors leaked from the administration, the media seemed more concerned with whether the march would remain nonviolent than with the catastrophic violence of the war we were protesting.

The months leading up to the November 15 March were very intense politically, but also personally for Trudi and me. My own self-doubts and insecurities surfaced strongly several times while Trudi and I were living in an apartment in Washington. There were nights when I hardly slept and I kept Trudi awake as I battled bouts of anxiety from feeling overwhelmed by my responsibilities. Our deep respect and love for each other and our common commitments, as well as our ability to laugh at ourselves, helped us cope.

Clearly there were legal issues related to the government delays restricting our exercise of our constitutionally guaranteed right of free speech, issues which Mobilization lawyers worked on in the courts. There were many days when negotiations with government officials moved forward at a snail's pace or not at all. We learned that one of our meetings was cancelled so that John Dean could go duck hunting in Canada. At our next meeting, Stewart Meacham of the AFSC personally challenged Dean's sense of priorities and appealed to his better self on the basis of moral conscience to help resolve issues related to logistics for the March.

In the 1970s John Dean was convicted and served time in prison for his role in the Watergate scandal. Subsequently, he wrote several books analyzing and warning about authoritarian rule in Washington, including *Worse Than Watergate: The Secret Presidency of George W. Bush*, in which he argued that Bush should be impeached. I wonder if during his personal transformation, John Dean remembered his meetings with us in fall 1969, and especially the personal appeal to his conscience by Stewart Meacham.

One huge logistical challenge was that until a week before the march the government did not agree to designate parking areas for the very large numbers of chartered buses bringing participants to the District. Finally, Washington's black mayor, Walter Washington, was able to bring pressure on the White House and on the attorney general's office to break the deadlock. In addition to his personal opposition to the Vietnam War, obviously the mayor had a pressing political interest in assuring that the march came off with a minimum of disruption to the city.

Putting up logistical roadblocks was not the worst problem the government caused for us. We learned later from documents obtained under the Freedom of Information Act that in October and early November the Nixon administration leaked several false reports about the influence of communists and threats of violence in the march. Even worse, the government deployed black FBI agents posing as local D.C.

community leaders, in secret meetings with Mobilization leaders, to demand that we pay them a dollar head tax for each marcher coming into Washington. Despite physical threats, in a very tense face-to-face meeting, the Mobilization refused. It was only much later that we learned that these so-called local leaders were actually FBI agents. In August 2013, news coverage of the fiftieth anniversary of the 1963 March on Washington for Jobs and Freedom revealed how the government used similar scare tactics about the influence of communists and threats of violence to discourage participation in that march. The government's repressive tactics failed to work then and didn't work in 1969.

Ironically, the political context for organizing the November 15, 1969 march was further complicated by differences and tensions between the Mobilization Committee and the more politically centrist Vietnam Moratorium Committee, tensions which the Justice Department tried to exploit.[13] The Moratorium was a much better funded project with close connections to the dovish wing of the Democratic Party. Starting in October 1969, the Moratorium organizers called on people to interrupt (declare a moratorium on) their normal activities in schools and workplaces on the fifteenth of each month and organize public anti-war activities on that day, including rallies, teach-ins, and vigils for peace. The Moratorium strategy was very creative and effective. On October 15, 1969 more than a million people nationwide and many more worldwide participated. Bill Clinton, then a Fulbright Scholar in England, organized a teach-in at Oxford University.

Because of their links to cautious Democratic Party leaders, the Moratorium Committee avoided calling for immediate withdrawal and excluded radical youth and old leftists from any leadership roles. The Moratorium coordinators, Marge Sklenkar, David Hawk, David Mixner and Sam Brown (a former National Student Association president whom I took to Saigon a year later) had offices on the seventh floor at 1029 Vermont Avenue NW in Washington. My office and those of the irregularly paid, much smaller Mobilization staff were located on the ninth floor. While many of us had warm personal relations, some of the Moratorium's political advisors and financial backers were cool toward the Mobilization. Mirroring charges by the Nixon administration, they were worried that we were too leftist and that our march might lead to violence, thereby hurting the overall anti-war effort. Unfortunately, their worries, combined with Nixon administration allegations and the violent October "Days of Rage" sponsored by the Weathermen (a radical split from SDS) combined to increase public and particularly media apprehension about possible violence at the upcoming November 15th march.

One day in October, the Moratorium coordinators invited me and a couple of other key Mobilization staffers to come to their office to meet with two of their important, older politically savvy backers. In a lecturing tone, the two explained to us that they assumed at most 250,000 people would participate in the Mobilization march on

13. Gray, "The Moratorium and the New Mobe," 32–42.

November 15, but even that number required substantial logistical support. Saying they were worried about the possibility of violence, they presented us with a list of what they claimed were the absolute minimal logistical resources to assure a peaceful event: a specific very large number of portable toilets, walkie-talkies, water and first aid stations, and trained marshals for security. When I called on Brad Lyttle, the Mobilization's logistics coordinator, he indicated, category by category, that we only had verbal commitments for approximately a quarter of the resources the Moratorium leaders said were absolutely necessary. By the day of the march, we may have doubled these numbers, but we still came up quite a bit short of their absolute minimum, and the number of Americans who participated in the march turned out to be double what they had predicted.

More than 500,000 people participated in the November 15 march, making it the largest peace march on Washington in American history. Another estimated 250,000 people marched in San Francisco. The logistical resources for the march, including the number of toilets, turned out to be sufficient and our program from Thursday through Saturday came off smoothly and free of violence. Moratorium staffers warmly congratulated the Mobe staff. Most news media reported that the vast majority of marchers were entirely peaceful. *The New York Times* and *Washington Post* ran front page photos and stories of the 500,000 people gathered for the rally and speeches at the Washington Monument. Other photos focused on people in the March Against Death carrying names of Americans from their home state who had been killed in Vietnam Ironically, on the day of the march, I got so caught up in pressures of phone calls in the Mobilization office that, even though I was coordinator, I never got out of the office to participate in the march.

Two incidents at the end of the march posed additional logistical and political challenges. As the massive rally at the Washington Monument ended, a few hundred marchers, led by the radical pacifist David Dellinger, headed to the Justice Department to engage in nonviolent civil disobedience. They were demanding an end to the trials of anti-war activists and Black Panthers then taking place in several cities, including the Chicago Seven trial which resulted from confrontations at the Democratic National Convention in August 1968. Dellinger and the other demonstrators were prepared to be arrested. They were confronted by police who, instead of arresting them, used tear gas to disperse them. The tear gas clouds spread quickly over a wide area. While the demonstration at the Justice Department was a small, isolated event, the police response created confusion and disruption for tens of thousands of marchers who were walking back from the rally to board buses or trains to take them home.

As dusk turned to dark, several people called the Mobilization office with urgent concern about the growing confusion and chaos on the streets. Realizing that the situation was becoming very dangerous, I called Deputy Attorney General Kleindienst's office and told the receptionist who I was. I said that there was an emergency and I needed to speak directly with her boss. She put me through. I described the situation and asked for his help in getting the police to assist people trying to get back to their buses and trains. Kleindienst said, "What's happening now on the streets is not the federal government's problem. If you need help, why don't you try getting it from that nigger mayor?" I hung up abruptly, called Mayor Washington and repeated word for word what the deputy attorney general had said to me. The mayor cursed Kleindienst, told me not to worry, and said he would take care of the problem. Within fifteen minutes, I began getting reports from the streets that the police suddenly had changed tactics, and now were helping rather than hindering marchers getting to their buses.

The second incident was humorous in retrospect, although it could have been disastrous. In the days before the march, with all the expenses adding up, we discovered that the Mobilization was $50,000 in debt. Bradford Lyttle, an extraordinary organizer and tactician, who years earlier had organized a walk from San Francisco to Moscow to protest the nuclear arms race, developed a complicated plan for collecting funds at the rally. The plan was kept secret because of fears, especially after the confrontation with the FBI agents posing as local black leaders, that the collection might be stolen by a gang, government agents or even a crazy faction in the anti-war movement. Lyttle proposed having scores of young ushers wearing distinctive arm bands circulating through the crowd with five gallon collection buckets. As their buckets filled, they were to dump the contributions into larger receptacles, which in turn were to be brought to the back of a large rented truck, locked and guarded from the inside by an unarmed but very well built labor union security guy. The plan was for Sid Peck, one of the primary leaders of the Mobilization, to drive the truck to a downtown bank where, late in the afternoon after the rally ended, special arrangements had been made to safely deposit the money.

The first problem was that Sid left the keys to the truck in his jacket which he hung on a hook inside the back of the truck. At the end of the rally, Sid could not convince the guard to let him in to get the keys. After several frustrating minutes of loud argument through the locked door, Brad Lyttle came along to vouch for Sid who then was able to get the keys.

The second, more serious problem occurred as Sid drove the truck down the block to the side entrance of the bank, where by pre-arrangement an official was waiting to receive the deposit. As he approached the bank, Sid heard a noisy confrontation at the front of the bank. He could see a contingent of police and he smelled tear gas. While Sid was trying to deposit the Mobilization's collection at the bank's side door, members of the radical Weathermen faction of SDS were at the front engaged in an ugly, violent confrontation with the D.C. police The Weathermen were wearing helmets, brandishing sticks and shouting, "Down with Imperialism!" and "Down with the Banks!" Sid successfully managed to make the deposit, which turned out to be a surprising $150,000, more than enough to pay off our debt and support ongoing Mobilization activities for the next several months.

It was a crazy scene that I wish someone had filmed, and it reflected the sometimes bizarre conflicting strategies and styles within the anti-war movement. While I believed at the time that the violent rhetoric and actions of the Weathermen and similar factions seriously hurt the movement, there probably was not much that could be done about it. Given the persistent ugly realities of racism, the awful events of the war, and the government's clear determination to pursue it despite growing popular opposition, some different and contradictory styles and strategies were inevitable. I felt sure that violence, the use of drugs in peace protests, and demonstrations that expressed hostility against returning soldiers were all counterproductive.

Those strategies and actions abandoned fundamental lessons learned from the nonviolent civil rights movement, including the essential importance of projecting a very clear message and seeking to win over people who hadn't yet made up their minds, or who still supported the war. Violent protests and drug-related actions undoubtedly alienated many Americans who had doubts about the war, but still had not decided to oppose it. Some of the confrontational actions may have contributed to prolonging the war by providing arguments for our opponents, discouraging prospective allies, and providing additional excuses for government repression.

Those of us who believed deeply in nonviolence, both as a matter of principle and as the best practical strategy for social change, may be faulted for not having been bold and consistent enough in providing more creative, effective, nonviolent ,strategies and tactics. Given my own moral outrage, I was troubled by my lack of imagination and maybe my lack of courage to conceive and organize more serious nonviolent action. Objectively, I recognized that part of the problem had to do with the differences between the issues addressed by the civil rights movement and those of the anti-war movement. Acts of civil disobedience such as sitting in at lunch counters or being arrested at a voter registration center demonstrated a clear connection between the action taken and the goals being sought, i.e., desegregation of public facilities and the right to vote. Moreover, in the case of civil rights, activists could appeal directly to the US Constitution to support their cause. Eventually, the courts, including the Supreme Court, Congress, and most Americans supported the changes being advocated.

Challenging the Vietnam War policies of our government was very different, more complex and controversial. Except for young men resisting the draft, soldiers refusing to fight, and citizens refusing to pay taxes specifically designated for the war, the connection between acts of civil disobedience and stopping the war was less clear. Moreover, in actions demanding basic civil rights we could appeal to people's sense of patriotism and national pride, while civil disobedience related to issues of war, the draft, and foreign policy challenged, or even offended deeply-ingrained popular understandings of patriotism. It was also much more difficult to appeal to the Constitution for support. Massive nonviolent civil disobedience to stop the war may have been morally appropriate, but winning broad public support and making a Constitutional case for such action was a lot more difficult. As rage against racism, the war and government intransigence intensified, and many youth became increasingly alienated, whatever ideas we may have had about appropriate or politically effective forms of protest, the possibility to influence, much less control, the forms of protest became quite limited.

In any case, public support for the Vietnam War did steadily decline during the late sixties and early seventies, especially after the Tet Offensive in January 1968, when North Vietnamese and NLF forces simultaneously attacked 100 locations in South Vietnam and even briefly penetrated the American embassy compound in Saigon. A month later, Walter Cronkite returned from Vietnam and declared the war to be unwinnable. In an unprecedented editorial at the end of his nightly newscast Cronkite said, "It seems now more certain than ever that the bloody experience of Vietnam is to end in a stalemate."[14] After hearing Cronkite's broadcast, President Johnson is reported to have said, "That's it. If I've lost Cronkite, I've lost middle America."[15]

On March 31, 1968, facing challenges for his party's nomination from Senators Eugene McCarthy and Robert Kennedy, both strong opponents of the war, Lyndon Johnson announced that he would not seek and would not accept nomination for a second term as president On June 5, on the night he won California's presidential primary and pretty much assured his candidacy, Senator Robert Kennedy was assassinated. Two months later, with thousands of anti-war protestors in the streets of Chicago, the Democrats nominated Vice President Hubert Humphrey. The Republicans chose Richard Nixon as their nominee. He and Spiro Agnew, the vice presidential candidate, ran a campaign opposing counter-cultural protests and promising that they would achieve "peace with honor" in Vietnam. With victory having lost its credibility, peace with honor sounded plausible and appealed to many Americans, as did Agnew's angry, anti-protest rhetoric. In November 1968, with less that 50 percent of the popular vote, but almost 56 percent of the Electoral College, Richard Nixon became the thirty-seventh president of the United States.

President Nixon continued the war. The government's stubborn determination reinforced the growing sense of public frustration and outrage. Despite more than one million participants in the Moratorium on October 15 and three-quarters of million people who participated in the Mobilization Committee's November 15 Marches in Washington and San Francisco, as well as polls showing that by late fall 1969 public support for the war had shrunk to 30 percent, President Nixon made it very clear that he was not going to be swayed by majority public opinion against the war. The war went on and anti-war protests continued, including demonstrations of a more confrontational nature.

Following the November 1969 march, I resumed my regular FOR travels and speaking engagements. Three experiences stand out in my memory. The first was in February 1968, following my indictment for draft resistance, when I was invited to

14. Cronkite, *We Are Mired in Stalemate.*
15. Johnson on Cronkite's Commentary.

read my poem, "We Are America," at the national CALC gathering in Washington. The three-day gathering concluded with 2,000 clergy and lay people, walking arm in arm to Arlington Cemetery to commemorate those killed in the war and pray for peace. Each of us carried a small American Flag. We were led by Rev. Martin Luther King Jr. and Rabbi Abraham Joshua Heschel. Two months later, Dr. King was murdered in Memphis.

The second experience involved three successive visits I made to East Lansing, Michigan to speak at the public high school. In the fall of 1965, a sixteen-year-old East Lansing student who was a member of the FOR invited me to address a small group of students opposed to the war. When I arrived in town, the student called to tell me that I would not be allowed on school property, so the plan was for the interested students, along with one of their teachers, to meet with me on a public sidewalk. The next year this teacher invited me to speak in his world history class. A few years later, I was invited to address an all-school assembly. While it wasn't equally true in all regions of the country, this experience reflected how, like the growth of teach-ins and anti-war protests on college campuses, high schools responded to pressures from their students to allow for greater debate about the Vietnam War.

A third significant experience was in March 1970 when I participated in a "Theatre of Ideas" panel discussion sponsored by *The New York Review of Books* on the topic of "Civil Disobedience." The two other panelists were former Attorney General Ramsey Clark and Dr. Hannah Arendt. In the early 1960s, I had been privileged to participate in a seminar with Hannah Arendt when she spent a year doing research and writing at Wesleyan University's Honors College. I was very interested in her political philosophy, particularly as expressed in *The Human Condition* and *On Revolution,* which were a central focus of my undergraduate thesis that got interrupted by my going to Selma.

As recorded in Elizabeth Young-Bruehl's moving biography, *Hannah Arendt: For Love of the World*, the panel discussion that evening became quite lively.[16] While Arendt was personally warm toward me, she also gave me a friendly scolding in the discussion. At a time when the right to protest was being publicly attacked by Vice President Agnew, I argued that the best way to defend the First Amendment was "a vigorous struggle against the Vietnam War, including organized nonviolent civil disobedience." Arendt believed I was naïve. She said that I seemed to be ignoring the Constitutional guarantee of free speech and underestimating the dangers of confrontation, even if nonviolent. While she agreed that people needed to act on their guaranteed rights in order to preserve them, she was also concerned about what she viewed as dangerous confrontational politics advocated by some young anti-war activists. Arendt argued: "Your right to carry out this struggle is guaranteed precisely by the First Amendment. Without that you would have to rely on the good will of the government." Then, smiling slyly in a way that I'm sure brought images of Nixon and

---

16. Young-Bruehl, *Hannah Arendt*, 426–427.

Agnew to the minds of everyone present, Arendt added, "I wouldn't do that if were you." This evoked appreciative laughter from the audience and a smile of recognition from me. Two months later, after the invasion of Cambodia, as the crisis in society deepened, Arendt became more sympathetic towards nonviolent civil disobedience.

Invasion of Cambodia/March on Washington May 1970

On Saturday May 2, 1970 I participated in a meeting with other leaders of the National Mobilization Committee at the home of Peter and Cora Weiss in New York City to discuss strategy for the coming months. Peter Weiss was a very active and important civil rights attorney, while Cora was a major leader of Women Strike for Peace and a co-chair of the national anti-war coalition. During the meeting Cora got a call from Sam Donaldson of ABC news, reporting that the United States had invaded Cambodia. While the White House had been claiming publicly that no such action was contemplated, news leaks had been hinting that this expansion of the war was under consideration. Given mounting evidence that the war in Vietnam was failing and that substantial North Vietnamese forces were coming south through Cambodia, there was growing speculation that America might expand bombing raids there as a new way to try to win the war. Upon hearing the news, the focus of our meeting immediately shifted from longer range plans to planning a mass protest march in Washington for the following Saturday. I was asked to coordinate the march.

Given this dangerous escalation of the war and very strong negative public reaction against it, the committee also decided that the upcoming march would include massive, nonviolent civil disobedience. Even in this new context, the Mobilization Committee's decision was surprising. While I believed that nonviolent civil disobedience could play a positive role in anti-war strategy, old left ideologues and some mainstream liberals consistently opposed civil disobedience based on their fear that it would alienate potential middle class and working class supporters who they argued were essential to the prospects for political success. This was the first and only time that the national Mobilization coalition decided to sponsor nonviolent civil disobedience.

A small sub-group, including Brad Lyttle, who had worked on logistics for the March Against Death in November 1969, was charged with developing a plan and tactics for the nonviolent civil disobedience. I went to work immediately with others to organize a press conference for Monday May 4, and enlist support for the march among key activists across the country, especially student leaders. The public reaction to the invasion was very emotional and angry. Demonstrations were occurring all over the country, especially on college campuses. My phone calls to campus leaders indicated that, even with less than a week's lead time, large numbers of students would come to Washington the very next Saturday. Furthermore, the student leaders' responses indicated that the idea of massive nonviolent civil disobedience not only wouldn't discourage them from coming, but was making many students all the more determined to participate.

By Monday, Brad Lyttle had developed a plan. With or without a permit from the government—and we guessed that we wouldn't get a permit—the Mobilization would hold a mass protest rally on the Ellipse, immediately behind the White House. People coming into Washington would be advised to park their cars or buses wherever they could and then walk toward the Ellipse. If they made it all the way, fine. If they were stopped by police or the military, the plan called for them to sit down wherever they were stopped and nonviolently refuse to move. We assumed, given the angry public mood, that the government would not allow a mass demonstration so close to the White House. The image of thousands of citizens essentially converging on the White House and willing to engage in nonviolent civil disobedience would be very dramatic and powerful. Given potential responses by the police and the military to anything which might even seem to threaten the president, the plan also was clearly provocative. While mass civil disobedience should never be undertaken lightly, I believed that the invasion of Cambodia and the angry public reaction created a political context in which this potentially confrontational scenario was justified and appropriate.

To our surprise, Mobilization's lawyers succeeded in obtaining a permit for the rally on the Ellipse. I think government officials probably understood the public mood and gauged that it was necessary to provide a controlled outlet for people to vent their anger. Getting a permit complicated our plans, but we still were committed in principle to including some form of massive nonviolent civil disobedience.

As events unfolded that week, initial enthusiasm and support for massive civil disobedience declined. On May 4, Ohio National Guard troops fired on student protesters at Kent State University, killing four students. Ten days later, two black students were killed and twelve were wounded when police fired on unarmed protesters at Jackson State in Mississippi. It was very revealing of persistent, pervasive racism that the killing of black students at Jackson State never got the media or public attention that the killings at Kent State did. Reaction to the killings at Kent State was swift and strong. Hundreds of student demonstrations erupted, completely shutting down many campuses. In Seattle, 10,000 students marched in protest; 1,000 or more, (including my future wife) sat down on interstate I-5, shutting down the major north-south freeway for several hours. But people on many campuses also became more fearful about what might happen in Washington on Saturday. We received many calls from nervous campus leaders. After the killings at Kent State, they were worried about the civil disobedience scenario. With the rally permit in hand, as pressures mounted and with no time adequately to prepare or train participants in the discipline of nonviolence, our efforts focused more and more on the legal rally and less on mass civil disobedience.

As it turned out, 100,000 people, most of them students, did come to Washington on May 9. And despite their anger, the rally on the Ellipse was peaceful. However, many of us felt a palpable sense of frustration. There seemed to be a psychological and political gap between all our militant speeches reflecting anger over the invasion of Cambodia and the killings of American students, and the non-confrontational nature of the rally. In part moved by that disconnect, in my speech that day, I explicitly urged resistance to the draft and called on anyone committed to resisting the draft to drop their draft cards in the collection baskets as they were passed around. Knowing that I was going to South Vietnam in July, I announced that I would take the draft cards with me and present them to Vietnamese students in Saigon. More than 200 young men deposited their draft cards in the baskets that day. At the end of the rally, a few hundred demonstrators, led once again by David Dellinger, carried out a nonviolent sit-in at a major downtown intersection and were arrested.

Most participants at the rally walked back to their buses and returned home. I believe they felt glad that they had come to Washington on such short notice, but also frustrated that we had not done enough to confront the government over the invasion of Cambodia and the murders at Kent State. In retrospect, once we had the rally permit, I think we made a serious mistake by not developing an alternative plan for massive nonviolent civil disobedience. For example, we might have urged participants to remain on the Ellipse, nonviolently confronting the White House, and inviting arrest. While there would have been risks, including the possibility that the protest might turn violent, the risks of not pushing hard enough in response to the Nixon administration's dramatic escalation of the war were also very real. For many who believed deeply that the war against Vietnam was morally wrong, their feelings of frustration and anger over not being able to stop it intensified in the early 1970s. For a small minority of activists, the sense of outrage at the government's intransigence led to support for violent actions to stop the war. While sharing their frustration, the vast majority of anti-war activists remained committed to nonviolence.

From 1970 to the end of the war five years later, anti-war activism basically took three different forms. While some people chose to participate in only one, many others, including myself, participated in several different kinds of action. Some anti-war organizations, including especially the Student Mobilization Committee, with support of the Socialist Workers Party, with a view to attract more working class participation, continued to concentrate on organizing even larger legal demonstrations, such as the mass march and rally in Washington, on April 24, 1971 that drew 200,000 participants.

Other activists focused on direct actions to stop the war. In December 1970 representatives of the US National Student Association and the National Student Unions of North and South Vietnam cooperated in formulating a "Peoples' Peace Treaty," the key principle of which called for immediate and unconditional American withdrawal from Vietnam.[17] During 1971, student leaders on many campuses nationwide, some anti-war organizations including Vietnam Veterans Against the War, and several of the strongest anti-war members of Congress endorsed the Peoples' Peace Treaty.

17. *Peoples Peace Treaty.*

Supporters of this treaty often cited a quotation from Dwight D. Eisenhower from a radio broadcast dialogue with British Prime Minister Macmillan on August 31, 1959: "I think that people want peace so much that one of these days governments had better get out of their way and let them have it."

Many members of SDS and the Youth International Party (Yippies) were drawn toward more confrontational direct action. In spring 1971, supporting the People's Peace Treaty, they organized Mayday in Washington. Possibly in part inspired by Eisenhower's idea, but also by their own outrage at the ongoing war, they adopted the deliberately provocative and, in my view, presumptuous slogan, "If the government won't stop the war, we'll stop the government." The Mayday strategy, while mostly nonviolent, included guerilla hit-and-run tactics that clearly reflected the growing frustration and anger over the government's intransigence. Personally, I believe that the Mayday demonstration was also a response to the not-confrontational-enough May 1970 demonstration in response to the invasion of Cambodia and the killings at Kent State.

Other activists organized nonviolent civil disobedience actions at draft boards and induction centers, including several raids on local Selective Service offices in which participants poured blood on draft board files or stole the records and publicly burned them. While some nonviolent actions were carried out in ways that tried to communicate with Americans who were still undecided about the war, other actions unfortunately seemed to totally disregard the potential negative effects on public opinion.

Many people opposed to the war concentrated their energies on Congress and efforts to affect the election of 1972, by working with the Coalition to Stop Funding the War and Senator George McGovern's campaign for president. While I think some of the more confrontational actions and the lack of more coordinated anti-war strategy may have helped re-elect President Nixon, given the range of popular anger and frustration at the time, I doubt that a nationally coordinated, creative strategy was possible.

In addition to cooperating with some of these diverse efforts, in 1971, on behalf of the FOR and Clergy and Laity Concerned, I organized the Daily Death Toll project. With the number of American casualties declining and the Nixon administration claiming that it was ending the war, the Daily Death Toll focused on memorializing approximately 300 Vietnamese who were being killed every day and called on Congress to cut off funding for the war. Modeled on the November 1969 March Against Death, each day a delegation of 300 Americans came to Washington from a different city and, after visiting their Representatives to urge them to cut funding for the war, engaged in nonviolent civil disobedience by lying down in the White House driveway. On most days, including the day I lay down in the driveway, participants were arrested and released later the same day. While the Daily Death Toll project was largely symbolic, by combining nonviolent civil disobedience with political action aimed at

Congress, the project reflected the combination of urgency and political realism felt by many people working to end the war.

On a much larger scale nationwide, in 1972, taking inspiration from Vietnam Summer in 1967, anti-war activists organized Indochina Summer, another public grassroots education and anti-war action campaign. Despite seventy percent or more of Americans being opposed to the war, increasing support in Congress to cut-off funds for the war, and all of the diverse anti-war activities, the US continued its war in Vietnam for three more years, compounding the destruction in Vietnam and adding thousands more American and Vietnamese casualties.

5

Visiting Saigon and Hanoi and Returning Twenty Years after the War is Over

Leading an interfaith, interracial study mission on repression in South Vietnam; travelling to Hanoi at Christmas to carry mail for American POWs; ending of my marriage; visiting North Vietnam again to observe use of medical aid; celebrating the war is over; and returning to Vietnam in 1995 to celebrate the fiftieth anniversary of the Vietnam-USA Friendship Society.

IN JULY 1970, AMIDST the ongoing debate about the war and how to end it, I organized and led an FOR-sponsored interfaith/interracial delegation of American religious and student leaders to South Vietnam. Our goal was to interview Vietnamese in Saigon and some surrounding areas who were part of the vast non-communist majority about their experiences and views, and to investigate reports of repression by the Saigon government.

One of the core debates in the anti-war movement during the late 1960s was framed by the extent to which one viewed the South Vietnamese National Liberation Front (known in the media as the Vietcong) as distinct from and a threat to the majority of South Vietnamese who were not communists, and whether the US war was helping or hurting this non-communist majority. Supporters of the war argued that the Vietcong were simply an extension or pawn of communist North Vietnam. Some went further, arguing that both the Vietcong and North Vietnam were pawns of "Red" China and/or the Soviet Union. According to this view, anchored in the Cold War, the American counter-insurgency war, in alliance with the Saigon government, was essential to protect the non-communist majority and prevent South Vietnam from falling (like dominoes) under North Vietnamese (and by extension, Chinese and/or Soviet) control.

Opponents of the war held diverse views about communism and the Vietcong. However, increasing numbers of people opposed to the war argued that American support for dictators in Saigon and our nation's military action in South Vietnam, including massive B-52 bombing and defoliation campaigns in the countryside, were alienating or killing large numbers of non-communist South Vietnamese whom the United States claimed to be protecting. Some prominent experts believed that the war was in fact driving more South Vietnamese to support the National Liberation Front, which they believed was indigenous in the South as well as imported from the North. They also asserted that the division of Vietnam into North and South was externally imposed rather than based on Vietnamese history and culture. The 1967 book, *The United States in Vietnam,* by George McTurnan Kahin and John W. Lewis was one very authoritative, critical source for these views.[1] In this context, FOR decided it was important to understand more about the experiences and views of non-communist South Vietnamese. For me, being strongly opposed to the war included considering the complex conflicting arguments about the best way to end it.

Motivated by wanting to keep South Vietnam free from communist control, some older peace movement leaders, including Al Hassler, believed that key leaders and groups among the non-communist South Vietnamese majority constituted an important and politically relevant middle way or "third force" that could play a crucial role in ending the war while preventing a communist government from coming to power. For some, preventing a communist takeover was as important as ending the war. Hassler and others argued that activist, engaged Mahayana Buddhist monks, including Thich Tri Quang and Thich Nhat Hanh, were key leaders of what they saw as an important and politically viable third force.

In the early 1960s, Thich Nhat Hanh organized Van Hanh University and the Buddhist School for Youth for Social Service, which trained young Vietnamese to do community service and oppose war and violence. As the conflict expanded, the Buddhist schools were careful not to align with either the NLF or the Saigon government. In 1965, students at Van Hanh University issued a Call for Peace, appealing to both sides to work together to end the war. In response, the Saigon government put increased pressure on the school and Thich Nhat Hanh was forced into exile. His successor, Sister Chan Khong, was falsely accused of being a communist by a chancellor with ties to the Saigon government. The school experienced increased difficulty raising funds and several people associated with the school were arrested.

Al Hassler met Thich Nhat Hanh at a symposium at Cornell University in 1966. Deeply moved by Nhat Hanh's pacifist beliefs and work in Vietnam, Hassler introduced him to Martin Luther King Jr. who nominated the monk for the Nobel Peace Prize. King privately acknowledged that his April 4, 1967 speech at Riverside Church, "A Time to Break the Silence," was inspired in part by their meeting. Al Hassler developed a close, complex relationship with Thich Nhat Hanh, including helping him write and then publish his book, *Vietnam: Lotus in A Sea of Fire.*[2]

1. Kahin and Lewis, *The United States in Vietnam.*
2. Hanh, *Vietnam: Lotus in A Sea of Fire.*

In July 1970, encouraged by Thich Nhat Hanh and his Buddhist colleagues, the FOR asked me to organize a delegation of religious and student leaders to meet with their non-communist counterparts in South Vietnam. Our delegation included Dr. David Hunter, deputy general secretary of the National Council of Churches; Episcopal Bishop Paul Moore (soon to become bishop of New York City); Rabbi Balfour Brickner, director of the commission for interreligious affairs of the Union of American Hebrew Congregations (Reform); Sister Mary Luke Tobin, of the Sisters of Loretto and president of the Leadership Conference of Women Religious; Sam Brown, of the Vietnam Moratorium Committee; Dorothy Cotton, director of US citizenship education for SCLC; Bernard Lafayette, coordinator of the Poor People's Campaign; Tim Butz, Vietnam War veteran and Kent State student; and Charles Palmer, president of the National Student Association. Palmer had been carrying on a correspondence for several months with student leaders in South Vietnam. We were joined in Saigon by religious and student leaders from Australia, New Zealand and the Netherlands.

We planned to spend a week in South Vietnam, primarily in Saigon, but also in the countryside meeting Buddhist and Roman Catholic religious leaders, representatives of women's groups, university students, and staff of international voluntary aid agencies, such as Catholic Relief Services and International Voluntary Services (IVS). We also planned to meet with South Vietnamese government officials, American embassy officials, and journalists. A one-week trip obviously would not make any of us experts, but we believed that we could gather valuable impressions and insights about the South Vietnamese whom many believed were caught in the middle of the war.

The South Vietnamese religious leaders we met were quite explicit in distancing themselves from the NLF, but also spoke very critically about the Saigon government and President Nguyen Van Thieu who, with American support, had replaced General Nguyen Cao Ky in 1967. Their strongest criticism was about the war itself—especially the bombing campaign—and the horrendous toll it was taking on the Vietnamese people. We learned more about the Buddhist monks who had immolated themselves in protests and others, including the leader of a women's organization, who were imprisoned and tortured by the Saigon regime. South Vietnamese students also clearly expressed non- or anti-communist views, as they told us more stories of repression, incarceration and abuse perpetrated by the Saigon government. American journalists corroborated most of what we heard about the extent of the repression.

Saigon government officials dismissed these stories as "communist propaganda." Aware of the dangers faced by many of the people with whom we met, our delegation did not disclose the names of any of our Vietnamese contacts so as not to further endanger them. However, when the Saigon officials clearly knew all their names and claimed that several of the people we had met were Vietcong agents, it became very clear that we were being closely followed. American embassy officials dismissed some of the stories of repression, and then asserted that, in any case, Vietcong practices were even worse. They argued that the counter-insurgency strategy was working and that, despite some problems, the United States was making progress in winning the hearts and minds of most South Vietnamese. In contrast with this official view, a month before we arrived (and partly as a result of an earlier FOR delegation) the US embassy had been forced to publicly acknowledge that the Saigon regime was holding approximately 50,000 political prisoners.

Coincidentally, the stories we heard about imprisonment and torture provided additional context for a dramatic incident that occurred just before we arrived in Saigon. A small congressional delegation had come to investigate the pacification program and reports of arrests and torture of dissidents by the Saigon regime. Don Luce, who worked in Vietnam for International Voluntary Services (IVS) and the World Council of Churches, served as their interpreter when they visited Con Son prison on an island off the coast of South Vietnam. While there, Don helped the delegation discover a set of small cells below ground level that were definitely *not* on the official tour. Known as "tiger cages," they housed prisoners who were frequently tortured. One of the Vietnamese we met had been held in the tiger cages and had been tortured.

Tom Harkin, who later served for many years as Senator from Iowa, was staff for a member of the congressional delegation. Harkin managed to photograph some of the prisoners down through the bars of the tiger cages. His photo was published in the July 17, 1970 issue of *Life* magazine. US officials who admitted that prisoners were tortured claimed that Americans did not participate in the torturing, but sometimes were present as advisors and observers. There were reports, however, of Americans throwing Vietnamese prisoners out of helicopters and directly participating in other forms of torture. Thirty-five years later at Abu Ghraib prison in Iraq, despite tight military control over journalists covering the war, we learned that Americans directed and carried out torture themselves. In April 2009, as part of protests against the war in Iraq, Don Luce wrote an essay, "The Tiger Cages of Vietnam," comparing American experience in Vietnam and Iraq."[3]

On one day during our visit, our delegation experienced an ironic, peaceful interlude. Don Luce arranged for us to take small boats to an island in the Mekong River inhabited by the Coconut Monk and his disciples. We were told that one bank of the Mekong was controlled by Saigon's military forces and the other by the NLF. While because of its small size, the island itself had not been occupied by either faction, both sides regularly fired artillery shells across the river, and scores of shells that fell short landed on the island. The monks set up a small industry soldering them into bells and decorative sculptures. I carried one of their large sculptures back to display at the FOR headquarters in Nyack. These monks literally, physically were sitting in the middle of the war and turning swords into plowshares.

Two days before our departure from Saigon, we were invited to attend a song and dance presentation by Saigon University students. We arrived a bit early and were ushered to the front of the auditorium where we watched a wonderful, spirited

3. Luce, *The Tiger Cages of Vietnam.*

performance. About a half an hour into the show, with the house lights out, a student appeared at the end of our row and motioned to me that we should follow him. I passed the word along to others, and we got up and followed. He led us out through a small door under the stage, down a dark hall to a low maintenance tunnel under the building. Bishop Moore and I, who were the tallest members of our group, had to bend over to get through. After a few minutes, we emerged into a lighted basement room where we were met by other students, including Huynh Tan Mam, president of the Saigon University Student Council, whom we had met earlier. With Judy Danielson, an American who worked with the Quakers, serving as interpreter, Mam thanked us for coming to Vietnam and then invited us to participate in a public meeting and manifestation for peace scheduled for the next morning at the University's School of Agriculture.

At one point, Judy translated what Mam said as, "After the public meeting at the School of Agriculture, we all will march together and confront the Independence Palace." Bishop Moore grabbed my arm and anxiously asked, "What was that, Ron? What did Judy say Mam proposed about confronting the Independence Palace?" Paul Moore, a decorated Marine Captain in World War II who had marched with Martin Luther King Jr. was not one to shrink from confrontation, but he was about to become the thirteenth Bishop of New York City, and, quite understandably, was not expecting on this trip to lead some sort of charge on Saigon's Independence Palace. I turned to Judy, who I think overheard Bishop Moore's nervous question, and asked her to clarify. She explained, "What Mam actually said is that we will walk together and then all stand in front of the Independence Palace." As it turned out we didn't get to do either scenario, but Judy's clarification helped to calm Bishop Moore and others.

The next morning we arrived at the School of Agriculture to find an auditorium already filled with several hundred Vietnamese, mostly students, who stood and applauded as we entered. Huynh Tan Mam briefly introduced the program and our delegation. Several Vietnamese spoke briefly about their experiences of arrest and torture as a result of speaking out and demonstrating for peace. They were followed by Rev. David Hunter, Sister Mary Luke Tobin, and Charles Palmer bringing greetings. Each speaker had to be translated to be understood, so even these brief remarks took fifteen or twenty minutes. Students passed through the audience offering participants placards with peace slogans on them in Vietnamese and English. Fearing that the police would arrest anyone photographed carrying one of these placards, initially, no one volunteered to take one. Then, simultaneously, a teenage boy and an elderly woman whose husband was paralyzed from being tortured in a Saigon prison, stood up, took placards and raised them high over their heads. The crowd cheered and then many students reached out eagerly to follow suit. I was reminded of the black teenagers who played leading roles in the marches in Selma, and the old people I met in Mississippi and Alabama, who courageously agreed to go down to the Court House to register to vote.

Mam was worried about what plainclothes police might do. He whispered that we needed to cut the program short. On his signal, I went to the microphone holding up a brown paper bag and told the crowd that it contained the draft cards of 200 young Americans, including Sam Brown, a member of our delegation. I announced that all of them had declared that they would not come to Vietnam to fight. As my announcement was translated, the youth and the elderly woman who had been the first to take up a peace placard came forward to join me in burning the draft cards. We took turns with a cigarette lighter. Then, as the Vietnamese students erupted in enthusiastic applause and cheers, a Vietnamese Catholic priest and a Buddhist monk came forward and joined us in burning the cards. Recalling my feeling two months earlier—that the mass demonstration protesting the invasion of Cambodia, where the draft cards had been collected—was too timid and mild, it felt very good to engage in this act of solidarity with Vietnamese youth, some of whom almost certainly would become future victims of the war.

Mam hurriedly guided us to the front of the march. Another student handed me a large white paper-mâché dove with blue and red ribbons on a long pole. As we turned onto the avenue that led to the Independence Palace, we could see rows of Saigon police wearing helmets, carrying shields, and armed with some sort of guns. They began coming toward us. When they were fifty to seventy-five yards away, we heard shots and saw projectiles flying over our heads. Tear gas filled the air. Apparently, more police were attacking us from behind. We saw students escaping to the left and to the right; everyone started running any way we could. A tear gas projectile hit the dove, causing it to smoke. Rabbi Balfour Brickner, Bernard Lafayette, and I, along with several Vietnamese students began climbing over a six-foot-high black iron fence. I was still holding on to the pole with the smoking dove attached. As we climbed over the fence, I remember Rabbi Brickner shouting, "For God's sake, Ron, let go of the bird."

We escaped down a narrow alley into an empty garage, where we met up with other members of our delegation and several more Vietnamese students. Despite the precariousness of our situation, Bernard Lafayette, who had led voter registration efforts in Selma, Alabama, began to try to conduct a workshop in nonviolent tactics with the Vietnamese students. He didn't speak any Vietnamese and the students spoke very little English. Bernard was frustrated when I pulled him away, arguing that we needed to get out of there and back to our hotel. I think he may have thought that I was being a bit of a white wimp. I reminded Bernard that we had a flight back to the US later that day.

Later we learned that the confrontation had ended when one of the Vietnamese student leaders walked out into the middle of the avenue alone, no more than twenty-five yards from the approaching line of police. Showing no fear, he shouted loudly that he knew that many of the police wanted peace just as much as he did. Then he announced that the demonstration was over and appealed to the police to cease their attack. They seemed to understand. They removed their gas masks and left. After things calmed down, several Vietnamese students walked the streets picking up spent tear gas shells which they presented to our delegation, urging us to take them home with us. Each shell was imprinted with the words, "Made in the USA."

On the flight home, I wrote a draft report about our experience and circulated it among members of the delegation. By the time we reached New York, we had our "Report of the Mission on Repression in South Vietnam" that FOR released publicly and sent to every member of Congress. A week after we returned, Bishop Moore and I appeared on the *Today* show and met with Senator Edward Kennedy. Kennedy listened carefully and told us that our report confirmed his views about how the war was terribly misguided. He made reference to our report in several speeches opposing the war. For most Americans who were following events in Vietnam and were already critical of the war, we didn't say anything dramatically new. Still, our emphasis on how the US was supporting Saigon's violent repression of non-communist South Vietnamese may have pushed some people who were still undecided about the war to oppose it and strengthened the views of others opposed to the war. The FOR received letters of appreciation from several members of Congress, including Republican Senators John Sherman Cooper and Edward Brooke, and Democratic Senators Harold Hughes, William Proxmire, Alan Cranston, and Daniel Inouye.

For Al Hassler and those who believed that a Vietnamese third force offered a way to end the war while avoiding a communist victory, our "Report on Repression" was disappointing. We had not found evidence of a politically viable third force. It was very clear to us that most South Vietnamese did not actively identify with the NLF and many were critical of it. But the main thing we learned was how much ordinary people were suffering from the war and from repressive policies of the Saigon government backed by the United States. I concluded that the idea of a viable Vietnamese political third force was more a creation of American anti-communist ideology and wishful thinking by Al Hassler and other, older, liberal, peace movement leaders, rather than an accurate reading of Vietnamese history or contemporary politics. I believed, as our report concluded, that the vast majority of South Vietnamese simply wanted the war and repression to end. I believe the Buddhist-inspired nonviolence that Thich Nhat Hanh advocated was a better form of resistance than violence, but Hassler's idea of a politically viable Vietnamese third force was a wishful fantasy.

A few months later, I accompanied Thich Nhat Hanh on a speaking tour in Minnesota and asked him, rather aggressively as I recall, "Isn't it true that the US war is destroying any middle ground and forcing more and more Vietnamese to become Vietcong?" Nhat Hanh smiled and responded softly to what I said in a noncommittal way that I found both frustrating and enlightening. While, in one sense, he seemed to agree with me, I think he also was trying to teach me that the whole truth of the situation was more complex and nuanced. More than anything, most Vietnamese desperately wanted all the suffering to end. Just as my anger at the war caused me to underestimate Nhat Hanh's Buddhist wisdom, I believe Al Hassler's rigid anti-communism caused him to overestimate Nhat Hanh's political importance.

The Vietnamese Buddhist delegation, with whom Thich Nhat Hanh was associated, played a minor role on the fringe of the official peace negotiations in Paris, and a third force military figure, General Duong Van "Big" Minh, became the interim president of South Vietnam for a few days in April 1975, helping to ease the transition from the American occupation to the takeover by the NLF and North Vietnam. However, the rapid dissolution of the Saigon government and army, and the swift and relatively peaceful process by which the country was reunited after the American withdrawal, tended to confirm that there had never been a politically viable third force and that the division between South and North had been artificially imposed by foreign powers. I am convinced that if the United States had continued the war based on the illusion that we could win, or that a third force could save South Vietnam from becoming communist, many more people would have been killed and wounded. The destruction in Vietnam would have been even more catastrophic, but the war would still have ended with victory for a unified, independent Vietnam under a communist government. Given four decades of Ho Chi Minh's leadership, including his determination and relative popularity, as well as effective military and political strategies, this outcome seemed relatively certain.

Tragically, almost four decades after the Vietnam War ended, many Americans still believed the United States could have won the war. Some criticized our government for not being willing to use sufficient military force, possibly including nuclear weapons; and they blamed the media and the anti-war movement for weakening the country's resolve. I recently saw a bumper sticker that reflected the sad illusion that America could have won the war. The bumper sticker on a Vietnam veteran's car declared, "When I left Vietnam, we were winning."

Trip to Hanoi, North Vietnam December 1970

IN DECEMBER 1970, I travelled to Hanoi, with my wife Trudi, who was then national co-director of CALC, and Ann Bennett, a prominent leader of Church Women United and wife of John Bennett, president of Union Theological Seminary. Our purpose was to carry more than 300 cards and letters to American servicemen who were being held as prisoners of war (POWs) in Hanoi from their families back home and to bring back their letters. During our week in the north, we visited sites that had been bombed by the United States, were introduced to several survivors of the bombings, met for an hour with Prime Minister Pham Van Dong, and had a face-to-face meeting with three American prisoners.

The Committee of Liaison (COL) that sponsored our trip was organized in response to the failure of the United States to reach an agreement with North Vietnam on exchange of mail between prisoners of war and their families, in part because our government refused to recognize the government of North Vietnam. While COL was controversial and under investigation by the FBI because it worked openly with the government in the north, most detained servicemen and their families appreciated that it provided the only available mail exchange. Unlike the North Vietnamese government, which cooperated with COL for mail delivery to American prisoners, the US government never made any arrangements for North Vietnamese prisoners captured by the Saigon government or by the American military to have contact with their families.

Despite the illogical argument, in the late 1960s and early 1970s the Nixon administration used the issue of American servicemen who were prisoners or missing in action (POW/MIAs) as an additional rationale for continuing the war. Some of officials' statements actually made it seem as if the war was being waged to retrieve missing Americans. Obviously, the ongoing war was responsible for creating more prisoners and more missing servicemen, while an end to the fighting would bring the POWs home and make possible some accounting for the MIAs. Some of their families were used by the administration to bolster public support for continuing the war. Whatever their views about the war or the anti-war movement, and despite significant government pressure, many families of American servicemen detained in the north valued the COL for making some exchange of communication with their loved ones possible.

Our small delegation was greeted at the Hanoi airport by representatives of the Vietnam Peace Committee, a semi-official government organization and partner with COL in the mail exchange. We stayed at the Hoa Binh (Peace) Hotel. Since it was late December, our hosts asked us about traditional American customs to celebrate Christmas. When we returned to the hotel from a day trip on Christmas Eve, we discovered that the hotel staff had decorated the dining room with pine branches, lighted candles, and a small pine tree. For dinner the waiters proudly brought out a roasted turkey, with its head still on and a carrot curl in its beak. After showing us the Christmas turkey, they returned it to the kitchen from where it soon reemerged chopped up in a Vietnamese-style stir fry with rice.

Ann, Trudi and I found it deeply moving to be together on Christmas in Hanoi, the capital of a country with which our nation was at war and which had been massively bombed by American B-52s. After a couple of days, we realized that, ironically, we felt more relaxed there than we often did at home, where we almost always felt the intense pressures of wanting desperately to stop the war and felt the frustration at our inability to do so. Our Vietnamese hosts' warm welcome and their calm, confident manner made being in Hanoi at Christmastime a surprisingly hope-filled and peaceful experience.

We were taken by car to see some of the destruction caused by B-52 bombing raids, and to meet several badly maimed victims. We also were taken to a museum where we saw displays of weapons, including anti-personnel bombs and bomblets, tens of thousands of tons of which had been dropped by our country on Vietnam, Cambodia and Laos. Having seeded the earth with these weapons, unexploded anti-personnel bombs would continue to kill and maim Vietnamese, Cambodians and Laotians long after the war was over. Fred Branfman, who worked as an educational advisor for the US government in Laos, had documented the devastating effects of the air war, including the use of anti-personnel weapons. A research project of the AFSC produced a slideshow based on his work, entitled "The Automated Air War." Over the next few years, whenever Trudi or I showed this slideshow at churches or on campuses, we would recall our Christmas 1970 visit in Hanoi and our personal encounters with some of the automated air war's victims.

In contrast with visiting scenes of devastation and underground bomb shelters, on several occasions Trudi and I walked freely and peacefully in the center of Hanoi, including around the lovely Lake of the Returning Sword with its unique One-Pole Pagoda. We were struck by how friendly Vietnamese were toward us and how little hatred or hostility they expressed. We were told that this was partly a reflection of Vietnamese Buddhist culture, but also a reflection of Ho Chi Minh's teachings about resistance strategy. During decades of occupation by the French, Japanese, and Americans, Ho Chi Minh urged Vietnamese not to hate foreigners once they no longer posed a threat. Resistance—even violent resistance—to foreign occupation was essential, but he taught that once the battle was won, persistent feelings of hatred and vengeance were ineffectual and wasteful. Ho Chi Minh's strategy was very different from Gandhi's in India. Both Gandhi and Martin Luther King Jr. believed in resisting evil, but they focused on nonviolent resistance, saying that even during the struggle hatred and vengeance were morally wrong and impractical. We learned that Ho Chi Minh taught that Vietnamese should resist and, if necessary even kill their attackers, but once servicemen were captured and no longer posed a threat, they should be treated humanely. While this may have been Ho's philosophy, it is a matter of record that American prisoners of war suffered much poor treatment and that some prisoners, including John McCain, were severely tortured.

One of the high points of our visit to Hanoi was an hour-long meeting with Pham Van Dong, a close associate and friend of Ho Chi Minh, and prime minister of the Democratic Republic of Vietnam (North Vietnam) from 1954 to1976. Dong was born and grew up in Quang Ngai Province in what became part of South Vietnam after 1954. He joined the resistance as a young man and was jailed by the French for seven years. Dong had actually been imprisoned on Con Son Island where the infamous tiger cages were discovered in July 1970. Following the Vietnamese defeat of the French at Dien Bien Phu in 1954, Ho Chi Minh chose Dong to go to Paris to sign the peace accord with French president Pierre Mendes France, and then named him prime minister. Listening to his and Ho's aspirations, political philosophy and strategy provided Ann, Trudi and me with firsthand personal experience of the Vietnamese leaders' profoundly patient determination and confidence that they would succeed finally in freeing Vietnam from control by any foreign power, including the United States. Meeting with Pham Van Dong reinforced our views that the American war in Vietnam was not only morally wrong, but fundamentally unwinnable. Following the Vietnamese victory and end of US occupation in 1975, Pham Van Dong served as prime minister of reunited Vietnam from 1976 to 1987.

On our fourth day in Hanoi we learned that we would meet some American POWs. In 1969, a COL delegation had met with four of them, including John McCain. One of the prisoners we were scheduled to meet had broken his eyeglasses when he landed by parachute in North Vietnam. We brought replacement glasses from his mother. It felt strange and awkward to prepare for visiting American POWs in Hanoi. Appreciating the sensitivity of the meeting, including the possible propaganda value to North Vietnam, the intense media focus on POW/MIAs at home, and our government's opposition to our mission, the three of us carefully considered what we would ask the servicemen and what subjects we would avoid. Our main purpose was to bring loving greetings from their families, to let the men know that people back home were thinking of them and praying for them, and that we all were looking forward to the war's end, so that they could come home. Given that they were prisoners and that our conversation would likely be monitored, we decided not ask about how they were being treated.

We did decide to ask each man to tell us how he was captured. One of the men was a bomber pilot who had flown several missions from an aircraft carrier stationed in the China Sea. He told us that he had never been in Vietnam and had never even met a Vietnamese before his plane was shot down and he parachuted into North Vietnam. Until then, he experienced the war from several thousand feet above the earth in a cockpit surrounded by the most advanced technology. "Until my plane was hit and I parachuted down," he told us, "the war wasn't real; it was more like a very dangerous arcade video game." He told us that he broke his ankle when he landed in a field. Local villagers quickly surrounded him and began to argue loudly among themselves. While he couldn't understand what they were saying, he could tell that they were debating what to do with him. After several minutes, they roughly bandaged his ankle with cloth strips and carried him some distance through fields and then down into a deep underground bunker. He told us, "Very soon after we were underground, there were very loud, thunder-like booms and the earth shook violently. I knew that these were bombs being dropped by our B-52s." He confessed candidly and rather convincingly, "You know, before that day, I had never experienced a B-52 raid from the ground. I wouldn't want—and I wouldn't want anyone else—to go through that ever again."

When Ann, Trudi, and I arrived in Seattle for a brief stopover on our flight home, we experienced how intensely the Nixon administration opposed the peace movement's humanitarian efforts. As soon as our plane pulled up to the gate, immigration authorities and armed police boarded the plane and ordered us to come with them and bring the bag containing hundreds of letters. As we walked off the plane, Ann whispered to me in a very determined voice that I should give her the bag. We were escorted into a small room where the authorities threatened us with legal penalties and demanded that we give them the mail. I realized why Ann had insisted that she carry it. She was a small woman in her seventies, who two days earlier had a serious health scare on our flight out of Hanoi. She held the bag tightly against her chest and said, "We are carrying this mail for American servicemen who are prisoners of war and we promised them that we would send it to their families. There is no way we are turning their letters over to the government. You will have to beat me to take the bag of mail." The authorities seemed to understand her seriousness. They let us go; we re-boarded our plane and continued our flight home. On our arrival at Kennedy Airport, leaders of the COL greeted us and we held a press conference. The very next day, the letters were placed in new envelopes and mailed to all the prisoners' families.

Clearly, traveling to North Vietnam in 1970, a country with which our government was at war, represented a big boundary crossing, but when we were asked to undertake this mission, Trudi and I didn't hesitate. Trudi's parents had fled Austria on the eve of the Nazi invasion, and along with my parents were quite worried about our physical safety while in North Vietnam as well as the possible political or even legal repercussions when we returned. But to Trudi and me, the decision seemed relatively clear and simple. In contrast with the trip to Hanoi that I had turned down in 1967, it certainly helped that this visit had a very clear humanitarian purpose. Because of that, Al Hassler supported my participation in the mission and I went representing the FOR, but he was glad that the COL paid for my travel.

By December 1970 public opposition to the war in Vietnam was so broad and deep there was a very substantial anti-war subculture that provided a safe, even supportive, popular context for our mission. While some Americans certainly were critical and even hostile, many admired and supported us. Trudi and I recognized that the trip involved some personal, political, maybe even legal, risks, but we didn't feel fearful. Going to Hanoi with Ann Bennett, a much older, prominent church woman who seemed fearless, wise and very confident also helped.

The ongoing existence of this anti-war subculture, and its willingness to challenge the government, helps to explain how, in 2003, months before the United States invaded Iraq and before there were any American casualties, more than 1 million Americans marched in protest. Compared with Vietnam, the Iraq protest movement arose very swiftly. While these pre-war protests did not prevent the Bush/Cheney administration from preparing, nor Congress from authorizing invasions of Afghanistan and Iraq, the disastrous experiences and uncertain outcomes of these wars will make it much more difficult for the United States to go to war in the future. I believe this represents substantial and hopeful progress.

Separation and Divorce

The next time I travelled to Vietnam, in late summer of 1974, Trudi and I were separated and I feared on our way to getting divorced. Our differences, including that Trudi had experienced an intimate relationship before and I had not may have been part of our initial attraction and may have helped keep us together for a time, but I believe they also contributed to our breakup. Starting in fall 1972, we were living in Philadelphia where I went to work for the American Friends Service Committee. Trudi commuted by train to New York City, where she worked with Dick Fernandez as national co-director of CALC. In spring 1974, Trudi took a studio apartment in New York City so she would not have to commute from Philadelphia every day. I think she enjoyed her time away from me and, after a while, she began a relationship with a Vietnam veteran. On a spring weekend in 1974 when she was back in Philadelphia, Trudi told me she wanted to try living separately. I felt devastated but I didn't know how I could change her mind. This did not seem to be something she wanted to discuss or negotiate. She was already seeing a good psychotherapist and I also started seeing him after her announcement. We had a few sessions together, but nothing seemed to alter Trudi's decision. For the first time in my life, I began to keep a journal, including recording and working to understand my dreams.

I still have the print by Sister Corita that Trudi gave me when we were splitting up. It portrays the image of a fully grown tree with its roots reaching down deep into the earth, and includes a quotation from Carl Jung, "A tree grows downward as well as upward, for every self-respecting tree must honor its roots." I think that the process of growing downward deeper in ourselves and honoring our roots as we grow older has a lot to do with how we manage to get through troubled waters without bridges. Trudi and I have done quite a lot of growing downward since then, and I'm grateful that we have maintained a close, warm friendship.

Trip to South and North Vietnam July/August 1974

In 1974, I was working as national peace education secretary of the AFSC, the largest American peace organization with thirty staffed regional and area offices across the country, as well as international relief and development programs abroad, including in South Vietnam and Laos. Despite the government's ban on trading with the enemy and threats of legal action, on grounds of religious conscience AFSC had begun providing medical supplies for civilian victims of the war in North Vietnam. In July 1974, AFSC's executive secretary Louis Schneider asked me to accompany him and Dr. Marjorie Nelson on a trip to visit the staff in Vientiane, Laos, the AFSC prosthetics center in Quang Ngai, South Vietnam, and then go on to North Vietnam to observe the use of donated medical supplies. We also planned to ask the government of North Vietnam for permission to place a permanent representative in Hanoi.

I had tremendous respect and affection for Lou Schneider who represented yet another surrogate father figure for me with his deeply spiritual, very steady and accessible leadership qualities. In staff and committee meetings he exhibited a quiet centeredness out of which he often offered probing moral and strategic questions and advice. For many years, Lou helped to shape AFSC's program and personnel decisions, including one that involved me. In 1972, I had been hired to be co-peace education secretary with Lyle Tatum, an older, solidly pacifist, but no longer activist Quaker. Together, the two of us were replacing Stewart Meacham—a giant in the peace movement whose active, radical political leadership was controversial among some Quakers. Stewart had retired, and replacing him was not an easy task. Apparently, the decision to hire co-secretaries, one older and one younger, had been some sort of compromise between more and less activist members of the search process. Two years later, in the midst of a budget crisis, Lou played the decisive role in asking Lyle Tatum to retire; and, despite the fact that I was just thirty-two and lacked Quaker credentials, Lou made me the sole AFSC national peace education secretary.

I was pleased that Lou invited me to go to Laos and Vietnam and looked forward very much to the trip, in part because I knew it would be an emotionally engaging experience that would help distract me from the deep hurt and sadness I was feeling over Trudi's decision to separate.

Marge Nelson was a medical doctor. Both in her appearance and approach to issues and concerns, she was a model of compassion, courage, gentleness, and integrity, who fit my positive, if still somewhat stereotyped, image of a middle aged, Midwestern Quaker. She had worked at the AFSC prosthetics center in Quang Ngai, South Vietnam. In January, 1968 (during the Tet offensive) while on a brief vacation with a friend a bit further north in Hue, she was captured by soldiers of the National Liberation Front. Two months later, Marge and her friend were released unharmed. They flew home to be with their families and then Marge returned to Quang Ngai to complete her term of service. Our 1974 trip was her first return to Vietnam and it was clearly a very emotional experience.

Our visit began in Vientiane, Laos where we stayed a few days with AFSC's representative. From Laos, we flew to Saigon and then traveled by car to Quang Ngai, South Vietnam. We met with very dedicated American and Vietnamese staff and with patients at the prosthetics center who had lost limbs as victims of US bombing raids or Vietcong booby traps. I was extremely impressed by the way the Vietnamese staff and patients seemed to ignore distinctions between those who might be sympathetic to or even possibly active supporters of the NLF, and those who weren't. Almost everyone we met was primarily critical of the Saigon government, the American occupation and the war. When I considered that these views were probably typical of many more Vietnamese, the immorality and futility of the war was brought home to me again, in yet a new personal way.

Returning overnight to Laos, the next day we took the thirty-minute flight from Vientiane to Hanoi. On a beautiful sunny day, with few clouds in the sky, our small Russian prop plane flew relatively low and I could see lovely geometrical rice fields that reminded me of the American Midwest, though the Vietnamese fields were much smaller. As we got closer to Hanoi, the landscape below us changed dramatically. We saw more and more signs of destruction, including huge bomb craters scarring the earth. Arriving in Hanoi on July 31, I was painfully reminded of my Christmas visit with Trudi and Ann Bennett. Although I had written her a letter urging that we work on getting back together, I think by this time both Trudi and I believed we were headed for divorce.

At the airport we were greeted by a North Vietnamese host committee including Lien, a lovely young Vietnamese translator, toward whom I immediately felt fresh stirrings of attraction. Being with her as she regularly translated for us and travelled with us to the South, I even fantasized about writing Lien a letter, confessing my love and saying that if she felt at all as I did, I would somehow return for her. I didn't write the letter and my love for Lien remained on the level of a dreamy fantasy, but the feelings I experienced helped me to know that there would be romantic love after Trudi.

We came to North Vietnam to observe how the AFSC medical supplies were being utilized. Our hosts informed us that, if security conditions permitted, they planned to take us south across the Demilitarized Zone (DMZ) which from the 1950s had divided North from South Vietnam. We left Hanoi very early the next morning in two Russian built six-passenger jeeps, the first carrying Lou, Marge and me, and our hosts and translators—the jovial Phan and lovely Lien—plus our military driver, Khoa. The second jeep carried our luggage, food, and a supply of lemonade and beer. As we drove out of Hanoi, we passed Bach Mai Hospital, badly damaged by a US bombing raid two years earlier. After the war ended, in part with American donations, Bach Mai was rebuilt and it became Vietnam's largest and most sophisticated medical center.

We drove for four or five hours on very bumpy roads past dozens of bombed bridges, making our way across rivers and streams by means of small ferries or temporary bridges, or by slowly slogging through shallow water and mud. The further we travelled the more we saw the war's devastation. We stayed the first night at a simple new provincial guest house, where we were told we were the first foreign guests. The next day, we arose early and continued on a very curvy road through groves of pine trees on a ridge overlooking the China Sea that reminded me of winding roads in Oregon and Northern California overlooking the Pacific. During a picnic lunch, Phan played a tape of Joan Baez singing folk songs, including one with the line, "We haven't been the best of lovers," which naturally caused me to think of Trudi and evoked a wave of deep regret and sadness.

As we got closer to the DMZ, the road became even worse. At one point, the second jeep bounced off the side of the road and got stuck in sand; we all had to help push it out. The destruction caused by years of heavy US bombing raids was awful. In some places the repeated pounding had destroyed structures and then pulverized the rubble into dust. Near the DMZ the Vietnamese had rebuilt whole villages and small industries underground so the people could maintain "normal" lives. We visited a fully equipped hospital that functioned entirely underground, where we were able to observe AFSC medical supplies being used to treat war victims. The combination of determination and imagination that went into this underground existence was quite extraordinary and provided yet another indication of why the American war was unwinnable. We were told that during the heaviest US bombing, children and old people on both sides of the DMZ had been evacuated further north, but in 1973 the government allowed them to return.

Crossing the DMZ, we transferred to vehicles belonging to the Provisional Revolutionary Government (PRG) of South Vietnam. As we were making the switch, Phan pointed down the road, and called out, "Look Ron, there's Tri." We ran to greet and embrace each other. During the Christmas 1970 visit to North Vietnam, Tri had been our daily companion and translator. He immediately asked, "How is Trudi?" I said, "She's fine," and then when we were alone later, I explained that we had separated. In part reflecting Vietnamese culture, but also his memories of us as a couple from four years earlier, Tri insisted that I take a message to her from him. "As an order from a Vietnamese comrade, I say that Trudi and Ron should stay together." I said that I appreciated his concern, but I didn't feel right taking his message to Trudi and, in any case, I didn't think we would get back together. I actually did give Trudi the message. We both were moved by it, but we knew our marriage was over.

Early the next day we headed back to Hanoi. In the face of the terrible destruction and suffering we witnessed, I found the patience, personal warmth, and sense of humor of many Vietnamese to be quite extraordinary. As an example, returning on that same curvy road, in the afternoon we stopped our vehicles in a small grove of trees overlooking the sea. It was very hot and Phan asked if we wanted to go swimming. Lou and Marge decided to remain in the shade, but I joined him on the beach, first talking quite intensely about nonviolence and Marxism and then going in for a swim. After a few minutes, Phan returned to the beach and urgently yelled at me to get out of the water right away. When I complied and ran up on the beach, he laughed and said, "Oh, sorry, I thought I saw US navy frogmen swimming toward you." I marveled that Phan's lightness of being and his humor contrasted so dramatically with the terrible realities of the war.

On at least two occasions, it was I who did something that was unintentionally pretty funny. One evening Lou, Marge and I were special honored guests at a program in a large auditorium filled with Vietnamese military officers and filmed by Chinese television. We were escorted down the center aisle, introduced on the stage, and then escorted back to our seats, with all eyes and cameras focused on us. I discovered that all that time, my fly was wide open. I guessed that many who witnessed this in person or via Chinese television came away better able to understand why we Americans hadn't been able to end the war sooner.

A second incident occurred during a dinner with government officials to discuss the AFSC's request to place a permanent representative in North Vietnam. Understandably, the Vietnamese were concerned that an American might not be able to cope with the difficult life in Hanoi during the war. We three tried to convince them that American Quakers could be tough too. Just before dinner was served, it seemed that we were making progress. Dinner was announced and we all got up to walk into the dining room. I was feeling a bit woozy from something I ate or drank the day before, and when I stood up I fainted and fell backward, spilling a small chocolate liquor drink down the front of my new white Laotian jacket. I tipped over a large stuffed chair, and landed upside down on the floor. I wasn't hurt, but being considerably taller and heavier than our Vietnamese hosts, my fall was quite dramatic. The Vietnamese were frightened and leaped to help me. I recovered quickly and, remembering what was at stake in our conversation, said loudly, "Don't worry, I'm okay and, besides, the American Quaker we will send to live in Hanoi will be much tougher than me." Everyone enjoyed a good laugh, and I was driven back to our hotel where I slept for twelve hours. A short time after our visit, the Vietnamese government agreed to have an AFSC representative in Hanoi. Lady Borton, another Midwestern Quaker who had worked in South Vietnam and spoke Vietnamese fluently, represented AFSC there for many years. She authored two unique books based on her experiences in Vietnam, *Sensing the Enemy*, and *After Sorrow: An American Among the Vietnamese.*

One of the most moving experiences on this trip occurred at another dinner in Hanoi when Marge Nelson was reunited with two young NLF soldiers who had been her captors in 1968. They apologized profusely for their actions in Hue; Marge equally profusely thanked them for how well they had treated her and her friend during the ordeal. They shared hugs, tears, and laughter as we all sat down to dinner together.

The next day we left Hanoi to return to Vientiane. Lou and I were going to Bangkok and then on to Tokyo for meetings with leaders of a North Korean civil association about AFSC's desire to visit Pyongyang. From Laos, we crossed the Mekong River to Thailand in a ferry that resembled a very tippy Native American canoe and then traveled overnight on an old, dilapidated wooden train to Bangkok. Our train trip was made more pleasurable by small bottles of Johnnie Walker Black and Drambuie I had brought along. On the SAS flight from Bangkok to Tokyo, I experienced a few deliciously flirtatious moments of conversation with a beautiful Swedish stewardess that offered further reassuring evidence for my future love life.

In August 1974, none of us knew that the war would be over in less than a year, that American forces would withdraw, and that Vietnam would be reunited and finally free of foreign occupation for the first time in more than a century. Then the Vietnamese would begin the enormous, complex work of healing and rebuilding their country. For the vast majority of Vietnamese, the end of the war brought tremendous relief, but for many the suffering continued. Thousands of veterans on both sides were physically wounded and/or psychologically traumatized by their experiences. Most prisoners of war were soon reunited with their loved ones, but many families of soldiers missing in action waited months or even years for reports on what had happened to them. The remains of some Americans who were killed were found and identified; others still are missing today. Untold numbers of Vietnamese were killed and the vast majority of their bodies were never found. Many Vietnamese civilians lost everything in massive B-52 bombing raids. Even after the war ended, many survivors suffered severe injuries and loss of limbs due to unexploded anti-personnel bombs. Still others discovered they had cancer, most likely as a result of exposure to the defoliant Agent Orange which American planes had sprayed over large areas of the countryside.

Vietnamese refugees experienced other forms of postwar trauma and suffering. In April 1975, dramatic photos appeared in the media, showing Vietnamese desperately clinging to US military helicopters on the eve of the NLF/North Vietnam victory and takeover of Saigon. More than 150,000 Vietnamese, most closely affiliated with the American or South Vietnamese military, fled at the war's end to escape retribution. The communist victors set up re-education camps for thousands who remained. Over the next few years more than 2 million out of approximately 60 million Vietnamese, as well as many Cambodians and Laotians, fled their homelands, often as "boat people," to refugee camps in Thailand and the Philippines. Eventually, the United States made it easier for them to come to America and the new Vietnamese government adopted regulations to ensure more orderly and safer departures. 58,000 Americans and an estimated 3 million Vietnamese, Cambodians and Laotians were killed in the war.

Weeks after the Vietnam War ended in April 1975, a massive "The War is Over" celebration was organized in New York City's Central Park, where I had burned my draft card eight years earlier. Having spent ten years struggling to end the war and remembering all that Trudi and I had been through together, I would have loved to be together with her for that celebration, but I just couldn't do it. My tears of joy that the war was finally over were too mixed with deep sadness that my marriage was over. Trudi and I spoke by telephone that day, sharing immense relief and joy about the war's end. The celebration, attended by 100,000 people, concluded with everyone singing the sobering lyrics of Phil Ochs's song, *The War is Over*. Ochs first released the song in 1968 during the darkest days of the war. At the time, the song seemed a kind of defiant declaration of his personal and the anti-war movement's collective intention. The war went on for seven more years before it finally was over. Those years took a heavy toll on many lives. A year after the war ended, at 36, Phil Ochs was dead by suicide.

A Return Trip to Vietnam in August 1995

In spring 1995, twenty years after the Vietnam War ended, I received a call from John McAuliff, director of the Indochina Reconciliation Project, inviting me to participate in a conference in Hanoi, to celebrate the fiftieth anniversary of the Vietnam-USA Friendship Society. John had served in the Peace Corps in Latin America in the mid-sixties and was a founder of the Committee of Returned Volunteers who publicly opposed the Vietnam War. From 1972 to 1976, while I was the AFSC national peace education secretary, he coordinated AFSC's Indochina Program. Even after the war ended, John's commitment to the people of Indochina remained strong and he understood that much work still needed to be done. John organized, raised funds for, and directed the Indochina Reconciliation Project, which focused on public education and advocacy, including urging normalization of US-Vietnam relations. John also did extraordinary work arranging for American veterans to visit Vietnam and supporting a variety of constructive reconciliation projects involving school teachers and other groups.

As background for attending this conference, I learned that at the end of World War II, Ho Chi Minh and other Vietnamese leaders organized the Vietnam-USA Friendship Society, hoping that America would recognize Vietnam's independence and oppose the return of French colonial rule. It was supported by several Americans who had been sent into Vietnam during 1944 and 1945 by the Office of Strategic Services (OSS), the predecessor to the CIA. Their assignment was to work with Vietnamese military resistance led by Ho to defeat the Japanese. The conference in Hanoi would reunite several prominent Vietnamese who had been involved in founding the Vietnam-USA Friendship Society with five octogenarian American former OSS officers, who had served in Vietnam in 1944 and 1945. In addition to John McAuliff and the former OSS men and their wives, the American delegation included three anti-war activists: Nick Eggleston, former president of Students for a Democratic Society; Carol Brightman, former editor of the anti-war magazine, *Viet Report*, and me, representing the religious wing of the American peace movement.

By 1995 I had already been working for more than ten years on the Arab-Israeli-Palestinian conflict, but this invitation seemed so special that I could not turn it down. As the five former OSS men, their wives, all in their eighties, and the three anti-war activists in our fifties, gathered at Kennedy Airport for the first leg of our long flight to Hanoi, we realized that we had many more stories than we could conceivably have time to tell one another. We would share many stories in the conference sessions, and over meals and drinks. After years of war and occupation in Vietnam, it was incredibly ironic to be revisiting Vietnam with Americans who had been assigned to support Ho Chi Minh's Vietminh forces. Two of them had walked alongside Ho as he returned from China to fight the Japanese. Another, an Asian American from the Seattle area, had served as the main radio operator for General Vo Nguyen Giap, commander of the Vietnamese military forces. Two others had parachuted from an American plane into Vietnam. On their way down to a clearing where a squad of Ho Chi Minh's men waited for them in military formation, they got entangled in a very tall Banyan tree. Vietnamese soldiers had to climb up to free them before the welcoming ceremony could begin.

One day all of us travelled by bus about seventy-five miles northwest of Hanoi to the village where the two Americans had landed fifty years earlier. They had an emotional reunion with a seventy-year-old Vietnamese woman who had been their cook. Without saying anything, I think we all experienced the tragic irony of the contrast between the warmth of their reunion and the decades of death and destruction Vietnamese suffered as a result of the Japanese, French and American invasions and occupations.

On the last day we were in Hanoi, we were invited to have lunch with eighty-four-year-old General Vo Nguyen Giap. For more than thirty years, he commanded Vietnamese military forces that defeated the Japanese in 1945, the French in 1954, and finally the Americans in 1975. As we sat around the table, I experienced a complex set of emotions. I was in awe of General Giap's incredible accomplishments and his strategic military leadership during four decades of struggle to achieve his country's independence. But I also felt a screaming sadness as I thought about the 58,000 American lives lost and more than 1,000,000 young Vietnamese who never returned home. I revisited the grief and anger I felt at my country's arrogance, its blinding anti-communism and the paradox of attempting, in the name of freedom, to impose our will on Vietnam.

At lunch General Giap acknowledged and appreciated the fact that in July President Clinton had announced normalization of diplomatic relations with Vietnam. Clinton took this historic step with very significant bipartisan support from two prominent Vietnam War veterans: Senator John Kerry, Democrat of Massachusetts, who had joined other Vietnam War veterans in 1971 in a protest where they tossed their service medals over a fence onto the Capitol steps; and Senator John McCain, Republican of Arizona, who had been a prisoner of war in North Vietnam for six years, and was tortured. As our time together came to a close, General Giap reached out his tanned, bony hands and took hold of the aging, white wrists of the two eighty-year-old American former OSS officers seated on either side of him. Very quietly, almost as if it was too painful to acknowledge, he said, "Finally, our two countries will have normal relations but it has taken us too long."

From Hanoi, several of us flew to Ho Chi Minh City (formerly Saigon), a trip that no longer involved crossing a boundary. With help from John McAuliffe, I phoned Huynh Tan Mam, who had been president of the Saigon Student Association when I brought American religious and student leaders to Saigon in July 1970. He was now an executive in the Vietnam Red Cross. As a result of the demonstration for peace in 1970, Mam had been arrested, so I wasn't sure how he would react to hearing from me after all these years. When he heard my name, he exclaimed, "Ron Young, I've been missing you, where have you been all these years?" The next day, when we met, we embraced and then walked the same route from the School of Agriculture to the Independence Palace that we had planned to march twenty-five years earlier. As we sat together having a cold drink, Mam turned to me and said, "It's strange, Ron, how things work out. In 1970, as students we used to paint anti-imperialist slogans on the streets in Saigon demanding 'USA Go Home!' Today, I and most Vietnamese welcome the start of normal relations and we want American investments and tourists to come to Vietnam."

This trip helped bring closure to the ten years I worked to end the war. At the same time, learning about the American OSS officers' pre-Cold War experiences and the hopes for normal relations that they shared with the Vietnamese in 1945, evoked renewed sadness over all the suffering in the intervening three decades. It also prompted a few profoundly challenging questions and ideas that I carry with me today. Looking back, how might our country and the world be different if, at the end of World War II, the United States had not supported France's effort to re-impose colonial rule but had recognized Vietnam's independence and established normal, peaceful relations? Looking ahead, I continue to ask myself, what are the most important lessons from the Vietnam War and our efforts to stop it that can help guide us toward creating a more peaceful future? I believe an essential part of honoring all the lives lost and shattered by the Vietnam War is that we work imaginatively and determinedly to prevent war in the future.

Ron's parents, Edie and Jim Young

Ron and sister, Judy

Fishing with their grandpa
on the Delaware River

Ron's grandparents,
John and Mae Hofer

Ron with Rev. Jim Lawson and Rev. Edwin Sanders in Nashville 2008

Ron with former members of the Youth Fellowship
at Centenary Methodist Church in Memphis 2008

Ron, as Associate Youth Minister, leading
morning service at the Congregational Church
In East Hampton, Connecticut 1965

Ron speaking in front of the Justice Department
October 21, 1967 Photo by John Goodwin

Reading his poem, "We Are America"
At Clergy and Laity Against the War gathering
in Washington, DC February 1968 Photo by John Goodwin

Ron and Trudi on their wedding day
October 5, 1968 releasing "Amnesty for War Resisters" balloons
Photo by John Goodwin

March to Ron's draft resistance trial February 1970
Photo by John Goodwin

Rev. William Sloane Coffin at Ron's trial date
Photo by John Goodwin

Woman calling name of American killed in Vietnam
March Against Death November 13–15, 1969
Photo by John Goodwin

Flag draped coffin containing names of Americans killed in Vietnam
March Against Death November 13–15, 1969 Photo by John Goodwin

FOR interfaith/interracial fact-finding delegation
focused on repression in South Vietnam July 1970

GAS AND BIRD

Tear gas clouds driving trapped students against
a fence when police broke up international
peace march. Ron Young flees with dove he
helped carry at head of march.

What the F.O.R. fact-finding mission to South Viet Nam did and saw

FOR Delegation with Vietnamese Students
in peace march tear gassed by Saigon police

Ron, Trudi and Ann Bennett meeting with Prime Minister Pham Van Dong in Hanoi on a mission carrying mail for American POWs December 1970

Ron lying in the White House driveway to protest the Vietnam Daily Death Toll November 1971 Photo by John Goodwin

Ron, Marjorie Nelson and Lou Schneider of AFSC with Vietnamese hosts
On their way from Hanoi south to the Demilitarized Zone August 1974

Archbishop Oscar Romero meeting Ecumenical Delegations
a day before he was assassinated March 1980

6

Moving to the Middle East: Learning Israeli and Palestinian Stories and Hopes

Marrying again and welcoming the birth of our son; taking on a Quaker assignment to live in Jordan and travel in the region listening to Arab and Israeli views of the conflict and prospects for peace; experiencing each side's story as true, including Jewish memories of the Holocaust and Palestinian memories of the Nakhba; holy sites and unholy encounters; meeting people on each side who want to know more about people on the other side; witnessing awful violence and signs that peace is possible; meeting peacemakers who are politically sidelined or killed; reflecting on Israeli and Palestinian hopes and disappointments over the Reagan initiative.

Marriage to Carol, Birth of a Son

I FIRST MET CAROL Jensen in 1973 when I was the AFSC peace education secretary, and she represented Northern California on our nationwide committee. In 1974, as my marriage with Trudi was ending, I began keeping a personal journal and I remember writing a note about Carol. Attracted to her and impressed by her strong independent thinking and sharp instincts about social change strategies, I wrote: "Carol is a woman with whom I will have to contend, but I think I'm going to enjoy it." In May, 1978, following her divorce, Carol moved from Seattle to Philadelphia and, at the suggestion of our mutual friend Gail Pressberg, she came to live in a communal house I had organized two years earlier. She joined the national staff of Clergy and Laity Concerned and during 1979–80 was a founder of the nuclear freeze movement. While CALC's offices were in New York City, Carol preferred living in Philadelphia, commuting several days a week or spending some nights with friends in the City.

From the time she moved into our house, Carol and I often ended our evenings together in the living room, sipping scotch and talking politics, sometimes with other housemates, but more often just the two of us. We shared a deep commitment to work for justice and peace, and enjoyed discussing strategies about worthwhile objectives and goals. We both are idealists, but we also understood that to succeed at social change you have to engage in messy practical political realities. While we held many political views in common, we also sometimes argued strenuously over strategies. While Carol was very good at understanding and being focused on accurately describing a situation as it is, I tended to see how a situation could be changed for the better and be focused on how to get there. Our differences caused creative tension between us that enriched our subsequent work together, including our work in the Middle East. Carol had a good sense of humor and, most of the time, seemed to appreciate mine. The fact that we both enjoyed getting to know very different people, regardless of their political views, would prove to be essential in our listening assignment among Arabs and Israelis in the Middle East. This love of people also turned out to be very helpful to Carol's subsequent vocation as a Lutheran parish pastor and to my work with American Jews, Christians and Muslims for Middle East peace. After only a few months, in addition to sharing long evenings together talking about social change, we also occasionally shared a bed.

Since both Carol and I had been married before, we approached our developing relationship cautiously and, especially in my case, with deliberate slow speed. Six months into our relationship, when we decided to move in with two married couples in a larger, much nicer old Germantown stone house, we were quite conscious that it signified our deepening commitment to one another. Still proceeding cautiously, we asked our housemates to refer to us as "Carol comma Ron" rather than "Carol and Ron." As I had with Trudi, I told Carol that I was bisexual. By this time, I mostly had dropped the categories—straight, bi, gay—and simply accepted sexuality as a fluid, wonderful and somewhat enigmatic dimension of human relationships. Carol accepted this and even encouraged a male friend of hers to talk with me about his own bisexual inclinations. We met one evening for dinner and he seemed to genuinely appreciate hearing my experiences and advice. While I matured a lot over the years about these issues, I'm still aware sometimes of the irony that both women I married seemed more accepting and relaxed about my bisexuality than I was. While I believe that sexuality is as important for women as for men, I think my ongoing ambivalence in part reflects how sex is often a more fraught dimension of relationships for men than it is for women. Given the importance of family to both of us, over the next year and a half, Carol and I made trips to Florida, Washington State and Maine to meet each other's parents and siblings. Those were joyous times that strengthened our relationship and confirmed its seriousness.

In May 1980, crossing on a ferry from Lewes, Delaware to Cape May, New Jersey, I proposed marriage and Carol accepted. We decided that Carol would keep her family name, and that we didn't need clergy to officiate, although we did invite a few close clergy friends to celebrate with us. We designed our own wedding invitation, wrote our own vows, and chose a recording of Pachelbel's *Canon in D* to play during the ceremony. We married each other in a simple Quaker-style wedding at our communal house in Philadelphia on October 11, 1980. Denise Levertov's poem *Movement*[1] expressed the hope Carol and I had for our marriage that we'd love each other in ways that provide support for each other while not becoming the other's center.

As this was a second wedding for both of us, everyone, including our families, seemed more relaxed. With help from our housemates, we prepared most of the reception food ourselves and served everything informally on paper plates to the sixty guests in our living room. Carol's dad, Emil, brought King Salmon from Washington State that he grilled in our backyard. I remember my dad being visibly eager for the ceremony to be over so he and several others could get back to watching the fifth game of the World Series, between Kansas City and the Philadelphia Phillies.

Since Carol's sister Mary and their parents came all the way from Seattle, we decided to invite them along on our honeymoon. The day after the wedding we drove together in my Dodge Dart to a lovely country inn in the Poconos and then spent the next night in New York City, where we saw the musical, "Barnum." The next morning, we drove up to the Berkshires along the Taconic Parkway, applauding as every curve along the winding, wooded highway revealed a new movement in the symphony of fall colors.

Both Carol and I were ready and eager to have children. It was not an accident that our first son was born July 11, 1981, nine months to the day from our wedding. While I don't recall the border crossing of my own birth, I will never forget the awe and joy I experienced as our son's head and then whole body emerged from Carol's. Even after watching for nine months as her belly swelled with him, we both greeted his arrival as if it was a miracle. After considering many Biblical names, we decided to name him Jonah because, with all that prophet's stubbornness and often humorous confusion about God's purposes, Jonah was a prophet with whom we could imagine living. We couldn't imagine being parents of Isaiah or Jeremiah. We didn't know that less than a year later we would be living and traveling in the Middle East with our Jonah, visiting many of the places featured in the biblical story of *Jonah and the Whale*.

In January 1982, Carol and I were appointed by the AFSC to be the international affairs representatives in the Middle East on behalf of American, British and Canadian Quaker service organizations. We were enthusiastic, but also humbled and nervous because we had no Middle East academic background or practical experience working on Middle East issues. As AFSC national peace education secretary, I had supervised Gail Pressberg, director of our Middle East peace education program, but I had no direct, personal involvement with the complex, emotional and often extremely contentious issues of the Arab-Israeli conflict. My closest experience was when I participated in a series of tense senior staff dialogues between representatives of AFSC and the American Jewish Committee, and when I helped negotiate a peaceful

1. Levertov, "Movement," 115.

outcome to a physically threatening sit-in by Meir Kahane's Jewish Defense League at the AFSC's Philadelphia headquarters. I knew it would be quite challenging to go from being a peace activist to becoming a sensitive listener to people on different sides of the conflict. At a roast at my last meeting as peace education secretary, fellow staff and committee members parodied me trying to sell "Make Love Not War" bumper stickers to rich princes in Saudi Arabia. None of us could possibly have imagined that thirty years later I would still be working on the Arab-Israeli-Palestinian conflict.

For three years, beginning in Spring 1982, as Quaker international affairs representatives we would live in Jordan and travel regularly in Israel, the West Bank and Gaza, Egypt, Jordan, Syria and Lebanon, to meet with Arabs and Israelis—civilians and government officials—to *listen* to their views about opportunities and obstacles for achieving peace, and how they believed America could help. Carol and I were expected to write a newsletter every two months that the Quaker agencies would send out to a few thousand key contacts and opinion makers in the United States, Canada and Great Britain. In AFSC, our reports would contribute to the development of advocacy positions on American policy. AFSC also expected us to explore possibilities for communicating information and perspectives between people on different sides of the conflict, and to seek out individual Palestinians and Israelis who might be interested in face-to-face meetings.

Orientation for Our Middle East Assignment

Aware of our lack of experience, AFSC wisely scheduled us for a three-month period of orientation, during which we did a lot of reading and had several briefings with experts involved with the conflict. The readings were very helpful, especially *A Middle East Reader*, edited by Irene Gendzier; *The Zionist Idea: A Historical Analysis and Reader,* edited and with an introduction by Arthur Hertzberg; *Orientalism* by Edward Said; and *The Arab Predicament* by Fouad Ajami. AFSC also scheduled dozens of appointments for us with very knowledgeable experts on the Middle East and conflict resolution, as well as Jewish American and Arab American leaders who had personal and organizational bonds to different sides of the conflict. I especially remember going to New York City to meet with Tahseen Bashir, Egypt's ambassador to Canada, who had flown down from Ottawa to brief us. He had been a senior advisor to President Anwar Sadat in the late 1970s during the entire process of making peace with Israel. Tahseen was personally sympathetic with the Palestinians and, at the same time, in very principled and practical ways, firmly committed to helping build a comprehensive Arab-Israeli-Palestinian peace. He had deep respect for Quakers. Given their small numbers and the fact that neither of us was a Quaker, Carol and I were surprised by how often people we met expressed a high regard for Quakers. We would learn more about the Quakers' reputation and reach as we took up our assignment. Another high point of our orientation was when we met two American academics at Harvard, Dr. Herbert Kelman and Dr. Everett Mendelsohn, who had been actively engaged in informal, unpublicized "track-two diplomacy" for several years. They had arranged, hosted and facilitated some of the earliest unpublicized conversations between Israelis and Palestinians to discuss the requirements for peace and how to get there. They helped us understand how Palestinian and Israeli perceptions of the conflict were changing and why spring 1982 was a very interesting and opportune time to be taking up this unique assignment.

One incident during our trip to Boston illustrated our inexperience. It also inspired us with the appreciation people felt for our work and their generosity in sharing both their personal stories and their hopes for the future. We met for lunch at the Harvard Club with several members of the AFSC committee responsible for our appointment. Our very special guest was Dr. Walid Khalidi, preeminent senior Palestinian scholar and advisor to Palestine Liberation Organization (PLO) Chairman Yasser Arafat. Dr. Khalidi's 1978 article in *Foreign Affairs*, "Thinking the Unthinkable: A Sovereign Palestinian State,"[2] was widely recognized as the earliest, most authoritative statement projecting Palestinian willingness to accept a resolution of the conflict based on a demilitarized Palestinian state in the West Bank and Gaza that would live alongside Israel in mutual security and peace. While many supporters of Israel considered Yasser Arafat to be an implacable enemy, it was widely known that Walid Khalidi had written this important article with the PLO Chairman Arafat's full approval and support.

Walid Khalidi was very gracious and soft-spoken. As we sat down for lunch, he warmly congratulated us on our assignment, and said, "I presume you've travelled in the Middle East and in Arab countries." A bit embarrassed, we answered, "No, we haven't." Trying a more minimalist approach, Khalidi then asked, "Well, perhaps then, at least you have been to Israel?" "No," we said, "we haven't." Carol and I looked around nervously. The thought crossed both our minds that maybe our appointment would end even before it began. Instead of reacting negatively or skeptically, Dr. Khalidi calmly drew a breath and responded quietly, "Well, I think it's very good to have new people in this role. All of us involved in the conflict could benefit from some fresh perspectives."

After completing our orientation, Carol and I, and nine-month-old Jonah were to set up our home base in Amman, Jordan. Initially, we worried that having Jonah might complicate our assignment and we were disappointed not to be based in Jerusalem, as the couple who preceded us had been. However, given the family-oriented cultures of the Middle East, it turned out that Jonah was often an asset. On several occasions his presence led to wonderfully warm, informal and very informative encounters with people whom we probably would not have met otherwise. Perhaps because Bible stories made Jerusalem seem familiar, we imagined that living there would be easier and better. However, as it turned out, we really appreciated living in

2. Khalidi, "Thinking the Unthinkable, 695–713.

Amman. We discovered there was an advantage to reviewing our interview notes and writing our bi-monthly reports from relatively peaceful Jordan, rather than from the deeply conflicted and frequently tense city of Jerusalem. We came to understand that if we were based in Jerusalem, the pressures to take sides might have been much more intense, tangible and tempting, and that could have compromised our assignment to be sensitive and objective listeners.

Appreciating that we might be nervous about moving to the Middle East, on the day before we were scheduled to leave, staff at AFSC's headquarters planned a Quaker meeting for worship as a supportive send-off. That morning, Carol and I went to our bank to get traveler checks. While we were speaking with an officer, a man entered the bank, jumped over the counter near us waving a gun, and shouted, "This is a holdup, everybody keep quiet and stay right where you are." He filled a couple of bags with money and fled. Within minutes, the police arrived and told everyone to remain until they had a chance to interview each of us. We were able to call the AFSC to explain that we were safe but unfortunately a bank robbery meant we would have to miss the meeting for worship sending us off to the dangerous Middle East. The irony and humor of this coincidence was lost on no one.

On our way to the Middle East, our itinerary included stopovers in London and Paris. Traveling with Jonah, we very much appreciated that the usually cost-conscious AFSC had booked us in business class on the trans-Atlantic flight. In London, our minimalist Quaker budget was reflected in simple accommodations at William Penn House, where we stayed in dormitory-like rooms and had to insert five pence coins to get a limited amount of hot water for a shower. We met with the staff and committee members of our British Quaker sponsoring agency. In Paris, Gail Pressberg had arranged for us to meet separately with Major General (ret.) Mattityahu Peled, an Israeli, and Isam Sartawi, a member of the PLO leadership and senior advisor to Yasser Arafat. Gail informed us that Peled and Sartawi happened to be in Paris at the time for important, private discussions.

General Matti Peled had commanded logistics in the Sinai during the June 1967 war, and subsequently served in occupied Gaza. He publicly opposed Israel's settlement construction in the newly conquered territories. He studied Arabic, and was instrumental in starting the Arabic literature department at Tel Aviv University. In 1975, he was a co-founder, along with Arie (Lova) Eliav and others, of the Israeli Council for Israeli-Palestinian Peace (ICIPP) that called for withdrawal from the territories captured in 1967, the establishment of an independent Palestinian state in the West Bank and Gaza, and for sharing Jerusalem. ICIPP adopted crossed Israeli and Palestinian flags as its symbol, despite the fact that displaying the Palestinian flag in Israel was illegal and the only Israeli flags in the occupied territories were those carried by Israeli soldiers or settlers. Despite his war record, many Israelis hated General Peled for his outspoken dovish views. He was so outraged by one Israeli critic who publicly accused him of being anti-Zionist that he sought and won a court judgment against his accuser. Peled supported the 1993 Oslo Declaration, although he later criticized the negotiations process for moving much too slowly. He believed the slow pace created a context that allowed extremists on both sides to act provocatively, and almost inevitably reignite violent conflict. Matti Peled died of cancer in 1995.

Isam Sartawi was born in 1935 in Acre, Palestine. He trained as a medical doctor in Baghdad and the United States. In response to the June 1967 war, he left his medical practice to join the Palestinian national liberation movement. Believing that armed struggle was necessary to combat Israel, he formed a new military group, the Arab Command for the Liberation of Palestine. In the mid-1970s, he abandoned the military approach in favor of dialogue with moderate Israelis, and became a major advisor to Yasser Arafat. Arafat consistently defended Sartawi from attacks on his dovish views by PLO hardliners. In 1979 Isam Sartawi was awarded the Austrian Kreisky Prize, along with Lova Eliav, for seeking a peaceful resolution to the Israeli-Palestinian conflict. In April 1983, Sartawi travelled to Portugal to attend a Socialist International conference that Shimon Peres from Israel also attended. While waiting in the hotel lobby in the hope of meeting Peres personally, Sartawi was assassinated. Most knowledgeable Palestinians believed he was killed on orders from a small, Iraqi-based, extremist Palestinian faction headed by Abu Nidal.

When we met each man separately, both Peled and Sartawi expressed warm respect for Gail Pressberg and for the Quakers. Over the phone, both men suggested meeting at the same small quiet café, to which we brought Jonah in his blue stroller. We guessed that this was where they also were meeting each other. Meeting these two heroes of early Israeli-Palestinian peacemaking efforts was an extraordinary and inspiring start to our Middle East mission.

Getting Settled in Amman

We landed at the old, rather tired-looking airport not far from the city center of Amman, in the late afternoon. On our taxi ride through the old downtown, as we passed through narrow streets in the crowded market, we were struck by many new sights and smells, and by all the brightly colored signs in Arabic that we couldn't read. A series of seven roundabouts or circles, starting with First Circle in the old downtown, defined the layout of streets in Amman. Our taxi delivered us to the small, Shepherd's Hotel between the second and third circle. Exhausted from our flight, we lay down on the bed with Jonah between us. As we dozed, we were startled awake by the loud Muslim call to prayer, *Allahu Akbar, Allahu Akbar,* coming from a minaret right outside our hotel window. Carol asked in a tone of doubt and puzzlement, "Where are we, Ron? What have we done?" I responded sleepily, "I don't know, Carol, I don't know." We slipped back into a restful sleep. An hour or so later, we were down in the hotel's casual dining room eating a tasty Middle Eastern dinner and drinking Egyptian beer.

One of the wonderfully friendly waiters carried baby Jonah off on a tour of the hotel kitchen. It was all very new but in just a few hours, we felt welcomed and relaxed.

The next morning, at Gail's suggestion, we called Peter Salah, Jordan's deputy minister of information. He greeted the three of us graciously, clearly pleased that we had brought Jonah along, even after he spilled cracker crumbs on the carpet. Peter became our good friend as well as an important contact in the Jordanian government. Through him we gained an introduction to Adnan Abu Odeh, then Jordan's minister of information and a very smart, independent-minded key advisor to King Hussein on Palestinian and Arab affairs. During our three years in Amman, we met regularly with Abu Odeh and learned a great deal from his candid, critical perspectives. Intellectually honest, in one of our early meetings with him, Adnan told us about the large and, in his view, shameful gap between realistic private Arab assessments of the need to make peace with Israel and loud, public warlike Arab pronouncements. I will never forget the crude image he used to describe this disconnect, "It's like a little boy who won't admit that he's wet his pants."

On a family trip to the Middle East in the summer of 2002, Carol and I re-connected with Adnan Abu Odeh, who was then somewhat out of favor with the palace because he criticized some Jordanian government policies. I highly recommend Abu Odeh's book, *Jordanians, Palestinians and the Hashemite Kingdom in the Middle East Peace Process,* published by the US Institute for Peace.

In the afternoon of our first full day in Jordan, we visited Rebecca and Amr Salti, who had volunteered to help us find an apartment. Over tea, the Saltis gave us advice and introduced us to their neighbor, Zaki, owner of an automobile repair shop, who offered to sell us his faded yellow 1971 Volkswagen beetle. The following day, we walked around Jebel Webdeh, a very pleasant, older, tree-lined, neighborhood. We met an elderly Palestinian man who was very friendly and spoke English. He told us that his daughter had an apartment for rent. Then, learning that we worked for the Quakers, he announced enthusiastically, "I also am a Quaker." He explained that, as a youth, he had attended the excellent Quaker school in Ramallah in the West Bank.

Within a week, we had moved into his daughter's small walk-up apartment located over a bakery and a cleaner. The appetizing aroma from the bakery that drifted up into our living room and the less pleasant smell from the cleaner that seeped up into our bedroom were a kind of yin/yang experience. We walked Jonah in the small neighborhood park just around the corner, while in the other direction we discovered a wonderful, inexpensive restaurant that served great grilled chicken, fries, and cold beer. We found a well-stocked supermarket several blocks away and a small fresh fruit and vegetable store, where sometimes we waited to make a purchase while the lone clerk finished his Muslim prayers on a small carpet in the back of his store. We enjoyed fresh-squeezed Jordanian orange juice almost every morning. We did our laundry in a small Japanese washing machine and hung clothes up on the roof to dry. We enrolled

Jonah in a daycare, run by Mrs. Fakhouri, a friendly, middle-aged Palestinian woman. In a very short time our family felt quite at home in Amman.

During our second week, we arranged to meet Rami G. Khouri, editor of the *Jordan Times*. A Palestinian, born in Nazareth, Rami also held American citizenship. His family had lived in New York City for several years while his father worked for the United Nations. Despite his anti-imperialist politics, Rami had become an enthusiastic fan of the NY Yankees. He attended Syracuse University, where he majored in journalism. Very personable and warm, Rami was also highly knowledgeable about Palestinian and Arab affairs, and had a relatively sophisticated understanding of American society and politics. As a reporter and journalist, he was thorough, and often offered courageous, independent perspectives in his *Jordan Times* columns. This meant that he sometimes got into trouble with the Jordanian government over Palestinian and human rights issues. He believed in dialogue with Israelis and in the necessity of negotiations for a two-state solution, and he wasn't afraid to say so publicly. In 1983 an Israeli professor named Shimoni wrote an Op-Ed article in the then liberal Israeli *Jerusalem Post* urging that Israel talk with the PLO. In response, Rami Khouri wrote an editorial in the *Jordan Times*, boldly headlined "I Extend My Hand to You, Professor Shimoni." A few years earlier, this positive, public exchange would not have happened. In 1983, it still was considered unusual and courageous.

Rami was very interested in following our work as we began our visits in Israel, the West Bank and Gaza. He agreed to meet with us regularly to brief us about developments in the region and to hear our reports. While in our travels we met with a wide variety of Arabs and Israelis, both in government and out, we were helped enormously by finding someone in each society who could brief us on the political lay of the land, provide relatively objective perspectives about current issues, and suggest additional issues we should explore or new people we should meet. Rami Khouri performed this important role for us in Jordan. He and his wife, Ellen, became personal friends.

In 2002, on our family trip to the Middle East, Carol and I had dinner with Rami and Ellen in Amman while our sons joined theirs at a holiday barbeque. Later, Rami moved to Beirut to be an editor for the *Beirut Daily Star,* and Director of the Issam Fares Institute for Public Policy and International Affairs. He writes a regular email column distributed by *Agence Global* to an international list of contacts. Several of his columns on the popular, democratic, largely nonviolent Arab uprisings in spring 2011 were profoundly insightful and moving.

Jordan's population in 1982 was approximately 4 million (about the same as Israel's), of whom 60 percent or more were of Palestinian origin. The rest came from families who for many generations lived east of the Jordan River. It is a relatively small country, surrounded by four much more powerful nations (Israel, Syria, Iraq and Saudi Arabia). Jordan's longest border is with Israel and Jordan had legal claims to the West Bank, which Israel had occupied as a result of the June 1967 war. In 1988, King Hussein relinquished those claims in favor of the Palestinians. Unlike other Arab states that kept Palestinians in refugee status, Jordan absorbed them as citizens, and many have played important roles as professionals and business leaders.

Early in our time in Amman, we were struck by how much daily news in Jordan focused on events and issues related to the Palestinians and developments in the region. For example, most of King Hussein's 1982 annual address to the National Consultative Council (roughly equivalent to an American president's State of the Union address) was devoted to the Israeli-Palestinian conflict and the Iran-Iraq war, then in its second year. Despite its small size, many believed that Jordan could play a pivotal role in resolving the Israeli-Palestinian conflict. King Hussein, like his father Abdullah, had a strong personal and strategic interest in a negotiated resolution but, given Jordan's size and vulnerability, the King was understandably very cautious and unlikely to act alone.

Jordan had endorsed UN Security Council resolutions 242 and 338 calling for a negotiated end to the Arab-Israeli conflict based on the interdependent principles of Israeli withdrawal from territories it captured in the 1967 war, and recognition and security of all states in the region, obviously including Israel. On several occasions King Hussein had implied that Jordan was willing to recognize Israel within pre-1967 borders. In one of our early meetings with the King's brother Crown Prince Hassan, he repeated to us what he had written earlier in *Foreign Affairs*. "We understand the Palestinian problem must be dealt with in the context of the existence of Israel." Despite this realism, Jordan did not officially recognize Israel until 1994, when the two nations signed a peace treaty in the context of the Israel-PLO declaration and the Oslo peace process. As Israeli-Palestinian negotiations bogged down, criticism in Jordan over peace with Israel intensified, but just as with the Egyptian-Israeli treaty, the Jordanian-Israeli treaty held.

Our Initial Visits to Israel, the West Bank and Gaza 1982

Several of our trips coincided with major developments in the countries we were visiting. We made our first visit to Israel in June 1982, a week after Israel invaded Lebanon. While initially most Israelis supported the invasion, others were critical of what they believed was Israel's first war of choice, in contrast to the wars of 1948, 1967 and 1973 which they believed were wars of necessity or of survival.

We prepared for our visit by briefing ourselves on some background to the invasion. Recent history in Lebanon, how that history related to the Israeli-Palestinian conflict, the Israeli rationale for the invasion and the US view of it all were important elements we sought to understand before crossing the Jordan River to the West Bank and Israel. During the 1970s, after King Hussein ejected Palestinian military forces from Jordan, the PLO established its headquarters in Lebanon and operated a kind of state-within-a-state in the south. Between 1978 and 1981 the PLO military mounted sporadic attacks and raids into Israel that inevitably provoked counter attacks by the

Israel Defense Forces (IDF), in which Lebanese civilians generally suffered more casualties than the Palestinians. These skirmishes were finally halted by a ceasefire in July 1981 negotiated by President Reagan's special envoy, Philip Habib, a prominent Lebanese American businessman from San Francisco. The ceasefire raised hopes for starting negotiations between Israel and the Palestinians, but they were soon frustrated. Despite the key American role in achieving the ceasefire and our country's commitment to pursue peace, regrettably, there was no serious US diplomatic effort to get negotiations going. Instead, despite Israeli objections, the Reagan administration pressed ahead with selling airborne warning and control systems (AWACs) to Saudi Arabia and enhancing strategic military cooperation with Egypt. These moves reflected the administration's policy goals of seeking to contain Soviet and Iranian influence in the region as apparently higher priorities than helping to negotiate Israeli-Palestinian peace.

Immediately after President Sadat's funeral in October 1981, the Reagan administration ignored another opportunity to help move Israelis and Palestinians toward negotiations. Flying home from the funeral, former Presidents Jimmy Carter and Gerald Ford issued a joint statement saying that eventually the US would need to talk with the PLO and urging the Reagan Administration to find a way of bringing the Palestinians into negotiations. Lead editorials in *The New York Times* and the *Washington Post* echoed their call. The former presidents' statement raised Palestinian and Israeli hopes that peace negotiations might be launched, but President Reagan did not respond.

Despite occasional violations, the PLO-Israel ceasefire in Lebanon continued to hold through late 1981 and early 1982. It was widely suspected at the time that Ariel Sharon, then Israel's defense minister, wanted Israel to invade Lebanon to totally eliminate the PLO's military threat. While Alexander Haig, President Reagan's secretary of state, spoke publicly about US interests in negotiated peace, many believed that Haig privately agreed with Sharon. According to this view, an Israeli invasion would not only destroy the PLO's military capacity to attack Israel once and for all, but also would pull Lebanon out of the Syrian, and by extension Soviet orbit, thus allowing for greater American and Israeli influence over Lebanon.

On June 3, 1982 we awoke to the news that Palestinian gunmen had attempted to assassinate Shlomo Argov, Israel's ambassador to London, providing the excuse that Sharon needed to convince Prime Minister Begin to order an invasion of Lebanon. Subsequent reports suggested that the extremist Palestinian faction that carried out the attempt on Argov's life and opposed any negotiations with Israel, was also planning to assassinate Nabil Ramlawi, the PLO representative in London. In 1978, the same extremist Palestinian faction was suspected of murdering Said Hammami, the PLO representative in London who was known to support a negotiated two-state resolution of the conflict. On June 6, Israel invaded Lebanon and the PLO launched a barrage of artillery attacks on northern Israel. While Secretary of State Haig publicly urged restraint, dovish Israelis believed that he privately gave a green light to the invasion. Ironically, Ambassador Argov later expressed reservations about Israel's decision to invade. Many prominent Israelis believed it was a terrible mistake. This was not the only time we witnessed Washington policymakers tacitly or explicitly supporting hawkish Israeli policies which many Israelis publicly criticized as harmful to Israel, including its essential interest in negotiating peace with the Palestinians.

In preparation for our first trip across the river to the West Bank and into Israel, we needed a permit from the Jordanian interior ministry. This was our first encounter with the governmental fiction denying Israel's existence. Arab governments and schools still omitted Israel from regional maps. According to the official Jordanian government view, after we crossed the Jordan River into the West Bank, we would simply be visiting occupied territory. There would be no official acknowledgement of or reference to our visiting Israel, and if we wound up getting Israeli stamps in our passports, we would then not be allowed to reenter Jordan or any other Arab country except Egypt. The fiction of non-recognition became even more ironic after we returned to Amman, when senior Jordanian officials we met were very interested to hear our perceptions about developments *in Israel.*

The unrealistic nature of this legal fiction was brought home to us in another way a few days before we left Amman. Abdel Jawad Salah, the exiled Palestinian mayor of El Bireh in the West Bank, asked us to find out more about *Oz ve Shalom-Netivot Shalom*, an Orthodox religious Israeli peace movement that publicly opposed Israel's invasion of Lebanon. When we asked Salah how he knew about the group, he told us that he had read about it in an Israeli newspaper passed on to him earlier that week by a friend in Jordanian intelligence.

We learned that since shortly after the 1967 war, every day Israeli and Jordanian intelligence services exchanged all their nations' daily newspapers on the Allenby Bridge across the Jordan River. Early one morning when we were waiting to cross, Carol and I watched as an Israeli soldier carried a bundle of that day's Israeli newspapers out onto the bridge, placed them on the center line, and returned to his side. Then, a Jordanian soldier carried a bundle of Jordanian newspapers out to the center of the bridge, set his bundle down and picked up the Israeli stack. The Israeli soldier then returned for the Jordanian bundle. The two soldiers never met or spoke. The official myth was maintained. Jordan did not recognize Israel's existence, but both governments wanted to know as much as possible about what was happening on the other side of the river.

Very early in the morning on June 14, 1982, Carol, Jonah and I took a taxi from our apartment in Jebel Webdeh to nearby Abdali where we boarded a minibus for the drive down to the Jordan River. Our bus driver that day was Ali, with whom we became friendly and with whom, on subsequent trips, we often shared our breakfast of soft cheese, sesame seeded rolls, and a thermos of coffee. During our three years living in Jordan, we probably made this trip fifteen or more times, and on almost every trip, Ali was our driver.

The route down to the Allenby Bridge passed a bit north of Mt. Nebo, where, according to the Bible, Moses looked across the Jordan Valley and saw the Promised Land. On the Israeli side of the river there was a large, relatively new concrete building that dwarfed the rather old military post on the Jordanian side. The Israelis separated people into two lines: "foreigners" and "Palestinians," for whom the process of interrogation and inspection of luggage was very different. Palestinians, many of whom came from the very land they were now reentering, were subjected to a variety of verbal and physical indignities, occasionally including strip searches, while the search of our belongings was routinely much simpler.

Once we cleared security, we joined other passengers in a shared taxi for the trip through Jericho and up the west side of the Jordan Valley. We passed through the village of Bethany, rounded a curve in the road and then, looking down over the Mount of Olives, we had our first view of the old walled city of Jerusalem, which included remains of the Temple Mount and Western Wall from the ancient Second Jewish Temple; the Church of the Holy Sepulchre, on the location where some believe Jesus was crucified; the silver-domed Al Aksa Mosque, second holiest site in Islam; and the magnificent gold Dome of the Rock where Jews believe God ordered Abraham to sacrifice his son, Isaac. Muslims believe it was Abraham's son Ishmael that God ordered sacrificed. Muslims also believe that Mohammed touched down on this rock during his night journey on horseback up to heaven and back.

On that and many subsequent visits, Carol and I enjoyed walking with Jonah through the Old City. We often ate outdoors at a small pizza shop where ruts from the wheels of Roman chariots were still visible in the narrow cobblestone road. On several Fridays, from our perch at the pizza shop, we watched Christian pilgrims visiting a station on the Via Dolorosa, Jews going to pray at the Western Wall, and Muslims walking to midday *Jum'ah* prayers at Al Aksa Mosque. While walking in very close proximity, sadly, they hardly seemed to notice one another.

Carol and I were worried that our first visit to Israel coincided with their invasion of Lebanon. We feared that Israeli opposition to the war, combined with our own anti-war bias, might lead us to develop simplistic, negative feelings that would compromise our Quaker mission to be good listeners to people on all sides. We were very grateful to meet Israelis who, whatever their opinions about the war, were able to help us appreciate a wide range of Israeli views, as well as the experiences and reasoning that motivated them. I think that our learning about Israel directly from Israelis, rather than from American Jews who often tend instinctively to be more defensive, helped Carol and me to develop a deep, complex understanding and love for Israel and its people.

At the start of the war in Lebanon, most Israelis believed that the invasion, codenamed "Peace for Galilee," was justified because of the ongoing threat of cross-border

PLO attacks. Despite the treaty with Egypt and Israel's demonstrated military supe-riority, Israelis understandably still felt insecure and fearful about Arab, particularly Palestinian Arab and PLO intentions. When I first read it during our orientation and ever since, I've appreciated the following passage in Fouad Ajami's book, *The Arab Predicament*, a passage which seemed to apply to both Israeli and Arab/Palestinian societies. Its wisdom provided an important guiding principle for our work listening to people on both sides. Ajami wrote:

> It is easy to judge but hard to understand the ghosts with which people and societies battle, the wounds and memories that drive them to do what they do. Even if we disagree with people's choice of allegiance, we must understand the reasons for their choice, the odds they fight against, the range of alternatives open to them.[3]

One of our most moving and memorable experiences on this first visit to Israel was the morning we spent visiting Yad Vashem, the memorial to victims of the Ho-locaust. Photos, documents and a narrative traced the development of Nazi ideology and their sophisticated and efficient plan to eradicate the Jewish people.

Beginning in 1987 whenever I led interfaith delegations to Yad Vashem, we al-ways concluded by walking meditatively through the darkened hall lit only by what seemed like a million tiny candles accompanied by small photos and names being recited, commemorating more than 1,500,000 Jewish children who were murdered in the Holocaust.

During many visits to Israel, Carol and I met Jews who had lost their entire fami-lies in the Holocaust. We also met Jews who had survived horrendous experiences before escaping or who had been rescued at the end of the war. We were struck by the pervasiveness of the personal and learned memories of the Holocaust, but equally by the realization that it was not possible to predict people's views about the conflict with the Arabs simply based on their past experiences. Some Holocaust survivors believed bitterly that Arabs, like Nazis, were implacable enemies of the Jewish people and Israel would have to continue to fight them to survive, while others believed peace was pos-sible and they were doing what they could to help achieve it.

After Yad Vashem, we went to the Hebrew University campus on Mt. Scopus to meet with Yaron Ezrachi, a brilliant and highly respected Israeli political scientist. Yaron's family, with both Eastern European (Ashkenazi) and Middle Eastern (Sep-hardic) roots, came to Palestine in the nineteenth century. He patiently described to us what being a Jew and a Zionist (Jewish nationalist) meant to him. For Yaron, despite all the history of suffering, the story of the Jewish people fundamentally was about hope for the future. In contrast, he explained that many Israeli Jews, includ-ing Prime Minister Menachem Begin, who led the extreme Irgun faction during the 1948 war, are driven by wounds and memories of long persecution culminating in the

3. Ajami, *The Arab Predicament*, 198.

extermination camps a mere forty years earlier. Yaron told us, "For them, the accumulation and weight of so much suffering defined what it meant to be a Jew. For Begin, to be a Jew means to fight and die." Yaron believed that both his view and Begin's had deep roots in Jewish history and experience, but that his perspective was more realistic and helpful in moving Israel toward a peaceful and normal future. Yaron Ezrahi's 1997 book, *Rubber Bullets: Power and Conscience in Modern Israel*,[4] addressed the complex and contradictory themes that he described to us during our first visit. Knowing him contributed a lot to our understanding and love of Israel. Later, when I brought interfaith delegations to the region, I frequently arranged for them to meet Yaron.

Although a majority supported the invasion of Lebanon, by the time of our second visit in July 1982, large numbers of Israelis were holding weekly anti-war demonstrations, including one outside the Knesset where hundreds of IDF reservists solicited signatures on petitions opposing the war. At one rally of 50,000 Israelis in Tel Aviv, Carol and I met a young woman who reminded me of American soldiers' wives whom I had met at anti-Vietnam War demonstrations. This Israeli wife and mother explained to us that she was there to protest the war with her son, who was one year old, just like our Jonah, precisely because her husband was serving in Lebanon. He also was opposed to the invasion. It was dramatic news in Israel that summer that for the first time, some Israeli soldiers refused orders to fight in Lebanon and formed an organization called *Yesh Gevul*, which means, "There is a limit."

During our time in the West Bank and Gaza that summer Carol and I met several Palestinians from whom we learned a lot about their story and situation, and for whom we developed deep respect and admiration. One of these was Professor Sari Nusseibeh, who would play a key leadership role during the first Palestinian intifada in 1987 and 1988, and later become president of Al Quds University in Jerusalem. We visited him and his wife, Lucy Austin Nusseibeh, at their home in Jericho. As we sat outside on a very warm, sunny afternoon, Sari and Lucy inquired about my earlier experiences with nonviolence in the civil rights movement. While not pacifists, they both believed that nonviolent strategies and tactics offered more effective strategies to resist the Israeli occupation. Unfortunately, Palestinian nonviolent resistance was often overshadowed by acts of violence against Israelis or crushed by harsh Israeli responses to any real resistance to the occupation.

Sari is the son of Anwar Nusseibeh, a Palestinian widely respected for his integrity, despite straddling conflicting realities as a Palestinian nationalist who served important posts in the government of Jordan. After the 1967 war, Sari's father was one of the first prominent Palestinians to publicly support a two-state resolution of the conflict with Israel. Sari has written about his personal experience as a nineteen-year-old confronting conflicting Palestinian and Israeli realities shortly after the end of the 1967 war. The Nusseibeh family home was located very near the Mandelbaum

4. Ezrahi, *Rubber Bullets.*

Gate, on the Green Line dividing West (Jewish) Jerusalem from East (Arab) Jerusalem. Sari told us, how before the war, he used to stare across the border into the Jewish neighborhood in West Jerusalem. When the war ended he decided to walk there. As he crossed the open space, he looked in front of him toward the Jewish neighborhood and back toward his home. Ever since then, as a Palestinian nationalist committed to making peace with Israel, Sari has felt he lives straddling the boundary reflecting on both Palestinian Arab and Jewish Israeli realities and aspirations.

In 1998, Lucy Austin Nusseibeh became Director of the Middle East Nonviolence and Democracy Project. In 2002, Sari joined with Ami Ayalon, the former head of Shin Bet, Israel's domestic security service (like our FBI) to launch the People's Voice peace campaign, based on principles for a two-state peace agreement the two men co-authored. As president of Al Quds University in Jerusalem in 2003, Sari organized a round-the-clock soccer game and nonviolent public gathering to block the Israeli government from building its security wall through the Al Quds campus. Sari Nusseibeh's 2007 memoir, *Once Upon A Country: A Palestinian Life*[5] is an honest, sad, wise and inspiring testimony to his love for his people and his commitment to justice and peace. His 2011 book, *What Is a Palestinian State Worth?* raises profound questions about the failure to achieve a two-state solution and explores possible alternative nonviolent options for the future.[6] Over the years, I observed that Sari was often sidelined (or he sidelined himself) from day-to-day politics in order to remain true to his convictions. His isolation was both a testimony to his integrity and a sad commentary on Palestinian and, specifically PLO politics.

On that first visit to the West Bank we also met Saeb Erekat, vice president of An Najah National University in Nablus. In 1980 and 1981, Saeb had quietly arranged unpublicized meetings between Palestinian students from An Najah and Israeli students from Tel Aviv University. The Israeli military threatened him with arrest if he continued. On our second visit, Saeb told us about a disturbing dream he had. In his dream, the two-state option had failed, and he was organizing protests demanding equal rights for Palestinians within Israel. He said that he woke up sweating and trembling. He told us, "If the two-state solution is not achieved soon, Palestinians would go back to demanding equal rights in a single state." He knew that Israel would not accept a one-state solution with equal rights, since that would mean Jews would once again find themselves in a vulnerable minority status. So, he believed if there is not a two-state solution, the conflict would go on much longer and many more people would be killed. Saeb had this disturbing prophetic dream in 1982.

A decade later, Saeb became a prominent negotiator and spokesperson for the Palestinian Authority. Following several missed opportunities for peace since Saeb had his dream, many peace-oriented Palestinians and Israelis were warning that, as a result of demographic developments, continued Jewish settlement expansion, the

---

5. Nusseibeh, *Once Upon A Country.*

6. Nusseibeh, *What Is A Palestinian State Worth?*

route of the Israeli security wall cutting through Palestinian territory, and the increasing strength of radical religious factions on both sides, time was running out for a two-state resolution. On July 30, 2013 Saeb Erekat, representing the Palestinian Authority, stood with Tzipi Livni, the lead Israeli negotiator, on either side of Secretary John Kerry as Kerry announced the goal of achieving a two-state final status agreement in a period of nine months.

On most of our trips across the river, Carol and I also travelled down to Gaza to visit Mary and Mohammed Khass, refugees from Haifa. Mary was a Christian Palestinian who worked for the AFSC as an educator and community organizer with women in the refugee camps. In her fifties, Mary was attractive, full of energy and a very strong, feisty woman, whether she was confronting Israeli military officials or local conservative Islamic Palestinian leaders. Mary's husband Mohammed was a Muslim, an independent journalist, and a former member of the Arab Communist Party. In 1948, he and most other Arab communists followed the Soviet Union's lead in recognizing the State of Israel. Since that was against the policies of all Arab governments at the time, he was arrested and briefly imprisoned by Egypt. Beginning in the 1970s, Mary and Mohammed occasionally arranged to meet with Israelis in private homes to engage in conversations about the occupation, Palestinian aspirations, and possibilities for a two-state resolution. During our visits in Gaza, Mary often took care of Jonah while Carol and I went together on our appointments. In the midst of Gaza's terrible poverty and Israel's military occupation, Mary and Mohammed Khass were irrepressible beacons of positive determination and hope.

Everywhere we traveled, we had to arrange for someone to take care of Jonah during our appointments. In Jerusalem, we came to rely on the Kuttab family—especially their teenage daughter Grace and their youngest son, Danny—who lived near where we usually stayed at the Palestinian YWCA in Sheik Jarrah. We learned a lot over the years from the Kuttabs' second son, Jonathan, who was a lawyer with Al Haq, a Palestinian human rights group, and from his brother Daoud, an independent journalist who sometimes got in trouble with the PLO for his critical reporting on Palestinian corruption. Daoud worked with Israeli and Palestinian artists to create an Israeli-Palestinian version of Sesame Street.

In the summer of 1982, responding to the Israeli invasion and occupation of Lebanon, not surprisingly conflict intensified with Palestinians in Gaza and the West Bank. Student demonstrations broke out on campuses, the largest of which was at Bir Zeit University, north of Ramallah. In response, the Israeli military ordered Bir Zeit closed for the third time that year. On one of my visits to Bir Zeit, I met Marwan Barghouti, a popular, politically savvy and charismatic young Palestinian leader, who was elected to head the Bir Zeit Student Council. It was clear to me, even after meeting with him only that one time, that Marwan would become an important leader in the Palestinian nationalist movement.

Marwan Barghouti was a co-founder of the Fateh Youth movement and played an active leadership role in the first intifada in 1987–88. A consistent critic of Palestinian Authority corruption, Marwan was often in conflict with Arafat. While he supported violent resistance to Israeli occupation, he also believed in negotiations with Israel for a two-state solution based on the 1967 borders. After initially supporting the 1993 Oslo Declaration, he became disillusioned with the Oslo negotiating process and increasingly turned toward militant action. In 2002, during the second Palestinian intifada, Israel arrested Barghouti and charged him with responsibility for murdering five Israelis, even though no evidence was presented that directly connected him to the murders. Asserting that the trial was illegitimate, Barghouti refused to offer a defense. He was sentenced to five life terms in prison where he continued his political leadership. In 2006 he played the central role in forging the "prisoners' document,"[7] which outlined ideas for resisting Israeli occupation and negotiating a two-state peace agreement. It was endorsed by prisoners from across the Palestinian political spectrum, including leaders from both Fateh and Hamas. In November-December 2009, related to Israel's negotiations for the release of Gilad Shalit, the young Israeli soldier held prisoner by Hamas for four years, several prominent Israeli peace advocates and a *Haaretz* editorial compared Marwan Barghouti's potential role to South Africa's Nelson Mandela and called for his release from prison. The idea of freeing Barghouti was raised again publicly in 2014. Opinion polls have indicated that if he were a candidate, Marwan Barghouti would easily win the Palestinian presidency, over both Mahmoud Abbas of Fateh and Ismail Haniyeh of Hamas.

While Palestinians debated how best to resist the Israeli occupation, there also were debates among Israelis about how best to contain Palestinian resistance. In 1976, the Israel Labor government allowed municipal elections to be held in the West Bank and Gaza, thinking they might produce a more malleable alternative leadership to the PLO. It turned out that all the elected mayors supported the PLO. After Likud came to power in 1977, Likud governments tried controlling the territories by deposing and expelling some of the Palestinian mayors who had been elected in 1976. By the summer of 1982, having already deposed elected mayors of Hebron, Halhoul, Ramallah, El Bireh and Jericho, the Likud government removed the mayors of Nablus, Jenin and Gaza City. Ironically, during this same period, in its desperate efforts to build up an alternative to the PLO, Israeli governments initially allowed funds to come into Gaza from outside to support development of the religiously-based Hamas movement.

Early in our assignment, we got to know two of the deposed Palestinian mayors personally: Mohammed Milhem, mayor of Halhoul, and Fahd Qawasmeh, mayor of Hebron. Both had been forcibly removed from their elected offices and exiled by Israel in 1981. They lived not far from us in Amman. While they both supported the PLO, they also were known for their advocacy of strikes and other nonviolent tactics to resist occupation and for their quiet support for a negotiated two-state solution. I

---

7. *National Conciliation Document of the Prisoners.*

often said to Israelis that it seemed very shortsighted to have exiled two of their best enemies. The conflict would likely have developed differently and might even have been resolved in the 1980s if Israel had offered to negotiate with the popularly elected Palestinian mayors rather than removing almost all of them from office.

Probably the most important Israeli we met on our first visit related to our work was Naomi Chazan, professor of African Studies at Hebrew University and a leader in Peace Now, the mainstream Israeli peace movement. As a political scientist, Naomi had a unique ability to put aside her own leftist politics to offer an analysis of the current situation that was objective, thorough and incredibly succinct. Like Rami Khouri in Jordan, Naomi regularly provided us with a clear, coherent picture of the current political context in Israel and often suggested additional issues for us to focus on and other Israelis for us to meet.

In 1992, Naomi was elected a member of the Knesset from the peace-oriented Meretz Party and served for a time as deputy speaker of the Knesset. In 2009 she became president of the New Israel Fund (NIF), a mainstream organization committed to democracy and equality for all Israeli citizens, Jewish and Arab. In 2010 and 2011, as anti-Arab racism played a more explicit, public role in Israeli politics, Naomi and the New Israel Fund were targets of vicious rightwing political attacks.

During our first visit to Israel, Naomi suggested that we visit Kiryat Shemona, a major Israeli development town in the Northern Galilee near the border, to get a better understanding of why many Israelis supported the invasion of Lebanon. Most Kiryat Shemona residents had come to Israel in the 1950s as refugees from Morocco. Like other Jews from Arab countries, they generally supported Prime Minister Begin and his conservative Likud coalition, in part because they felt they had been treated as second class citizens by the Israeli Labor Party from 1948 to 1977. The invasion of Lebanon was named "Peace for Galilee" to indicate that its goal was to achieve security for Kiryat Shemona and other northern Israeli towns. We visited a community center that had been hit by PLO rockets fired from Lebanon and rebuilt with contributions from American Jews. We walked past entrances to dozens of bomb shelters scattered throughout the community. Understandably, residents of Israel's northern cities and towns feared more PLO rocket attacks and hoped the IDF invasion would put an end to them.

The complex diversity of Israeli views was dramatized for us one evening at a beautiful kibbutz hotel in the Galilee, south of Kiryat Shemona. After dinner in the parking lot a group of conservative American Christian evangelicals serenaded appreciative Israeli kibbutz members in Hebrew. While the "End Times" theology of this group would not have been comforting to any Jews, the group's enthusiastic and material support for Israel's war in Lebanon was very much welcomed and appreciated. Meanwhile, inside the hotel, an Israeli guide energetically appealed to an American Jewish group that had just toured the border area, pleading for funds to help Israel pay for the war. In yet another room, an Israeli Jewish Socialist who fled Germany during

WWII, showed slides and lectured on the history of the kibbutz movement. He openly criticized the war in Lebanon, supported a two-state solution with the Palestinians, and expressed his conviction that the Likud government was a disaster for Israel. Each of these vignettes represented an authentic face of Israel, and, as we learned, there were many more.

Just as our visit to Kiryat Shemona helped us understand Israeli fears of cross-border attacks, our visit to Kiryat Arba, a large, rightwing Jewish settlement in the southern West Bank, near Hebron, helped us understand some Israelis' radical nationalist/religious commitment to the idea of "Greater Israel," with borders extending from the Mediterranean to the Jordan River. Kiryat Arba was founded by Rabbi Moshe Levinger and other religious nationalists in 1968, shortly after Israel captured the West Bank from Jordan. Levinger was a leader in the ultranationalist movement that sought to plant Jewish settlements throughout the captured territory. From residents of Kiryat Arba we heard hard line views that all of the West Bank, which they referred to as Judea and Samaria, belonged to Israel, and that Palestinians would either have to accept this reality or leave. There were frequent confrontations between Jewish settlers from Kiryat Arba and nearby Palestinian residents. We also observed Israeli soldiers patrolling around Hebron, to protect the Jewish settlers. While overlooking violence by Jewish settlers against Palestinians, the Israeli forces responded harshly to any acts of Palestinian resistance.

On a 1996 visit to Hebron to observe Palestinian elections, I stepped in the way of two teenage Jewish girls from Kiryat Arba who cursed and then spit at a Palestinian woman journalist with whom I was walking. This is one of many examples of the power relationship in the occupied territories, with its explicit racist dimension, between extremist Jewish settlers, the Israeli army, and Palestinians. As bad as the occupation is, it is important to remember how the occupation happened. Some pro-Palestinian Americans focused entirely on ending the occupation tend to ignore the historical context. Israel did not plan to occupy the West Bank and Gaza; the occupation was a consequence of Israel winning the 1967 war against the surrounding Arab states of Egypt, Jordan and Syria, all at that time publicly committed to destroying Israel. That's a very different story from the white South African government intentionally establishing the Apartheid regime. In contrast to efforts pressuring Israel to act unilaterally, the way to end the occupation is spelled out in UN Security Council Resolution 242 with its twin interdependent principles. It is true and many Israeli peace advocates acknowledge that some specific conditions Palestinians face under Israeli occupation resemble apartheid conditions. Beyond that, a number of prominent Israelis have acknowledged that if Israel holds on to the West Bank territory and doesn't grant Palestinians equal rights, this outcome would represent a situation more fully analogous to an apartheid state.

In part, the rationale for Jewish settlement in the Hebron area is based on the fact that there was a very long history of Jews living there and on the experience of an

Arab Palestinian riot in 1929 during which sixty-seven Jews were killed. Learning a different version of this piece of history from Avraham (Avrum) Burg showed me yet another face of Israel. Berg was the most moving and memorable speaker at a 1982 conference in Tel Aviv sponsored by *New Outlook*, a magazine devoted to the goal of Arab-Israeli peace. In his speech, he cited a centuries-old rabbinic teaching that "the highest and most noble patriot is one who turns his enemy into a friend." Burg's father, Joseph, had been a conservative mainstream leader of the National Religious Party and his mother had survived the 1929 riots in Hebron, so I was surprised by Avrum's strong dovish views. When I met him privately in Jerusalem a few days later, I asked him to help me understand how he came to hold such views. He explained that, in fact, his mother and her family all had been hidden and saved by a Palestinian Muslim family during the 1929 riot. I later learned that as many as 400 Jews may have been hidden and saved by Palestinians. So, while many Jews cited the Hebron riot as evidence of deep and unalterable Arab hostility to Jews, Avrum's mother's experience provided a basis for a different view.

In 1986 Avrum Burg was elected as a Labor Party member of the Knesset. He served as head of the Jewish Agency and as speaker of the Knesset from 1999 to 2003. He believed deeply in the positive values of Jewish nationalism and that a just peace with the Palestinians was essential for Israel's future. Deeply discouraged and frustrated by developments in Israel, especially by the government's relations with the Palestinians, he withdrew from formal politics in 2004. In 2008, he wrote a passionate, prophetic, and very controversial book titled, *The Holocaust Is Over: We Must Rise from Its Ashes*.[8] In a testimony on the cover, Howard M. Sachar, the highly respected author of *A History of Israel*, described Burg's book as "a compelling and eloquent *cri de coeur* from a veteran of Israel's wars and politics." As chairman of the Israeli Center for Renewal of Democracy, Burg still believes "two neighboring states for two peoples that respect one another would be the best solution," but he also believes, "if our shortsighted leaders miss this opportunity, the same fair and equal principles should be applied to one state for two peoples."[9] Like Sari Nusseibeh on the Palestinian side, Avrum Burg's principled, realistic positions and his increasing political isolation are a reflection of his integrity and also a sad commentary on Israeli politics.

Reflecting on our initial experiences in Israel and the Palestinian territories, Carol and I were struck by two basic realities. On the one hand, Israeli military occupation combined with continuous expansion of Jewish settlements objectively represented *de facto* Israeli annexation of the territories and there seemed to be little the Palestinians could do to stop it. On the other hand, despite Israel's power, the steadfastness of Palestinian resistance to occupation and their determination to create an independent state showed signs of becoming stronger. We were surprised that even on the Israeli side of the 1948 armistice line, we found pervasive, persistent tension

8. Burg, *The Holocaust Is Over.*
9. Burg, "Israel's Fading Democracy."

between invincible Israeli power and immovable Palestinian resistance. One day on a driving tour around West Jerusalem, as we were passing through the lovely German Colony neighborhood of old Arab homes that were taken over by Israel in 1948, we asked our English-speaking Palestinian driver who lived near Bethlehem, "Isn't all of this a *fait accompli?*" He responded sharply, "*La! La!* (No, no), I have not accepted this. . . .The Israelis must accept our Palestinian right of self-determination, our right to an independent state, and either permit refugees to return or provide compensation to them." He answered firmly, "If the Israelis are willing to do this, then I am willing to accept Israel, but not until then."

We soon recognized that for Israelis and Palestinians to have confidence that negotiations would lead to peace, first there would have to be a halt or at least a dramatic reduction in threats of Palestinian violence against Israelis, accompanied by Israel halting expansion of settlements and easing the conditions of occupation faced daily by Palestinians. We came to understand that weighing Israeli experience and Palestinian experience against each other or deciding whose suffering was worse or whose fears more justified was simply not useful. Clearly, for progress toward peace, the suffering and fears of people on both sides would need to be addressed and reduced.

We also came to appreciate how UN Security Council resolution 242 fundamentally and fairly outlined the requirements for peace. Adopted unanimously in the aftermath of the June 1967 war, it calls for Israeli withdrawal from occupied territories and recognition and security for all states in the region, obviously including Israel. Resolution 242, and resolution 338 which was adopted after the 1973 war, have consistently been the accepted international legal basis for all Arab-Israeli and Israeli-Palestinian peace negotiations. Palestinians and their supporters tend to focus on the first principle, i.e., ending the occupation; Israelis and their supporters tend to focus on the second, i.e., achieving recognition and security for Israel. Early in our Quaker assignment, we became convinced that the two goals were inextricably linked and that it would be impossible to implement one without simultaneously implementing the other.

It was encouraging to us that we met people, including political leaders on both sides, who were interested in learning more about the other side and possibly even meeting face-to-face with them. Their numbers were small, and there were all kinds of popular, political, and legal constraints that made direct contacts very difficult, even dangerous, but people's interest and determination to meet one another was growing. In this context, our moving back and forth, crossing boundaries, meeting and listening to Palestinians and Israelis seemed more important, relevant, and timely than we could possibly have anticipated when we took the assignment.

We also came to appreciate that there was an advantage to our doing this work on behalf of Quakers, who had a very positive reputation. In these early visits, we met Palestinians who gratefully recalled that Quakers were among the first to arrive with tents in Gaza to house refugees from the 1948 Arab-Israeli War. Several Israeli

Jews we met, including several who had quite hawkish views on the conflict, warmly remembered Quakers for their aid to Jewish refugees in Europe during World Wars I and II. Their positive personal experiences and/or memories of Quakers contributed to their being willing to meet with us and share their stories, even though recounting their stores often meant remembering and recounting suffering

Visit to Beirut, September 1982 – Sabra and Shatila

In early September 1982, Gail Pressberg came to visit us in Amman. On September 9, I celebrated my fortieth birthday and much to my surprise, Palestinian mayors Mohammed Milhem and Fahd Qawasmeh came to our small apartment to help celebrate. After a few days in Jordan, Gail planned for me to travel with her to Damascus, Syria and then make the eighty mile trip by car to Beirut. In Lebanon, we planned to visit with other American Quaker service staff working on humanitarian and development assistance projects.

By late August, Israeli military forces occupied large areas of Lebanon, but they had not entered Beirut. Through a combination of American and Saudi mediation, Chairman Arafat had agreed that the PLO would withdraw its military forces from Lebanon and take most of them to Yemen. In exchange, Prime Minister Begin assured the United States that Israeli forces would relax the siege around Beirut and that Palestinian civilians remaining in refugee camps would be safe. The US passed this message to the PLO and sent American Marines to oversee the PLO's withdrawal. On August 23, Bashir Gemayel, leader of the anti-Syrian, anti-Palestinian Phalange Party became president of Lebanon. With Israeli and American support, it was hoped that Gemayel would be able to restore some stability and order. This was the context as we left for my first visit to Beirut.

After an overnight in Damascus, we were to travel by car to Beirut, but during the night, the Israeli air force bombed the main highway, so we had to cross the mountains further north, allowing us to see a few of the remaining magnificent Cedars of Lebanon. Arriving at our Beirut hotel in early evening, we learned that President Bashir Gemayel had been assassinated, possibly by Syrian agents. Everyone expected that Israeli forces would now attack and occupy the city. From our refuge in the hotel basement, throughout the night we heard Israeli planes flying overhead and the screaming sounds of falling bombs. The next day, the Israeli army entered Beirut and set up several military checkpoints.

Over the next few days Gail and I moved around the city discretely meeting with Quaker staff and others, trying as much as possible to avoid Israeli military checkpoints and patrols. Gail was nervous. Being Jewish and having many Israeli friends and acquaintances, she feared we might run into an Israeli soldier who would recognize her and greet her. Such an encounter with a soldier in the occupying army obviously would not have gone over well with our Lebanese hosts.

On the night of September 16, as we were having dinner with several NGO representatives at a Chinese restaurant in West Beirut, Janet Lee Stevens, a young, independent American journalist, burst into the dining room claiming hysterically that a massacre was occurring in the Sabra and Shatila Palestinian refugee camps. After she left the room, several people assured us that she was probably exaggerating. Later, we learned that she was not. Israeli forces had allowed Lebanese Christian militia who hated the Palestinians to enter the two refugee camps where they slaughtered several hundred Palestinians. The next day, on a trip south to Sidon and Tyre to visit Quaker projects, we stopped at one of the camps. Many of the bodies still lay where they had been killed. I remember walking through the camp taking photographs, including one of a family of nine people representing three generations—grandparents, parents and children—all gathered around a low table with food still on it, as if they might still be eating, but all of them were dead. Although I spoke about Sabra and Shatila in public lectures, I could never show the photographs to anyone. Less than a year later, on April 18, 1983, Janet Lee Stevens was killed along with sixty-two other people in a suicide bombing attack on the American embassy in Beirut.

After our visit to the refugee camps and two development projects, our colleagues insisted on driving Gail and me to see the only newly paved road in southern Lebanon. It was built by the Israeli army to thank right wing American Christian evangelicals for supporting Israel's invasion. The narrow strip of brand new black macadam led up a hill to a small concrete building housing a radio transmitter that broadcast "Good News about Jesus Christ" to the devastated, largely Shiite Muslim population of Southern Lebanon. Residents of the area might be forgiven for being a bit confused about the meaning of this good news.

In Israel, public response to Sabra and Shatila was immediate and extraordinary. Since the start of the invasion, the numbers of Israelis participating in weekly anti-war demonstrations had been steadily increasing. News that Israeli military forces had facilitated the massacres touched a central Jewish nerve. Ten days after the massacres occurred, more than 400,000 Israelis (approximately 10 percent of the population) participated in a protest rally in Tel Aviv, calling for the resignation of Defense Minister Sharon and other responsible senior officials. Awed by the size of the Israeli demonstration, I couldn't help thinking about the My Lai massacre in Vietnam and what a difference it might have made if the anti-war movement had been able to mobilize 10 percent of the American population in simultaneous mass demonstrations. In response to this huge public outcry, the Israeli government established the independent Kahan Commission to investigate Israeli responsibility. Five months later, the commission concluded that both Defense Minister Ariel Sharon and IDF Chief of Staff Lt. General Rafael Eitan were indirectly responsible and that both should resign. At first, Sharon refused; however, after a right-wing Israeli threw a hand grenade at a Peace Now demonstration in Jerusalem, killing Emil Gruenzweig, a graduate student, and wounding Avrum Burg, Sharon stepped down.

Sabra and Shatila seared the consciousness of Palestinians as well. Understandably, they focused mainly on Israel's responsibility rather than the fact that Lebanese Christian militia did the actual killing. Photos of the massacres circulated widely among Palestinians.

Years later, speaking with Palestinians who were children or teenagers when the events occurred, I learned that photographs from the camps radically disabused many of them of the idea that older Palestinian leaders would (or could) somehow protect and take care of them. Sabra and Shatila pushed many young Palestinians to become activists. I have no doubt that the images and memories contributed to the eruption of the first Palestinian intifada in December 1987.

A few weeks after I returned to Amman, in early October 1982, Carol and I had our first meeting with Yasser Arafat, Chairman of the PLO. We were joined by Everett Mendelsohn, a professor of the history of science at Harvard University, who had been involved with Quakers and Middle East issues for many years, and was visiting us in Amman. Arafat had come to Jordan for meetings with King Hussein and was staying at the King's guest house. As he was running late, and packing to fly out of Amman, Arafat invited us upstairs into his apartment. Thanking the Chairman for seeing us, we expressed sympathy for the Palestinians killed in Lebanon. Arafat was very emotional, explaining to us that as an essential condition for his agreement to take PLO fighters out of Lebanon, America had provided assurances for the safety of those remaining behind in the camps, based on Israeli assurances to the United States. Becoming even more agitated, Arafat told us that the American guarantees were essential for him to be able to convince his younger military commanders to leave their families behind. Many Lebanese, including the president and prime minister, had urged Reagan to leave the American Marine force in Beirut until the situation was more stable, but he withdrew the Marines as soon the PLO military left Beirut. Near the end of our meeting, Chairman Arafat angrily characterized what had happened as an American betrayal. At one point, he declared, "The US military has lost its honor." We understood Arafat's sense of betrayal and felt we had nothing to say in response.

Visit to Cairo, October 1982

In October 1982 Carol, Jonah, and I crossed again into the West Bank and Israel, spent a night in Jerusalem, and then boarded an early morning bus in Tel Aviv for the twelve hour trip across the Sinai desert to Cairo. At that time, public travel between Israel and Egypt—a product of the Camp David treaty—was relatively new and rare. As our bus crossed the Sinai, we were startled by what looked like a giant birthday cake floating through the desert. In fact, it was the lighted top of a freighter moving slowly northward through the Suez Canal.

As we arrived in the outskirts of Cairo we began to see large factories and big office buildings, some old and drab, and others newer. It was the evening rush hour.

People were everywhere, some riding atop crowded trains, some packed tightly in buses, cars and taxis, and others making their way on foot while traffic barely moved in the clogged streets. Sometimes, walking was the only way to get where you needed to go.

On our first day in Cairo, we took a taxi to visit the Pyramids and Sphinx at Giza. They totally surpassed photos we had seen or anything we had imagined. Beginning in 1985, whenever I led interfaith trips to the region, in addition to an exhausting schedule of appointments related to the conflict, I always arranged for participants to experience some of the magnificent sites in each country, including the pyramids in Egypt, Petra and Jerash in Jordan, the Omayyad Mosque in Syria, and, of course, the Old City of Jerusalem.

On our second day in Cairo, we left Jonah with the housekeeper at the Ford Foundation Guest House where we were staying, and took a taxi for our appointment with the Political Affairs Editor of *Al Ahram*, Cairo's biggest daily newspaper. As the taxi made its way along busy Cairo streets, Carol leaned close to me and whispered, "I'm sure this is the same way we went yesterday to the Pyramids." I repeated our destination, *Al Ahram*, to the driver, who smiled and said, "*Aywah* (Yes), *Al Ahram*," and continued in the same direction. After another ten minutes, it seemed clear we were headed to the Pyramids, so, nervously utilizing the few Arabic words I knew, I said "*Jaride* (newspaper) *Al Ahram*." The driver seemed to understand. He pulled the taxi off to the right side of the busy boulevard and, risking life and limb, darted through the traffic across the street to a kiosk. He returned smiling, and handed us a folded copy of that morning's *Al Ahram* newspaper. By now, we were already late for our appointment. I said to the taxi driver with even more urgency, "*Maktab* (office), *Jaride Al Ahram*." Finally grasping the problem, he executed a daring U-turn and headed back into the city center. "*Al Ahram*" is the name of the big daily newspaper, but it also means "The Pyramids." When we finally showed up for our appointment almost an hour late, the editor initially seemed annoyed, but hearing our story, he graciously laughed with (or perhaps at) us. In Jordan many people spoke English; in Egypt, our inability to speak Arabic was definitely a handicap.

Experiencing the size of Cairo, its enormous population, along with the obvious challenges of massive poverty and modernization helped us to understand why Egypt couldn't afford more wars and why it was willing to defy popular Arab sentiment to make peace with Israel. On that first visit to Cairo, we asked Boutros Boutros Ghali, then Egypt's foreign minister and later UN secretary general, about the challenges facing Egypt because of other Arab states' hostility to the peace treaty. Ghali responded confidently and proudly, reflecting Egypt's importance in the Arab world. He told us, "Egypt will not run to be with the other Arab states. You will see, all the Arabs will come to follow Egypt." In fact, a month earlier all the Arab states had officially expressed willingness to negotiate peace with Israel in the Fez Declaration based on UN Security Council resolutions 242 and 338.

In the aftermath of the assassination of President Anwar Sadat in October 1981, many Israelis feared that the new Egyptian president, Hosni Mubarak, might abrogate the peace treaty. Three specific Israeli actions generated intense Egyptian and broader popular Arab anger: Israel's bombing of Iraq's nuclear reactor near Baghdad, its annexation of the Golan Heights captured from Syria, and the invasion of Lebanon. It seemed clear to us from meeting with Boutros Ghali and many others in Cairo that Egypt's aversion to another war and its commitment to peace with Israel were solidly based on perceived strategic national interests. Despite popular Egyptian outrage at Israeli policies, we expected that Egypt would maintain its agreement with Israel, although it would be a much colder peace than many initially hoped. Even after the January 2011 Egyptian uprising that toppled Hosni Mubarak, the massive popular opposition demonstrations, the military's ouster of President Morsi in 2013, and the election of the head of Egypt's military as president in 2014, Egypt's treaty with Israel continued to hold.

On this first visit we were especially grateful to meet Saad Eddin Ibrihim, a professor of sociology at American University in Cairo, and highly respected sociologist, independent political analyst and leading advocate for human rights. He was one of the founders of the Arab Organization for Human Rights. Like Rami Khouri in Jordan and Noami Chazan in Israel, Saad helped us by orientating us to the current political context in Egypt and suggesting additional Egyptians for us to meet. In 2000, Saad's principled advocacy for human rights and his criticism of the government led to his arrest, conviction and imprisonment by Mubarak's regime. Following an international campaign, he was cleared of all charges by Egypt's highest civilian court in 2003. Persisting in his human rights advocacy, in 2008 Saad was convicted *in absentia* of "defaming Egypt." Except for a brief trip to Cairo in 2010 to visit family, he remained outside the country. During the 2011 massive popular uprising against Mubarak, Saad was a visiting professor at Drew University in New Jersey and was interviewed several times on CNN.

Reagan Initiative for Peace: Focus on Jordan and the PLO

While the focus of Middle East peacemaking had been on Egypt and Israel, in the wake of the 1982 invasion of Lebanon the focus shifted to possible peace efforts involving Jordan, the Palestinians, and Israel. The Reagan Initiative for Peace announced on September 1 and the Arab Fez Declaration on September 9 raised hopes that negotiations between Israel and the Palestinians might get started. The Fez Declaration, initiated by Saudi Arabia's King Fahd and adopted unanimously by the Arab states at their summit in Morocco, did not include an explicit reference to recognition of Israel. However, consistent with the language of UN Security Council resolutions 242 and 338, it called for recognition and security for all states in the region in exchange for withdrawal of Israeli forces from territories occupied in 1967. A senior advisor at the palace in Amman, quoted King Hussein as saying that Fez "certainly amounts to Arab willingness to recognize pre-1967 Israel."

We met many peace-oriented Israelis, including important senior Labor Party leaders, who believed that Israel should respond positively to the Fez Declaration. Prime Minister Begin's official response was negative and President Reagan's response was, at best, indifferent. Two decades later in 2002, this same sad pattern of rejection by a Likud government and seeming indifference by the American government was repeated in response to the much more explicit Arab Peace Initiative. Peace advocates on all sides viewed these responses critically as missed opportunities. In April 2011, former senior Israeli government, intelligence and military leaders announced an Israeli Peace Initiative as an appropriately positive, even if unofficial response to the Arab Peace Initiative.

In late 1982, Jordanian and Palestinian leaders were frustrated and angry over ambiguous US policy in response to Israel's invasion of Lebanon and the massacres at Sabra and Shatila. Nevertheless, both King Hussein and Chairman Arafat viewed the combination of the Reagan Initiative and the Arab Fez Declaration as providing a possible basis for progress. On September 1, Reagan said, "The time has come for a new realism on the part of all the peoples of the Middle East." As we interviewed Jordanians and Palestinians, we found many of them encouraged by Reagan's initiative, including its more explicit attention to the needs and rights of Palestinians, as in this statement by the President: "The question now is how to reconcile Israel's legitimate security needs with the legitimate rights of the Palestinians." Reagan also declared a freeze on Israeli settlements as an essential step to create the confidence needed to get negotiations going.

Most Palestinians were critical that President Reagan spoke only about "autonomy" for Palestinians. The US still did not support the Palestinian people's right of self-determination or their right to an independent state, but stated that the Palestinians' future should be linked with Jordan.

Between September 1982 and April 1983, Carol and I interviewed dozens of Jordanian, Palestinian, and Israeli political leaders. We met regularly with American embassy officials wherever we traveled. After a few months, many who were initially encouraged by the Reagan Initiative began to complain that, while Jordan and the PLO were taking the Initiative seriously and were working actively to develop a positive coordinated response, the Reagan administration seemed to have lost interest. During the years we lived in the Middle East and several times since then I've observed the United States actively engaging in peacemaking and then switching focus or engaging with much less determination and energy. Sadly, this pattern first raises and then frustrates both Palestinian and Israeli popular hopes for peace, and each time this happened extremism increased on both sides and it became harder to raise people's hopes again.

King Hussein expressed Jordan's willingness to work with the Reagan Initiative, but his flexibility was limited. Palestinians believed that the PLO, not Jordan, should represent them in any negotiations. Even Elias Friej, the very moderate Palestinian mayor of Bethlehem (and the only mayor of an important town not deposed by Israel) was adamant that, if there was to be a joint delegation with Jordan, the PLO must have a public role in naming the Palestinian participants. This was essential both to give the Palestinian negotiators legitimacy and to protect them from those who suspected that a joint delegation might negotiate away Palestinian national rights.

Two other important questions arose in regard to the Reagan Initiative: Would the United States come around to support the principle of the Palestinians' right of self-determination, a principle most European governments were prepared to support; and would the United States pressure Israel to freeze settlement construction? As it became clear that America was unwilling to take either of these steps, hopes for the Reagan initiative diminished. Jordanians and Palestinians were frustrated by the Reagan administration's inability to grasp the limitations on King Hussein's and Chairman Arafat's flexibility. While some American officials understood the need for more active, creative and determined follow-up diplomacy, others seemed to hold the simplistic, unrealistic and arrogant view that if the United States simply stood firm, eventually Jordan and the PLO would accept American terms.

It seemed to us that the Reagan administration overestimated the Arab side's capacity for flexibility; and, at the same time, the administration seemed to underestimate the potential for Israeli flexibility, thereby frustrating many peace-oriented Israelis. Leaders in the Israeli Labor alignment and the Israeli Peace Now movement were very critical of the Likud's hard line positions and wanted the United States to push Israel harder to be flexible. They believed that most Israelis understood how expansion of settlements was an obstacle to negotiations, and that most would accept the idea of the PLO naming non-PLO West Bank and Gaza Palestinians to participate in a joint Jordanian-Palestinian negotiating team. If the United States accepted such a delegation, they believed Begin's government would be hard pressed to reject negotiating with it. Many Israeli moderates with whom we met were worried that the Reagan administration was not exerting enough creative, tough diplomatic energy. On the eve of Prime Minister Begin's visit to Washington in November 1982, a *Jerusalem Post* editorial compared Reagan's efforts with Carter's and concluded,

> There is no evidence as yet that Mr. Reagan and his team are prepared to devote to the Middle East conflict the same single-minded effort which President Jimmy Carter brought to bear on it and without which peacemaking is probably impossible.[10]

Many prominent Israeli moderates were worried that the opportunity for negotiations for a two-state solution was slipping away and they wanted the United States

10. *Jerusalem Post* Editorial.

to exert real pressure on Begin's government. These views were substantiated dramatically in two columns by Max Frankel in *The New York Times* in November. Frankel's views were based on interviews he conducted with prominent Israelis, including Shimon Peres and Abba Eban. His columns were especially noteworthy because Frankel himself was a Holocaust survivor and because the *Times'* editorial policy generally supported Israel. David Shipler, then the Jerusalem correspondent for *The New York Times*, told us he had heard Israeli Labor Party leaders express views very similar to those Frankel reported.

In his first column, "Looming Over Israel,"[11] Frankel described the intense debate among Israelis about the dangers to Israel of holding on to the West Bank and Gaza. He reported that prominent opposition leaders clearly understood that continued Israeli occupation and rule over 2 million Palestinians would eventually make Israel "either democratic and un-Jewish or Jewish and undemocratic." Even more dramatic, Frankel reported that some of these leaders, on a "not for attribution" basis, were advocating means of pressuring Israel's government "that would have been unthinkable even a few weeks ago." The title of Frankel's second column the next day was, "Help Us By Cutting Aid,"[12] Frankel reported that Israeli opposition leaders supported "sharp cuts in America's non-military aid of $800 million a year"—that is, cuts that would not endanger Israel's security—as a way of undermining support for the Likud government and forcing Israelis to take a hard look at the Reagan Initiative. Max Frankel's column created a huge controversy in Israel. Labor party leaders denied giving Frankel such advice, but Frankel defended his columns' accuracy.[13] Frankel believed that Israelis speaking out, albeit timidly, reflected their sense of hope that an important opportunity for movement toward peace existed and that the United States could help by pressuring Israel, as well as the Arab parties, to be more forthcoming.

Ignoring the advice of Israeli advocates for peace, President Reagan and leading members of Congress, both Republican and Democrat, declared their opposition to cuts in aid or any pressure on Israel. US policy of refusing to pressure Israel was viewed as a victory by Israel's Likud government, by AIPAC (the Israel lobby), and several mainstream American Jewish organizations; at the same time, Israeli Labor Party leaders, as well as many peace-oriented Israeli and American Jews viewed this policy as shortsighted and dangerous for Israel in that it contributed to a major missed opportunity to get Israeli-Palestinian negotiations going. It was a clear case when not only Palestinians but many Israelis as well were disappointed and frustrated by US policy. While obviously it would be better if Israel and the Palestinians moved toward peace on their own, by late 1982 Carol and I were convinced that creative, engaged, and determined US leadership was absolutely essential for achieving peace.

11. Frankel, "Looming Over Israel."
12. Frankel, "Help Us By Cutting Aid," *The New York Times* (November 16, 1982).
13. "Israeli Dispute Erupts Over Columns in the Times," *The New York Times*, November 18, 1982.

On April 10, 1983, King Hussein announced that he was unable to reach an agreement with the PLO on a joint approach to peace negotiations, meaning they could not agree on something that would be acceptable to the Reagan administration. Reflecting his sensitivity about mutual relations, the King did not publicly blame the United States for the failure. However, Adnan Abu Odeh and other senior advisors to the King spoke candidly to us about their deep disappointment and frustration over the lack of American creativity and determination. King Hussein's announcement was a serious blow to Jordanians, Palestinians, and Israelis who hoped for a negotiated peace. In a tragic coincidence, on the same day that the King made this announcement in Jordan, Isam Sartawi, the PLO peace advocate whom Carol and I met in Paris a year earlier, was assassinated in Portugal by Palestinian extremists.

7

The Other Side Won't Disappear:
Negotiations and Problems Getting to Peace

Hearing strong doubts about the Lebanon-Israel peace agreement; visiting Damascus and starting to understand Syria; witnessing violent factional fighting in Lebanon and the US being forced to withdraw; following the Jordan-PLO agreement on a joint approach to negotiations, Israeli elections that lead to a unity government, and a second chance for the Reagan Initiative; understanding what it will take to get to peace and how the Cold War ideology and other problematic tendencies in US foreign policy make getting there difficult.

FOLLOWING KING HUSSEIN'S APRIL 1983 announcement, American diplomatic activity and our focus shifted back to Lebanon. On May 17, after thirty-five rounds of talks, the Reagan administration finally convinced the Lebanese government of Amin Gemayel (the older, politically more moderate brother of Bashir Gemayel, who had been assassinated) to sign a peace agreement with Israel. It called for phased Israeli withdrawal, contingent on withdrawal of Syrian forces, even though the United States never negotiated this with Syria.

During the fall of 1983, Carol and I spent a week in Beirut and made two separate trips to Damascus. Not surprisingly, many Lebanese and Syrians were skeptical or sharply critical of the so-called peace agreement. We were quite surprised, however, that the first really strong critique of the agreement we heard was from Abba Eban, senior Labor Party leader and former Israeli foreign minister. In a memorable meeting with him at his home in Herziliya, as he paced his living room floor, Eban impatiently declared, "the May 17 Agreement is totally unrealistic; it won't work." He characterized Alexander Haig's approach to negotiating the agreement as ignorant and arrogant. "How could the United States be so stupid," Eban asked us rhetorically, "to assume that Syria would do what they wanted and get out of Lebanon without any negotiations?"

Over the next eight months, we met several European and American diplomats who also expressed skepticism about the agreement, although their views were offered off the record and they used much more guarded language than Abba Eban.

Israel's occupation of Lebanon, the PLO military defeat and withdrawal to Yemen, the Sabra and Shatila massacres, the May 17 agreement, and the presence of a US-led multinational force generated heightened tensions and violent confrontations in Lebanon. The tensions were compounded by growing popular pressure to revise the old power sharing formula that privileged Christians over Muslims and Sunni Muslims over Shiite Muslims in Lebanon's governmental structure. Syria had important interests and played an active, generally covert role in relation to all these issues.

Visits to Syria and Lebanon

Except for my overnight stop en route to Beirut in September 1982, Carol and I had been in the Middle East more than a year before visiting Damascus. We realized that we didn't appreciate Syria's significant role in the region, in part because we had little understanding of its history and interests. In addition, Syrian ties with the Soviet Union meant that Cold War blinders distorted our vision, as they did the understanding of most Washington-based policymakers. Some American diplomats on the ground in Syria and most diplomats from European countries had more nuanced and realistic understandings of Syrian interests and policies. Our first trip to Damascus showed us how dangerous misguided and unrealistic assumptions about Syria could be. The United States tended to see Syria's role as strictly negative and often failed to engage seriously with Syria, an approach which posed a significant danger for America, Israel, and for the Middle East region.

Our initial contact in Damascus was with Mahat Khoury, Syrian liaison to the Middle East Council of Churches and owner of the Family Bookstore, a short walk from the Vendome Hotel where we stayed near the center of the city. As the widow of a highly respected and popular writer, Mahat was very well connected in Syrian intellectual and political circles. She operated her bookstore like a French intellectual salon. Mahat often invited us into her small office sitting room to have coffee and meet her friends, including Syrian and Palestinian officials and religious leaders. However, she was quite cautious talking about politics herself. Given the Syrian security regime, we never asked Mahat for the kind of briefing that we relied on from Rami Khouri in Jordan, Naomi Chazan in Israel, and Saad Eddin Ibrahiim in Egypt, but thanks to her incredible connections we got to meet George Jabbour, director of President Hafez al-Assad's research bureau; Bushra Kanafani, director of the Americas section of the Syrian foreign ministry; Tarek Shallah, a very successful Syrian businessman; several Syria orthodox Christian leaders, and Ahmed Kuftaro, the grand mufti of Syria.

Mahat also introduced us to major PLO leaders including Khaled Fahoum, head of the Palestine National Council, and two leaders of the small, but important Marxist

PLO factions. We met several times with Bassam Abu Sharif and Jamil Hilal, spokespersons respectively for the Popular Front and Democratic Front for the Liberation of Palestine (PFLP and DFLP), who were regular customers at Mahat's bookstore. In 1972, Bassam lost an eye and fingers on one hand as a result of an Israeli Mossad letter bomb delivered to his Beirut office. During the 1960s and 1970s, both men supported violence against Israel, including terrorist attacks, but in the 1980s they began to support the idea of negotiations. In our meetings with them in 1983–84, we gained direct, personal experience of changes in perspective taking place even in leftist, radical Palestinian factions. Frequently, in our conversations with Jamil Hilal, he would ask us if we wanted to hear the official position of the DFLP or his own personal view. Usually they were somewhat different and frequently Jamil's personal view was the more nuanced and interesting.

In the mid-1990s, reflecting progress in the Oslo process, Jamil Hilal was able to move to Ramallah in the West Bank to teach sociology at Bir Zeit University, and despite having helped coordinate plane hijackings in 1970, Bassam Abu Sharif was permitted to move back to Jordan. In 1988, Bassam began meeting with Uzi Mahnaimi, an Israeli journalist who previously had served as a military intelligence officer and recruited Arab spies for Israel. This is only one of several striking examples of Israeli and Palestinian enemies who developed relationships and became friends. In 1991 Bassam Abu Sharif and Uzi Mahnaimi collaborated on writing their memoirs in a book titled, *Best of Enemies*. In 1972, while he was recovering from Israel's Mossad letter bomb attack, Abu Sharif made a decision: "I would still fight, with all I had, for a Palestinian state. But now, having suffered it, I knew violence would never work. . . . Having suffered it firsthand, I knew violence was not the way. Peace was the way."[1]

The most interesting religious leader we met in Syria was Grand Mufti Ahmed Kuftaro. Like chief rabbis in Israel, the grand mufti is appointed by the government, so it was particularly interesting that he (and his students) publicly espoused moderate, orthodox Islamic views. Kuftaro had deep respect for Christianity and Judaism, was a prominent public advocate for interfaith cooperation, and quietly supported negotiating peace with Israel. I believe that President Assad probably chose Kuftaro to be the Grand Mufti because his understanding of Islam led him to be sensitive to minority communities. Syrian society includes several minorities and Assad, himself, was from the minority Alawite community.

Between 1987 and 1998, I organized and led several interfaith trips to Syria, where American Jews, Christians and Muslims had opportunities to meet Grand Mufti Kuftaro. I especially remember one visit where an American Jesuit and a rabbi engaged in intense dialogue with him about passages from the Bible and the Quran that mandated work for justice and peace. Carol and I became friends with one of Ahmed Kuftaro's outstanding students, Imam Mohammed Bashar Arafat (no relation to Yasser Arafat). Bashar moved from Damascus to Baltimore, Maryland where he

---

1. Abu Sharif and Mahnaimi, *Best of Enemies,* 101–102.

became a leader in interfaith activities. Bashar founded the *Civilizations Exchange and Cooperation Foundation,* a worldwide interfaith program. With State Department sponsorship, he has given lectures about Islam and America in several Muslim countries and helps host delegations from Muslim countries that come to the United States.

Carol and I did not devote all of our time to politics in Syria. Like Baghdad and Cairo, Damascus is a great historic center of the Arab and Muslim world, and it was much busier, livelier, and more cosmopolitan than Amman, which sometimes felt like a mid-sized, Midwestern American city. As in Jerusalem, we enjoyed walking a lot, especially around the Old City, visiting Al Azzam Palace, a wonderful bakery on the Street Called Straight, the house of Ananias where Paul is believed to have stayed after his revelation on the road to Damascus, and the spectacular eighth-century Omayyad Mosque, with its beautiful gold and green mosaic walls, supposedly depicting a vision of Paradise. Dabdoub's crafts shop adjacent to Al Azzam Palace seemed to have the best quality crafts, even if also somewhat higher prices than other shops. A visitor in our home today would discover a lovely brass, copper and silver platter, a hundred-year-old wooden Syrian wedding chest with inlaid mother of pearl, and several large copper pieces, all from Dabdoub's. On one of our early visits to the shop, as we described our work for the Quakers, we learned that the co-owners of the shop were an old Syrian Jewish family and a Palestinian Christian family who fled from Palestine to Beirut and then to Damascus in 1948 during the first Arab-Israeli war.

Late October 1983 was a very interesting time to visit Syria, which slowly but surely was reasserting its historic influence in Lebanon. Syria provided overt and covert political and armed support for Lebanese factions that opposed the Israeli occupation, rejected the US-brokered peace agreement, and demanded revision of Lebanon's national power sharing formula. Working with and through these political factions, Syria's objectives included abrogation of the Israel-Lebanon agreement and withdrawal of Israel and of the US-led multi-national force. Syria wanted a stable Lebanon, but one where Syrian interests, both legitimate and not so legitimate, would be restored and respected.

Important changes were also taking place in Syrian views of Israel. For example, when we first visited Damascus, their newspapers were beginning to carry stories about Israeli political developments. Previously, the state-controlled media had consistently and crudely referred to Israel simply as "the Zionist entity," and refused to acknowledge the possibility of diverse Israeli views. For anyone who knows Israel's complex and frequently fractious politics, this simplistic perspective was both comical and sad. Beginning in the summer of 1982, Syrians became interested in the growing, popular Israeli opposition to the Lebanon war, including especially *Yesh Guvul* ("there is a limit"), composed of Israeli soldiers who refused to serve in Lebanon. Stories about Israeli anti-war demonstrations helped Syrians learn about the diversity of Israeli public opinion.

Carol and I had a very interesting direct confirmation of this shift. In preparation for our first visit to Damascus, the AFSC office in Philadelphia warned us not to speak often or openly about Israel because that might make Syrian authorities suspicious. Our many visits to Israel might cause them to deny us entry. We learned that this caution certainly would have been very important a few years earlier, but almost all the Syrians we met were extremely interested in hearing about Israel. We came to appreciate that just as our Syrian contacts made us more interesting to Israelis, our Israeli experiences helped us to gain access to relatively high level Syrian officials, including the foreign minister and senior Bath Party officials. On an official level, the shift was reflected in Syria's support for the Fez Declaration of September 1982 which, despite its ambiguities and limitations, reflected new united support by Arab governments for negotiations with Israel based on UN Security Council resolutions 242 and 338.

While occasionally we met with Foreign Minister Farouk al Sharaa, our regular contact in the Syrian government was Bushra Kanafani, head of the foreign ministry's Americas section. It is noteworthy that both it and the Soviet section of the Syrian foreign ministry were headed by women, reflecting the government's secular, socialist orientation. Although she felt a deep personal antagonism toward Israel, Bushra explained that it was in Syria's strategic national interest to engage in peace negotiations based on U.N Security Council resolutions 242 and 338. While clearly Syria's motivations and reasoning were similar to Egypt's several years earlier, given Syria's still-strained relations with Egypt, Bushra did not explicitly make this comparison and we didn't press the analogy.

At one of our early meetings, I told Bushra that I had met several Syrian university students who said that they looked forward to peace and an opportunity to visit Israel. Bushra said she had bitter personal memories of Israel's creation and the 1948 war, and she never would want to go there. At the end of the 1948 war, her parents had invited a Palestinian refugee family with young children —forced by the Israeli army to abandon their home and orchard in Palestine—to live with them in Damascus. The family had fled first to Beirut, and then to Damascus where for several months they slept on the Kanafani's living room floor. Bushra's experiences and feelings reflected the genuine sympathy and solidarity many Arab people felt for Palestinians.

In the 1990s, when Bushra Kanafani became deputy Syrian ambassador in Washington, she twice invited me to join her for dinner, once at a Lebanese restaurant and once at the Syrian embassy. Both times we discussed prospects for the Oslo peace negotiations. While I was consistently hopeful and she skeptical, I have no doubt that Bushra sincerely believed peace with Israel was in Syria's national interest and she genuinely wanted negotiations to succeed.

A third important development that we witnessed in fall 1983 was Syria's involvement in the political and military conflicts between different Palestinian factions. Arafat and forces loyal to him in Tripoli (Lebanon, not Libya) had been attacked by rebel Palestinians supported by Syria who were motivated by a deep sense of betrayal over the decision to withdraw from Lebanon and the resulting Sabra and Shatila massacres. They were also suspicious of Arafat's talks with King Hussein about forming a joint Jordanian-Palestinian approach to negotiations with Israel. The Syrian government tended to think of itself as the Palestinians' most important and indispensable strategic ally; eventually Hafez al-Assad pulled back from intervening in Palestinian factional fighting and accepted Palestinian efforts to reunify the PLO.

Carol and I spent many hours interviewing Palestinian and Syrian officials about this split. We also witnessed the Palestinian factional fighting firsthand on a car trip with several colleagues from Beirut to Tripoli in northern Lebanon to interview Yasser Arafat. We were scheduled to return to the United States in early December 1983 for two months of home leave and a nationwide speaking tour, and we assumed that saying we had interviewed Arafat would significantly increase interest in our talks. We knew the trip north entailed some risks, so we left Jonah with a baby sitter at our Beirut hotel, with a note to call Gail Pressberg if something happened to us. For both of us, instead of just one, to make this trip clearly was not the wisest or most responsible decision. Thankfully, our driver and very knowledgeable guide was Wa'il Kheir, Lebanese staff of the Middle East Council of Churches.

As we approached Tripoli from the South, we heard machine gun fire. Not seeing any evidence of fighting nearby, Wa'il simply took an alternate route around the city. At Arafat's office in a refugee camp north of Tripoli, we had a very useful hour-long interview with Ahmed Abdul Rahman, his cabinet secretary. Although Rahman assured us that we were not in any danger, the artillery fire sounded very close. While we could have—and probably should have—been satisfied with Rahman's perspective, we still wanted to interview Arafat in person.

On Rahman's advice, we drove to a private home in Tripoli that was serving as a temporary field hospital for wounded Palestinians, where Arafat was supposed to be meeting with Abu Jihad (Khalil al Wazir). Abu Jihad, a very senior PLO leader, lived in Amman. Carol and I regularly met with him and frequently discussed possible contacts between Israelis and PLO leaders. At the house, we sent a brief hand-written note to him via one of the security guards posted outside. A few minutes later, he came out, greeted us, and told us that he and Arafat would be leaving very soon and we should follow them. When they came out, Arafat's driver took off quickly and drove at high speeds. He knew exactly where he was going and, of course, we did not. Within a few minutes we lost sight of their jeep. Wa'il stopped several people on the street and asked in Arabic, "Which way did Arafat go?" Their hand signals and verbal responses seemed to point in every possible direction. We guessed that Arafat had been seen sometime earlier that day heading in each of the different directions people pointed. As we continued onto a side street and down a hill, we heard loud explosions and saw several fires ahead of us. At that point, Wa'il declared that our pursuit of Arafat was over and he was taking us back to Beirut. We didn't argue.

As we drove south, we were stopped several times at armed checkpoints, in one case by several men in their twenties wearing ski masks and carrying AK-47s. Their bleary, reddish eyes suggested that they might be high on drugs. Wa'il somehow seemed to distinguish the identity and political orientation of each different faction and cleverly used different explanations about who we were and what we were doing there. All his explanations seemed to work. At one checkpoint, he said we were journalists, at another, relief workers and then, in the funniest and most shameless explanation, Wa'il claimed that the two women in the back seat were his harem. The gunmen laughed loudly, said some things in Arabic that he chose not to translate, and then waved us through. Over dinner we laughed about our experiences that day, but we all knew that they really weren't funny until we had safely returned to Beirut.

The everyday threats of violence faced by people in Lebanon during this period came home to me personally on January 18, 1984 when we learned the news that Malcolm Kerr, president of American University in Beirut, was gunned down on the lawn outside his office. Three months earlier, I had interviewed him on that same lawn. Malcolm Kerr was a longtime supporter of the Palestinian national struggle and had authored an important book, *The Arab Cold War: Gamal Abd al-Nasir and His Rivals, 1958–1970*. Not surprisingly, he expressed strong opposition to the Israeli invasion and occupation of Lebanon, but he also was very critical of Syria's role in Lebanon. No one was ever arrested for Kerr's murder. One theory was that he was killed by a gunman on orders from Iran; another was that Syrian intelligence had ordered his assassination.

In late 1983 and early 1984, conflict in Lebanon came to a head. Despite the Israeli military occupation, American support for the government of Amin Gemayel, and the presence of the US-led multinational force, Syrian-supported factions that opposed the May 17 agreement steadily gained greater strength. The multinational force was accurately perceived as operating in collusion with the Israeli occupation. Political pressure and violent resistance increased to force the Lebanese government to abrogate the May 17 agreement with Israel. On October 23, 1983, just a week after our time in Beirut, suicide bombers rammed trucks loaded with explosives into the US Marine compound and the French barracks, killing more than 240 American servicemen and fifty-eight French paratroopers, and wounding many more. Hezbollah, the radical Shiite political movement, grew stronger. There were threats of further attacks on the multinational force and Amal, a more moderate Shiite faction, joined the demands for the May 17 agreement to be cancelled and the US-led multinational force to be withdrawn. Initially, President Reagan and American officials were adamant in declaring that the United States absolutely would not be pressured into leaving Lebanon. As a demonstration of US resolve, the battleship USS New Jersey fired more than 300 huge rounds at Druze and Syrian positions in the hills overlooking Beirut. Then, in February 1984, under mounting pressure from Congress, Reagan ordered

American forces to withdraw. A month later, the Lebanese government abrogated the May 17 agreement.

Reflecting on the Lebanese government's dependence on America during this period, a Lebanese friend said to us, "Having the United States as your enemy may be dangerous, but having it as your main friend can be suicidal."

The Israeli occupation of Lebanon continued for sixteen more years despite the erosion of popular support and continuous Hezbollah attacks on Israeli soldiers. Finally, in 2000, the government headed by Ehud Barak withdrew Israeli forces, except from a small border area claimed by both Lebanon and Syria. While in 1982 many southern Lebanese Shiites welcomed Israel's invasion that ended the PLO military presence, the long occupation generated two outcomes not anticipated by either Israel or the United States: popular support increased for violent resistance to the Israeli occupation and Hezbollah gained a much larger role in Lebanese national politics.

The Reagan Initiative, Round Two

In 1984, the United States again showed interest in getting Israeli-Palestinian negotiations going. As we had two years earlier, Carol and I focused on the Reagan Initiative and on the prospect of a joint Jordanian-PLO approach. As Israeli forces continued to be bogged down in Lebanon, and no resolution with the Palestinians seemed possible, the political fortunes of Prime Minister Begin's governing Likud coalition declined. Depressed by his wife's death in November 1982 and the apparent stalemate in relations with the Arabs, Begin seemed increasingly exhausted and isolated. Faced with protests by mothers and wives of some of the Israeli soldiers killed or captured in Lebanon, reports surfaced that Begin was troubled by misgivings about the invasion. He resigned in October 1983.

I learned of Begin's doubts about the Lebanon war in private conversations with Lova Eliav, former secretary general of the Labor Party and outspoken opponent of Israel's settlement policies. Despite his very different political orientation, Prime Minister Begin called on Lova to serve as his unpublicized personal mediator with PLO Chairman Arafat in very sensitive, secret negotiations about prisoner exchanges. During many one-on-one meetings Lova learned that Begin felt he had been misled by Ariel Sharon over the decision to invade Lebanon.

Lova Eliav dedicated his life to service of Israel and to his vision of peace with Israel's Arab neighbors. He told me that since the late sixties he had recognized that the Palestinian nation was an evolving fact. He argued that if the Arabs were ready for peace, Israel must be ready to relinquish territory. He believed, as a matter of principle, Israel must not try to suppress the Palestinians' right of self-determination. While his ideas would gather political and popular support later, they were initially strongly rejected by Prime Minister Levi Eshkol and by his successor, Golda Meir. When we knew him, Lova had been pushed out from mainstream Israeli politics and was doing development work in the Negev. As noted earlier, he was a co-founder of the Israeli Council for Israeli Palestinian Peace, and a winner, along with Issam Sartawi, of the Kreisky Prize for Peacemaking. In 1986, Lova wrote *New Heart, New Spirit: Biblical Humanism for Modern Israel,* which challenges nationalist, rightwing interpretations of the Bible, and instead emphasizes the Bible's humanism. In 1988 Lova was awarded the Israel Prize for his contributions to Israeli society. He died in 2010.

In the context of shifting political dynamics in Israel, in early 1984 the United States sought to revive the Reagan Initiative. Despite Syrian opposition, King Hussein and Chairman Arafat resumed their talks about a joint approach to negotiations. As interest in the Reagan initiative revived, Carol and I regularly interviewed American, Jordanian and PLO officials, as well as diverse Palestinians and Israelis. Sadly, it seemed to us that the American approach was no more creative or determined than it had been two years earlier.

Jordan and the PLO did sign a formal cooperation agreement on February 11, 1984, moving the PLO closer to acceptance of UN Security Council resolutions 242 and 338, which they finally formally endorsed in 1988. While the agreement provided for a joint negotiating team, it also put Jordan clearly on record as supporting the Palestinians' right of self-determination and recognizing the PLO as their sole legitimate representative. Importantly, the agreement also called for an international conference involving the five permanent members of the UN Security Council to launch the peace negotiations. The involvement of UN Security Council members would help protect King Hussein and Chairman Arafat politically from suspicions and criticism from leftist Palestinians and from Syria. For many moderate Arabs and Israelis, this Jordan-PLO agreement represented a promising new opportunity to get negotiations going.

Israeli elections in July 1984 resulted in Likud and Labor winning an equal number of seats in the Knesset. The two major blocks agreed to form a government of national unity, in which Shimon Peres of Labor would serve as prime minister for the first two years, while Likud's Yitzhak Shamir would serve as foreign minister, and then they would reverse roles for the next two years. Combined with the Jordan-PLO cooperation agreement, the Israeli unity government with Peres as prime minister appeared to create a positive context for launching Israeli-Palestinian peace negotiations.

While Likud opposed having the United Nations play any role in negotiations, Prime Minister Peres believed Israel should respond positively to the Jordan-PLO agreement, including the call for an international conference to launch the negotiations. Despite the domestic political risks, Peres addressed the UN General Assembly in September 1985 and declared that Israel would accept the idea of the five permanent members of the UN Security Council launching the peace negotiations. While King Hussein and Arafat, and Israeli peace advocates, saw Peres's speech as encouraging, President Reagan soon made it clear that the United States opposed the idea of an international conference and rejected any role for the Soviet Union in relation to the negotiations. Evidently, Prime Minister Peres was more interested in getting negotiations started than he was in keeping the UN or the USSR out of the process, while Reagan's priorities were the opposite. Despite diplomatic efforts, round two of the Reagan Initiative ended in failure. This missed opportunity dramatically showed how, when an Israeli government demonstrated flexibility, American Cold War policies and priorities remained major obstacles to peace. This experience and the experience in 1982 when the Reagan Administration refused Israeli Labor party leaders' advice to put pressure on Israel by cutting aid, made it clear to me that the problems with US efforts for Arab-Israeli-Palestinian peace are much deeper than AIPAC and overly zealous, sometimes misguided pro-Israel lobbying; indeed, these examples demonstrated that misguided US policy not only frustrated Palestinian aspirations but put Israel's future at risk. I recalled what a Lebanese had said to Carol and me about Lebanon's dependence on the US: "Having the United States as your enemy may be dangerous, but having it as your main friend can be suicidal." I wondered and worried if this might also be true for Israel's relationship with the United States.

In April 1985 Carol and I and Jonah came home from Jordan, having completed our three-year assignment for the Quakers. We had been closely following diplomatic efforts to start negotiations while we lived in the Middle East, but we were back home when we witnessed the sad, final fizzle of the Reagan Initiative for peace.

After three years living in the Middle East and listening to Arabs and Israelis speak about opportunities and obstacles for peace, including their hopes and disappointments with the US role, I was convinced that America, in part precisely because of its special relationship with Israel, has a unique responsibility and an indispensable role to play in helping to resolve the Arab-Israeli-Palestinian conflict. Indeed, almost no past progress to resolve this conflict had been made without US leadership, facilitation, and resolute support. I also believed if the United States was going to play that role there would need to be broad public support, especially from American religious communities. I came home in 1985 committed to the idea of working with American Jews, Christians and Muslims to organize active interfaith cooperation for peace in the Middle East.

Before turning attention to my interfaith work for peace from 1987 to the present, I need to set the context for that work related to my understanding developed over many years of what getting to peace requires, and both the problems and the possibility of the United States playing a positive role in helping Israelis and Palestinians get there.

Getting to Peace

After a particularly difficult day of negotiations leading up the Oslo Declaration in 1993, as they walked together to dinner, the two chief negotiators, Uri Savir, representing Israel, and Abu Ala (Ahmed Qurei), representing the PLO, had a very interesting and revealing personal exchange.

> Savir: You know why we don't like you? It's because you remind us of ourselves.

> Abu Ala: Really! That's also my problem with you.

> Savir: Perhaps it's because we're the sons of suffering peoples.

> Abu Ala: And perhaps it's because we're from the same place.[2]

During the three years Carol and I carried out the Quaker assignment of listening to Arabs and Israelis and in my work for peace since then, I've felt continually challenged to develop deeper understanding of the Arab-Israeli conflict and particularly the core conflict between Israelis and Palestinians. The exchange between Uri Savir and Abu Ala revealed a feature of the Israeli-Palestinian conflict that may be unique, i.e., Palestinians and Israelis sometimes see themselves as mirror images of each other.

The conflicts in Vietnam and El Salvador I witnessed up close were essentially between liberation movements and colonialist or neo-colonialist military regimes. In contrast, I believe the Israeli-Palestinian conflict fundamentally is a conflict between two national liberation movements. Both the Jewish people and the Palestinian people have compelling authentic historical connections and nationalist claims in the same small land, making their conflict morally more complicated and much more difficult to resolve. In 1983, an exchange I had with David Hartman, a modern Orthodox Israeli rabbi and founder of the Hartman Institute in Jerusalem, poignantly revealed the conflict's unique character. Knowing that Carol and I regularly met with Palestinians, Rabbi Hartman said, "You need to get Palestinians to understand that when we Jews come to this land, we don't come as foreigners or colonizers. We are coming home." I replied, "I think I understand David, and I do try to help Palestinians understand that. What Palestinians want you to understand is that when you came here, they *were* home."

In an article in the summer 1988 issue of *Middlebury Magazine,* entitled "Twice Promised Land," Rabbi Arthur Hertzberg wisely wrote: "The difficulty with the Arab-Jewish, or Israeli-Palestinian, conflict is that both of the protagonists in this conflict, in terms of the logic of their own underlying premises, are absolutely right."[3]

Given the two peoples' bone-deep sense of connection to the same land and the suffering both peoples have endured, it is not surprising that from 1948 to 1988, the vast majority of Israeli Jews and Palestinian Arabs refused to recognize the legitimacy of the other side's claim; indeed, most did not view the other side as a people with any legitimate nationalist claim. In 1947, the Arab states universally rejected the UN partition plan and the creation of Israel. Twenty years later, following their defeat in

---

2. Savir, *The Process,* 32.
3. Hertzberg, "Twice Promised Land."

the 1967 war and despite Israel being firmly established, the Arab states formally and unanimously adopted three Arab no's: "No negotiations with Israel, no recognition of Israel, and no peace with Israel." In 1948, while some Jews believed the partition plan was only a first step, most Jews thought it provided an important international legal foundation and a sensible compromise, so the vast majority of Jews accepted it. Two decades later, as a result of the June 1967 war, Israel captured Gaza, Sinai, the Golan Heights, and the West Bank including Jerusalem. While some few clear-eyed and courageous Palestinians saw this situation as the basis for negotiating a two-state solution, most Palestinians and the PLO continued to reject the idea of recognizing or negotiating with Israel. For some Israelis, their swift and decisive victory in the "Six Day War" fueled fantasies of achieving greater Israel, from the Mediterranean Sea to the Jordan River. In the wake of the war, almost all mainstream Israeli political leaders adopted three Israeli no's: "No recognition of the PLO, no negotiations with the PLO, and no Palestinian state." For forty years, most Israelis and Palestinians were exclusively attached to their own side's compelling, emotional narrative, while denying the legitimacy of the other's. Each side wanted the other side to disappear. In my view, the best book for gaining an in-depth understanding of both peoples is David K. Shipler's *Arab and Jew: Wounded Spirits in a Promised Land*, for which he won a Pulitzer Prize in 1987.

Israelis and Palestinians delegitimized and demonized one another by pointing to the other's most negative statements and actions, sometimes even equating them with the Nazis. Israelis saw Arab rejection as reflecting their desire to drive Jews into the sea, an obviously frightening reversal of the biblical Exodus story. Palestinians viewed Israel, like European powers before it, as carrying out colonialist, settler policies. Supporters of each side became skilled at portraying the other side's rhetoric and action in ways that justified their own worst interpretations. However, following five Arab-Israeli wars, growing numbers of people on both sides saw that they could not make the other side disappear. They began to recognize that their simplistic self-justifying views would not lead to victory, but to interminable conflict, with more violence, suffering, and death.

During our time living in the Middle East, from 1982 to 1985, Carol and I encountered growing numbers of Israelis and Palestinians who were coming to accept, even if grudgingly, that the other side was here to stay and what each side needed most—for Israelis, recognition and security, and for Palestinians, an end to occupation and an independent state—could only be achieved through a negotiated two-state solution. This represented a seismic shift away from a zero-sum view, in which every loss for one side was viewed as a gain for the other, to a new recognition that in order for one side to achieve what it needed and deserved, the other side also had to get what it needed and deserved. Growing numbers of people on both sides recognized that achieving those goals would require negotiating. The "three no's" began to dissolve.

As Israeli and Palestinian perspectives changed, third parties including unofficial actors like the Quakers facilitated communication and direct contacts between them, a process which both reflected and reinforced new thinking about the conflict and how to resolve it. Carol and I were privileged to play a small part in this process. For three years, we routinely shared information and perceptions of people we met on one side with people we were meeting on the other side. We also had a few opportunities to help individual Israelis and Palestinians meet face to face. For example, in 1983 we arranged for Mordechai (Morela) BarOn, former chief of staff for General Moshe Dayan and one of the founders of Peace Now, and Mohammed Milhem, exiled Palestinian mayor of Halhoul in the West Bank (who a short time later became a member of the PLO executive committee), to go on an AFSC-sponsored speaking tour in the United States. The two men spoke in several synagogues, where individual rabbis braved controversy in their community by inviting the two men to speak. Since BarOn lived in Jerusalem and Milhem was exiled in Amman, they could not meet before their tour, so Carol and I tape recorded each of them responding to the same ten questions. They listened to each other's responses before agreeing to undertake the tour. Subsequently, Morela and Mohammed became personal friends, and partners in working for peace.

Carol and I regularly met in Jerusalem with Tzali Reshef, Janet Aviad, and other leaders of the Israeli Peace Now movement and in Amman with the PLO leader, Abu Jihad to carry messages and explore possible meetings between Israelis and PLO representatives. Abu Jihad, his wife Um Jihad, and their two teenage daughters, Iman (Faith) and Amal (Hope) always welcomed us very warmly in their home. Everyone approached the prospect of meeting their enemies very cautiously and seriously, in part because of the political, legal and even physical risks involved. Abu Jihad always took very careful notes of our conversations and made sure he had the correct spelling and pronunciation of Israeli names. Adding to the potential impact of this work, several of the Peace Now leaders had close relations with Israeli Labor Party leaders, while Abu Jihad was a very senior leader in the PLO and a trusted, close colleague of Arafat. When the first intifada erupted in 1987, he became the main coordinator between the PLO leadership outside and Palestinians in the West Bank and Gaza. It was clear to us that, while he supported resistance, including violent resistance to Israeli occupation, Abu Jihad also supported the idea of negotiating with Israel for a two-state peace agreement. Tragically, on April 16, 1988 Israeli commandos carried out a daring nighttime raid, and assassinated Abu Jihad at his alternate home in Tunis.

As more Israelis and Palestinians changed their views, internal debates in both societies intensified. More people advocated negotiations and accepted the need for compromises, while others still could only see a determined and unchangeable enemy that needed to be defeated. Just as during the Vietnam War some Americans promoted an unrealistic third way between continued war and communist victory, some Israelis and Palestinians advocated unrealistic alternative solutions that fit their own partisan preferences and prejudices. For years many Israeli leaders denied that Palestinians were a people and promoted the idea that Jordan is Palestine, which meant that Palestinians should or could create their state in that already sovereign nation. This was not only clearly unacceptable to King Hussein, but it also disregarded the Palestinians' bone-deep connections to the land west of the Jordan River, seventy-five percent of which became Israel in 1948. Israeli leaders also pursued the illusion that they could find or create an alternative, more malleable leadership to the PLO. Ironically, the Likud governments in Israel initially allowed funds to come into Gaza to support Hamas as an alternative to the PLO.

Palestinians also adopted or advocated unrealistic solutions. For many years they advocated a single state between the Jordan River and the Mediterranean, with equal rights for all, despite the fact that a vast majority of Israelis would never agree. While this idea had a certain theoretical appeal, it completely ignored the Jewish people's profound aspiration and almost universal support for a country with a Jewish majority and character. Even more unrealistic, some Palestinians latched on to the views of *Neturei Karta*, the tiny, anti-Zionist Hassidic religious faction that for theological reasons did not and still does not recognize the Israeli state. Some Palestinians found support in small, radical, Jewish peace groups, whose members sympathized more actively with Palestinians and may have been or seemed to be less firmly committed to the idea of preserving a specifically Jewish state.

Carol and I discovered during the early 1980s that people would reveal their evolving views in subtle or surprising ways, sometimes even surprising themselves. In 1984 I met Yehuda Ben Meir, member of the National Religious Party and at the time deputy to Likud foreign minister Yitzhak Shamir in the Israeli unity government. I had been warned that Ben Meir was very conservative and probably wouldn't meet with me, and if he did meet that he would not show any interest in peace with the Palestinians. Looking at the business card I handed him, Ben Meir frowned and said, "I don't think this is your card." I had mistakenly handed him the card of Mohammed Milhem, member of the PLO executive committee. I took back the card, apologized, and offered my own. Ben Meir then asked whether I met regularly with the PLO. After repeating the Israeli mantra that "the PLO is a terrorist organization and Israel will never negotiate with them," he leaned across his desk and asked me quietly, "What are PLO leaders saying about negotiations?" It seemed that my accidentally handing him the wrong card provided the occasion for him to acknowledge that he was interested in the possibility of Israel talking with the PLO. In 1988 Yehuda Ben Meir joined with Rabbis Yehuda Amital and Michael Melchior in forming Meimad, a religious Zionist movement that believed in working actively for peace with the Palestinians, including the PLO.

At my meeting in Tunis with Abu Iyad, one of the five founders of the PLO, I brought personal greetings from our Israeli friend, Mordechai (Morela) BarOn. BarOn and he had met privately in Europe a few months earlier. Abu Iyad responded:

"Please give Morela my greetings. I am very glad to have met him but, you know, if we want to achieve a Palestinian state, we must also meet with members of the Likud, not just with members of Peace Now or the Labor Party." Later, as Abu Iyad's aide drove me back to my hotel, I asked whether he agreed about the need to meet with more hawkish Israelis. He explained that, growing up in Lebanon, he had never met an Israeli until he was captured by a patrol on the outskirts of Beirut during the Israeli occupation. During two weeks as a prisoner, he said he listened in amazement as Israeli soldiers passionately debated the merits of the war. "They didn't know that I understood Hebrew. I was shocked to hear the intense debate among Israeli soldiers and this helped to convince me that peace is possible. So, yes, I agree with Abu Iyad: the PLO should talk with any Israelis willing to talk with us."

I was privileged personally to get to know a few Palestinian and Israeli leaders whose views changed dramatically over the years and who played major roles in advocating for peace. Nabil Shaath was born in Safad, Palestine in 1938 but was living in Cairo when Carol and I first met him in 1982. He founded Team International, a very successful high tech consulting firm, and wanted to participate in the economic development of a Palestinian state. On one of my visits in Cairo, Nabil confessed: "For most of my life, I believed Zionism was simply another form of European colonialism." Then, after getting to know many Israeli Jews, listening to their life stories, and accepting their deep sense of connection to the land, Nabil changed his view. He told me, "I came to accept that Jews feel as deeply connected to this land as we Palestinians do, and I also recognized, if the Jewish people are colonialists, they have the oddest history of any colonialists in the world."

Throughout the 1980s and 1990s, Nabil participated in many unofficial dialogues with prominent Israelis and American Jews, and played a major role in both formal and informal negotiations. In 2003 he was appointed foreign minister of the Palestinian Authority. In early 2010, Nabil—who had a home in Gaza although he didn't live there after the violent Hamas takeover—was invited by independent Gazans to explore ideas for reconciliation and a possible unity government between Fateh and Hamas.

Yehoshafat Harkabi served for years as Israel's director of military intelligence and was one of few senior Israeli intelligence officers fluent in Arabic. Over the years, he closely monitored changes in Arab and PLO policies, gradually concluding that Israel should negotiate with the PLO and accept an independent Palestinian state in the West Bank and Gaza. Like Matti Peled, whom Carol and I met on our way to the Middle East in April 1982, Harkabi was a deeply devoted Zionist. He told me that his father, who immigrated to Palestine in the early 1900s, was so moved by being back in the land of Israel that he refused to wear shoes for most of the rest of his life. Harkabi argued passionately that Zionism was not colonialism, but he told me that Israel had made a terrible mistake by building settlements in the occupied territories after the 1967 war. He believed that Israel should negotiate with the PLO for a two-state solution.

In the 1990s Harkabi was appointed a visiting professor at Princeton University and he lectured in many American cities. I travelled with him and his son Danny, who piloted our rented piper cub plane, on a speaking tour in the Midwest. In St. Louis, I was the only non-Jew in his meeting with local Jewish leaders who challenged him about why he changed from a hawk to a dove, arguing that his dovish stance was dangerous for Israel. Harkabi responded impatiently, "I was never a hawk and I am not now a dove. I was always a realist and I am still a realist today." He believed that the more conservative views of AIPAC and many mainstream American Jewish leaders were out of date and, to the extent that they influenced US policies, they posed a grave danger to Israel's future as a Jewish and democratic state. In his 1988 book, *Israel's Fateful Decisions*, Harkabi made his case for the urgency of Israel negotiating with the PLO. Toward the end of the St. Louis meeting, he angrily told the local Jewish leaders: "It's you who are not being realistic and it's your views that are putting Israel's survival at risk." Because he had served for years as Israel's chief of military intelligence and helped orchestrate Israel's victories in wars with the Arab states, while Harkabi may not have changed their minds, the Jewish leaders found it hard to argue against him.

Carol and I also encountered American diplomats, including some ambassadors, who in the course of their postings developed views that differed with those of Washington-based policymakers and members of Congress. These encounters reminded me of meeting Ambassador Robert White in El Salvador in 1980. Several State Department representatives in Arab countries and Israel told us off the record that they believed America should recognize the Palestinain people's right of self-determination, and that America and Israel would have to talk with the PLO. This was several years before the United States finally agreed to talk with them in 1988. Since they were officially prohibited from meeting PLO officials, some American officials were very interested in hearing what Carol and I learned in our meetings. We were frequently impressed by staff in our Middle East embassies and occasionally may have played a small role in the evolution of their views.

Daniel Kurtzer was the chief political officer at the US embassy in Tel Aviv when we lived in Amman. Dan later became US ambassador to Egypt and then to Israel. On one of our visits to Tel Aviv, Dan told us that he would be coming across the river on a familiarization visit to Jordan. Following diplomatic protocol, the US embassy in Amman would only arrange meetings for him with Jordanians, not with Palestinians. Dan accepted my offer to arrange a meeting for him with Fahd Qawasmeh, the very popular, elected Palestinian mayor of Hebron, whom Begin's Likud government had deposed and exiled in 1981. I drove Dan to Qawasmeh's home in our yellow 1971 beetle, joking about how our Quaker car was not adequately armored to transport an ambassador. Shortly after Dan's meeting with him, at Arafat's invitation, Qawasmeh joined the PLO executive committee. Clearly, Dan would not have met him if the mayor had been on the PLO executive committee at the time. While many factors influenced Kurtzer's thinking, including his own deep American and Jewish concern for Israel's future, I believe the meeting with Mayor Qawasmeh, a principled, public supporter of a negotiated two-state solution with Israel, was important in his developing perspective about Palestinian aspirations, the PLO, and what the United States needed to do to provide effective leadership for peace. In 2008, Dan Kurtzer and Scott Lasensky co-authored *Negotiating Arab-Israeli Peace*, published by the US Institute for Peace.[4] Former Senator George Mitchell, who at that time was about to be named President Obama's special envoy for Mideast peace negotiations, praised the book's analysis as providing "a solid framework from which American policymakers and mediators can work to facilitate a comprehensive Arab-Israeli peace settlement."

Israelis and Palestinians who met each other during the early 1980s often faced harsh criticism and were even labeled as traitors by extremist elements within their own societies. On December 29, 1984, while Carol and I were on a visit in Jerusalem, we got a telephone call late at night from our Israeli friend, Morela BarOn, who said that he just heard the terrible news that Mayor Qawasmeh had been assassinated outside his home in Amman, in front of his six year old son. Most Palestinians believed that, like Isam Sartawi, Qawasmeh was killed on orders from the small, extremist faction headed by Abu Nidal. When we returned to Amman, Carol and I participated in a memorial march of several thousand Palestinians and heard an impassioned graveside eulogy by Chairman Arafat honoring Mayor Qawasmeh. Following the march, Carol went to a gathering of women at the Qawasmeh home. Fahd's wife, holding back tears, came over to where she was seated, knelt next to her and pleaded, "Why did this happen?" I attended a gathering of men at the PLO office where Arafat eulogized Qawasmeh a second time as a "Palestinian national hero." Seeing that I was crying, Qawasmeh's teenage son embraced me, as if he were the father and I the son, and told me reassuringly, "It will be alright Ron, it will be alright."

There was sad irony in the fact that the Israeli government deposed and exiled this moderate, very popular, elected Palestinian mayor of Hebron who advocated non-violent methods to resist Israeli occupation and supported a two-state solution. Irony turned to true tragedy when a Palestinian extremist assassinated Mayor Qawasmeh. During the 1980s growing numbers of Palestinians and Israelis turned toward greater realism and willingness to accept the idea of negotiations to achieve a two-state peace agreement. While political leaders on both sides, at least in private, were also coming to accept the idea of a negotiated two-state resolution of the conflict, most lacked courage to press forward publicly. Meanwhile, extremist minorities worked feverishly and violently to torpedo peace efforts.

4. Kurtzer and Lasensky, *Negotiating Arab-Israeli Peace*.

United States Policy: Part of the Problem or Part of the Solution?

Before sharing the story of my work organizing interfaith cooperation for peace, I want to explain how my understanding developed over many years about the role of US policy in the search for Middle East peace. Simplistic pro-Palestinian or pro-Israel explanations of the failure to achieve peace are not convincing. In the sixties, speaking about race relations, Eldridge Cleaver told whites: "You're either part of the solution or you're part of the problem." In contrast, in relation to resolving the Arab-Israeli-Palestinian conflict, I believe America is both part of the problem and essential to finding a solution. Some critics, particularly those with a pro-Palestinian orientation, blame US failure to achieve peace on the influence of AIPAC and other powerful, partisan "pro-Israel" organizations. Some supporters of Israel put all the blame on the ambivalence and/or failure of Palestinian political leadership. I do not discount the failures of leaders on both sides to lead or the negative effects of misguided "pro-Israel" influence as factors harming chances for peace. I do believe these simplistic explanations have produced some ironic results. Palestinian supporters often fail to look past antagonistic, over-zealous Israel supporters to appreciate and work as allies with Israeli and American Jews who support creation of a Palestinian state and support pressure on Israel to achieve it. Supporters of Israel who put all the blame on the Palestinians often seem not to appreciate that in the long run failure to achieve a two-state resolution of the conflict is more dangerous for the future of Israel than it is for the Palestinians and Arab states.

In addition to the factors mentioned, I believe the failure of US peacemaking efforts in the Middle East is the result of complex, problematic tendencies in American foreign policy, tendencies that have been responsible for seriously flawed and in some cases disastrous US policies in Africa, Asia and Latin America. Further complicating the situation is the fact that America and Israel share some of the same problematic tendencies. In pursuing what it believes to be Israel's interests and guided in recent decades by a politics closer to the hawkish Likud than the more peace-oriented Israeli Labor Party, AIPAC often works in ways that reinforce and magnify these problematic tendencies in both countries' policies. Simple partisan explanations of the failure to achieve peace ignore or give far too little attention to other important factors shaping US policy. These include the profoundly negative influences on US policy of the Cold War and War on Terrorism; America's dependence for decades on access to Mideast oil; pressures from powerful American military hardware manufacturers that reap huge profits from arms sales and US arms aid in the region; and active, strong neo-conservative political influence on US foreign policy worldwide.

It puzzles and troubles me how, especially for people who are critical of the US role in other parts of the world, it seems so easy in this particular conflict to put so much of the blame for what's wrong with US policy on Israel and American Jews. While not the major factor, from my experiences, I am convinced that deeply rooted, persistent anti-Jewish prejudice plays a role in fueling this bias. A basic question for anyone who sees serious problems with US policy in other areas of the world is: why wouldn't these problems also pertain and have serious negative consequences on the search for peace the Middle East? Also, specifically, related to possibilities of resolving the Arab-Israeli conflict, how does one explain occasions when prominent Israeli political leaders were critical of the US for not doing enough to help Israel achieve peace? Two major examples in the 1980s were when senior Israeli Labor party leaders in 1982 quietly suggested to *The New York Times* columnist Max Frankel that the US should cut non-military aid to Israel to pressure Begin's government to respond positively to the Reagan Initiative; and then in 1985, these same Israeli leaders were frustrated when, despite Prime Minister Peres's acceptance of the idea, the Reagan initiative died when President Reagan opposed any role for the Soviet Union or the UN Security Council in launching peace negotiations. In the 1990s Prime Minister Rabin had serious differences with AIPAC during the Oslo process related to negotiations with the PLO, including in 1995 when Rabin appealed openly to American Jewish leaders to oppose AIPAC's support for the Dole/Gingrich bill to move the US embassy to Jerusalem. Encouraged by Rabin and by her own hopes for the Oslo peace process, Jewish Senator Diane Feinstein introduced an amendment to the bill that allowed President Clinton to ignore implementing it.

In addition to underestimating political differences among Israelis about the priority and path for peace, blaming Israel and American Jews for the failure to achieve peace doesn't take sufficient account of the divisions in the American Jewish community over what it means to be pro-Israel. As an example, the Union of American Hebrew Congregations and it successor body, the Union of Reform Judaism, largest of the national Jewish religious organizations, has been on record for three decades as opposed to expansion of settlements in the occupied territories. It certainly is fair to be critical that mainstream Jewish opposition to settlements has not been publicly and politically strong enough. However, it also is true that no administration, except that of George H.W. Bush has applied tough pressure on Israel to stop expansion of settlements. Sadly, as will become clear in the next chapter, in that case, rather than appealing to American Jews and all Americans for support, President Bush spoke about the issue in a way that reminded Jews of an old anti-Jewish stereotype. Several administrations failed to act on opportunities when pressure on Israel to halt settlement expansion would have helped chances for peace and when Jewish and non-Jewish advocates of peace might well have helped the administration win that political fight.

As will become evident in chapters 8 and 10, major Jewish religious leaders of Reform, Conservative and Reconstructionist national movements have played key roles since the mid-1980s in national interfaith coalitions that have consistently and publicly advocated for the kind of balanced US policies also supported by many Israeli and Palestinian peace advocates. Active public support for fair, determined US policy for peace, including support for pressure on Israel, by Americans for Peace

Now over many years and more recently by JStreet provides further evidence that American Jews, like other Americans, are divided over what policies the US should pursue to help achieve Arab-Israeli-Palestinian peace. A bold, balanced, and determined push by the United States to achieve peace would test the commitments and relative strength of Jewish and other larger non-Jewish pro-peace constituencies, but so far no administration has determined that peace is an important enough priority to risk this political fight.

If I am right that there are more complex, deeper problems in American foreign policy that help explain the failure of US peace efforts in the Middle East, it should be clear to everyone that neither AIPAC nor the American Jewish community is the source of these problems. A more detailed account of the negative effects of these problems on peace prospects in the 1980s can be found in my book, *Missed Opportunities for Peace: United States Middle East Policy, 1981–86.*[5] For an insightful analysis of a basic problematic tendency that America and Israel share, I encourage you to read Todd Gitlin's and Liel Leibowitz's 2010 book, *The Chosen Peoples: America, Israel and the Ordeals of Divine Election.*[6] In my view, it is essential to understanding the history of the Arab-Israeli-Palestinian conflict, including the history of failed attempts to resolve it, and the challenges and opportunities for interfaith cooperation for peace, that one takes account of five fundamental problems in US foreign policy.

The first profoundly problematic tendency in US foreign policy is a simplistic, good vs. evil vision of the world. For America, this delusional virtue is derived from viewing our nation as "a city set on a hill." Israel's version is viewing itself as "a light to the nations." Both exceptionalist visions have roots in dangerously prideful misappropriations of biblical images. In the American case, for decades this tendency has been combined with foreign policy rigidly guided by the Cold War. In the aftermath of the Iranian revolution in 1979, and then reinforced after the 9/11 terrorist attacks, the War on Terrorism has been added as another rigid, controlling strategy for US policy. These frameworks frequently have distorted US policymakers' understanding of people, political movements and whole countries. Policies based on Cold War ideology and priorities contributed significantly to the failure of the Reagan Initiative in the 1980s. Cold War blinders significantly limited and distorted American policies toward the PLO and Syria. The War on Terrorism led the US to declare Hamas a terrorist organization and refuse to deal with them, despite the fact that Hamas won 40 percent of the Palestinian popular vote in 2006 and the reality that peace eventually will have to be negotiated with a united Palestinian government that represents both the West Bank and Gaza. How the US refusing to deal with Hamas has been harmful to Israel, as well as to the Palestinians, was dramatically demonstrated in 2008 when there were no US diplomatic efforts to prevent the breakdown of the Israel-Hamas ceasefire, which led directly to the deadly war in Gaza. In 2011, in an article in the

5. Young, *Missed Opportunities for Peace.*
6. Gitlin and Leibovitz, *The Chosen Peoples.*

New Republic, Efraim Halevy, the former head of Mossad, noted that a majority of Israelis supported Israel negotiating with Hamas for the release of Gilad Shalit; and Halevy argued, "This should be the beginning, not the end, of Israel's negotiations with Hamas."[7]

In addition to their negative effects on prospects for Arab-Israeli peace, the Cold War and War on Terrorism have had distorting, and in some cases disastrous influence on US policy over decades in many countries on every continent. To cite only some examples: Brazil, Cuba, Chile, the Dominican Republic, El Salvador, Guatemala and Haiti in Latin American; the Congo, Namibia, and South Africa in Africa; Korea and Vietnam in Asia; and Iraq and Iran in the Middle East. For years, the US viewed Iraq through the prism of the Cold War and Iran through the prism of the War on Terrorism. During the decade-long Iraq-Iran war in which 1 million people were killed, Henry Kissinger chillingly quipped, "It's a pity they both can't lose." In visits to several of these countries, I've personally witnessed the negative consequences of US policies guided by these simplistic, rigid frameworks. Critically understanding the political and cultural origins and sources of support for the Cold War and War on Terrorism is essential to challenging their controlling and destructive influence, and that's essential for generating more realistic and creative US foreign policy worldwide, including in the Middle East.

A second problem in American foreign policy is the tendency to overestimate what military power can accomplish. Clearly, this was a major factor leading to US intervention and eventually to the US defeat in Vietnam. In the Middle East, decades of American military aid to the Shah of Iran and to Arab dictators finally didn't prevent popular uprisings from overthrowing authoritarian regimes, leaving a legacy of popular anti-American sentiment. American overestimation of military power also reinforced Israeli illusions of what its military could accomplish. In Lebanon in 1982, and again in 2006, those illusions resulted in extended Israeli military intervention that generated greater suffering and destruction, and led to outcomes diametrically opposed to the inflated, unrealistic goals of Israeli military action.

A third problem in US foreign policy, again most dramatically exposed by the American defeat in Vietnam, is the tendency to underestimate ordinary peoples' aspirations for independence and peace. Most Americans, including most policymakers, were blind to how most Vietnamese viewed Ho Chi Minh as the father of Vietnam's movement for independence from colonialism. Over the years of conflict in the Middle East, I believe Israeli and American policymakers profoundly underestimated the determination and staying power of Palestinian nationalist aspirations; and I believe Palestinian and American political leaders underestimated popular Israeli aspirations for peace. There were several times in the 1980s and 1990s when Palestinian aspirations for an end to occupation and an independent state and Israeli aspirations for recognition and security converged in ways that created a context in which, if the

7. Halevy, "This Should Be the Beginning, Not the End, of Israel Negotiating with Hamas."

US had engaged in more creative and more muscular diplomacy, our country could have helped Israelis and Palestinians achieve peace. By failing to appreciate the power of popular aspirations for independence and peace and engaging in intermittent or weak diplomacy, the United States contributed to missing opportunities that left many practical, peace-oriented Israelis and Palestinians deeply disappointed and frustrated.

A fourth fundamental problem in US policy is the American inclination to act alone, rather than in cooperation with allies or with the United Nations. Starting in the 1970s, most European governments understood that the search for peace had to be based on the Palestinian people's right of self-determination as a twin principle with Israel's right to recognition and security. Ignoring our allies' wisdom, it took the United States until the 1990s to support the principle of Palestinian self-determination. In 1982, in the wake of Israel's invasion of Lebanon, the United States opposed the idea of UN peacekeepers, insisting instead on a US-led multinational force, which immediately was perceived as operating in collusion with Israel's occupation, and soon suffered terrible casualties, and was forced to withdraw. In 1985, despite Israeli Prime Minister Peres' acceptance of the idea, President Reagan opposed the idea of UN Security Council members launching the peace negotiations, thereby leading to the final failure of the Reagan Initiative. In 2011, a UN Security Council resolution condemning expansion of Israeli settlements and calling for a resumption of negotiations was defeated by a lone US veto, thereby blocking this relatively mild international pressure on Israel and further undermining America's credibility in the region. While the American veto was viewed as a victory by AIPAC, rightwing Christian fundamentalists, and political neo-conservatives, Palestinians and many mainstream Israeli and Jewish American peace advocates, including pro-Israel, pro-peace JStreet, viewed the veto as unwise and harmful to chances for negotiated peace.

A fifth basic problem has been the pattern of American diplomatic peace initiatives initially coming on strong and then soon losing focus or fading. For more than three decades, Republican and Democratic administrations have failed to act with the kind of creativity and consistent determination in relation to Israeli-Palestinian peace negotiations that President Jimmy Carter demonstrated in achieving peace between Egypt and Israel.

At several times over the last thirty years, these five problematic tendencies in US policy seriously hurt chances for peace. Failed American peace initiatives frustrated Palestinian and Israeli peace advocates, and disappointed majorities on both sides who continue to long for peace and still support a two-state solution. In 2014, during President Barack Obama's second term, America's commitment and determination to help Israelis and Palestinians resolve their decades-old conflict, in the form of a two-state peace agreement was again being tested.

I turn now to the story of founding and building the US Interreligious Committee for Peace (1987–2003) and helping to organize and serving as consultant to the National Interreligious Leadership Initiative for Peace (2003 to the present), both broad-based coalitions of prominent American Jewish, Christian and Muslim religious leaders united in advocating active, fair, and determined US policies for peace in the Middle East. I am convinced if US administrations had been more determined in pursuit of peace and we had been more effective in getting administrations to adopt policies advocated by these interreligious coalitions, Arab-Israeli-Palestinian peace could have been achieved in the intervening years.

8

American Jews, Christians and Muslims: Conflict or Cooperation for Peace?

Carol on a path to becoming a Lutheran pastor; welcoming and caring for our second son; writing a book on missed opportunities for peace; organizing the US Inter-religious Committee *for Peace in the Middle East (USICPME); reaching agreement on a founding statement; arranging and leading interfaith trips to the region that sometimes were emotionally wrenching but helped build relationships for work-ing together; organizing interfaith convocations for peace in Washington DC and other cities; attending the White House signing ceremony of the Israeli-Palestinian Oslo Declaration; people's hopes are raised high, but then they crash hard when the Oslo process ends, without achieving a peace agreement.*

CAROL, JONAH, AND I returned to the United States in spring 1985 after stopovers in England and Ireland where we reported on our extraordinary three years in the Middle East. Leaving the tan, desert environment of Jordan, we particularly relished visiting the green, wet landscape of Ireland just before Easter. In Belfast, Northern Ireland, we were hosted by an Irish Quaker family and gave a talk in their home about the Arab-Israeli conflict. Both Catholics and Protestants seemed frankly relieved to hear about an "in-tractable" conflict different from their own. Thirteen years later, former Senator George J. Mitchell successfully negotiated the Belfast peace agreement resolving the conflict in Northern Ireland.

Our family initially moved back into the shared house in Philadelphia where we were married five years earlier and lived just before moving to Jordan. The experience of being in Jordan for three years and listening to Arab and Israeli views had profound effects on both of us. Following up on interest kindled by a course she had taken be-fore we went to the Middle East, Carol decided to go to Union Theological Seminary in New York, where she started on a five-year path that would lead to ordination and an extraordinary second career as a Lutheran Pastor and leader in the Evangelical Lutheran Church in America. Before leaving Jordan, I decided to write a book about the role of US policy in relation to missed opportunities for peace that we had witnessed. I also planned to explore forming a national interfaith organization to advocate for US policies to help achieve peace. The discipline, appreciation for different views, and patience we learned working for the Quakers in the Middle East would turn out to be invaluable on the new paths Carol and I decided to pursue.

We moved into Union Seminary housing on Riverside Drive in New York City, two blocks from Riverside Church where Dr. King preached his famous sermon against the Vietnam War and directly across the Hudson from West New York, New Jersey. After all my travels and boundary crossings, living across the river from the city where I spent my first nine years, I felt I had come home.

It was a very small seminary apartment. Jonah, who turned four in July, slept in the tiny bedroom while Carol and I slept on a convertible couch in the combination living room, eating area and kitchen. Our tight quarters reminded me of my experience as a child. An inlaid mother of pearl and wood wedding chest and an engraved three-foot-wide copper tray, both bought in Damascus, served as our breakfast counter and coffee table. During the day, I used Jonah's bedroom as an office to write my book on our new Kaypro computer, with a six-inch square screen and a daisy wheel printer.

In March 1986, Carol, who was enjoying her first year of graduate theological studies, discovered she was pregnant. We calculated that Jamie had been conceived while she was immersed in Hebrew language study, which may explain his later intense interest in Judaism and Islam. Fortunately, just before Jamie was born in October, we were able to move into a two bedroom apartment, where Jonah had his own room and Jamie slept in a crib in our bedroom. The apartment's eighth floor windows faced west across the Hudson River, giving us a wonderful view of my old home city, the George Washington Bridge and spectacular sunsets. Jonah started kindergarten at P.S. 75, a really good magnet school on Broadway. We took Jamie to daycare in the mornings and I took care of him while Carol was in classes or at the library.

My hope was to write a book that would look critically at US Middle East policy, in ways that an American supporter of Israel or the Palestinians could appreciate. I believed there was a need for a new effort within American religious communities, drawing on shared core values of our three Abrahamic traditions, to work together advocating for active, fair and firm US leadership for peace in the region. Based on my earlier organizing against the Vietnam War and my experiences and relationships with many Israelis and Arabs, I felt I might have the skills, sensitivities, and set of relationships to organize such an effort.

By spring 1986, I had completed a 200 page draft of *Missed Opportunities for Peace: US Middle East Policy, 1981–86*. I included 300 footnotes, in part to reassure readers and myself that my analysis was not based only on forty notebooks of our personal interviews and experiences, but also could be substantiated in readily accessible mainstream news sources. I sent the draft off to the AFSC for final editing and a forward. I also submitted it to the College of Social Studies at Wesleyan University as the senior thesis required for my Bachelor of Arts degree. Finally, at forty-four, I was going to graduate from college. I also sought feedback on the book from several knowledgeable leaders representing different experiences and perspectives. I received responses from William Quandt, national security advisor to President Carter during the Egyptian-Israeli peace process and editor of *The Middle East: Ten Years After Camp David*; Rabbi Arthur Hertzberg, vice president of the World Jewish Congress; Dr. Rashid Khalidi, Palestinian American Professor of History; Rita Hauser, international lawyer and member of the board of the Rand Corporation; Reverend W. Sterling Cary, African American minister in the United Church of Christ; and Reverend J. Bryan Hehir, from the US Conference of Catholic Bishops. Their positive responses encouraged me to push ahead with the idea of organizing a national interfaith organization for peace in the Middle East. Bryan Hehir wrote,

> A just peace in the Middle East is a regional and global necessity. It will require the best efforts of political leadership . . . and the intelligent support of religious leadership in many places . . . particularly in the United States. Ronald Young's book makes a cogent case for the role of religious communities and institutions in pursuit of a just peace.

What Bryan Hehir wrote in 1986 remains true today.

US Interreligious Committee for Peace in the Middle East

Between 1985 and 1987 I met with scores of national and local American Jewish, Christian and Muslim religious leaders. Given the historical and moral complexity of the Arab-Israeli-Palestinian conflict, and the deep community ties and emotional volatility among supporters of each side, I understood that development of an interfaith effort would need to proceed carefully and slowly. Rather than seeking leaders who might already agree, I knew that I had to involve prominent, highly respected national leaders from the three Abrahamic communities to assure the viability and sustainability of the project. I want to mention and honor several religious leaders who played key early roles in what became the US Interreligious Committee for Peace in the Middle East (USICPME). In each of the communities, unfortunately, there were, and continue to be, leaders whose narrowly partisan perspectives pull our communities apart and tend to generate conflict rather than cooperation. It was clear to me that this initiative required a more balanced, nuanced, and reconciliatory approach.

Rabbi Arthur Hertzberg was one of the first prominent Jewish leaders to support my idea. During the time Carol and I lived in Amman, he and his wife, Phyllis, lived part of the year in Jerusalem, where I made an appointment to visit him. As part of our

AFSC orientation in 1982, we had read *The Zionist Idea*, edited by Arthur, and found it immensely helpful in analyzing the deep cultural, historical and religious roots, and diverse tendencies within Jewish nationalism. Arthur was born in Poland, and many of his relatives perished in the Holocaust. He was raised in Baltimore, Maryland where his father was an Orthodox rabbi, though Arthur chose to be ordained in the Conservative movement. He was a highly respected Talmudic scholar, author of several important books, and a major leader in the worldwide Jewish community.

From shortly after the 1967 war, Arthur was concerned over Israel's treatment of the Palestinians and publicly critical of the construction of Jewish settlements in the captured territories. In 1968 he called for the creation of an independent Palestinian state in the West Bank and Gaza alongside Israel. Over the next two decades, he clashed publicly with several Israeli leaders, including both Golda Meir and Menachem Begin, as well as with many prominent American Jewish leaders. Arthur's profoundly moral and deeply Jewish criticism of Israeli policies, as well as his oversized ego is reflected forcefully in this passage from his autobiography, *A Jew in America.*

> I was largely in opposition to the dominant policies. I found myself restating this view year by year, as repeated attempts were made to silence me in Jerusalem and by its lackeys in New York and Washington. I insisted that we in the Diaspora could represent the best interest of the Jews worldwide — never mind the political and moral foolishness that governments in power might be proclaiming . . . I also had no fear that I was committing treason by denouncing what I knew was wrong and foolish, and I laughed off the label "maverick."[1]

As a very articulate and tough dissenter from mainstream American Jewish views about the Israeli-Palestinian conflict, Arthur was also an ardent Zionist who profoundly loved Israel, the Jewish people and Jewish traditions. He was equally tough in challenging anti-Jewish prejudice wherever and whenever it arose. In 1991, prior to the Madrid peace conference, President George H.W. Bush and Secretary of State James Baker announced that, unless Prime Minister Shamir agreed to halt expansion of Jewish settlements, they would oppose loan guarantees requested by Israel to help Jews emigrating from Russia. A USICPME delegation, including Hertzberg, was scheduled to meet with the deputy secretary of state to express support for the administration's position. At his press conference the day before our meeting, President Bush reacted angrily to reports about an AIPAC lobbying effort urging Congress to provide the loan guarantees without conditions. In the course of his remarks the President said, "I heard today that there were something like a thousand (Jewish) lobbyists on the hill working the other side of the question. We've got one lonely little guy down here doing it." Bush's characterization of himself—president of the most powerful country in the world—as "one lonely little guy" facing a thousand Jewish

---

1. Hertzberg, *A Jew in America*, 454.

lobbyists, evoked old negative Jewish stereotypes. It generated a wave of anxiety in the Jewish community, and was publicly denounced by many prominent Jewish leaders. What the president said, and the way he said it, caused many rabbis who otherwise supported putting pressure on Israel to remain silent.

The next day as our USICPME delegation gathered in the lobby of the State Department, Rabbi Hertzberg asked our delegation to allow him a few minutes at the beginning of the meeting to explain to the deputy secretary how the president's choice of language and his tone echoed historic anti-Semitic stereotypes about Jews controlling the country, and how that took a terrible toll on Jewish support for the administration's laudable stance. While Christian and Muslim members of our delegation understood Hertzberg's view, I don't think they would have addressed the president's implicitly anti-Jewish rhetoric at all, and certainly not as eloquently and effectively as Hertzberg. Rabbi Hertzberg served as the first Jewish national chairperson and then as honorary co-chair of USICPME, providing me with steady personal support and wise political counsel until his death in 2006.

Dawud Ahmed Assad, a Palestinian American Muslim and executive director of the Council of Mosques USA, served as our Muslim national co-chair for many years. I was introduced to him at a dinner in New York City in 1986 by Moisul Matin, an Indian Muslim American who appreciated the imperative of involving Palestinian Americans in this interreligious peace effort. I went to meet with Dawud a few days later. After I described the project and invited him to help us, Dawud said to me:

> I will do this Ron, even though it will be very hard for me. You don't know that I come from the village of Deir Yassin in Palestine. I was sixteen years old in 1948, living with my family, when Begin's forces came into our village and carried out a massacre. Several members of my family were killed that day. I escaped with my mother and we went to live in Jordan.

Dawud's story made me feel utterly presumptuous as a white American Christian asking him to work with Jews for peace. Seeing my discomfort, Dawud came around his desk, put his hand on my shoulder and said, "It's alright, Ron; I am a Muslim and I know that it's my Islamic duty to work with Christians and Jews for peace between Palestinians and Israelis." In the months leading up to the founding meeting of our committee, Dawud provided me with essential advice and support for enlisting many other American Muslim leaders in this effort.

In September 1993, we were together at the White House for the Oslo Declaration signing ceremony. A few days later Dawud attended a celebration of the Declaration in New York City sponsored by the National Conference of Christians and Jews. Dawud told me how, after dinner, an Orthodox American rabbi came up to him with tears in his eyes. Having heard Dawud introduced as a Palestinian survivor of the Deir Yassin massacre, the rabbi confessed that, as an eighteen-year-old in 1948, he had personally participated in the attack on Dawud's village. The two men embraced and then, both crying, pledged to work together for peace. Several times over the next twenty-five years I saw how Dawud's memories of Deir Yassin continued to haunt him, but he remained faithful to his conviction that core Islamic teachings commanded him to engage in interfaith work for peace.

Several Christian leaders played important roles in formation of USICPME. Reverend Dr. Joan Brown Campbell, general secretary of the National Council of Churches of Christ (NCCC), and Dr. Charles Kimball, director of the Council's Middle East Office, were very helpful in reaching out to enlist endorsements from major Protestant and Christian Orthodox church leaders.

Charles Kimball had a lot of experience in the Middle East. He knew the major Palestinian and Arab Christian leaders personally, and was responsible for several projects supporting the Palestinians. At the same time, he believed strongly and engaged sensitively in interfaith cooperation with Jews and Muslims. In 1991, Charles wrote *Striving Together: A Way Forward in Christian-Muslim Relations,* and in 2002, he wrote *When Religion Becomes Evil*, examining the relationship of religion and violence. While Charles served as an active member of our executive committee, Joan Campbell served as the Christian national co-chair of USICPME for several years. After leaving the National Council of Churches and becoming director of the religion department at the Chautauqua Institution, Joan invited me to give a major morning lecture and twice serve as the chaplain for a week. Several years later, Joan told me that the recording of my morning lecture, "Religion: Source of Violence or Source of Peace?" continued to be one of the most popular in Chautauqua's audio library.

Reverend J. Bryan Hehir, a senior staff with the US Conference of Catholic Bishops, played a key role in getting early endorsements from prominent Roman Catholic leaders, including Archbishops Bernardin, May, Mahoney, and Weakland. Participation by Roman Catholic leadership was especially important because the Catholic Church was perceived by American Jewish leaders as often more sensitive than some Protestant leaders when they addressed the Arab-Israeli conflict. The hierarchal structure of the Catholic Church assured that any statements about the conflict were very carefully vetted for possible effects on interfaith relations. Especially after the 1967 war, some statements by more loosely structured Protestant denominations were perceived by American Jewish leaders, sometimes fairly and sometimes unfairly, as insensitive toward Israel. Several of the Catholic leaders who endorsed the USICPME were both very knowledgeable about the history of the Arab-Israeli conflict and had long histories of positive engagement with American Jewish leadership.

At our founding meeting in June 1987, two Roman Catholic leaders made important specific contributions. Fr. John Pawlikowski, OSM, professor of ethics at the Catholic Theological Union, gave an inspired, nuanced opening lecture on the complexities of addressing the Arab-Israeli-Palestinian conflict in an interfaith context. Dr. Eugene Fisher, who spent many years working on Catholic-Jewish relations for the US Conference of Catholic Bishops, made the important suggestion relative to the name of our committee that the "I" in USICPME should stand for *interreligious* instead of interfaith as I originally had proposed. Gene explained, "Since all three of our communities trace our roots to Abraham, in a sense, we share a common faith—the faith of Abraham—but we come from different religious traditions." To my surprise, all fifty leaders readily agreed with Fisher's suggestion; thus, the committee became known as the US *Interreligious* Committee for Peace in the Middle East.

In addition to Rabbi Arthur Hertzberg, major American Jewish religious leaders who endorsed USICPME in 1987 included Reform leaders Albert Vorspan, senior vice president of the Union of American Hebrew Congregations, and Rabbi Eugene Lipman, president of the Central Conference of American Rabbis; Rabbi Wolfe Kelman, executive vice president of the Conservative movement's Rabbinical Assembly; and Rabbi Mordechai E. Liebling, executive director of the Jewish Reconstructionist Federation, as well as scores of congregational rabbis. While we were not able to attract leaders of national Orthodox Jewish organizations, Rabbi Joseph Ehrenkranz, a prominent modern orthodox rabbi and executive director of the Center for Christian-Jewish Understanding at Sacred Heart University in Connecticut, participated in our interfaith trip to the Middle East in 1992 and then for several years played an active role in the committee's leadership.

One of the most challenging and interesting parts of organizing the Committee was getting to know leaders in the American Muslim community. Dawud Assad introduced me to Imam Warithuddin Mohammed, formerly Wallace Deen Mohammed and son of Elijah Mohammed, leader of the Nation of Islam. After the assassination of Malcolm X, Warithuddin became the most prominent and popular African American orthodox Muslim leader. We got the endorsement of Dr. Fazlur Rahman, professor at the University of Chicago and author of *Islam*, the highly respected and widely read, single volume introduction to the Islamic religion. In Los Angeles, I was introduced to Maher and Hassan Hathout, revered Egyptian American Muslim community leaders. In Philadelphia, I met Dr. Mahmoud Ayoub. Born in Southern Lebanon and blind from birth, Dr. Ayoub is an acclaimed scholar who has written several books on Islam and interreligious relations.

In fall 1987, as part of my effort to generate local interreligious cooperation, I arranged for Dr. Mahmoud Ayoub and Rabbi Eugene Lipman to speak at a program co-sponsored by the Islamic Center of Kansas City and Congregation B'nai Jehudah, the largest Reform synagogue in the city. The two speakers surprised and inspired a mixed audience of Jewish and Palestinian Americans with their warm personal interaction and converging visions for Israeli-Palestinian peace. I have no doubt that it was the first event at the synagogue that was attended by a dozen middle-aged Palestinian American men wearing black and white checkered keffiyehs, like the one worn by Yasser Arafat.

The willingness of highly respected national and local religious leaders to endorse this effort reflected their understanding that working together for peace is a core imperative of their religious traditions. The USICPME would not have gotten off the ground in 1987 and certainly would not have been sustainable without their support. Of course, over the years, some leaders withdrew because of the pressures of other commitments; others may have left out of frustration with our practice of always seeking consensus on advocacy positions and/or with our inability to be more successful in getting policymakers to adopt the policies we advocated.

In the 1980s, cooperation for peace between leaders of communities that had strong bonds with Israel or the Palestinians was rare or nonexistent. Even in cities where there was a history of interfaith cooperation, the prevailing pattern was—and largely still is—that interfaith organizations avoid dealing with the Arab-Israeli conflict out of fear that tensions between those communities would jeopardize cooperation on other issues. Thus, it was encouraging and somewhat surprising how many prominent religious leaders agreed to become involved in forming the USICPME. They certainly knew that seeking agreement on specific advocacy positions would not be easy, but they agreed to work together because, like Dawud Assad, they believed that their traditions commanded them to do it. Reflecting the idea found in the book of Zechariah in the Hebrew Bible, they are prisoners of hope. When I was preparing one of our first publicity brochures and asked board members for brief quotations, one rabbi sent me a note that simply read, "God commands peace; therefore peace is possible!" That spirit of hope and determination permeated our work and helped to sustain us through episodes of bitter, violent conflict on the ground in the Middle East.

After two years of exploration and preparation, in June 1987, I gathered fifty American Jewish, Christian and Muslim religious leaders at the Crystal City Marriott Hotel in Alexandria, Virginia, for the unpublicized founding meeting of the USICPME. Following my brief remarks about the purpose of the meeting, the opening session included talks by Samih K. Staitieh, Palestinian American Muslim businessman from Kansas City; and Arnold Jacob Wolf, a reform rabbi from Chicago. Everyone very soon understood that, while the idea for the committee might be a matter of clear moral and religious principle, the actual experience of working together would be much more complicated and challenging. It would require a lot of patient listening and careful crafting of consensus statements, as well as dedicated, faithful determination.

In his opening remarks, Samih Staitieh said, "As a Palestinian American Muslim, I want to be very clear and honest that I've always had the deepest respect and love for Judaism, but that I also have been bitterly opposed to Zionism." In his opening statement, Rabbi Wolf looked directly at Samih and said, "I very much want to work with Samih Staitieh for peace, but I, too, want to be honest. The left side of my heart is Judaism and the right side of my heart is Zionism; and I can't take my heart apart for Samih or anyone else." Although this confrontation made everyone nervous, it was encouraging that immediately after their talks, rather than escaping to their respective hotel rooms, Arnie and Samih headed straight toward each other. Surrounded by a small circle of conference participants, the two men engaged in intense dialogue. I wondered several times during that first conference whether my vision was really workable. Could the leaders agree on enough basic principles and practical advocacy positions to make working together worthwhile?

Following two days of deliberations, including dozens of late night and early morning intense one-on-one conversations, the fifty leaders were able to reach consensus on a founding statement entitled simply, *A Time for Peace.* Here are excerpts:

A TIME FOR PEACE (excerpts)

Founding Statement of the US Interreligious Committee
for Peace in the Middle East
June 1987

We are Jews, Christians and Muslims who believe working for peace in the Middle East is a moral imperative of our common Abrahamic faith.

We call upon our own US government . . . to promote negotiations for a just peace based on the following:

Israel's right to secure borders and peace with her neighbors, as an expression of the Jewish people's right of self-determination . . . UN Security Council Resolution 242 provides an agreed formula to achieve security and peace for all states in the area in exchange for withdrawal from territories occupied in 1967.

The Palestinian people's right of self-determination . . . Evidence that Palestinians are willing to exercise their right of self-determination in the West Bank and Gaza alongside Israel encourages prospects for peace.

Jerusalem is of vital significance to Israelis and Palestinians, and to Jews, Christians and Muslims worldwide. **We believe negotiations, rather than unilateral action, can help assure that Jerusalem will be a city of peace.**

A Time for Peace reflected the consensus that interreligious work for peace is imperative, not optional, and that common advocacy positions must and can be developed. While obviously dialogue and developing relationships would be essential to the Committee's work, we were not undertaking this effort simply to foster communication. From its founding, the USICPME was committed to advocating for US policies that we believed were essential for achieving peace. We were united in principled support for both the Jewish people's and the Palestinian people's rights of national self-determination, for a two-state solution, and for negotiating a way to share the holy city of Jerusalem. Throughout the history of the USICPME, we consistently worked to reach agreement on the highest common denominator advocacy positions. Six years before the Oslo Declaration, *A Time for Peace,* was a principled, realistic and remarkably forward-looking document.

Aware that *A Time for Peace* would also likely be controversial in their communities, the fifty participants at the June conference set a goal of enlisting endorsements for it by 500 national and local religious leaders before going public with the statement. We made tentative plans to sponsor a national press conference and public meeting in Washington in January 1988, six months from the founding meeting, to publicly announce formation of the US Interreligious Committee for Peace.

We knew we had to be particularly sensitive not to get so many Christian leaders involved that Jewish and Muslim leaders would feel overwhelmed. Since we couldn't possibly include all the Protestant denominations, we gave priority to those that had constituencies and/or long-standing involvement in the Middle East. Shortly after the founding meeting, I went to Atlanta to meet with former President Jimmy Carter. I explained the purpose of USICPME and showed him the founding statement and initial list of endorsers. Carter looked troubled. He said, "Why Ron, you left out the most important religion of all." Then, after a pause, smiling he continued, "Of course, I mean Southern Baptists." The former president expressed strong support for our work and more than once wrote letters of introduction to Arab and Israeli heads of state, and to PLO Chairman Arafat seeking meetings on behalf of delegations I arranged to take to the Middle East.

Formation of the USICPME in 1987 was also inspired by significant changes in the attitudes of people in the Middle East. Ten years earlier, when President Sadat offered to go to Jerusalem and announced that Egypt was prepared to negotiate peace with Israel, he broke out of the rigid Arab consensus of hostility toward Israel and he broke through the prevailing Israeli fear of Arabs. Despite Sadat's assassination, the treaty between Egypt and Israel had already held for nearly a decade, creating one significant building block for Arab-Israeli peace, although the core Israeli-Palestinian conflict had yet to be seriously addressed. Based on my three-year experience in the region, I knew that Sadat's decision, though universally denounced by Arab governments and the PLO, was consistent with privately held views of a growing number of Arab leaders. On the Israeli side, Sadat's initiative had led a group of IDF reservist to form *Shalom Achshav* (Peace Now) and urge Prime Minister Begin to respond positively to Sadat. They, in turn, would seek to build popular Israeli support for peace with the Palestinians. Indeed, by the mid-1980s, some Israeli Peace Now leaders and PLO leaders were meeting face to face to discuss the possibility of a two-state solution. Carol and I were privileged to have been involved in some of their early contacts and exchanges.

A month before the scheduled launch of USICPME, in December 1987, the first Palestinian intifada erupted in Gaza and the West Bank. It demonstrated that, despite Israel's overwhelming military power, Palestinian resistance to occupation and determination to achieve an independent state were growing stronger. During 1988, as we were getting the committee off the ground, there were behind-the-scenes efforts to get the PLO to reject terrorism and show more flexibility in relation to Israel. In November, the PLO took the historic step of officially declaring their acceptance of a Palestinian state based on the 1947 United Nations partition plan, and their support for negotiations with Israel based on Security Council resolutions 242 and 338. In a December statement, Yasser Arafat renounced terrorism and promised Palestinian recognition of Israel. In response, the United States agreed to talk with the PLO.

These developments created a context that made organizing the USICPME all the more important and timely. In January 1988, our press conference coincided with a visit to Washington by President Mubarak of Egypt and Hanna Siniora, Editor of *Al Fajr* (the Dawn), a Palestinian newspaper in Jerusalem. As a result, the USICPME launch was reported by David Shipler with a photograph on page three of the *New York Times*. Major Associated Press and United Press International wire service stories were carried in scores of newspapers across the country. In addition to focusing on our founding statement, the articles featured names of some of the 500 Jewish, Christian and Muslim leaders who endorsed *A Time for Peace*.

Following the press conference, 300 people gathered in an auditorium at the National Cathedral in Washington. I served as moderator for a conference that included presentations by an Egyptian, three Palestinians and two Israelis, all of whom Carol and I had come to know personally during our time in the Middle East. They included: Ambassador Tahseen Bashir, who had been President Sadat's senior advisor at Camp David; Hannah Siniora, Editor of *Al Fajr*; Fayez Abu Rahme, a prominent Palestinian lawyer from Gaza; Rami Khouri, former editor of the *Jordan Times*; Dr. Moshe Maoz, Israeli expert on Syria; and Mordechai BarOn, former chief of staff for General Moshe Dayan and one of the founders of Peace Now. An important measure of the event's success and of the changing context was how many attendees expressed surprise that such a gathering could take place and directly address central issues in the conflict, without generating the usual narrowly partisan and emotionally rancorous debate.

Another sign that the USICPME represented responsible, mainstream views was the willingness of former American ambassadors and senior State Department officials to participate. They are typically hesitant to endorse or join any non-governmental initiatives concerned with issues that they addressed in their official capacities. However, Alfred (Roy) Atherton, Edward P. Djerejian, Samuel W. Lewis, Richard W. Murphy, Robert Pelletreau, Robert Oakley, William B. Quandt, and Harold H. Saunders all gave USICPME constructive support.

Similarly, and despite the risks of controversy in their respective communities, prominent leaders of Arab American and Jewish American national organizations also became involved, including Michael Berenbaum, David Cohen, Rita Hauser, Khalil Jahshan, Philip M. Klutznick, Jacqueline Levine, Hamzi K. Moghrabi, Albert Mokhiber, Sulayman S. Nyang, Henry Siegman, Daniel Thurz, Jacqueline Wexler, and James J. Zogby. The USICPME continued to play a unique and important role in advocating active, determined US policies for peace until 2003, when it was succeeded by the National Interreligious Leadership Initiative for Peace in the Middle East, known as NILI.

Interfaith Trips to the Middle East

Based on my experiences in the region, I decided to arrange interfaith trips to the Middle East as a project of USICPME. Most Americans who visited the Middle East went on holy land sightseeing tours, or traveled with like-minded people from their own community, with schedules that reinforced their prior biases. I knew it would be psychologically and politically challenging for a religiously diverse delegation to travel together to visit Israel, the West Bank and Gaza, Egypt, Jordan and Syria, and meet people with very different experiences and conflicting points of view. However, knowing how meeting and listening to people on different sides had affected Carol and me, I was confident that such trips would creatively unsettle participants' certainties about the conflict, help them develop more complex and nuanced understandings, and hopefully encourage them to work together for peace when they returned. I sometimes said simply that my twin goals for the trips were that participants would come back a little less certain about their views of the conflict and a little more hopeful that peace was possible. Between 1985 and 1998, I led ten trips which I believe accomplished those goals and a lot more. Many participants provided core leadership and support for the USICPME, both nationally and in a number of American cities.

Two important and inspiring examples of successful local efforts occurred in Portland, Oregon and Syracuse, New York, where determined, sensitive community leaders played key roles. In Portland, Rev. Rodney Page, director of Ecumenical Ministries of Oregon, Joshua Stampfer, senior rabbi of Neveh Shalom, the large Conservative congregation, and Frank Afranji, a Palestinian American Muslim, worked together to form a local committee. Coincidently, my first meeting with them took place in a generously Buddhist-themed Chinese restaurant. Together, we arranged an interfaith trip to the region, sponsored local programs, including a few where I spoke, and organized an annual interfaith caravan for Mideast Peace that traveled to a local church, mosque and synagogue in Portland on New Year's Day.

In Syracuse, the key leaders were Ahmad El Hindi, a successful local Palestinian American businessman, and Richard (Red) D. Schwartz, professor of law and sociology at Syracuse University. A few years before formation of the USICPME, Ahmad and Red had organized a dialogue group that reached consensus on support for a negotiated two-state solution. They and others from Syracuse participated in one of my trips to the region. The Syracuse group, known as SAMED (Syracuse Area Middle East Dialgoue) played an important role in Upstate New York and served as a model for similar efforts in other cities. Over several years, both Red and Ahmad did fundraising and served as active members of USICPME's national board. Their deep personal commitments to working together for peace were, and still are, inspirational.

One big problem with my work during these years was that I did it all on a shoestring of funding. Participants paid their own travel costs for the trips, plus a supplement to cover my expenses and sometimes an honorarium. In all my years at the FOR and AFSC, I had never done substantial fundraising and I didn't know any obvious sources to tap for support. Interreligious work for Mideast peace did not seem to be a priority for any major funding source that I was able to identify. Indeed, most funders seemed to concentrate on supporting efforts in their particular community. Our work survived on small grants from national religious organizations, generous personal contributions from several trip participants like Red Schwartz and Ahmad el Hindi, and contributions of thirty-five dollars a year from many of the approximately 2,000 individual supporters across the country. As there were times when I was not able to take a regular salary, Carol's support on her pastor's salary was crucial. Doing this work alone, sometimes with the help of a part time secretary or poorly paid student intern, meant that important follow up work, including nurturing fledgling local interfaith organizing efforts often was neglected. I have no doubt that interreligious work for peace could have been substantially more effective, if I had been able to tap larger sources of funding. Nevertheless, what we did accomplish was quite significant.

One of my fundraising experiences illustrates my lack of luck. Fr. Ted Hesburgh, CSC, president of Notre Dame University and member of our board, told me he had once made a speech in California about developing a center at Notre Dame to work for peaceful resolution of international conflicts. An elderly woman came up to him afterwards, said how much she appreciated his vision, and handed him a note promising a very large contribution (I believe $1,000,000) to support what became the Kroc Institute for International Peace Studies. A year after hearing Hesburgh's story, an elderly woman came up to me after a talk I gave and asked if she could speak privately with me. Of course, I agreed. Taking me aside, she asked me to put my foot up on the desk where she could see it. I was puzzled but complied. Then, she said, "Yes, I thought so, you have very large feet just like my husband. He died and I have several pairs of his shoes I would like to send to you." I thanked her and gave her my address. Two weeks later, two pairs of shoes arrived.

On several of our trips participants had dramatic encounters which caused them to rethink simplistic, long-held views about the conflict. Jewish, Christian and Muslim participants, with bonds to different sides in the conflict, travelling together and interacting for days with one another challenged stereotypes and developed personal relationships. Even taking into account the self-selection and good intentions of people who were willing to engage in these issues, the trips not only changed views; they were also often psychologically and emotionally wrenching.

In1985, after very good visits in Israel, the West Bank, Gaza, and Egypt, our interfaith group traveled to Amman, where we were invited to the home of Abu Jihad to meet Hani al Hassan who was visiting from Kuwait. Both were senior leaders of the PLO and close colleagues of Chairman Arafat. Before talking politics, Abu Jihad served us Kanafi, a famous, very rich Palestinian dessert. Following brief remarks by Hani al Hassan, members of our delegation asked tough questions about Palestinian violence and the PLO's stance on accepting Israel's existence. The PLO leaders explained that violence arose out of the daily oppression that Palestinians experienced under Israeli occupation and, while not explicitly acknowledging the legitimacy of Israel, both men spoke positively about the idea of a two-state solution.

Rabbi Leonard Beerman, an outspoken advocate for justice and peace who supported a two-state solution, was moved by what he heard. He said he looked forward to reporting the PLO leaders' views to members of Leo Baeck Temple, his large Reform congregation in Los Angeles. Then, in a relaxed tone he asked Hani al Hassan, "Looking ahead, say fifty years, how do you view the relationship between a Palestinian state and Israel?" Hani responded in a similarly casual tone, "Well, fifty years from now, I don't see Israel existing the way it does today." The response was obviously ambiguous. Clearly upset, Leonard replied: "Ouch! I feel as if I've just been punched in the gut." He assumed Hani's response probably meant that in the long run he supported a one-state solution, in which, once again, Jews would be a minority.

Rev. George Regas, rector of All Saints Episcopal Church in Pasadena, a very close friend and longtime social action partner with Rabbi Beerman, expressed surprise at Leonard's anxious response. Beerman turned to his friend and said tensely, "George, if you don't understand my reaction, you don't understand much about me." Returning to our hotel after the meeting, Leonard and George, and most of the delegation, including Rev. William Sloane Coffin Jr., minister of Riverside Church in New York City, and Stephen Cary, chairman of the AFSC, stayed up on the hotel's veranda until three in the morning, trying to sort out what they had heard and why they responded so differently to what Hani al Hassan had said. They had all been encouraged by much of what they heard from the two PLO leaders, but the different ways they heard Hani al Hassan's remark about the future reflected deep, possibly unbridgeable differences in experience and perception between Jews and non-Jews.

This incident reflected a tension at the core of the conflict that continues today, even among those who share a principled moral commitment to working for peace. While over the years, a substantial majority of Palestinians have accepted the idea of a two-state solution, many would prefer a single democratic state between the Jordan River and the Mediterranean in which Palestinians and Jews would live together as citizens with equal rights. Most American Christians (and probably most American Muslims) view either a two-state or one-state solution as morally acceptable. Most tend to view Jews as a religious group, rather than the way Jews view themselves, as a people, like the Danes or the Irish. Given Jews' perception of themselves as a people, the persecution of the Jews over centuries, the positive Zionist vision of developing a Jewish state, and the experience of the Holocaust only seventy years ago, for most Jews, preserving the Jewish majority and Jewish character of Israel is essential and basically non-negotiable. Anything that seems to threaten the legitimacy of Israel as a majority Jewish state understandably evokes deep fears and defensiveness. Inter-religious cooperation for peace involves really listening and understanding each other, but the gap in experience and perception between Jews and non-Jews is real and can easily erupt as a source of serious tensions between individuals and our communities.

On some trips, people experienced what I call the bone-deep connections that both Palestinians and Jews feel for the land and how this affects the conflict. Meeting with several older Palestinian women in Jerusalem, including the sister of Dr. Ha-nah Nasser, the president of Bir Zeit University, members of one interfaith delegation were deeply moved, but also discouraged by the Palestinian women's steadfast, even fierce, emotional attachment to properties their families had lost in 1948. The women showed us old, rusted keys from their family homes in areas that forty years ago had become part of Israel. Coming away from that meeting, the idea of these Palestin-ian women accepting Israel seemed impossible. On another visit, I heard several of these same women speak candidly about the very hard compromises people on both sides, including themselves, would have to make to achieve a durable two-state peace agreement. However, in the meeting with our delegation, the women had passionately insisted that those family properties lost in 1948 would always belong to them. Their connections and rights to their parents' and grandparents' properties felt bone-deep and inalienable. Deep connections to the whole land and, at the same time, willing-ness to accept very difficult compromises, are at the core of the conflict and the brave possibility for peace.

On another occasion, the bone-deep connection that Jews feel to the land was revealed in the physical effects experienced by a rabbi who met PLO Chairman Yasser Arafat. At the conclusion of a late night meeting in Amman in which many tough is-sues were discussed, Arafat singled out Rabbi Eugene Mihaly, academic vice president of Hebrew Union College in Cincinnati. Remarking that that the two of them shared a certain physical resemblance, Arafat said smiling, "We must be cousins." Gene did his best to respond politely, if a bit nervously, saying he was sure that he was much older than Arafat and so, "I must be your uncle." Arafat laughed and embraced the reluctant rabbi. A few days later, when Gene returned to his summer home in Michigan, he ex-perienced terrible back pain and could hardly get up from his bed. Unable to find any physical explanation, his doctor asked him, "Rabbi, have you had any recent traumatic experiences?" Gene responded, "Well, a week ago, I was hugged by Yasser Arafat." The doctor laughed and said, "If you had told me that earlier, I could have saved you a lot of money." Rabbi Mihaly's extraordinary back pain surely indicated how deeply

Arafat's embodiment of Palestinian claims threatened his bone-deep Jewish connection to the same land.

Jewish nationalism (Zionism) and Palestinian nationalism are not simply ideas or theories. They reflect profoundly powerful attachments and commitments that these two peoples with different but intertwined histories feel to the same small land. Geography and history have joined Jews and Palestinians at the hip. Given their bone-deep attachments and the suffering both peoples have experienced, it is not surprising that appreciating the other's narrative is very difficult or impossible. When Americans, who say we are working for peace, are unable or unwilling to understand and empathize with both narratives the outcome is often passionately partisan advocacy that replays and reinforces the conflict.

On some trips, interfaith delegations were able to experience difficult back-to-back encounters with Jewish and Palestinian narratives in ways that deepened participants' understanding and sympathy for both sides. At other times, encountering one side's narrative or people's suffering was so compelling and disturbing that it made it almost impossible to comprehend the other side's perspective. Often our schedule called for us to visit Yad Vashem, Memorial to Victims of the Holocaust, one day and Palestinian refugee camps in Gaza the next. That presented a very hard psychological and emotional challenge for participants. Our interfaith delegations were blessed on several trips by gracious, inspired help from our Israeli and Palestinian guides.

Several delegations benefitted enormously from being guided through Yad Vashem by Shalmi BaMor, the education director, who was deeply committed to Arab-Israeli peace. Some in our delegations worried or were even suspicious that revisiting the history of the Holocaust would evoke such strong sympathy that it might have the effect of softening or neutralizing people's empathy for what Palestinians were suffering under Israeli occupation. In guiding us through the memorial, Shalmi presented a more complex and sensitive picture, explaining how since the founding of modern Israel, the Holocaust and the issue of Jewish resistance or lack of resistance to the Nazis was interpreted very differently at different times, depending on the current conflict and whether Israelis were feeling more or less confident or besieged. He never suggested that the Holocaust could be used to explain or excuse the suffering Israel caused to Palestinians in 1948 or after the 1967 war in the occupied West Bank and Gaza He spoke sympathetically about Palestinian suffering, their right of national self-determination, and the urgent need for a negotiated two-state agreement. On the Avenue of the Righteous commemorating gentiles who saved Jews during the Holocaust, Shalmi told us about his personal project of wanting to add memorials to honor Arab Muslims in North Africa who had saved Jews during the Nazi occupation. He believed that resolving the Israeli-Palestinian conflict would free Jews emotionally to want to know about these Arab Muslim heroes and would encourage Arabs to want to provide the information.

At Yad Vashem, I had the extraordinary privilege of introducing Shalmi to Abdelwahab (Heba) Hechiche, professor at the University of South Florida and member of the USICPME board of directors. Heba was born and raised in Tunisia. During the Nazi occupation of Tunis, his mother hid Jews in their basement and in a nearby building belonging to the Red Cross. While teaching in Paris in the 1960s, Heba organized secret meetings between Arab and Israeli students. He and Shalmi embraced, and Heba promised to arrange for Shalmi to visit to Tunisia to pursue his idea of adding memorials to Tunisian Arab Muslims who saved Jews during the Nazi occupation.

After visiting Yad Vashem, we often went next to Gaza, where we were fortunate to be guided by Mary Khass, a courageous advocate for women's and children's rights. Mary knew Palestinian suffering in Gaza firsthand and she believed deeply in nonviolence and in reaching out to Israelis for peace and reconciliation. It was always inspiring and challenging to visit Gaza and meet Mary who somehow managed to be morally and emotionally sensitive to both peoples' narratives. Still, hearing the Palestinian narrative of the *Nahkba*—their catastrophic expulsion during the 1948 war—and witnessing their suffering under military occupation one day after hearing the Jewish narrative of the Holocaust, was a challenge for all of us. I encouraged people to try hard not to compare or weigh one side's narrative or suffering against the other, but to listen deeply to what they were learning in each situation. Having Shalmi BarMor and Mary Khass as our guides helped us a lot, but it wasn't always sufficient.

Despite good intentions and careful planning, not all our experiences were positive. On one trip, we spent a day in Gaza where we heard numerous stories of Palestinian teens and children who threw stones at Israeli jeeps being chased and beaten by soldiers. The next day we were scheduled to meet with leaders of the Israel Council for Peace and Security, composed of retired, high ranking Israeli military officers who were united in publicly advocating Israeli withdrawal from the occupied territories, creation of a Palestinian state and an undivided, shared Jerusalem. Unfortunately, members of our delegation were still so upset by their previous day's experiences in Gaza that they angrily confronted the two retired Israeli generals, as if they had personally carried out the beatings of the Palestinian kids. There was very little genuine listening. By the end of the meeting, everyone was angry, exhausted, and very frustrated.

Sometimes, an American found an Arab or an Israeli with whom there was an unlikely personal connection in the past. On his second trip with us, Rabbi Leonard Beerman met Peter Salah, retired Jordanian deputy minister of information. As the conversation turned informal, Leonard told about being a young rabbinic student in 1948, studying with Martin Buber in Jerusalem. When the newly declared state of Israel was attacked by the armies of surrounding Arab states, Leonard signed up to fight and was sent to a post near the wall of the Old City in Jerusalem. Peter Salah told how as a young soldier in the Jordanian Army, he was stationed on top of the wall. As they shared the details of where they were positioned and where they aimed their guns, Leonard and Peter realized that they had probably been aiming at each other. They laughed heartedly, shook hands, and each thanked the other for being a poor marksman.

In 1996, as our delegation was meeting with Mordechai BarOn, a founder of Peace Now, Ahmad el-Hindi, a Palestinian American Muslim businessman who helped form and lead the USICPME local group in Syracuse, introduced himself and said he grew up in a Palestinian village. Morela asked the name of Ahmed's village. Ahmad replied that his village was very small and didn't even exist anymore, so he was sure Morela wouldn't know it. BarOn persisted and Ahmad responded, saying, "The name of my village was Yazour." Hearing the name, Morela dropped his head into his hands. When he looked up, tears were running down his cheeks. "What's wrong?" Ahmad asked anxiously, "Are you alright?" Morela stared at him and said, "Ahmad, I was part of a small Haganah military unit in 1948 that captured your village."

We also had extraordinary experiences in Egypt, Jordan and Syria. In Damascus, Tarek Shallah, a well-connected friend and successful businessman, hosted us for dinner with his counterparts and government officials. With my help, he developed a telephone and email connection with a successful Jewish travel agent in the United States. Over the years, the two exchanged ideas for post-peace plans that would bring groups of tourists to Israel and Syria. In the early 1990s, Tarek hosted a dinner at his lovely, large home outside Damascus for *Nishma* (Let's Listen) a delegation of prominent Jewish American leaders and twenty prominent Syrian businessmen and professionals. This did not happen without a green light from Assad's government.

Since the popular uprising in Syria in 2011 and the terrible violent repression unleashed by the regime, we have not had any contact with our friend in Damascus. Like many Syrians, he was initially hopeful that President Bashar al-Assad was interested in pursuing reform and ready to follow his father's footsteps in being willing to negotiate peace with Israel. Following trips they made to Syria early in 2009, both special envoy George Mitchell and Senator John Kerry reported similar impressions of President Assad. Looking back, it is worth asking whether a determined, effective US push for Syrian-Israeli peace at that time might have encouraged the regime to make a more rational, less violent response to popular demands for reform and thereby avoid the catastrophic war that has enveloped the country. The status quo in the Middle East is definitely not stable. A basic lesson from these years is that the consequences of not taking advantage of opportunities for bold, fair, determined peacemaking include the risk of new eruptions of devastating violence.

Thanks to letters of introduction from former President Jimmy Carter, various USICPME delegations met with Ezer Weizman, Israel's president from 1993 to 2000, Chairman Yasser Arafat of the PLO, King Hussein of Jordan, Syria's foreign minister Farouk al Sharaa and Vice President Abdul Halim Khaddam, President Hosni Mubarak of Egypt, and Amr Moussa, secretary general of the Arab League. In every country, we also almost always had informative meetings with the American ambassador, chief political officer and, in Jerusalem, with the US consulate general.

In 1995, our schedule in Cairo included a memorable meeting with Osama el-Baz, senior foreign policy advisor to President Mubarak. When el-Baz entered the rather cavernous, very formal meeting room at the Egyptian foreign ministry, he suggested that we pull our chairs together in a circle for a more informal conversation. We had arrived just a few days after a terrorist attack on an Egyptian tourist bus, and el-Baz was emotionally focused on this terrible event. He spoke authoritatively about how during the 1980s, the United States had funded and trained Muslim Mujahideen (militants) to fight the Russians in Afghanistan. El Baz said he feared that the extremists who carried out the attack in Cairo would eventually find ways to attack America. This was six years before the September 11, 2001 terrorist attacks. El Baz added, "I'm afraid these chickens are coming home to roost."

Some meetings severely stretched people's capacity to listen, but also were instructive about the importance of listening precisely when it is hardest to do. On one occasion in Damascus, while we were meeting with Khaled Fahoum, chairman of the Palestine National Council, he got a telephone call from Dr. George Habash, head of the Popular Front for the Liberation of Palestine (PFLP). The PFLP is a Marxist Palestinian faction that was responsible for several of the most infamous terrorist attacks on Israeli civilians. Habash was interested in meeting with us. I asked the group what we should do. The rabbi in the delegation responded, "We've already come this far Ron, I think we should go to meet with him." The group agreed. We walked from Fahoum's office to the basement of an apartment building where the PFLP office walls displayed posters of Palestinian fighters, including several women, holding A-K 47s. I introduced each member of our delegation, including the rabbi, individually by name to Dr. Habash. He invited the rabbi to sit next to him on a small, couch under a poster portraying a photo of V.I. Lenin.

Habash welcomed us and said that normally in a meeting like this he would present a talk about the Palestinian liberation struggle, but he had never before met an interfaith delegation and he imagined that we had many questions. Then he turned to the rabbi and said, "I'm sure you have questions for me rabbi, why don't you start?" Nervous, the rabbi thanked Habash and said, "You're right, I do have many questions, but I want to start simply by asking if you would be willing to tell us something about your life." George Habash told us about growing up in Lydda, Palestine (today's Lod, near Tel Aviv), and coming home from studying medicine at American University in Beirut in the summer of 1948 during the first Arab-Israeli war. Because of the strategic importance of the area where his family lived, the Israeli military rounded up Palestinians and forced them to leave their homes. Habash and his family became refugees. It was very hot and, while Habash didn't personally tell us this, I learned later that his young sister apparently died of dehydration on their journey. He told our delegation how the experience of being forced to flee his homeland led him to become a militant political activist. I don't think anyone's views about the conflict changed in that hour, but the rabbi's question and Habash's response helped everyone to appreciate that even my worst enemy is a real human being and, while we may strongly disagree with someone's loyalties and choices, it is important to listen and learn about the circumstances he faced.

National Interfaith Convocation for Peace in the Middle East

In March, 1989, two years after its founding meeting, the USICPME sponsored the first National Interfaith Convocation and Congressional Visitation for Peace in the Middle East. More than 700 people from thirty-eight states gathered for three days at the Omni Shoreham Hotel in Washington, where they heard lectures, attended panel presentations by Israelis, Palestinians and American religious leaders, and participated in workshops on organizing local interreligious cooperation for peace. On the second evening, rented school buses carried participants to a major program we organized at the National Cathedral. The speakers that evening were Dr. Walid Khalidi and Rabbi Arthur Hertzberg, two prominent, principled and articulate advocates for a negotiated two-state solution to the Israeli-Palestinian conflict.

The following day, participants attended a briefing at the Lutheran Church of the Reformation, and then went in interfaith delegations to Capitol Hill to visit their members of Congress. They were united in advocating for active American leadership to achieve Israeli-Palestinian peace, reflecting talking points based on *A Time for Peace.* In an evaluation session, several people reported that members of Congress, accustomed to narrowly partisan lobbying, were quite surprised and encouraged by interfaith delegations advocating a common message for peace. Almost fifteen years later Alvin Sugarman, rabbi emeritus at The Temple in Atlanta, told me how personally inspirational the convocation had been for him. As a token of appreciation for their commitment, everyone attending the Convocation took home a commemorative poster with artwork by Sister Mary Corita Kent, consisting of a white tree on a light blue background with bright green script that read, "The ground work doesn't show till one day." We adopted "Groundwork for Peace" as the name for the committee's quarterly newsletter. I think it was an appropriate phrase to describe what the US Interreligious Committee accomplished.

In the ongoing dynamics of Israeli and Palestinian efforts for peace and more active American support for a two-state solution, one of the most memorable and inspiring events occurred in 1989, when more than 25,000 Israelis and Palestinians linked hands around the Old City in a demonstration entitled "Hands Around Jerusalem," powerfully symbolizing the need for a solution in which the two peoples in two nations would share the city. In a sense, the USICPME was our American version of hands around Jerusalem. In 2010 and 2011, Israeli and Palestinian peace activists joined in nonviolent demonstrations opposing provocative and dangerous Israeli land grabs and settlement expansion in Arab East Jerusalem. Since 1987, Jewish, Christian and Muslim leaders of the USICPME and the National Interreligious Leadership Initiative for Peace (formed in 2003) have consistently advocated for an undivided, shared Jerusalem where both Israel and Palestine would have their capitals.

Following the March 1989 USICPME gathering in Washington, I used it as a model to organize convocations in New York City, Boston, Chicago, Kansas City, and St. Louis. At two of these events, Yehoshafat Harkabi, former chief of Israeli military intelligence, and Nabil Shaath, senior official of the PLO and close advisor to Chairman Arafat, were keynote speakers. Both advocated negotiations between Israel and the PLO and supported a two-state solution. The New York convocation on Sunday evening February 11, 1990, was at the Cathedral of St. John the Divine and drew more than 800 people. The program included prayers for peace and wonderful music, along with challenging and very moving talks by Harkabi and Shaath.

February 11, 1990 happened to be the day that Nelson Mandela—the most prominent leader of the anti-Apartheid movement—was to be released from Victor Verster prison in South Africa. He had been convicted of sabotage and treason by the all-white government in 1963, and spent twenty-seven years in prison. As a way of celebrating Mandela's release from prison, we arranged for a South African representative of the African National Congress to bring us their greetings. I went to her Harlem apartment to provide directions and explain a bit more about the evening's program. When I arrived, her door was open and she was seated on her couch, with her baby son next to her, sorting newly washed baby clothes and intently watching television. She invited me to sit with her. We cried and embraced when we saw Mandela walk out of the prison gates to freedom.

Exhibiting an extraordinary lack of bitterness or hatred and despite opposition from many of his colleagues in the ANC, following his release from prison, Nelson Mandela led the African National Party in peace negotiations with white South African President F.W. DeKlerk that resulted in free national elections and a multi-racial democracy. Elected President in 1994, Mandela invited a few of his former prison guards to attend as honored guests at his inauguration. While serving as president from 1994 to 1999, Mandela consistently advocated for cooperation and reconciliation between South African blacks and whites. In July 1993, Carol and I, and our sons attended the ceremony in Philadelphia where Mandela and DeKlerk were awarded the Liberty Medal. That same year, in October, they were awarded the Nobel Peace Prize. Two earlier South African Nobel Peace Prize recipients were Albert Luthuli (1960) and Desmond Tutu (1984), both deeply committed to nonviolence and, interestingly, both with some connections to the Fellowship of Reconciliation.

At the New York Convocation that evening, besides the content of their talks, Nabil Shaath and Yehoshofat Harkabi inspired all of us by how warmly they greeted each other and by the respect they showed for each other. Neither man was a Mandela, but everyone was moved by their reconciliatory tone. Nabil publicly confessed for the first time that as a young Palestinian he had admired Abba Eban, the famous South African-born Israeli foreign minister, and how he hoped someday to represent Palestinians even half so eloquently and effectively. Harkabi responded aloud, "Nabil, you're already doing that." These warm human encounters across the boundaries of the conflict were unusual but no longer unprecedented.

A similarly inspiring, informal encounter occurred at a program co-sponsored by USICPME and Congregation B'nai Jeshurun in New York City. 700 people gathered to honor the memory of Rabbi Marshall Meyer, a founding member of the USICPME. Colette Avital, then the Israeli consul general in New York, entered the synagogue and brushed past her security men to warmly greet Hassan Abdul Rahman, the PLO representative in Washington. They briefly embraced. When Ambassador Robert Pelletreau, former assistant secretary of state for near eastern affairs, rose to speak, he commented on the warmth with which Avital and Rahman had greeted each other, saying, "This is the role I've been waiting many years to play, standing up as an American ambassador in support of Israelis and Palestinians who want peace and are working hard together to make it happen."

Despite the committee's shoestring budget, I believe the interfaith leadership trips, the national and local convocations, and many other USICPME programs and speaking engagements built a network of Jews, Christians and Muslims committed to working together for Middle East peace. Even when they worked separately in their own communities, people who had these interfaith experiences at least knew someone else, someone with a personal or communal bond to the other side, equally committed to achieving a two-state peace agreement.

Al Vorspan, then senior vice president of the Union of American Hebrew Congregations (renamed the Union for Reform Judaism in 2003) was the second Jewish co-chair of the USICPME, and along with his wife, Shirley, participated in an interfaith delegation I led to the Middle East in 1992. Another participant in that delegation was a Muslim American professor, Abdelwahab (Heba) Hechiche, whose mother had hidden Jews during the Nazi occupation of Tunis. When everyone met for the first time at Kennedy Airport, Al and Shirley told me they were nervous about remembering and correctly pronouncing the names of the Muslim participants. By the time we had traveled together for a dozen days in Israel, Gaza and the West Bank, Egypt, Syria and Jordan, no one could forget the names of the other participants. Al wrote a moving reflection on the trip for *Reform Judaism*, a magazine that is sent to every household that is a member of a Reform Jewish congregation.

My work demonstrated three reasons why interfaith cooperation for peace was critically important. First, like early endorsers of the USICPME, I believed that this work is mandated by the core teachings of our three Abrahamic faith traditions. Second, I understood that, despite our best individual efforts, it is very hard to be objective and sensitive about both Israeli and Palestinian experiences and perspectives. If we are not involved in serious ongoing dialogue and relationships with people whose views are different from ours, our perspectives tend to be partial and prejudiced, which leads to advocacy that often is neither realistic nor constructive. Third, as in the lobbying experience in1989, it is clear that when American Jews, Christians and Muslims unite in advocacy for peace, it is significantly more effective than when they lobby separately and, frequently in opposition to one another. The USICPME helped prepare the groundwork for more informed and sensitive work for peace, and the personal relationships we cultivated also enabled us to cooperate on other issues, including united interreligious responses to the 9/11 terrorist attacks and their aftermath of hostility and violence against Muslims

Events in the wider Middle East sometimes demanded a change in focus. On August 2, 1990, Iraq invaded Kuwait. Based on a UN Security Council resolution calling for Iraq's withdrawal, the US organized a multi-country coalition, led by General Colin Powell, which attacked Iraq in January 1991 and forced Iraqi forces to withdraw. Until that crisis, the USICPME had focused exclusively on the Arab-Israeli-Palestinian conflict. We had not even addressed the ten-year war between Iraq and Iran that took the lives of more than a million people. In response to Iraq's invasion of Kuwait, we called for international diplomatic efforts combined with sanctions, and we sponsored a consultation on the theme, "The Crisis in the Gulf and the Israeli-Palestinian Conflict." We arranged presentations by Dr. James O.C. Jonah, assistant secretary general of the United Nations; Dr. Sergo Mikoyan, visiting Soviet scholar at the Woodrow Wilson Center; and Dr. Harold Saunders, former assistant secretary of state. Prominent Palestinian and Israeli peace advocates, Dr Sari Nusseibeh, from Bir Zeit University and Dr. Yaron Ezrachi, from Hebrew University also spoke. Conference participants adopted a "Common Agenda for Peace" resolution and conducted an interfaith prayer vigil for peace at the White House.

In the lead-up to the Gulf War, I invited leaders of the USICPME to write prayers for peace from their respective religious traditions.[2] They were sent to thousands of congregations across the country and were used as centerpieces in hundreds of services in the weeks before the war. On the night that the coalition launched its attack on Iraqi forces in Kuwait, I participated in a very moving interfaith service at Muhlenberg College in Pennsylvania that featured our prayers.

Interfaith Responses to the Madrid Peace Conference and Oslo Peace Process

President George H.W. Bush and Secretary of State James A. Baker had promised their allies in the anti-Iraq coalition that when the war was over, the United States would actively work to resolve the Arab-Israeli-Palestinian conflict. They launched a very ambitious effort to organize an international peace conference in Madrid, chosen to

2. "Prayers for Peace."

remind the world about Spain's golden years of interreligious cooperation during the fourteenth and fifteenth centuries. Convened by the United States and Soviet Union in October 1991, this was the first time that all of the parties in the conflict—Israel, Lebanon, Syria, Jordan and the Palestinians (the latter two in a joint delegation)—had agreed to engage in face-to-face negotiations. In a very creative diplomatic initiative, a second track of negotiations, involving a wider circle of countries, was also launched to address important regional issues, such as water, the environment, arms control, refugees and economic development. The USICPME worked actively in support of the Madrid peace conference, including publicly supporting the Bush administration's insistence that Israel freeze settlement expansion as a condition for receiving loan guarantees. As noted earlier, in response to AIPAC lobbying, President Bush had evoked an old anti-Semitic stereotype and thus significantly reduced American Jewish support for this focused form of pressure on Israel.

To encourage active diplomatic follow up to the Madrid conference, in December 1991 the committee sponsored an Interfaith Convocation for Peace at the National Cathedral in Washington that was attended by 500 people. The day before the event, I got a call from the State Department, informing me that Secretary of State James Baker and his wife, Susan, planned to attend. I knew that Susan had been personally very moved by meeting Palestinians on a trip to Jerusalem and Secretary Baker, with support of the President Bush, was intent on the Madrid conference succeeding. I took it as a reflection of their appreciation for the important role of religious communities that they decided to attend the Interfaith Convocation. The Madrid negotiations progressed very slowly. During midterm election campaigns in 1992, USICPME circulated an open letter to candidates, urging them to support an "active US role in the peace process," and cautioning them to avoid "irresponsible, partisan statements that could harm fragile negotiations."

All too often over the years, rather than praising Congressional support for peacemaking, religious leaders have had to plead with members of Congress not to take actions that would harm chances for peace. On many occasions members of Congress have shamelessly supported positions that have posed obstacles to chances for peace. In 2012, thirty American Jewish, Christian and Muslim leaders of NILI, the successor interfaith coalition to USICPME, urged candidates not to "use any rhetoric that could make prospects for peace more problematic, or harm chances for a two-state Israeli-Palestinian peace agreement."

Some Middle East experts and supporters of Israel argue that the United States cannot want peace more than the parties themselves and, because of the special US-Israel relationshiip, our government should never pressure Israel. In fact, the Bush administration's insistence that Israel freeze settlement expansion as a condition for loan guarantees contributed positively to political debate in Israel that led to new elections in 1992, which resulted in Yitzhak Rabin of the Labor Party becoming prime minister. This series of events demonstrated that carefully focused and timely

American pressure could positively affect Israeli politics and chances for peace. But American policymakers were very slow to recognize this lesson and many members of Congress, motivated by perceived political self-interest, seemed never to learn it at all. The USICPME united prominent religious leaders in support of consensus advocacy positions calling for active, creative, determined diplomacy to help and, as necessary pressure all the parties including Israel to move toward negotiated peace. We were able to do this because we found deeper and broader agreement among religious leaders and communities than often was assumed. American administrations (both Democratic and Republican) and Congress failed to adopt firmer initiatives for peace in part due to the conservative, hawkish influence of AIPAC and fundamentalist evangelical Christians, but also because of deeper problematic tendencies in US foreign policy that I identified in the last chapter.

As the Madrid Conference negotiations bogged down, PLO Chairman Arafat and Israeli Prime Minister Rabin accepted an offer from the government of Norway to host secret talks outside Oslo. In addition to its non-threatening size, Norway was trusted by Israel in part because of the courageous efforts by Norwegians to rescue Jews from the Nazis, and trusted by the PLO because Norway had provided generous humanitarian and development aid to Palestinians. The negotiating teams were headed by Uri Savir on the Israeli side and by Abu Alaa (Ahmed Qurei) for the Palestinians. After months of difficult negotiations, an Israel-PLO Declaration of Principles was signed on the south lawn of the White House on September 13, 1993. Uri Savir's 1988 book, *The Process*, is a perceptive and deeply moving account of the political and interpersonal process that led to success of the Oslo negotiations. Holding the signing ceremony at the White House reflected the understanding, by both the PLO and Israel that, while Norway hosted the talks that produced the principles, implementing the Oslo Declaration and actually getting to peace would depend on active, strong American involvement.

A week before the Oslo Declaration signing ceremony, I received a call from the White House inviting USICPME leaders to be present. Attending with me were our three national co-chairpersons: Rabbi Arthur Hertzberg, Rev. Dr. Joan B. Campbell, and Dawud Assad, as well as several members of our board. A very moving moment occurred at the end of the ceremony when, after a nudge from President Clinton, to everyone's surprise, Yasser Arafat and Yitzhak Rabin shook hands. The audience of 2,000 startled persons simultaneously sucked in a deep breath, which sounded like a collective, scripted, AMEN!

The Oslo Declaration raised high hopes for peace among Israelis and Palestinians and most American supporters of the two sides. But developments on the ground and in the negotiations pushed in contradictory directions, some towards a two-state agreement and comprehensive peace, and others toward renewed violent conflict. Seven years later the Camp David summit hosted by President Clinton failed to produce a peace agreement and a second Palestinian intifada erupted. Sweet hopes for peace turned sour and many people seemed to forget several important positive accomplishments of the Oslo declaration and process.

It is important to remember what Oslo achieved. Immediately after the signing ceremony, the United States hosted a conference of sixty countries that raised pledges totaling 5 billion dollars (including an American promise of $600,000) for development aid for the Palestinians. After living in exile for decades, national PLO leaders, including Chairman Arafat, returned to Gaza and the West Bank. In October 1994, encouraged by the Oslo process, Jordan signed a peace treaty with Israel. In 1995, in talks at the Wye Plantation in Maryland, Israel and the Palestinians successfully concluded phase one of the Oslo process; and, in separate talks, Israel and Syria came close to achieving agreement on principles for Syrian-Israeli peace. In January 1996 Palestinians held national elections and a freely elected Palestinian government began to exercise limited authority in Gaza and some areas of the West Bank. Despite widespread corruption in the Palestinian Authority, on visits to the West Bank and Gaza in 1995 and 1996, I observed improved roads, new commercial buildings, apartments and private homes, and other signs of economic development and more normal life. The education ministries in Israel, Jordan and the Palestinian Authority initiated a joint project to review and reform school curricula in anticipation of peace. Israelis, Palestinians and Jordanians began to forge civil society links for economic and professional cooperation, including a non-profit organization focused on regional environmental issues. And perhaps most important of all, for several months during the late 1990s there were very few violent incidents between Palestinians and Israelis. These signs provided hope for the future.

However, the pace of the Oslo negotiations was frustratingly slow. The Palestinian Authority was neither consistent nor energetic about halting violence by factions opposed to Oslo, and Israeli governments continued to expand Jewish settlements in the occupied territories. With more Israeli-only roads crisscrossing the West Bank, it became harder to imagine a viable, contiguous Palestinian state. Tragically, in a pattern reminiscent of the Reagan administration in 1982 and 1983, the Clinton administration called for halting violence and freezing expansion of settlements, but failed to act firmly to demand implementation of either goal.

The cycle of violence resumed. On February 25, 1994, five months after the Oslo Declaration, Baruch Goldstein, a Brooklyn-born Jewish extremist from Kiryat Arba, machine gunned Palestinians as they prayed in the mosque at the Tomb of the Patriarchs in Hebron, killing twenty-nine and wounding 150. In Gaza, Hamas, the radical Islamic movement committed by its charter to the elimination of Israel, became more popular. Along with smaller militant Islamic groups, Hamas launched new violent attacks against Israelis. Four Palestinian suicide attacks killed thirty-nine Israelis and wounded many more. The combination of continued settlement expansion and the escalating cycle of violence depressed post-Oslo hopes that peace was possible and seriously undermined progress in the negotiations.

During this period, the USICPME denounced all acts of violence, called for American efforts to achieve an effective, durable ceasefire, and urged pressure on Israel to halt settlement expansion. We called on the Clinton administration to redouble its efforts to advance negotiations. While some argued that Israeli-Palestinian violence meant the peace process should be slowed down, we asserted that the process should move faster.

In May 1995, the Committee strongly opposed a provocative initiative by Senator Bob Dole and Representative Newt Gingrich to move the US embassy from Tel Aviv to Jerusalem. While AIPAC supported this proposal, Israeli Prime Minister Rabin opposed it, recognizing that it represented a serious threat to negotiations. This was not the first or only time when a prominent Israeli leader and some important American Jewish leaders disagreed with AIPAC about what was in Israel's best interest. Fortunately, thanks to language introduced by Diane Feinstein, Jewish American senator from California, Dole's initiative was amended in a way that allowed the Clinton administration to ignore it.

The biggest blow to the Oslo peace process occurred on November 4, 1995. As he stepped off the stage of a huge peace rally in Tel Aviv, Prime Minister Yitzhak Rabin, whom most Israelis trusted as peacemaker in part because of his history as a tough military commander, was assassinated by Yigal Amir, a Jewish extremist opposed to Oslo. Shimon Peres became Israel's acting prime minister. Only a few months earlier, apparently concerned that the Oslo process was moving too slowly, Prime Minister Rabin and President Arafat had quietly authorized informal, unpublicized talks led by Yossi Beilin and Mahmoud Abbas, two architects of the Oslo accord, to develop ideas for resolving final status issues, including borders and security arrangements, settlements, refugees and the future of Jerusalem.

In January 1996, I traveled to the West Bank as an informal observer of the first national Palestinian elections, and then was joined in Jerusalem by leaders of the USICPME for meetings with several Israelis and Palestinians who were knowledgeable about the unpublicized Abbas-Beilin talks. We were surprised and very encouraged to learn how much progress had already been made on the two most emotional issues: refugees and Jerusalem. There was an emerging understanding that a negotiated agreement must allow for a Palestinian right of return that would not threaten Israeli demographics. That meant it would be exercised exclusively in the West Bank and Gaza Palestinian state, and while Israel might admit a small number of refugees (perhaps as many as 50,000) based on family reunification, in the vast majority of cases, compensation or resettlement would be the main forms of relief. A negotiated compromise on Jerusalem included a commitment to keeping the city open and undivided, with possible agreed adjustments of municipal borders, and making it the capital of both nations. Jerusalem's Jewish residents would be Israeli citizens and Palestinian residents would be citizens of Palestine, as had already been implicitly recognized in that they voted in Palestinian national elections. The major religious sites in the Old City would be overseen by religious authorities. Some version of these ideas for compromises on the issues of refugees and Jerusalem has been included in every subsequent set of parameters for Israeli-Palestinian peace.

Reported progress in these talks was good news, but it didn't compensate for setbacks on the ground. As Palestinian and Israeli popular frustrations intensified, so did their doubts about the other side's real intentions. Each side pointed to some action by the other as justification for their latest acts of violence. In spring 1996, a series of Hamas suicide attacks killed more than sixty Israeli civilians and wounded hundreds, intensifying Israeli disillusionment and contributing directly to Likud's election victory over Labor. Benjamin Netanyahu replaced Shimon Peres as prime minister, slowing the pace of negotiations even more. Once again, a basic lesson about the conflict was demonstrated: without real progress toward peace on the ground, violent confrontation is almost inevitable.

USICPME wanted to help concerned people see that there were possible compromise solutions for even the toughest issues. In the fall of 1997, I published a report of our delegation's findings about final status issues called "Israeli-Palestinian Ideas for Mutually Acceptable Solutions of Permanent Status Issues" in *Groundwork for Peace*. I organized a briefing in Washington on the theme, "Ideas for Resolving Jerusalem and Other Final Status Issues," for representatives of the Washington offices of more than twenty national organizations including the American Israel Public Affairs Committee (AIPAC), American Jewish Committee, American Muslim Council, Americans for Peace Now, Anti-Defamation League, Arab-American Anti-Discrimination Committee, Arab American Institute, Churches for Middle East Peace, National Council of Churches, Religious Action Center of Reform Judaism, and the US Conference of Catholic Bishops.

Despite their very different and often contentious public positions, the briefing went very well. The discussion was rational and respectful. It seemed that when they sat down quietly together in a room away from the media and seriously discussed practical compromises that were already being considered by Israelis and Palestinians, representatives of these organizations could be much more flexible than they were in their more rhetorical partisan public statements. In the afternoon, I arranged a similar briefing on Capitol Hill attended by twenty-five legislators and/or staff, which also was received very well. This helped to confirm that there was much broader public support than often is assumed for the compromises necessary to resolve the conflict, and more support than is assumed for active American leadership to help the parties get there.

"Don't Let the Light Go Out" – November 1998

It was important for the USICPME and other concerned groups to keep hopes for peace alive. In fall of 1998, we sponsored a second interfaith convocation with the theme, "Bless Peacemaking: Don't Let the Light Go Out." It was scheduled to take place on Sunday evening, November 22 at Foundry United Methodist Church in Washington, where President Clinton and his family worshipped. Unfortunately, the Clintons were out of the country, but he sent a warm letter of support that was read aloud by the White House associate director for public liaison. Our goal was to publicly highlight the main elements of a possible two-state peace agreement, and demonstrate American support for this vision by the presence of many prominent national Jewish, Christian and Muslim religious leaders seated in the Chancel and a large interfaith audience filling the church. The centerpiece of the program was to be a dialogue between Maj. Gen. (Ret.) Shlomo Lahat, popular mayor of Tel Aviv from 1974 to 1993 and leader of the Israel Council for Security and Peace, and Nabil Shaath, advisor to Yasser Arafat and a chief negotiator for the PLO during the Oslo process. Lahat and Shaath had clear, principled and public records of supporting a negotiated two-state solution, with security and peace for both Israelis and Palestinians. Having met with each man many times, I had absolute confidence in both the content and reconciliatory tone of what they would present. After Lahat and Shaath spoke, we planned for brief statements of support by several religious leaders. At the end of the program, as everyone in the church held lighted candles, Peter Yarrow of Peter, Paul and Mary would sing "Don't Let the Light Go Out."

Unfortunately, this was a case of the best intentions and best laid plans not happening. A week before the convocation, I received a call from Nabil Shaath that his schedule had changed and he would not be able to participate. Later that same day, I got a call from Friends of Tel Aviv University in Washington, saying that they had scheduled a program for that Sunday afternoon in which Dr. Hanan Ashrawi, a prominent and popular spokesperson for the Palestinian delegation during the Oslo process negotiations, was to speak and perhaps she would be willing to substitute for Shaath. Having met Hanan many times, I called her, explained the convocation and invited her to participate. She agreed to do it. Unfortunately, Hanan's dialogue program with the deputy Israeli ambassador in the afternoon turned into a rather nasty debate, so when she arrived that evening, she was in a confrontational mood.

Shlomo Lahat spoke first, calling for an end to Israeli occupation, an independent Palestinian state based on 1967 borders, removal of Israeli settlements, Jerusalem as the capital for both Palestine and Israel, and Israeli withdrawal from the Golan Heights as a basis for peace with Syria. In her presentation, Hanan made almost no reference to what Lahat had said but reiterated many of the same angry arguments against Israeli policies that she had made earlier that day in her debate with the deputy Israeli ambassador. Peter Yarrow's singing couldn't alleviate the discouragement and frustration a lot of people felt as they left the church. It wasn't the first time that a dialog effort turned sour, and it wouldn't be the last. The next morning when I dutifully asked Al Vorspan, the Jewish co-chair of the USICPME, what he thought about program, he answered honestly. Clearly sensitive to all my hard work, Al smiled and said, "It seems to me last night was a rare case in which the Israeli was willing to give away the store and the Palestinian kicked him in the guts." I felt as badly after that program as I had about anything I had ever organized that didn't come off as planned.

The very next evening in Baltimore we demonstrated that the design for the convocation was indeed constructive and workable. The original plan was for Lahat and Shaath to repeat their dialogue from Sunday evening at a dinner meeting on Monday sponsored by the Baltimore World Affairs Council. Lahat and I traveled to Baltimore by train; Hanan Ashrawi asked her good friend Dr. Najat Arafat Khelil, a prominent Palestinian-American activist, to take her place. Shlomo and Najat were magnificent together, presenting their complementary visions of a two-state peace agreement, differing on some relatively minor matters, but agreeing strongly on most points, including on the urgent need for more active, engaged and determined US leadership. They warmly parried skeptical challenges from a few impatient and partisan supporters of each side. For most people that evening, the content and tone of the Baltimore program was very welcome and helped to revive their hopes for peace and US leadership. If only we could have accomplished that on Sunday at the Clintons' church. Flying home to Seattle the next day I felt somewhat buoyed by Monday night's successful program, but exhausted by all the work I put into Sunday night's program and depressed by how it had turned out.

In 1999, early Israeli elections led to Ehud Barak of the Labor Party becoming prime minister by a narrow margin. Only a year later, largely a result of his hapless political leadership, Barak faced new elections. Believing that success in the peace process might revive his political fortunes, Barak decided to push for a summit to resolve the conflict with the Palestinians. Nearing the end of his second term and wishing to cap his presidency with a Mideast peace agreement, Clinton agreed to host the summit at Camp David in July 2000. The summit came closer to resolving the conflict than any previous negotiations. However, Arafat's ambivalence about accepting Israel's offer, the American tendency to favor Israeli positions rather than act as true mediator, and a serious lack of adequate pre-summit diplomatic preparations, particularly related to the vital and emotional issues of refugees and Jerusalem, caused the Summit to end without an agreement. Barak and Clinton publicly blamed Arafat for the failure, but that was too simple and politically self-serving. Nabil Shaath, the PLO leader Carol and I had known since 1982, told me that just before Clinton's press conference, he begged the president not to say that the summit failed, but rather that "the negotiations came very close to succeeding and that the United States would continue to work closely and urgently with the parties to finish the process."

Embittered by the continued occupation, with no peace agreement in sight, and furious about a provocative visit to the Temple Mount by Ariel Sharon who was then campaigning for election, in September 2000, a second Palestinian intifada erupted in Gaza and the West Bank. Tragically for all, this uprising was far more violent than the first one thirteen years earlier. While some Palestinians were convinced that non-violent resistance represented a more effective strategy, people's frustration and anger, combined with Hamas' radical ideology, led many Palestinians to support violent resistance. Ten years after the Madrid Peace Conference and seven years after the Oslo Declaration, there was still no Palestinian state and no peace agreement. A majority of Palestinians supported acts of violent resistance against Israeli occupation, to which Israel predictably responded with tough and very destructive military measures supported by a majority of Israelis. Keeping hope for peace alive became much more difficult. Just as some positive developments encouraged more active American support for peace, renewed violent confrontation between Israelis and Palestinians was an enormous source of discouragement.

In November 2000, in an effort to bridge remaining gaps from the July summit and get negotiations going again, to his credit, President Clinton presented a series of ideas that became known as the Clinton Parameters.[3] They were drawn from years of formal negotiations and informal talks between Israelis and Palestinians, and very similar to ideas the USICPME publicized in 1997. (Versions of these ideas would surface again in 2003 in the People's Voice Initiative and the Geneva Accord.) Building on the Clinton Parameters, official Israeli and Palestinian negotiating teams reached what became known as the Taba Agreement in Egypt in January 2001. But neither President Arafat nor Israel's new prime minister, Ariel Sharon, was prepared to sign on to the new agreement or to resume talks where they left off. Instead, Sharon refused to talk with Arafat and concentrated on military suppression of the intifada, while Arafat tried to use the intifada to his political advantage. Dramatically distinguishing his approach from Clinton's, George W. Bush made clear that working for Israeli-Palestinian peace would not be a high priority of his administration.

To his credit, President Bush did ask former Senator George Mitchell to study the causes of the second intifada and asked CIA Director George Tenet to develop a plan for achieving a ceasefire and restoring security. The USICPME viewed the April 2001 Mitchell report and the Tenet plan of June 2001 as thorough, fair documents with carefully crafted recommendations that could have led Israel and the Palestinian Authority to halt the violence and resume negotiations. Unfortunately, the recommendations never got the serious attention they deserved. Repeating a familiar pattern in American policy, after commissioning the reports and recommendations, the Bush administration did almost nothing to press for their implementation, and neither Prime Minister Sharon nor President Arafat seemed interested in resuming negotiations. Three months later, in response to the 9/11 terrorist attacks, the Bush administration became almost entirely focused on launching the war in Afghanistan and preparing the invasion and occupation of Iraq.

The Arab-Israeli-Palestinian conflict didn't go away. People's hopes for peace were raised again in June, 2002, when the United States, in coordination with the European Union, Russia, and the UN secretary general (known as the Quartet)

3. "Middle East: Peace Plans."

launched the Road Map for peace. In 2003, Israelis and Palestinians united in publicly launching two informal, popular model peace agreements, the People's Voice Initiative and the Geneva Accord.

The People's Voice Initiative, co-authored by Palestinian Sari Nusseibeh, president of Al Quds University, and Ami Ayalon, former head of Shin Bet, the Israeli equivalent of the FBI, offered an outline of basic, simple principles for a realistic peace between Israelis and Palestinians. Principles like these still serve as benchmarks for an equitable and viable two-state Israeli-Palestinian peace agreement. Here are the principles of the People's Voice Initiative:

> 1. *Two states for two peoples*: Both sides will declare that Palestine is the only state of the Palestinian people and Israel is the only state of the Jewish people.

> 2. *Borders:* Permanent borders between the two states will be agreed on the basis of the June 4, 1967 lines, UN resolutions and the Arab Peace Initiative. Border modifications will be based on an equal territorial exchange (1:1) in accordance with the vital needs of both sides, including security, territorial contiguity, and demographic considerations. The Palestinian State will have a connection between its two geographic areas, the West Bank and the Gaza Strip.

> 3. *Jerusalem:* Jerusalem will be an open city, the capital of two states. Freedom of religion and full access to holy sites will be guaranteed to all. Arab neighborhoods in Jerusalem will come under Palestinian sovereignty; Jewish neighborhoods under Israeli sovereignty. Neither side will exercise sovereignty over the holy places. The State of Palestine will be designated Guardian of the Temple Mount for the benefit of Muslims. Israel will be the Guardian of the Western Wall for the benefit of the Jewish people. The status quo on Christian holy sites will be maintained. No excavation will take place in or underneath the holy sites.

> 4. *Right of return:* Recognizing the suffering and the plight of the Palestinian refugees, the international community, Israel, and the Palestinian State will initiate and contribute to an international fund to compensate them. Palestinian refugees will return only to the State of Palestine; Jews will return only to the State of Israel

> 5. *The Palestinian State will be demilitarized* and the international community will guarantee its security and independence.

> 6. *End of conflict:* Upon the full implementation of these principles, all claims on both sides and the Israeli-Palestinian conflict will end.

On December 1, 2003 the Geneva Accord, a much more detailed two-state agreement, was presented in Washington. Two days later I coordinated a press conference at the National Press Club to announce formation of the National Interreligious

Leadership Initiative for Peace in the Middle East (NILI). Before describing the formation and history of NILI, for which I serve as staff consultant, I want to share some significant developments in my family, as they related to my ongoing work for Middle East peace.

9

Working for Peace from Home:
Family and Friends Kept Me Going.

Working sometimes without salary and for many years from our home; parents dying; raising our sons and taking them to the Middle East; meeting again with friends from when we lived there, including Morela BarOn, Mohammed Milhem, and Ambassador Daniel Kurtzer.

MY PERSONAL AND FAMILY life have been deeply intertwined with my professional life as a worker for peace. Often working alone without a real salary, and for the last sixteen years working from our home, there were many times when the two parts of my life overlapped.

After returning from the Middle East in 1985, for three years our family lived in New York City in campus housing while Carol attended Union Theological Seminary. Working from our seminary apartment, I did research and wrote my book, took care of our sons while Carol was in class or the library, and consulted with Jewish, Christian and Muslim leaders about the idea of an interfaith effort for peace in the Middle East. During two summers, our family spent time at my sister's home in East Boothbay, Maine and at Carol's parents' home overlooking Puget Sound in Washington State, both settings that provided beautiful, tranquil surroundings in which to work. In the summer of 1988 we moved back to Philadelphia, so that Carol could study at the Lutheran Theological Seminary. A year later, she graduated from Union—quite an accomplishment at forty, especially given that we also were raising Jonah who was eight, and Jamie who just turned three that fall. Jonah entered second grade at the local public school, and we enrolled Jamie in daycare at a local Presbyterian church, where I also rented a small space for the USICPME office.

After graduating from Union, while Carol waited for a call to pastor a church, we moved back into the shared house in Philadelphia where we lived before moving to the Middle East, and then as the process dragged on, we rented an apartment. In the Lutheran Church, the Bishop forwards your name to a congregation where he considers you to be a good match, and then the congregation decides whether or not to call you. In the Bishop's view, Carol's excellent academic record at Union, combined with her experience in the Middle East, and several earlier years as a religious community organizer for peace and justice made her a very strong candidate. But some of the congregations may have been reluctant to have a woman pastor. Carol's branch of Lutheranism had been ordaining women only since 1970 and there was still significant resistance. This was a hard and anxious time emotionally for Carol and me. As I was in the early stages of organizing and trying to raise funds for the newly formed USICPME, the delay was also hard for us financially. As contributions came in, I was able to take a modest monthly salary and Carol worked for several months at the AFSC as interim peace education secretary—ironically, the same national staff position I held from 1972 to 1982.

In September 1989, my mom died. My sister Judy called Carol with the news and she called me in New York City, where I was attending a planning meeting for the New York interfaith convocation for peace. From the time she suffered her first heart attack during the year my parents lived in Haiti, we knew that my mom had high blood pressure and a serious heart condition. Apparently, without any symptoms the day before, mom's heart simply stopped. In bed next to dad, she died peacefully in her sleep.

In the 1970s, my parents had moved from Rockland County, New York to Port St. Lucie, Florida, where they lived in a modest doublewide mobile home in a pleasant, inexpensive, senior community. Mom became a leader in the local League of Women Voters, which she said was partly inspired by visiting me when I worked with Rev. Lawson in Memphis. In retrospect, I credit her idealism and personal commitment to fairness as important influences on my decision in 1962 to move to Memphis and work in the black community. Mom and dad seemed happy in Florida. They regularly swam in the community pool, played tennis and rode bikes together. Dad occasionally played golf on the community's par-three course where, in violation of the rules, he regularly started on the fifth hole located across the street from their home.

Mom was such a strong, dominating emotional presence, it was hard to imagine our family without her. Her idealism, both in the compassionate sense of wanting the best for everyone and in the controlling sense of sometimes believing she knew what was best for others, clearly had a big influence on Judy and me. We felt mom's presence powerfully in our lives and still do. As a result of her positive idealism, genuine warmth and wonderful sense of humor, and despite her sometimes being overbearing and favoring me, Judy and I both continue to feel a lot of love for mom. We miss her.

The day after mom died, when I spoke with dad, he seemed to be in shock. I don't remember him ever crying before, but I could hear him sobbing over the phone. My sister and I flew down separately to Florida. She arrived a day before me and Dad picked her up at the airport. I rented a car and drove to the house. When I arrived, dad came out to meet me in the driveway. He looked so sad. I hugged him and told him I loved him. That evening, I recalled twenty-five years earlier visiting my parents when I had just learned Trudi's decision to leave me. Dad had come out of their house and, without saying a word, hugged me real hard. Judy and I stayed with dad for a few days, preparing meals which he could reheat in the microwave and arranging for a young couple to come by each week to clean house and check on him. We also got dad to agree to live with us for at least part of the year, dividing his time between Judy's home in Maine and ours in Philadelphia.

In early fall 1990 Carol received a call to be pastor of Trinity Lutheran Church, a small congregation in a conservative, predominantly white area in northeast Philadelphia where, coincidentally, Benjamin Netanyahu, who later twice served as Israel's Prime Minister, went to high school. Our family moved into the small three bedroom parsonage a few blocks from the church. Carol's ordination ceremony took place in November and was quite an event for her whole family. Her parents, Emil and Louise, flew in from Seattle; other relatives drove from Indiana and Virginia. Dad, who was living with us in the parsonage, seemed really to enjoy the ceremony and celebration. When I was growing up, dad only came to church on Christmas and Easter, but in Philadelphia he became a pretty regular participant in Sunday worship at Trinity. If mom had been alive, of course, she would have loved being at Carol's ordination, although she also might have been a bit confused since, for many years, she thought that I was going to become a minister.

It was important to Carol and me that our parents supported what we were doing. While dad was never explicitly enthusiastic about our vocations, except for worrying about when I would finally graduate from college, he never spoke negatively about our activities. Mom compensated for his relative passivity with her over-the-top enthusiasm. It felt good that both sets of parents seemed proud of our being chosen to do the overseas Quaker listening assignment, although they weren't happy about our taking their nine-month-old grandson so far away. I know for my parents it helped that they had really enjoyed their experience living in Brazil and Haiti. Still, given the realities and media images of violent conflict in the region, they were nervous about our going to the Middle East. On several occasions when there was news of violence somewhere in the region, even when it was nowhere near where we lived, one or both of our moms would call to find out if we were safe. Both sets of parents and my sister, Judy communicated regularly with us by letters and phone calls. Judy kept all the letters and photos we sent from the Middle East in an album that was very helpful in stimulating my memories as I worked on recalling our experiences for this book. They all came to visit us in the Middle East. Briefly sharing our life with them in Amman and traveling with them to Petra, Jerash, Jerusalem, and Cairo provided a special family grounding to our three years in the Middle East that complemented the more public, political dimensions of our work.

Mom took up quite a lot of emotional space in our family. After she died, I felt that dad was more fully present than he had ever been before. For the next six years, Judy and I got to experience dad's love for us and to enjoy him much more. While the change was less dramatic for them, I think the same was true for Carol and our sons. Even as he suffered from macular degeneration and increasing dementia, dad seemed warmer and more engaged than when mom was alive. I came to appreciate parallel paths in his life and mine. Just as getting those grants to study in California and Arizona, and then going to teach in Brazil and Haiti made him a more fulfilled and happy person, my travels in Vietnam and Latin America, and our years living in the Middle East broadened my vision and contributed to my own sense of professional and personal fulfillment. Despite occasional eruptions of impatience and anger, most of the time he lived with us, dad exhibited a simple kindness and appreciation for life that I hope I can emulate. One example occurred the day dad was formally diagnosed with Alzheimers disease, and he told me on our drive home from the doctor's office that he didn't want to tell Carol because it would upset her. I was discovering, or maybe rediscovering, sides of dad that I hadn't experienced for many years. I had a new appreciation of photos of us together from when I was young. I recalled that as a teenager I overheard junior high school students say that Mr. Young was their favorite teacher. I remembered the young couple in Florida who regularly came to check on him after mom died telling Judy and me very appreciatively, "Your dad is such a gentleman."

Jonah, who turned eight in 1989, attended local public schools in Philadelphia. After getting a great start at a magnet school in New York City, his years in Philadelphia public schools turned out to be very poor, frustrating experiences. Carol and I remember parent-teacher conferences where practically all Jonah's teacher talked about was how frustrated and tired she had become; it was painfully clear that she should have been retired. In fall 1991, even though we really couldn't afford it, we enrolled Jonah in fifth grade at Abington Friends (Quaker) School. Jamie, who turned four in 1989, attended Paley Day Care run by the Jewish Federation. He seemed to thrive there, including coming home enthusiastic about celebrating Jewish holidays and once performing in a play where he had the role of *abba* (father) in a Jewish family. The next fall, with generous scholarship help, we also enrolled Jamie in Abington Friends School. The creativity, devotion and personal attention of their teachers, plus the Quaker values-centered community engaged and inspired both boys. It was by far their best school experience. They played recreation league soccer, basketball and baseball in northeast Philly. They still remember their neighborhood friends, have regular e-mail contact with them, and have even traveled across the country to keep these friendships current. Jonah and his Philly friends have attended each other's weddings. In January 2012, Jamie reconnected with a close friend from Abington Friends School, who served six years in the US Navy. His friend is very respectful and genuinely appreciative of Jamie's becoming a Muslim, and the two continue to have frequent email and Facebook exchanges about their activities and their views of world events.

From 1990 to 1995 during times when my dad stayed with our family in the parsonage in Philadelphia, Jonah and Jamie shared a room, so dad could have a bedroom to himself. Dad's health clearly was deteriorating. His macular degeneration made it impossible for him to enjoy watching tennis on television. During bouts of dementia, he would sometimes see people who weren't there. One weekend, when Carol and I were both going away, we arranged for an elderly woman from her congregation to stay with dad and the boys. Worried about how this would work, Carol asked twelve-year-old Jonah what he would do if grandpa said he saw people. Demonstrating a remarkable emotional resourcefulness that has continued to be characteristic, Jonah said, "Don't worry mom, I'll just tell grandpa that you took the people with you."

In the summer of 1995, dad was staying with Judy and her boys in Maine, while we had driven to Seattle to visit Carol parents. Dad's dementia worsened and his health dramatically deteriorated. He was hospitalized in August. Judy stayed with him at the hospital every day as his life systems slowly failed, but I was still in the Midwest, driving back to Philadelphia. Based on dad's living will, Judy and I decided over the telephone not to order extraordinary measures. Dad died on August 23, 1995, two days after his ninetieth birthday. I regret not being with Judy as he slipped away. We miss him.

I rented space in the basement of Carol's church for the office of the USICPME. Carol's part time secretary, Fran Soslow, a middle-aged Jewish woman, also worked part time with me. Every three months, sometimes with the help of church volunteers, Fran and I assembled mailings of the committee's quarterly newsletter, *Groundwork for Peace*, and mailed it to 2,000 supporters across the country.

Most years, I arranged and led an interfaith trip to the Middle East, taking fifteen to twenty Jews, Christians and Muslims to visit Israel, the West Bank and Gaza, Egypt, Jordan and Syria. Some trip participants were national leaders, but most were local leaders often from the same city. I hoped that when participants returned home, they would be committed to working together for peace and that was the outcome of several trips. Each of these trips became the consuming focus of my work for two to three months since I did almost everything myself: recruiting the participants, making the travel reservations, organizing a full schedule of appointments, guiding the group, developing a consensus report, and arranging follow up appointments with the State Department and members of Congress. Doing all the communicating for these trips by fax and telephone was difficult and very time consuming.

Given the time difference between the US and the Middle East, one of the awkward and sometimes humorous experiences doing this work was that arranging appointments with officials in the Middle East—before email—often involved making international phone calls in the middle of the night. I particularly remember one time in New York when Carol's parents were visiting us in our small apartment. It was three in the morning; I was calling Cairo and loudly asking for Dr. Abdullah, while sitting in the bathroom with the door closed and a sleeping bag over my head to muffle the sound of my voice. Carol's mom, Louise, loved to tell this story as an example of "Ron's work for peace." Once when our family was on vacation in the Bay of Fundy in Canada, I was in an outdoor public phone booth very early in the morning, calling an Israeli official in Jerusalem and a Syrian official in Damascus, once again speaking very loudly over poor phone connections. After the 9/11 attacks, I guess some of these loud bizarre-sounding phone calls from public locations might have caused anxious, watchful citizens to report me to Homeland Security.

Carol, Jonah and Jamie put up with my intense involvement in arranging these trips, including the crazy middle-of-the-night phone calls, and with my being away for two to three weeks at a time. They were also gracious about my many public speaking trips in the United States. I'm not sure what our young boys thought I was doing. As an example, shortly after we came home from the Middle East in 1985, when Jonah was only four, we spent a weekend in Washington DC, where I spoke at a peace rally. Jonah got to meet Peter Yarrow backstage and sing a few bars of "Puff the Magic Dragon" with him. On Monday, back in New York, Jonah shared his version of our weekend trip at his day care. His teacher told us that Jonah reported, "We went to Washington, I met Peter and my dad gave a speech in an *alley*." The fact that I made numerous trips to other cities and often gave public lectures for much smaller honoraria than many friends told me I deserved contributed to our family's often very tight finances.

Over the years, the USICPME funding fluctuated with perceptions about prospects for peace in the Middle East. Ironically, dramatic positive developments that generated optimism, such as the 1993 Oslo Declaration, and negative developments such as waves of increased violence that generated pessimism, both often caused a decline in contributions. Whether people thought peace was imminent or that it would never come, unfortunately they didn't seem to think they needed to do much about it; moreover, many people were still skeptical about the idea of interfaith cooperation for Middle East peace I was very fortunate that Carol felt a strong personal commitment to my work. Without her encouragement and the support of her pastor's salary, I would not have been able to continue this work.

In 1996, with both my parents gone, the four of us and our dog Jake moved to Washington State to be closer to Carol's parents who were in their 80s. We moved ourselves across the country in our Dodge van and a rented truck, with a pair of walkie-talkies to communicate between the vehicles. At a ridiculous cost of $2,000, I arranged for my (way too many) books to be shipped separately. I remember as I was packing carton after carton, Carol looked over my shoulder and teased me: "Ron, with all the books you have, how come you're not smarter?"

Carol got a call to St. John Lutheran Church in Seattle, which she discovered was the same church where two of her great uncles had been confirmed decades earlier, and one of them had carved the hymn board that hung in front of the sanctuary. With her dad's help, we found a lovely house to rent at a small lake in Marysville, about fifteen minutes from her parents' home and an hour from Seattle. It had three bedrooms, a large sunny room that became my office, a great wood deck the length of the house and a lovely lawn, with automatic sprinklers that, unfortunately, we frequently busted by running over them with the lawn mower.

Two years later, when Carol's parents moved into a senior community, we moved into their home, on a hundred-foot bluff overlooking Puget Sound, with a magnificent view of the snowcapped Olympic Mountains and spectacular sunsets. Her parents had bought the property in the early 1950s for $2,800. After he retired, Carol's dad, Emil, built their home. Our family was very lucky to live in that place, surrounded by huge, old growth Douglas firs and cedars. It was a blessed place to live and do my work for peace in the Middle East. With Emil's supervision, Jonah and I turned the original small cabin into a simple guest cottage, where over the years various visiting family have enjoyed living for weeks at a time.

In the two years after we moved to Washington State, Carol's mother's health went downhill pretty fast and she died in November 2000. Louise was known for her warm hospitality, good cooking, love of singing and great sense of humor, including her loud laugh. At the end of her memorial service at our church, with a trumpet blaring from the choir loft, Carol led the family and the congregation out of the sanctuary marching and singing "When the Saints Go Marching In."

Emil was a civil engineer who worked for many years as the chief sanitary engineer for the state of Washington. Carol recalls a few family summer vacations when her dad would add visits to "interesting sewage treatment plants" to their vacation trip schedule. In 1960, Emil took an assignment for the World Health Organization in Ethiopia to help design the sewage treatment plan for Addis Ababa. Like mine, Carol's parents enjoyed international travel; even though it made them nervous sometimes, they appreciated our living and working in the Middle East. While peacemaking was no more Emil's vocation than engineering was mine, he was genuinely interested in my work. Emil read my book, *Missed Opportunities for Peace,* and took the time to write many thoughtful comments and questions in the margins with bright orange magic marker. I keep his copy of my book on a special shelf near my desk. Emil was always working on a project of some sort and hated getting to a stage in his late eighties when he couldn't do as much. I think he slowly came to accept that we loved simply having him here with us. Emil died in February 2006. Because he and Louise loved life and parties, after his memorial service, the family gathered together for much eating, drinking and dancing. On occasions like that, I discovered there must be a bit of the Irish in at least some Danes and Norwegians.

Our Sons, Jonah and Jamie, Growing Up

After our move to Washington State, Jonah entered tenth grade at the very large Marys-ville High School. Thanks to his piano lessons from a young, attractive Russian-Jewish immigrant in Philadelphia and a pied-piper high school music director, Jonah was soon signed up to be the pianist for the Marysville High School jazz choir, and a year later, also for the jazz band. Both groups were quite accomplished and travelled widely to perform, including going to the Lionel Hampton Jazz Festival at the University of Idaho. These groups also provided a small subset of good friends for Jonah in this very large and diverse high school. After graduation, Jonah attended Shoreline Community College where he met and fell in love with Elyse Kliedon, whom he married nine years later. Elyse is a nurse practitioner. Tiring of the pressurized schedules and too much administrative work in a hospital, Elyse put her profoundly patient-centered nursing style to work in hospice care. Jonah went on to Western Washington University and graduated with two degrees, one in education, with an emphasis on science, and one in music. For several years he worked as a substitute elementary school teacher and part time with Mattias, a young man with severe cerebral palsy. Then, more recently, he got a fulltime job in a private school, where his creative teaching skills seem very much appreciated. Jonah also has become a skilled mountain climber, leader of climbs, and kayaker. He has climbed Mt. Rainier twice and skied Mt. Baker several times. In his marriage with Elyse, his teaching of children, his work with Mattias, and in his outdoor avocations, Jonah continues to demonstrate a characteristic combination of eager enthusiasm, knowledge of the subject, and relaxed, emotional resourcefulness. I suspect his experiences as an itinerant baby for three years in the Middle East may have contributed to his positive, relaxed character.

We enrolled Jamie in fourth grade at Marshall, the local elementary school in Marysville. When district boundary lines changed, he was assigned to attend fifth and sixth grades at Quilceda Elementary School on the edge of the Tulalip Indian reservation, where he stood out as an excellent reader. He was often selected for various leadership roles, including in the DARE program, educating kids against alcohol-ism. In 1998, when we moved to Carol's parents' home, Jamie had to change schools again, entering seventh grade at Port Susan Middle School in Stanwood. Ninth grade was in a separate wing, while tenth through twelfth grades was in the main build-ing of the high school. Making all these changes was hard for Jamie. Having been a straight 'A' student, the combination of all this moving around and the mixed quality of the instruction and counseling at the high school meant that his experience in tenth through twelfth grades was pretty poor. Beginning when he was ten years old, Jamie played clarinet and then tenor saxophone. He was part of the high school jazz band and a special, select, countywide youth jazz band that performed several times in Seattle jazz clubs and once at the small symphony hall in Seattle. At 6'6," he also played basketball up through tenth grade.

Jamie has shown a keen intellectual interest in Carol's and my work. Even when he was seven and eight on Sundays after church, he frequently questioned or commented on Carol's sermons. As a teen, Jamie engaged me with very interesting questions about the Middle East and religion, sometimes going on the internet to discover information and perspectives of which I was unaware. Since high school, he worked successfully at several very different jobs, including volunteering with the Red Cross doing hurricane relief work in Florida, selling top-end frozen food by telephone, driving a large truck making early morning milk deliveries, and working in a machine shop in Seattle owned by Pakistani American Muslims. Like Jonah, Jamie attended Shoreline Community College where he pursued pre-engineering; then, having unsuccessfully battled calculus, in 2011, he shifted his focus to liberal arts. He loved the new focus; his grades soared; and he graduated from Shoreline in June 2012 and from the University Washington in 2013, with a B.A. in an interdisciplinary program of economics, international relations, philosophy and religion.

As I said, from a very young age, Jamie demonstrated serious interest in religion. In 2008, encouraged by friendships with several Muslims his age and after talking with leaders in a local mosque, Jamie became a Muslim by reciting the Shahadah: *There is no God but God (Allah) and Mohammed is God's prophet.* That same year, he took a four week course in Judaism taught by the rabbi of a local Reform synagogue. As a Muslim, Jamie prays faithfully five times most days, fasts devotedly during Ramadan and continues to have serious engagement with his Islamic faith. He frequently engages Carol and me in discussions about religious beliefs and practices, and about developments in the Middle East. Having met via an internet Islamic marriage site, Jamie carried on an email and skype relationship with Hena Parveen, a young Indian Muslim woman. In December 2012, our whole family travelled to Delhi where we met Hena's family and participated in a Muslim family wedding celebration. Returning to the United States, Jamie and Hena were legally married in Seattle and celebrated their marriage in the Fellowship Hall of Carol's church with a lovely Indian buffet dinner attended by Muslims from Jamie's mosque, members of our Lutheran church, and many relatives and friends. A year later Hena gave birth to their son, Omar, our first grandson.

I feel deeply blessed by both Jonah and Jamie. Interestingly, each has absorbed or adopted a passion of mine and lived it out more fully. I remember two incredible experiences I had in the Rocky Mountains in my thirties, one time going solo camping in a wind so strong that it blew the tent down flat over my body, and another time climbing in the snow to a high mountain cabin from which I skied down the next day, passing within twenty-five yards of a herd of big horn sheep. In 1998, when Carol turned 50 and I was 56, our family climbed Mt. St. Helens together. Jonah is a wonderful elementary school teacher and he's taken love of the outdoors to higher, much more challenging levels. I pray that his teaching, his enthusiasm and his practical, learned wisdom for venturing into the world's wildernesses will be a blessing to him and to others for many years to come.

As a new American Muslim, with an Indian Muslim wife and Muslim son, Jamie has certainly taken my interfaith work for peace to a much deeper, personal level. I remember the inspiration I felt as a Christian marching with Rabbi Abraham Joshua Heschel in Selma for civil rights and later in Washington for peace in Vietnam, and then reading his book, *The Prophets*. In my work for peace in the Middle East, I've continually been inspired by knowing Muslim religious leaders, including Dr. Sayyid Syeed, Dawud Assad, Warith Deen Mohammed and Imam Feisal Abdul Rahman. Jamie has met some of them, and Dr. Syeed has taken a keen interest in Jamie's academic and career path. Jamie reflects a profound awareness and appreciation of Allah's greatness, oneness and extraordinary mercy towards us all. The phrase from the Quran, recited in almost every Muslim prayer, that reflects this belief is, *"Bismallah al-rahman, al-rahim* (In the name of God, the most gracious, the most merciful). I am so grateful for Jamie's inspiration, and I pray that he may be blessed and be a blessing to others.

Family Trip to the Middle East

In the summer of 2002, Carol had a three month sabbatical from St. John United Lutheran Church. Jonah was twenty-one, and attending Western Washington University in Bellingham; Jamie was sixteen, entering his junior year of high school. We decided it was important for our sons to have firsthand experience with some of the people and places that were so familiar and so important to Carol and me. We decided to take a family trip to the Middle East.

In July we flew to England, where we spent a few days touring London. Early one morning, our boys took a fast train over to Paris, where they literally ran to visit Notre Dame, the Louvre, Musee de L'Orangerie, and the Eiffel Tower, all in one day. They got take-out food from McDonalds to eat on the train and returned to London late that night. The next day we all flew from London to Israel, where we had a reservation to stay at a small hotel in East Jerusalem.

Our first day in Jerusalem we walked for hours through the Old City, stopping at shops, visiting the Lutheran Church of the Redeemer, the Church of the Holy Sepulcher, the Western Wall of the Temple, and from a distance viewed the gray-domed Al Aksa mosque and golden Dome of the Rock, both of which were closed to tourists at the time. As there were very few tourists in the Old City, several times we were followed by local shopkeepers offering lower and lower prices for their wares. We wound up buying several items, in part to respond to their lowering the prices and, I suppose, to relieve our consciences over their desperate situation.

We telephoned Palestinian and Israeli friends whom we knew from twenty years earlier. Dr. Hanna Nasser, president of Bir Zeit University, insisted that we come to the university for lunch. Hana had been forcibly taken by Israeli military forces and dropped by helicopter into Lebanon in 1974. He made his way to Jordan and he and his wife Tanya wound up living a few blocks from us in Amman. They had been allowed to return home to the West Bank in 1993 as part of the Oslo peace process. We arranged for a Palestinian taxi to drive us to the university. Because his taxi had yellow Jerusalem plates, the driver was able to travel on a road reserved for Israelis and mainly used by Israeli settlers. When we neared Bir Zeit, he turned off the restricted road and drove very carefully over a dirt barrier to get into the village. Tanya had arranged a lovely luncheon for us, and our boys had a chance to see Palestinian students studying and walking about the campus on a beautiful sunny day when, as it happened, there were no clashes with Israeli soldiers.

The next day we took a taxi to the German Colony in West Jerusalem to visit Morela and Erela BarOn. In 1983, Carol and I had arranged for Morela to travel with Palestinian Mayor Mohammed Milhem on an AFSC-sponsored US speaking tour. Luckily, on this visit, Morela was able to give us Mohammed Milhem's phone number in Amman. We called him from Jerusalem, something we could not have done before the 1994 Jordan-Israel peace treaty. We arranged to visit Mohammed and his family when we crossed the river into Jordan. No less dedicated to a two-state solution than they were in 1982, like many peace-oriented Israelis, our Israeli friends, Morela and Erela were very frustrated by their government's and our government's policies. They were very discouraged by the lack of progress toward peace.

While we were in Jerusalem, we also called the US embassy in Tel Aviv to seek an appointment with Daniel Kurtzer, American ambassador to Israel. Carol and I regularly met with Dan in the early 1980s, when he was the embassy's chief political officer. We left a message on the answering service. A few hours later Dan's secretary called and told us that he would be delighted to see us, and suggested we come to Tel Aviv after we returned from Amman and Damascus.

We traveled north in Israel, swam in the Sea of Galilee and stayed in a hotel overlooking the sea. We visited the Mount of Beatitudes, where it's said Jesus gave the Sermon on the Mount, and we looked down into the house (now below ground level and covered by protective glass) where it is believed the apostle Peter lived. We saw the preserved hull of a fishing boat, believed to be 2,000 years old, which had been uncovered and carefully lifted out of the Sea of Galilee's mud bottom. Early the next morning an Israeli taxi driver drove us to the place where we would cross the Jordan River, saying that he looked forward to the day when he could drive us all the way to Amman. On the other side, we hired a Jordanian taxi driver who drove us, all too speedily and crazily, up the long, winding road to Amman.

After getting settled in our hotel, we took a taxi to our old neighborhood in Jebel Webdeh. It was about three o'clock in the afternoon. To our surprise, the mid-afternoon scene in front of the baker's and cleaner's shops below the apartment where we had lived for three years seemed exactly the same as twenty years earlier. Having started his day very early in the morning, the baker was sitting on a chair outside his shop. He immediately recognized us and called excitedly to the cleaner who was inside pressing clothes. Both greeted us very warmly with hugs and exclamations of disbelief at how much Jonah had grown. The baker asked the same incredible question Huynh Tan Mam had asked me in 1995 when I reunited with him in Saigon. "Where have you been all this time? We've been missing you." Someone ran to find Makram, our old landlord, who came from a prominent Jordanian family and was trained as a surgeon in Moscow. His father had served as doctor to King Hussein. Makram came quickly, and enthusiastically invited us for tea, and then dinner with his family at a new restaurant in a restored ancient neighborhood of Amman. That evening, after a delicious Middle Eastern dinner, Jonah, Jamie and I enjoyed watching Carol, encouraged by Makram, as she awkwardly tried to smoke a hookah (water pipe).

The next day, we travelled south by bus to Petra, the more than 2,000 year old Nabataean city in southwest Jordan that we entered on horseback down a ten-foot-wide path between high red sandstone cliffs. Sections of ancient clay pipes that carried water into the city remain embedded in the side walls above the path. Inside Petra, we were surprised to find remains of a newly unearthed Byzantine-era church, the floor of which was covered with incredible mosaics depicting leopards, monkeys, and lions. On our way out of the ancient city, perfectly in character, our sons did their own things. Jonah insisted on going off to climb a high overlook, and Jamie wandered off ahead, meeting a Jordanian guide his age and accepting his invitation to have tea with the young man's family on the outskirts of the city. We all met for dinner back at our hotel and watched a beautiful sunset over the red rocks of Petra.

Returning to Amman, we enjoyed a wonderful evening at the home of Palestinian Mayor Mohammed Milhem and his wife, and we brought him warm greetings from Morela. As noted earlier, Mohammed was elected mayor of the West Bank village of Halhoul in 1976, and then in 1981 deposed and exiled by Israel to Amman. He was always known for his principled politics and personal integrity. Although he joined the PLO executive committee at Chairman Arafat's urging, like Dr. Hanna Nasir and Mayor Qawasmeh, he was continuously frustrated by Fateh's corruption and often found himself in conflict with Arafat. Now, retired from PLO and Palestinian politics, Mohammed spoke sadly about all the opportunities for peace that had been missed and all the lives that had been wasted in the meantime. While he still hoped for a two-state agreement, given the lack of committed, capable, courageous political leadership on the ground and in the US in 2002, like our Israeli friends, Mohammed saw little prospect of progress.

The next day we left Amman by hired car for Damascus. We made a three hour stopover at Jerash, Jordan, one of the best preserved ancient cities of the Roman Decapolis. As at Petra, Carol and I were amazed at the new archeological discoveries. A beautiful second public theater on the north side of Jerash had been uncovered since our last visit.

In Damascus, where daytime temperatures were over 100 degrees, we stayed at a pleasant hotel with a pool. Despite the heat, we walked a lot in the Old City. We revisited the Street Called Straight, and Dabdoub's (our favorite craft shop), as well as a much smaller shop near the House of Ananias (now a small meditative chapel) where it's said Saul/Paul stayed after being temporarily blinded on the road to Damascus. On our visit to the spectacular Omayyad Mosque, Jamie, who insisted on wearing shorts because it was so hot, had to put on a black cape and long skirt to be adequately covered. His unusual dress didn't deter him from wandering off. We found him a bit later, sitting with a Syrian family, trying to carry on a conversation in broken English about Islam.

One day, while our boys were swimming in the hotel pool, Carol and I had lunch with a friend who had hosted us twenty years ago at his mother's home in the ancient Christian village of Mamarita, across the valley from the famous Crac de Chevallier, a Crusades-era castle. On a walk in the hills that day, he commented on the irony that while the Crac is now a minor tourist site, Mamarita is still basically the same, simple Christian village it was when the European Crusaders arrived. A Greek Orthodox Syrian, he loved the theology of Teilhard de Chardin and was working on a translation of David Bohm's book, *Wholeness and the Implicate Order.* Carol and I remembered how twenty years earlier, he had waited until the three of us were alone on a mountainside near Mamarita before he would talk about the human rights situation in Syria.

The next day we met an Iraqi businessman and his son, who was Jamie's age, visiting from Baghdad. While adamant in his negative view of Saddam Hussein, the dad seemed very appreciative that Carol and I opposed the US invasion and occupation of Iraq. Jamie and the boy, neither of whom spoke the other's language, played together enthusiastically in the pool. Even in this simple, brief conversation, we experienced the familiar, complex combination of Arab admiration for American principles and accomplishments, and expressions of frustration and anger at US Middle East policies.

I went to the US embassy to meet with the chief political officer. As had happened on many visits to the embassy in the early 1980s, I came away with a more complex, nuanced, and believable picture of Syrian interests and policies than the typical negative views commonly expressed by many Washington policymakers and members of Congress. In 2011, while there was considerable media coverage of the dramatic popular uprising in Syria and the Assad government's violent responses, Carol and I wished that the coverage had been accompanied by more knowledgeable political analyses, including more objective understanding of the diverse communities in Syria, the Syrian regime, and its relationship with Russia and Iran. In being slow to seek Russia's cooperation and opposing Iran's participation in a second Geneva conference, I believe American Cold War and War on Terrorism blinders contributed to the failure of US and international diplomacy that could have helped end the catastrophic conflict in Syria.

We visited Mohammad Bashar Arafat and his family who had come from Baltimore to visit his family in Damascus. Bashar took us to meet the vice president of the Abu Noor Institute, a center that annually trains more than 1,000 Muslims from many different countries in modern, moderate Orthodox Islam. We learned that he had played a role in convincing President Bashar al-Assad to open up the internet in Syria.

Late one afternoon, we joined Mahat Khoury, owner of the bookshop that we had regularly visited in Damascus, for tea at the Meridian Hotel. We thanked her again for introducing us to so many interesting Syrians. She met Jamie for the first time, and remembered that Jonah was only three years old and barely three feet tall when she last saw him.

On our last night in Damascus, Tarek Shallah, our travel agent, invited us to join his family for dinner at a restaurant popular among artists and theatre people in a newly renovated, lovely neighborhood in the Old City. Tarek spoke to us again about his vision, once peace was achieved, of his agency offering tourist packages that would include visits to Israel, Jordan and Syria. We drove back to Amman the next morning, and then took a minibus driven by our old friend Ali down to the Allenby Bridge. We crossed the Jordan River into the West Bank, and after a stop for lunch in Jericho, rode to Jerusalem in an Israeli taxi.

On our last day in Israel, we traveled down to Tel Aviv where Carol and I had an appointment with Ambassador Kurtzer. We left Jonah and Jamie in the old city of Jaffa, south of Tel Aviv. They didn't have swimsuits, but they couldn't resist the temptation of the Mediterranean, so they went swimming in their shorts. As a result, they both were still somewhat damp that night on our flight home.

When Carol and I arrived at the embassy, an aide to Ambassador Kurtzer was waiting to escort us in; a young Marine simply glanced at our passports and waved us through, and Dan's aide took us directly to his office. Greeting each other warmly, we spoke about our respective children and enjoyed a laugh about the time I had chauffeured Dan in our old, unarmored Quaker VW beetle in Amman to meet Palestinian Mayor Fahd Qawasmeh. Dan again thanked us very appreciatively for introducing him to Mayor Qawasmeh and the three of us shared a moment of sad remembrance.

We discussed current developments in the region and agreed that the United States needed to make providing more active, consistent and engaged leadership for Arab-Israeli-Palestinian peace a higher priority. Dan asserted that a special envoy would be needed to work continuously on the ground for the negotiations; he believed the parties had to be effectively monitored and held accountable for implementing their commitments; and he believed that the United States should coordinate with other countries. To its credit, in 2002 the Bush administration was coordinating with the European Union, Russia and the United Nations in pursuing the Road Map to peace, which also called for monitoring the parties and for holding them accountable, although those features of the Road Map were never seriously implemented. Dan acknowledged that the administration should listen to domestic advocacy groups, including religious groups, but he also believed firmly that no groups should be allowed to dictate American policy. For a fuller offering of Dan's views, see Daniel Kurtzer and Scott Lasensky, *Negotiating Arab-Israeli Peace*, published by the US Institute for Peace.

Dan encouraged me to organize and lead more interreligious delegations to the region, saying he believed these visits were valuable both for American participants who came away with more complex and nuanced understandings of the conflict, and for Arabs and Israelis who encountered these delegations as inspiring examples of uniquely American interreligious cooperation. Carol and I came away wishing that policymakers in Washington were listening more carefully to Dan and following his wise counsel more closely. I remembered having almost exactly the same feeling in March 1980 in El Salvador, meeting with Ambassador Robert White. In both cases, it was encouraging and inspiring to meet and listen to the views of these sensitive and wise American ambassadors, but very discouraging to discover how relatively little influence their views had in Washington on US policies.

Renewing our friendship with Dan Kurtzer in modern Tel Aviv while our sons swam in the Mediterranean off the shore of what had been the old Arab Palestinian city of Jaffa seemed a fitting way to end our family trip to the Middle East.

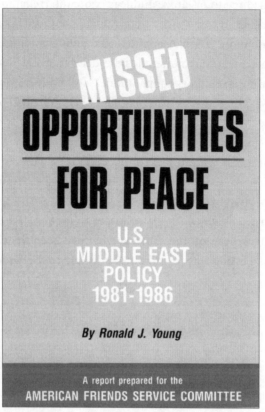

Ron's book, *Missed Opportunities for Peace*,
accepted as his Senior Thesis for graduation
from Wesleyan at forty-four years old

Ron with his mom, dad, and son Jonah
at Wesleyan Graduation June 1986

Ron with founders of the US Interreligious Committee for Peace in the Middle East:
Imam Warith Deen Mohammed, Fr. J. Bryan Hehir, Rabbi Arthur Hertzberg, and Dawud Assad.
(Co-founder Rev. Dr. Joan Brown Campbell is not shown.)

Ron with Mohammed Farivar in a US Interrreligious Committee delegation
being greeted by His Majesty King Hussein in Amman, Jordan

US Interreligious Committee delegation members Victor Kovner, Saul Sorrin,
and Sr. Margaret-Rose Welch, meeting Ezer Weizman in Tel Aviv 1987

Saul Sorrin and Victor Kovner in an intense conversation
with PLO leader Abu Jihad (Khalil Wazir) in Amman 1987

Secretary of State James Baker and his wife Susan attending
an Interfaith Convocation for Peace at the National Cathedral
in Washington, DC December 1991

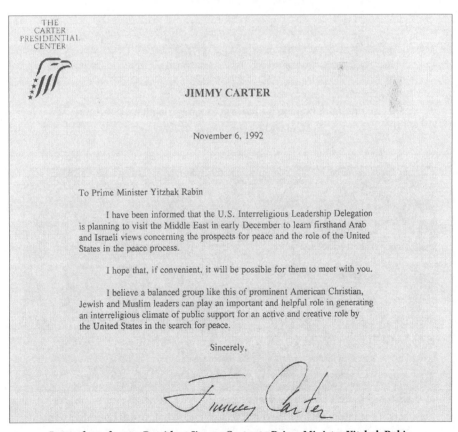

THE
CARTER
PRESIDENTIAL
CENTER

JIMMY CARTER

November 6, 1992

To Prime Minister Yitzhak Rabin

I have been informed that the U.S. Interreligious Leadership Delegation is planning to visit the Middle East in early December to learn firsthand Arab and Israeli views concerning the prospects for peace and the role of the United States in the peace process.

I hope that, if convenient, it will be possible for them to meet with you.

I believe a balanced group like this of prominent American Christian, Jewish and Muslim leaders can play an important and helpful role in generating an interreligious climate of public support for an active and creative role by the United States in the search for peace.

Sincerely,

Jimmy Carter

Letter from former President Jimmy Carter to Prime Minister Yitshak Rabin
introducing a US Interreligious Committee delegation November 1992

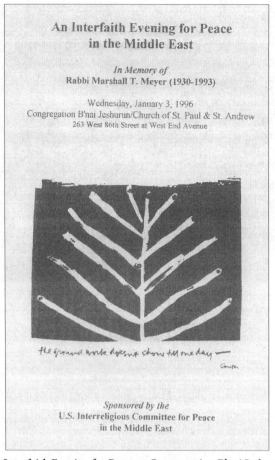

An Interfaith Evening for Peace at Congregation B'nai Jeshurun
In Memory of Rabbi Marshall T. Meyer

Speakers at the Interfaith Evening for Peace: Colette Avital, Israeli Consulate General
in New York; Ambassador Robert Pelletreau, former Assistant Secretary of State;
and Hassan Abdel Rahman, PLO Representative in Washington, DC.

Ron and Carol on their wedding day October 11, 1980

Carol and Ron with sons and daughters-in-law

Carol in alb, Pastor of St. John United Lutheran Church in Seattle

Ron, Carol and Jonah with the baker and cleaner in their old neighborhood
in Amman, Jordan on a family trip to the Middle East in 2002. Son Jamie took the photo.

NILI leaders delegation meeting with Secretary of State Hillary Clinton
September 2010

ISRAELI-PALESTINIAN PEACE BEFORE IT'S TOO LATE:
STRONG U.S. LEADERSHIP NEEDED NOW.

Mr. President,

We are Jewish, Christian and Muslim national religious leaders united in support of strong U.S. leadership for a two-state solution before it is too late.

We urge you to visit Jerusalem and the region soon to meet with Israeli and Palestinian leaders to restart negotiations focused on the principles and ideas in the Israeli Peace Initiative, the earlier Arab Peace Initiative and the Geneva Accord.

We believe the United States, in coordination with the Quartet, should continue to respond carefully to the new Palestinian unity agreement and not act precipitously to cut off aid to the Palestinians. The unity government must commit itself to rejecting violence and negotiating a two-state peace agreement with Israel.

We pledge our prayers and public support for active, fair and firm U.S. leadership for peace and we will urge Congress to support this effort.

NILI FOR PEACE IN THE MIDDLE EAST

See the full text of the Letter at the website of the *National Interreligious Leadership Initiative for Peace in the Middle East*: www.nili-mideastpeace.org

——— LIST OF ENDORSERS ———

CHRISTIAN LEADERS
His Eminence Theodore Cardinal McCarrick, Archbishop Emeritus of Washington *
Bishop Howard Hubbard, Chairman, International Committee, U.S. Conference of Catholic Bishops*
Archbishop Vicken Aykazian, Director, Ecumenical Affairs, Armenia Orthodox Church in America*
Fr. Mark Arey, Director, Ecumenical Officer, Greek Orthodox Archdiocese of America*
The Reverend Peg Chemberlin, President, National Council of Churches of Christ USA*
The Reverend Michael Kinnamon, General Secretary, National Council of Churches of Christ USA*
Bishop Mark S. Hanson, Presiding Bishop, Evangelical Lutheran Church in America*
The Most Rev. Dr. Katharine Jefferts Schori, Presiding Bishop and Primate, Episcopal Church*
The Reverend Geoffrey Black, General Minister & President, United Church of Christ*
The Rev. Dr. Sharon Watkins, General Minister, President, Christian Churches (Disciples of Christ)*
The Reverend Gradye Parsons, Stated Clerk, Presbyterian Church (USA)*
Bishop Sharon Zimmerman Rader, Council of Bishops, United Methodist Church*
The Reverend Leighton Ford, President, Leighton Ford Ministries, Board Member, World Vision US*
Richard J. Mouw, President, Fuller Theological Seminary*
David Neff, Editor in Chief and Vice-President, Christianity Today*
The Reverend John M. Buchanan, Editor and Publisher, Christian Century*

JEWISH LEADERS
Rabbi Peter Knobel, Past President, Central Conference of American Rabbis*
Rabbi Paul Menitoff, Executive Vice President Emeritus, Central Conference of American Rabbis*
Rabbi Alvin Sugarman, Vice President, A Different Future*
Rabbi Elliot Dorff, Rector, American Jewish University*
Rabbi Burton Visotzky, Professor of Midrash & Interreligious Studies, Jewish Theological Seminary*
Rabbi Freddi Cooper, President, Reconstructionist Rabbinical Assembly*
Rabbi Shawn Zevit, Director of Congregational Services, Jewish Reconstructionist Federation*
Dr. Carl Sheingold, Former Executive Vice President, Jewish Reconstructionist Federation*

MUSLIM LEADERS
Dr. Sayyid Muhammad Syeed, National Director, Islamic Society of North America*
Imam Mohammed ibn Hagmagid, Vice President, Islamic Society of North America*
Naeem Baig, Executive Director, Islamic Circle of North America*
Dawud Assad, President Emeritus, Council of Mosques, USA*
Eide Alawan, Interfaith Office for Outreach, Islamic Center of America*

*Organizations for Identification Only

NILI sponsored Ad in Politico.com on the day Israeli Prime Minister Netanyahu
spoke in Congress May 2011

10

Heads of Religious Organizations Unite for Peace: But There Is No Peace

Engaging the heads of twenty-five Jewish, Christian and Muslim national religious organizations in a new initiative for Middle East Peace (NILI); a consensus on "Principles of Cooperation" and "Twelve Urgent Steps for Peace"; cooperation or conflict within and between our three communities; why I continue doing interfaith work for peace; President Obama in Jerusalem; and the Kerry initiative for peace.

National Interreligious Leadership Initiative for Peace

IN MAY 2003 I got a telephone call from Dr. Bruce Wexler, a psychiatrist who teaches at Yale University. My friend, Rabbi Jim Ponet, director of the Yale Hillel Foundation, where I had lectured twice, had urged Wexler to contact me to discuss his idea of bringing together top religious leaders to provide a powerful united voice for moderation and peace in the Middle East. As Wexler and I talked, it was clear that his goals were very similar to those of the USICPME that I had organized and led since 1987, but Bruce wanted to increase the visibility and clout of this work by enlisting the heads of national religious organizations.

Based on my significant relationships with many Jewish, Christian and Muslim leaders, it made sense for me to help organize this new initiative. By the end of the summer, Bruce and I had received positive responses from heads of twenty-five national religious organizations to participate in what we were calling the National Interreligious Leadership Initiative for Peace in the Middle East (NILI). Given the similarity between the two efforts, after I consulted with the three co-chairs and the board of USICPME, we decided to put the older organization on hold, while I worked to develop the new initiative. The formation of NILI received initial financial support from the Nathan Cummings Foundation and invaluable assistance from the prestigious public relations firm of Ruder Finn.

In June 2003, President Bush met with Israeli Prime Minister Sharon and Palestinian President Mahmoud Abbas in Aqaba, Jordan to advance the Road Map to Peace, launched in 2002 by the United States in coordination with the Quartet. Despite earlier disappointments, peace-oriented Israelis and Palestinians responded favorably to the Road Map for several reasons. First, coordinated with the EU, Russia and the UN Secretary General's office, it was multilateral, not a unilateral US initiative; second, it called for clear benchmark steps by both sides and a timetable for progress; and third, it represented a performance based approach that was to include monitoring both sides' implementation of the steps they agreed to take. The biggest question was: would the United States follow through on this effort with more consistency, creativity and determination than it had on earlier initiatives?

In late summer and fall of 2003, I drafted and circulated proposed principles of cooperation and twelve specific urgent steps for peace for the religious leaders to consider.[1] In addition to grounding NILI's formation on fundamental moral imperatives for peace of the three Abrahamic faith traditions, one of the most important principles of cooperation realistically reflected the unique challenges of interreligious cooperation for Israeli-Palestinian peace

> Recognizing and appreciating the deep, precious bonds many of us have with different sides of this conflict and how these bonds cause us to have different and sometimes conflicting viewpoints, we believe our areas of agreement are more important than our disagreements, and we commit ourselves to work together conscientiously and sensitively to emphasize our common agenda for peace.

The twelve steps I proposed supported the Quartet's Road Map. Four steps were directed toward our own government, four toward the Palestinian Authority, and four toward the Israeli government. Following several email exchanges and conference calls, by Thanksgiving 2003, we achieved consensus on the principles of cooperation and the "twelve urgent steps" among thirty-two national religious leaders, including top officials from Jewish Reform, Conservative and Reconstructionist movements. Christians included top national leaders of the US Conference of Catholic Bishops, the Greek Orthodox and Armenian Orthodox churches, and six Protestant denominations, including the Evangelical Lutheran Church in America, Episcopal Church, Presbyterian Church (USA), United Methodist Church, Christian Church (Disciples of Christ) and the United Church of Christ. Conservative Christian evangelical leaders included the editor of *Christianity Today*, the president of Fuller Seminary, the president of Leighton Ford Ministries, and the president of World Vision. Muslim

---

1. NILI "Principles of Cooperation" and "Twelve Urgent Steps for Peace."

leaders included heads of the two largest Islamic umbrella religious organizations: the Islamic Society of North America and the Islamic Circle of North America, as well as the Palestinian American president emeritus of the Council of Mosques USA, the founder of the American Society for Muslim Advancement and the Cordoba Initiative, and the Palestinian American Muslim chaplain of Georgetown University and president of Clergy Beyond Borders. NILI represented an unprecedented coalition of Jewish, Christian and Muslim national religious leaders.

On December 3, 2003 I coordinated a press conference at the National Press Club, chaired by Cardinal Theodore McCarrick, archbishop of Washington, to announce formation of NILI, and our proposed twelve urgent steps for peace. At my suggestion, significantly, Jewish leaders addressed the actions we believed Israel needed to take and Muslim leaders addressed those the Palestinian Authority needed to take.

Two days before the press conference, the Geneva Accord was publicly presented in Washington. With support of the Swiss government over a period of two years, this informal, unofficial, model peace agreement had been negotiated by prominent Israelis and Palestinians, several of whom had been involved in the official Oslo process and in the negotiations that produced the Taba Agreement in 2001. Building on the Clinton Parameters and Taba, the Geneva Accord represented a comprehensive, detailed unofficial peace treaty for a two-state resolution, with specific solutions for resolving all issues in the conflict. Public opinion polls taken soon after the Accord's release indicated that the compromises proposed by it would likely be acceptable to popular majorities of both Israelis and Palestinians. The serendipitous timing of NILI's announcement, combined with excellent PR work by Ruder Finn resulted in our receiving extensive positive national and international media coverage.

On December 6, Peter Steinfels, Religion Editor of *The New York Times*, devoted his entire weekly column to NILI. Entitled "Mideast Initiative Pushes Beyond Platitudes,"[2] Steinfels wrote that he was particularly impressed that prominent, mainstream national Jewish, Christian and Muslim religious leaders were united in advocating specific policies rather than simply supporting general principles. NILI specifically urged the Bush administration to: 1) work urgently for an end to violence and an effective, durable ceasefire; 2) appoint a special envoy who would be consistently and actively engaged negotiating with the parties in the region; 3) insist on simultaneous specific steps by both sides, with timetables and public monitoring of their implementation (as examples, NILI called on Israel to freeze all settlement expansion and on the Palestinian Authority to halt all violent attacks); and 4) support benchmark principles and ideas, such as those in the Geneva Accord, for possible mutually acceptable solutions to resolve final status issues, including the crucial and emotional issues of refugees and Jerusalem. Steinfels concluded his column by saying that NILI's platform "suggested that a consensus might stretch a lot further across religious opinion in the United States and run a lot deeper than a few vague phrases." In its

2. Steinfels, "Mideast Initiative Pushes Beyond Platitudes."

specificity and fairness, NILI's consensus statement contrasted with many politically motivated congressional resolutions that are typically one-sided and often decidedly unhelpful to advancing negotiations for peace.

At the end of the press conference, anticipating challenges they might face from within their respective communities, three of the religious leaders summed up NILI's message by saying that it provided broad, interreligious support for active, fair and firm US leadership for peace.

The NILI consensus contrasted with the advocacy stance of Christians United for Israel (CUFI), the well-funded organization headed by Reverend John Hagee, a conservative fundamentalist Christian who loudly proclaimed "pro-Israel" and anti-Palestinian views. Disagreeing sharply with Hagee, David Neff, Editor of *Christianity Today*, the national Christian evangelical magazine founded by Billy Graham, said he believed 65 percent to 70 percent of Christian evangelicals would support a two-state solution. Predicting that there would be strong evangelical support for successful US leadership for peace, Neff said,

> If the Bush administration is able to seize this moment and provide American leadership that actually results in a stable and peaceful resolution between Israel and Palestine, I think almost all of America's evangelicals will praise him.

Rabbi Paul Menitoff, said he believed that there was more agreement than disagreement among American Jews about the likely compromises necessary to resolve the conflict. He, too, stressed the need for urgent and decisive US leadership. Referring to the Geneva Accord as an example, Menitoff said,

> The general outlines of a final peace agreement are widely recognized. . . .The question is how many more Israelis and Palestinians will be killed before the inevitable peace is achieved. Will President Bush act decisively with the Israeli and Palestinian leadership to lessen the body count?

Imam Feisal Abdul Rauf, Founder of the Cordoba Initiative, said he believed that resolving the Arab-Israeli conflict was essential to reducing the threat of terrorism, and concluded his remarks by emphasizing the futility of further violence by either side.

> We believe that 100 more years of Palestinian suicide bombings will not drive Israel into the sea, and we believe that 100 more years of Israeli targeted assassinations will never dry up the reservoir of young Palestinians willing to give up their lives.

The religious leaders promised to use all the instruments at their disposal, e.g., pulpits, worship bulletins, newsletters, publications, email messages, websites and networks with their colleagues to build a broad interfaith movement based on NILI's principles and its twelve urgent steps. They pledged their communities' active, public support for making pursuit of Arab-Israeli-Palestinian peace an urgent priority of US foreign policy.

During the next twelve months, I traveled to thirty-five American cities where I met with local Jewish, Christian and Muslim leaders to whom I was given introductions by the national leaders involved in NILI. They welcomed NILI as a very helpful model for cooperation, providing principled and practical guidelines for advocacy that they could copy at the local level. On several occasions when NILI's national leaders communicated consensus concerns to the president and secretary of state, many of the more than 500 local rabbis, pastors, priests, imams, and lay people to whom I sent email action alerts responded by sending similar specific messages to their Senators and Representatives.

Concerned about the continuing cycle of violence and the lack of progress, six months after NILI's public launch, we met with Secretary of State Colin Powell to press for more active and determined leadership by the Bush administration. In a friendly and candid exchange, Powell said he agreed with our call for a special envoy, but the administration was waiting for a more promising moment to appoint one. NILI leaders argued that sending an envoy promptly could help break the stalemate and get negotiations going. We also advocated that the administration, in coordination with the Quartet, should spell out specific, simultaneous steps each side needed to take, along with a timetable and procedures to monitor their implementation. While national NILI leaders were meeting with Secretary Powell, hundreds of local religious leaders and lay people sent similar messages to members of Congress. We felt that Colin Powell listened attentively and empathetically to our concerns. Unfortunately, President Bush and Vice President Cheney were almost totally focused on the invasion and occupation of Iraq, and they were not listening to advice from Powell.

Another very significant convergence of national and local interreligious efforts occurred at a practical level in February 2005 when I was asked to provide information about NILI to the US Conference of Catholic Bishops as they were preparing a nationwide Catholic campaign for peace in the Holy Land. A few months later, the Catholic campaign called on local diocesan bishops and Catholic leaders "to partner actively with local religious leaders in the Jewish, Muslim and other Christian traditions" and urged local bishops to be guided by NILI's principles and its consensus public policy advocacy agenda.

In June 2005, in cooperation with A Different Future (another new organization started by Bruce Wexler), NILI sponsored an innovative trans-national video conference broadcast on the web from Jerusalem and Washington. In fifty local synagogues, churches and mosques across the United States and venues in Australia, Brazil, Egypt, Jordan and the Netherlands, more than 3,500 participants witnessed prominent Israelis and Palestinians advocating for peace before a live audience in Jerusalem, and American religious leaders addressing a live audience in our nation's capital. In the run up to the video conference, NILI leaders persuaded Senator Richard Lugar (R-IN), chairman of the Senate foreign relations committee and Representative Henry Hyde

(R-IL), chairman of the House international relations committee, to initiate a "Dear Colleague" letter, urging more active leadership for peace by the Bush administration.

Despite these and other efforts, violence between Palestinians and Israelis, and Israeli settlement expansion continued. Tragically, between 2004 and 2006, more than 4,000 Palestinians and 1,000 Israelis, the majority of them civilians, were killed and many more wounded. The Road Map appeared to be going nowhere.

Israeli fears and frustration during this period were manifest in public support for their government's decision to build a "security barrier" the entire length of the West Bank and for Prime Minister Sharon's decision to unilaterally withdraw Israeli forces from Gaza. Sharon acknowledged the dilemma for Israel as a Jewish and democratic state posed by holding on to the occupied territories. Between 80 percent and 85 percent of Israelis, including many principled advocates for peace, supported both of these Israeli government initiatives. Ironically, Sharon's decision to withdraw unilaterally from Gaza—instead of negotiating the withdrawal with the Palestinian Authority—allowed Hamas to claim that it was their violent attacks that forced Israel to withdraw. The route of the Israeli security wall cut substantially into West Bank territory, and thus increased daily hardships for Palestinians and reinforced perceptions that Israel had no intention of negotiating a viable two-state solution. NILI religious leaders expressed understanding of Israel's need to protect its citizens, but called for halting construction of the security barrier "in areas that require confiscation of Palestinian land and threaten the viability of a contiguous Palestinian state."

Palestinian frustration with lack of progress towards peace and with widespread corruption in the Fateh-dominated Palestinian Authority was reflected in the 2006 Palestinian elections, in which Hamas won more than 40 percent of the votes and Ismail Haniyeh of Hamas became the new prime minister. While the Bush administration had pushed for the elections to be held and acknowledged that they were free and fair, the United States labeled Hamas a "terrorist organization" and, given the War on Terrorism as a guiding basis for foreign policy, the US refused to meet with Haniyeh's new government. To its credit, the White House did resist congressional pressure to cut off all aid to the Palestinians. However, as tensions between Fateh and Hamas intensified, the administration directed US aid exclusively to Fateh, thus clearly taking sides. In 2007, a violent confrontation erupted between the two factions, and Hamas took control of the Gaza Strip, effectively creating two governing authorities: Hamas in Gaza and Fateh in the West Bank.

The Bush administration continued to be preoccupied with Iraq. In March 2005, responding to international Arab and Muslim criticism, President Bush invited Karen P. Hughes, his Texas friend and advisor, to serve as undersecretary for public diplomacy and public affairs, to try to improve the image of America in Arab and Muslim countries. After traveling to the Middle East and South Asia in fall 2005, Hughes said that while many people she met were deeply troubled by the US invasion and occupation of Iraq, many were even more concerned over the urgent need for greater US efforts to achieve peace between the Palestinians and Israel. NILI leaders met with Karen Hughes in February 2006, just after Hamas's election victory. We expressed support for the administration's resistance to congressional calls for cutting off aid to the Palestinians, and advocated for more determined US leadership on behalf of the Road Map.

NILI also urged the administration to meet with leaders of the Council of Religious Institutions in the Holy Land, which was composed of the highest level Jewish, Christian and Muslim religious leaders in Israel and the Palestinian territories. These leaders had endorsed the 2002 Alexandria Declaration, condemning the killing of innocents, and they were committed to working together for peace and reconciliation. Hughes told NILI's leaders that she was certain the president would want to meet with these Israeli and Palestinian religious leaders.

The NILI leaders also expressed disappointment that they had not been able to get a meeting with President Bush. When Hughes learned that our request had been made through conservative deputy national security advisor Elliott Abrams, she looked skeptical and made a point of saying she would speak personally with the president on NILI's behalf. We never did succeed in meeting with Bush and, unfortunately, Karen Hughes left the administration in October 2007 to return to Texas.

In the fall and winter of 2005 to 2006, I arranged and/or participated in several programs that helped increase NILI's public visibility and further developed interreligious advocacy efforts for peace, and I spoke at dozens of congregations and community forums across the country. In October, 2005 the Kroc Institute for International Peace Studies at Notre Dame sponsored a major program entitled, *When Faiths Unite: Religion and US Policy Toward the Israeli-Palestinian Conflict.* Speakers included Rabbi David Saperstein, director of the Religious Action Center of Reform Judaism; Imam Feisal Abdul Rauf, founder and director of the Cordoba Initiative; and myself.

Over the next year, I arranged a series of conference call briefings, each time involving eighty to a hundred national and local religious leaders. Guest speakers on several of these conference calls included Ziad Asali, president of the American Task Force on Palestine, and M.J. Rosenberg, director of the Washington DC office of the Israel Policy Forum. Having representatives of mainstream, peace-oriented Jewish American and Palestinian American national organizations on the same call, and hearing their genuine support for each other's views helped concerned people learn that there was a hopeful convergence of advocacy positions among major national organizations in favor of Middle East peace. The calls also helped to support and encourage greater cooperation among local Jewish, Christian and Muslim religious leaders.

On July 12, 2006 Lebanese Hezbollah militants launched a rocket attack across the northern border of Israel, killing three Israeli soldiers and capturing two more. The IDF immediately responded with overwhelming air power, attacking Beirut and Southern Lebanon. Hezbollah rockets rained down on northern Israel. More than

1,000 people, mostly Lebanese, were killed; a million Lebanese and several hundred thousand Israelis were displaced. Some Israelis, including Amos Oz and David Grossman, two of Israel's most prominent novelists, called for an immediate ceasefire. Believing that given additional time, Israeli military forces could achieve a decisive victory over Hezbollah and a shift in the political balance in Lebanon to be more favorable to Israel and the United States, the Bush administration opposed calls for an immediate ceasefire. The war was ended by a ceasefire brokered by the United Nations. One of many personal tragedies was that two days before the ceasefire, David Grossman's son, Uri, a member of the IDF, was killed in Lebanon.

In the aftermath of the war in Lebanon, on September 7, 2006, Cardinal McCarrick hosted a meeting of twenty-five Jewish, Christian and Muslim national religious leaders in Washington, where they adopted a new consensus statement titled, "Arab-Israeli-Palestinian Peace: From Crisis to Hope," based on a draft that Steve Colecchi of the US Catholic Conference and I had prepared in consultation with the NILI Steering Committee. It urged strict adherence to the UN Security Council resolutions that ended the Hezbollah-Israel war, renewed and more determined US support for the Road Map, and efforts to restart Israeli-Syrian and Israeli-Lebanese peace negotiations. The NILI national leaders posted the statement on their organizations' websites and circulated it widely to their nationwide networks.

On January 29, 2007, a NILI delegation met with Secretary of State Condoleezza Rice to advocate for the messages in the new consensus statement. As a result, she asked Under Secretary Nicholas Burns to meet regularly with NILI leaders to continue the dialogue. NILI leaders sent a letter to every member of Congress about the new consensus statement, and I urged local leaders to communicate our message to their members of Congress.

In June 2007, on the fortieth anniversary of the 1967 war, NILI issued a press release reflecting concerns we had raised earlier with the State Department. We expressed support for the bipartisan Senate Resolution 321 co-sponsored by Senators Feinstein (D-CA), Lugar (R-IN), Dodd (D-CT), Hagel (R-NE) and thirty-three other senators, which echoed NILI's concern for more active US leadership for peace, including the appointment of a special envoy. Once again, NILI encouraged local religious leaders to send similar messages to their Senators and Representatives.

We met with Under Secretary Nicholas Burns in August and again in November 2007 to present recommendations for the Annapolis peace conference that the Bush administration planned to host in December. NILI urged the Bush administration to invite leaders of the Council of Religious Institutions in the Holy Land (mentioned above) to be observers, but no invitations were issued. A short time later, NILI hosted a delegation from the Council that had come to Washington. We were able to arrange good appointments for them with several key Senators, but we could not get a meeting for them with President Bush.

Despite hopes that the Annapolis conference would restart peace negotiations, the situation on the ground deteriorated. A shaky six month ceasefire between Hamas and Israel ended on December 19, 2008. There were no serious diplomatic efforts to extend the ceasefire, in part because the United States continued to refuse to deal with Hamas. Hamas launched hundreds of rockets from Gaza into southern Israel, to which Israel predictably responded with an air attack, followed by a ground assault, called "Operation Cast Lead." For the first time since its founding, NILI was not able to achieve a consensus statement in response. I fault myself for inadequate consultation in preparing a draft but more importantly, NILI leaders could not reach agreement because the three constituent communities reacted very differently to the fighting. To their credit, local Jewish, Christian and Muslim leaders in Boston, Chicago and Los Angeles did manage to issue interfaith statements calling for an immediate ceasefire.

Weeks later, Hamas and Israel initiated separate ceasefires and the fighting stopped. In less than a month thirteen Israelis and more than 1,300 Palestinians had been killed, and hundreds more had been wounded. The destruction in Gaza was terrible. NILI leaders reached consensus on a carefully crafted letter to newly inaugurated President Barack Obama in January 2009. Acknowledging the different reactions of our communities, NILI urged diplomatic efforts to achieve an effective and durable ceasefire, international measures to prevent resupply of rockets to Hamas, Israeli withdrawal from Gaza, opening of border crossings, and substantial humanitarian and reconstruction assistance.

In May 2009, NILI leaders sent a second letter to President Obama, this time strongly supporting his decision to make Arab-Israeli-Palestinian peace a priority of US policy and his appointment of former Senator George Mitchell as special envoy. Based on confirmed reports about improved performance of Palestinian security forces in the West Bank, we advocated that the US urge Israel to reduce the number of military checkpoints and we addressed the need for international monitoring. NILI reiterated its consistent call for a halt to Israeli settlement expansion and addressed the sensitive issue of the West Bank/Gaza split in governance between Fateh and Hamas. The religious leaders agreed on urging the United States to support efforts to form a Palestinian government capable of representing both the West Bank and Gaza, on the conditions that it would be committed to rejecting violence and negotiating a two-state peace agreement with Israel. We also urged the Obama administration to publicly support ideas, such as those in the Geneva Accord, for resolving Israeli-Palestinian final status issues; and we urged active US diplomacy to re-start peace negotiations between Israel and Syria.

In their messages to the newly elected president, the breadth of support by heads of major Jewish, Christian and Muslim national religious organizations for several, specific recommendations confirmed once again what Peter Steinfels had concluded in his *New York Times* column five years earlier, that NILI's "common platform suggests that a consensus might stretch a lot further across religious opinion in the United States and run a lot deeper than a few vague phrases."[3] In one meeting at the State Department, Rabbi David Saperstein, director of the Religious Action Center of Reform Judaism, spoke strongly on behalf of NILI when he told William Burns, "If the president presses actively and fairly for peace, he can count on majority support in synagogues, churches and mosques across the country." Christian and Muslim religious leaders strongly echoed Rabbi Saperstein's view. Clearly, there was a broad consensus; the problem was that the Bush administration had not provided the kind of active, determined leadership needed to reach a peace agreement.

President Obama seemed committed to provide such US leadership. Both as candidate and as president, Barack Obama declared Arab-Israeli-Palestinian peace to be an urgent priority of US policy. In his speech to the UN General Assembly in fall 2010, the president announced the goal of achieving a Palestinian state by September 2011. However, after failing to persuade Israel to extend a halt on settlement expansion and the breakdown of Israeli-Palestinian negotiations, the Obama administration backed off further efforts. The combination of intermittent violence and expansion of settlements, including in East Jerusalem, made a two-state agreement seem more remote.

Prospects for Peace

As 2011 began, while polls showed that majorities of Israelis and Palestinians still favored a two-state solution, and most knowledgeable observers agreed that it was the only realistic way to resolve the conflict, the chances for negotiated peace seemed to be slipping away. More people on both sides were saying that time was running out. Despite some progress on Palestinian security and economic development in the West Bank, Israeli actions—settlement expansion, Israeli-only roads, military checkpoints, and the security wall—were causing Palestinians to lose hope that a viable, contiguous, independent state was possible. The suffering in Gaza also contributed to bitter frustration, and not only among Palestinians. In many countries, empathy with the Palestinians' plight and popular anger against Israeli policies combined with persistent anti-Semitism to generate a troubling trend toward greater international isolation of Israel.

Simultaneously, Hamas' radical ideology and sporadic rocket attacks by various extremist Palestinian factions fed deep Israeli doubts about Palestinian intentions. Israeli fears and frustration were compounded by Iranian president Ahmedinejad's virulent denunciations of Israel, Iran's provision of more accurate and advanced rockets to both Hamas in Gaza and Hezbollah in Lebanon, and the threat that Iran might be developing nuclear weapons.

---

3. Steinfels, "Mideast Initiative Pushes Beyond Platitudes."

Since its founding in 2003, Jewish, Christian and Muslim leaders of NILI (and of USICPME from 1987 to 2003) have consistently advocated that more engaged, determined American leadership was essential for achieving peace. Early in Obama's Presidency, statements by Generals David Petraeus and Jim Jones that Arab-Israeli-Palestinian peace was vital to US national security and to reducing the threat of terrorism added new weight and urgency, yet there was little progress on the ground and none in negotiations. After the Obama administration's initial push failed, Israel refused to extend a freeze on settlements and the Palestinian Authority responded by refusing to rejoin negotiations unless there was a freeze. While the elements of a framework for comprehensive Arab-Israeli-Palestinian peace seemed clearer than ever, the possibility of actually achieving peace seemed as distant as ever.

It sometimes seemed as if Palestinian president Abbas wanted to get to a solution without negotiating, while Israeli Prime Minister Netanyahu wanted to negotiate without ever getting to a solution. Abbas was publicly committed to halting violence and achieving a two-state solution, but, with Gaza under Hamas's control, it wasn't clear how much support Abbas had among Palestinians. While Prime Minister Netanyahu said he accepted the idea of a Palestinian state and called for negotiations, he continued to add settlements while allowing provocative land confiscations and expansion of Jewish control in East Jerusalem. Most factions in the rightwing Israeli government publicly rejected compromises, including the idea of sharing Jerusalem. Calls to require Arab citizens of Israel to sign a special loyalty oath to the Jewish state and escalating political attacks on Israeli civil rights organizations intensified an explicitly anti-Arab, racist dimension in Israeli politics. On the Palestinian side, the divided government between the West Bank and Gaza, extremist rhetoric, and sporadic rocket attacks added to bleak prospects for progress toward peace.

Most leaders in Israel's governing coalition appeared to give little weight to the warning by former Prime Minister Ehud Olmert that Israel's existence as a Jewish and democratic state was threatened by failure to achieve a two-state solution. Peace Now had been issuing this warning since the 1980s, but to hear it coming from a former leader of the hawkish Likud was new. Like Ariel Sharon, who broke with Likud to form a new, more centrist party, Prime Minister Olmert, publicly acknowledged the demographic dilemma if Israel continued to hold on to the West Bank, ruling over 2,500,000 Palestinians there and another 1,500,000 Palestinians in Gaza. In an interview with reporters at the conclusion of the Annapolis conference in November 2007, Olmert dramatically declared, "If the day comes when the two-state solution collapses, and we face a South African-style struggle for equal voting rights (also for the Palestinians in the territories), then, as soon as that happens, the State of Israel is finished,"[4] Olmert has consistently made the same case ever since. Prime Minister Netanyahu and his rightwing allies in Israel and in America showed no signs that they shared Olmert's sense of urgency.

4. Olmert: "Two State solution or Israel is done for."

Popular frustration among growing numbers of Palestinians and their American and European supporters led to increased emphasis on BDS (boycotts, divestment and sanctions") strategies against Israel and increasing discussion of a one-state solution, even though that idea is a non-starter for the vast majority of Jews. As of 2014, while the BDS strategy gained almost no political traction in Congress, it generated support among many activists and provoked angry reactions by most supporters of Israel. The same was true for the idea of a one-state solution. It is critically important to understand why a "one-state solution" won't work. It is clear that Palestinians would not accept a non-democratic state, because it would be a version of apartheid; it is equally clear that a single democratic state from the Jordan River to the Mediterranean with equal rights for all would be unacceptable to the vast majority of Jews because it would mean once again Jews would be a minority in a non-Jewish state. Thus, pressing for a one-state solution actually would lead to further bitter, violent conflict. As difficult as it may seem currently for the parties to get there, a negotiated two-state peace agreement remains the only realistic resolution of the conflict.

Cooperation or Conflict in Public Advocacy for Mideast Peace

For more than twenty-five years, my interreligious work for peace consistently involved finding a highest common denominator for policy advocacy reflecting the convergence of views among American Jews, Christians and Muslims on what peace required and what the US should do. Frequently, we formed these united advocacy positions in the face of contentious conflicts both within and between our different communities. Since 2003, NILI reflected a substantial consensus among heads of major Jewish, Christian and Muslim national religious organizations both about the requirements for peace and the need for more engaged, determined US leadership to help the parties get there. In doing this, it is important to understand the points of common ground and also the different tendencies and disagreements both within and between our communities.

Beginning in the 1990s, a substantial consensus developed on what to advocate for Israeli-Palestinian peace among major national organizations working in Washington, including Americans for Peace Now, the American Task Force on Palestine, the Arab-American Institute, *Brit Tzedek v' shalom*, Churches for Middle East Peace, the US Conference of Catholic Bishops, and the US Interreligious Committee, then from 2003 to today, NILI. In spring 2008, JStreet, a new Jewish pro-Israel, pro-peace mainstream, national organization was formed, adding very significantly to the political clout of this constellation of groups. Viewing their websites, one can see that the language they use is appropriately different for their respective constituencies, but they generally agree about the requirements for peace and what the United States should do. At the same time, debates and tensions within each community and between our communities have continued over different views about the causes and history of the conflict, what action strategies to adopt, and what US policies to advocate. From 2010 to 2014, with few signs of progress on the ground or visible progress in negotiations, some of these intra- and inter-community conflicts intensified.

JStreet, the new "pro-Israel, pro-peace" American Jewish lobby founded in 2008, has achieved impressive popular and financial support. Wisely, JStreet sought to avoid direct conflict with the much more powerful AIPAC and some other long-established national Jewish organizations, although it was quite clear that JStreet had substantially different views from them about what it means to be "pro-Israel" and about what US policies to advocate. As an example, in March 2010 Prime Minister Netanyahu's government caused a serious rift with the Obama administration on the eve of Vice President Biden's visit to Israel by announcing plans to expand Jewish settlements in Arab East Jerusalem. AIPAC stood squarely with Netanyahu, declaring that settlement expansion in Jerusalem was legitimate and would go ahead, and urging the Obama administration to keep any disagreements with Israel "out of the public view." In contrast, JStreet publicly supported the administration standing firm in publicly criticizing Israel's settlements expansion.

While a majority of American Jews probably agreed with JStreet on settlements and the need for active US engagement, JStreet walked a fine line sometimes between firmly supporting American efforts for peace and positions viewed as "harmful to Israel" in much of the Jewish community. In February 2010, JStreet's decision to join with Churches for Middle East Peace and Arab American groups in calling for an end to the siege of Gaza, without making any reference to stopping the resupply of rockets to Hamas, was controversial among American Jews. Given widespread wariness about any UN role in resolving the conflict, it was also controversial when JStreet urged the United States not to veto the Security Council resolution in February 2011 condemning Israeli settlements as illegal and calling for resumption of negotiations. Especially after large Republican gains in the 2010 midterm congressional elections, JStreet aroused concern of some by allowing itself to be perceived as strategically allied with the Democratic Party, rather than maintaining a more strictly non-partisan or bi-partisan posture. During Obama's second term, support, including financial support, for JStreet's advocacy for peace increased. More conservative Jewish organizations including AIPAC, the American Jewish Committee and the Anti-Defamation League continued essentially to align with policies of Israel's right wing coalition government, while much smaller Jewish organizations on the left, including Jewish Voice for Peace, Jews Against Occupation and Jews for Justice for Palestinians became more outspokenly critical of Israel.

Encouragingly, JStreet's annual national conferences continued to grow in size and political impact. While JStreet concentrated almost all its energies in the Jewish community, I was invited to moderate workshops on interfaith cooperation at two of the national conferences. In the 2012 congressional elections, JStreet's lobbying arm demonstrated real political clout by exercising influence in several Congressional races. As Rabbi David Saperstein, director of the Religious Action Center of Reform Judaism, said in an address at the 2011 conference, "the strategic challenge for JStreet going forward is to advocate and organize for active, engaged US leadership for peace in ways that continue to gain greater traction with American Jews and with more members of Congress." Given the intense debate within the Jewish community and the often unthinking support for AIPAC among members of Congress, meeting this strategic challenge would require JStreet to exercise great care and creativity in deciding what and how to advocate.

In the Arab American and American Muslim communities the differences over the conflict were less focused and more complex. It is crucial to note that a majority of Arab Americans are Christians, and more than 85 percent of American Muslims are not of Arab descent. Forty percent are African American and approximately 10 percent are recent immigrants from African countries; 35 percent are from south Asia and only approximately 10 to 15 percent are from Arab countries. Most Arab Americans and most American Muslims sympathize with the Palestinians, but this is not necessarily their communities' highest priority. (It should be noted that in the West Bank, between 8 percent and 9 percent of Palestinians are Christians; in Gaza less than 1 percent are Christians.)

The Arab American and American Muslim organizations that make the Israeli-Palestinian issue a priority have important differences in emphasis and strategy. The American Task Force on Palestine and the Arab American Institute work intensively in Washington, pressing for administration policies and congressional support for a two-state solution. In contrast, *Al Awda* and the much newer American Muslims for Palestine, are both smaller, activist, grassroots organizations, that focus on supporting Palestinian refugees' right of return and a one-state solution. These latter activist Arab and Muslim groups generate serious tensions with the Jewish community since for the vast majority of Jews, advocating for the "right of return" of Palestinian refugees inside Israel or advocating for a one-state solution is tantamount to advocating the end of Israel as a state with a Jewish majority.

While top leaders of the Islamic Society of North America and the Islamic Circle of North America, the two largest North American Islamic organizations, consistently signed on to NILI statements supporting a two-state solution, constituents of these broad umbrella groups include American Muslims who hold diverse views. Furthermore, facing widespread popular ignorance and prejudice toward Islam, for many American Muslims working to protect their civil rights and struggling against Islamophobia are higher priorities than the Palestinian issue. Several developments in recent years, including the continued suffering of Palestinians in Gaza, expansion of Israeli settlements especially in Jerusalem, and explicitly anti-Arab or anti-Muslim statements and actions by Israeli officials, have exacerbated anti-Israel attitudes among American Muslims. Still, I believe most Arab Americans and most American Muslims support active, determined US efforts to achieve a negotiated two-state Israeli-Palestinian peace agreement.

Among American Christians actively concerned about the Arab-Israeli-Palestinian conflict, there is more than one division. Politically, the biggest division is between Christians United for Israel (CUFI) which often works very closely with AIPAC, and Churches for Middle East Peace (CMEP), a coalition of twenty-four Christian denominations and organizations, that works closely with Americans for Peace Now and JStreet. CUFI is a multi-million dollar rightwing campaign led by Reverend John Hagee with support from fundamentalist evangelical Christians. Based on dispensationalist "end times" theology, CUFI supports hard line, hawkish Israeli policies. While they identify themselves as Christian Zionists, their alliance with rightwing Israeli political forces indicate that they really should be considered "Christian Likudniks." On specific issues, CUFI creates alliances of convenience with AIPAC and occasionally with other American Jewish organizations. CUFI supports and even provides financial support for expansion of Jewish settlements in the Occupied Territories; CUFI enthusiastically supported Israel's 2006 war in Lebanon and in Gaza in 2008; Rev. Hagee and CUFI were publicly critical of Prime Minister Rabin working with the PLO for peace, and criticized Prime Minister Sharon's decision to withdraw from Gaza. CUFI speakers and programs regularly reinforce anti-Arab and anti-Muslim stereotypes. Recently, to their credit, some mainstream American Jewish leaders have begun distance themselves from CUFI. Most mainline Protestants, Roman Catholics, Orthodox Christians and many Christian evangelicals work with Churches for Middle East Peace, the US Conference of Catholic Bishops, the National Association of Evangelicals or Telos, a newer evangelical group, and with NILI for a resolution of the conflict. In general, these American Christians oppose expansion of settlements, call for an end to violence and support active US efforts for a negotiated two-state peace agreement. Given the huge gap between enormous rightwing financial support for CUFI and relatively modest funding for CMEP, it's not surprising that CMEP doesn't directly take on CUFI, but it is disappointing and frustrating that liberal Protestants and Catholics don't do more to challenge CUFI's pernicious influence in the conflict and on prospects for peace.

At times, there also are differences, albeit much softer ones, between mainstream, liberal Protestant denominations and the American Catholic Church, in part related to Catholic hierarchal versus Protestant more dispersed structures and authority. Catholic statements on the conflict are always very carefully vetted not only for content about the conflict, but also for their potential effects on interfaith relations. In Protestant denominations, sometimes a statement sympathetic to the Palestinians, in part based on the denomination's sister Palestinian communities, might be issued by a department or agency focused on justice and peace issues; however, the denomination's department concerned with interfaith relations might only become involved if the Jewish community responded critically to the statement. In the history of the conflict, especially since 1967, this difference between Protestant and Catholic responses has occasionally led to serious tension between Protestants and the Jewish community. Tensions are also caused by the experience of American Christians who may have been very supportive of Israel, but then go on a trip to the region where they personally encounter Palestinian suffering under the Israeli occupation. They come home, almost like new converts, angry at Israel and now in solidarity with the Palestinians. As I've written, each side's narrative of the conflict is morally and emotionally compelling, and seems to cancel out the other side's narrative. It is very difficult simultaneously to hold on to both Palestinian and Israeli narratives; but, in my view, effective work for peace requires that we do just that.

The second major division among concerned American Christians working on the Israeli-Palestinian conflict is between Churches for Middle East Peace and North American Friends of Sabeel. In recent years, as Sabeel and the boycott Israel campaign has gathered more support, particularly in Protestant denominations, it deserves a more serious, sensitive response. Sabeel is the Palestinian liberation theology center founded by Rev. Dr. Naim Ateek. Ateek's Palestinian Liberation Theology draws heavily on liberation theologies in Latin America and Southern Africa. To his credit, Rev. Ateek is very clear and principled in his firm commitment to nonviolence in the struggle against the Israeli occupation. The problem, in my view, is that, despite its appeal to some sincere peace and justice activists, modelling Palestinian liberation theology on struggles against Latin American military dictatorships and the South Africa Apartheid regime doesn't make moral or historical sense in relation to the Palestinian struggle with Israel. In contrast to the histories in Latin America and South Africa, from its founding in 1948, Israel has had both moral and international legal legitimacy. As I have written earlier, the Israeli-Palestinian conflict is a struggle between two peoples, Jewish and Palestinian, both asserting their claims and rights of national self-determination in the same small land, a land in which both peoples have bone-deep historical connections.

It might be possible to develop a liberation theology in this unique context, but I believe that analogies to Latin America or South Africa distort the history of the Israeli-Palestinian conflict and lead to advocacy strategies that exacerbate the conflict rather than help resolve it. Specific Israeli practices in the Occupied Territories or, even more so, an outcome to the conflict in which Israel would rule over one-state with less than equal rights for Palestinians can be viewed as analogous to Apartheid. Prominent Israeli political leaders from the right and the left, including Ehud Olmert, Ehud Barak and Shimon Peres all have publicly acknowledged that; indeed, that is why a negotiated two-state peace agreement that ends the occupation and provides peace, security, and mutual recognition for both Israel and a viable, independent state of Palestine is the just and realistic resolution of the conflict. Ateek's version of liberation theology leads almost inevitably to—and may in fact start from—the belief that

Zionism (Jewish nationalism) is fundamentally illegitimate. While I can understand this view based on the bitterly painful Palestinian experience since the founding of modern Israel, it's no more accurate or helpful to resolving the conflict than narrowly partisan Israeli Jewish views for years that have denied the legitimacy, and even the existence, of a Palestinian people and dismissed Palestinian nationalist claims. Both peoples are real and both peoples have authentic, legitimate claims to the right of national self-determination in the same land.

For a liberation theology to accurately and constructively address this conflict it would need to be based on the recognition that in the Middle East, the national liberation of the Palestinian people and the national liberation of the Jewish people are historically and morally intertwined and interdependent. This realistic, reconciliatory liberation theology would be based on the truth Martin Luther King Jr. taught us about race relations. Simply stated, King declared, "Strangely enough, I can never be what I ought to be until you are what you ought to be. You can never be what you ought to be until I am what I ought to be."[5] In the context of the Middle East, as bitterly opposed as they've been, Jewish and Palestinian national liberation movements need each other to succeed. Jewish national liberation in the land in the form of a democratic, majority Jewish state of Israel cannot be fulfilled apart from the achievement of Palestinian national liberation in the form of an independent, viable state of Palestine. And Palestinian national liberation cannot be fulfilled apart from acceptance of Jewish national liberation in a majority Jewish state of Israel. Not everyone who supports a two-state resolution understands the conflict in this way. Carol and I feel privileged personally to know Jews and Palestinians who understand this deeper, moral truth about the conflict and accept that this understanding must shape the vision and the path toward potential peaceful resolution of the conflict and reconciliation between these two peoples.

While Churches for Middle East Peace and North American Friends of Sabeel do not publicly criticize each other, they tend to keep their distance. In 2010, in preparation for CMEP's annual advocacy conference in Washington, CMEP's board had a heated discussion about how to deal with the 2009 Kairos Palestine declaration, written primarily by Naim Ateek and endorsed by many Palestinian Christians. The Kairos document supports an activist strategy of boycotts, divestment, and sanctions (BDS) to pressure Israel; it is ambiguous about supporting a two-state or one-state solution; and it raises moral and theological questions about the legitimacy of Israel. The declaration stirred up a wave of controversy with American Jewish organizations and was the subject of a long, serious critique by the Central Conference of American Rabbis. As a compromise, the CMEP Board decided to schedule an unofficial presentation and discussion of the Kairos document at their conference. At a Friends of Sabeel conference I attended in Seattle in fall 2010, the Kairos document was a featured resource and Naim Atteek a featured speaker. He and other speakers advocated BDS strategies

5. King Jr., "A Christmas Sermon for Peace," 254.

and several speakers advocated a one-state solution. During the deliberations, there was hardly any mention of Churches for Middle East Peace.

Churches for Middle East Peace works in Washington and maintains a network of supporters around the country advocating with the administration and Congress for continued aid to the Palestinians, halting settlement expansion, opposing the Israeli security wall where it poses serious blockage to the creation of a contiguous, viable Palestinian State, and negotiating a two-state solution, including a shared Jerusalem where both states would have their capitals. The North American Friends of Sabeel website says they also support a two-state solution, but they focus their energies almost entirely on echoing the Palestinian narrative of the conflict, reflecting Ateek's liberation theology, and advocating strategies to confront Israel rather than building public support for US policies to help the two sides achieve negotiated peace. In advocating BDS strategies, Friends of Sabeel works with the small, most pro-Palestinian Jewish organizations; but they tend to have very little influence on national politics and alienate themselves from many American Christians and the majority of American Jews. In contrast, Churches for Middle East Peace works cooperatively with Americans for Peace Now and JStreet, both more mainstream organizations that represent much larger numbers of Jewish Americans who support a negotiated two-state resolution of the conflict.

A particularly painful example of differences and tensions among American Christians and between Christians and Jews involves the Presbyterian Church (USA). Presbyterians have been active in the Middle East since the 1800s and played major positive roles in founding the prestigious American Universities in Beirut and Cairo. They have many institutional and personal connections with Arabs and Arab civil society projects which understandably affect their perspectives on the Arab-Israeli conflict and sometimes lead to tensions with the Jewish community over advocacy related to Israel.

In 2004, the Presbyterian Church General Assembly adopted a resolution that called for exploring divestment from companies involved in the occupation, as a way of putting pressure on Israel. While the resolution won majority support at the Assembly, it also angered many Presbyterians who strongly supported Israel. American Jewish organizations were very critical, charging that the resolution reflected anti-Jewish as well as anti-Israel bias. Following much consultation and dialogue, the 2006 General Assembly withdrew the resolution and backed away from the divestment strategy. A committee was asked to bring recommendations to the 2010 General Assembly. That gathering narrowly defeated a resolution calling for divestment from three major companies involved with the occupation. Instead, the Assembly adopted resolutions supporting positive investment in Palestinian economic development and calling for a boycott of Israeli products coming from the occupied territories. This more narrowly focused boycott strategy gained some understanding and support among Jewish American peace advocates. In June 2014, controversy among

Presbyterians and with major American Jewish leaders erupted again when the General Assembly voted by a very thin margin to sell stock in three companies whose products or services Israel uses in the occupied territories. The controversy became even more heated over a study guide for congregations, *Zionism Unsettled*, produced by the Israel/Palestine Mission Network, a subgroup of the national church. In addition to sharply critiquing specific Israeli policies, the seventy-seven page booklet represents a fundamental critique of the legitimacy of Jewish nationalism and of Israel.

In general, Protestant denominations have tried to find ways to protest Israeli occupation practices without causing counterproductive conflict with the Jewish community. In May 2012, the United Methodist Church's Quadrennial Convention voted down two proposals to support divestment from companies involved in Israel's occupation, and passed a proposal for positive investment in Palestinian economic development. The Episcopal Church and the Evangelical Lutheran Church in America have taken similar positions. However, in October 2012, fifteen leaders of American Christian churches signed a letter urging Congress to reconsider aid to Israel in light of Israeli violations of Palestinians' human rights. It was signed by heads of most Protestant denominations; leaders of the Episcopal Church and the US Conference of Catholic Bishops refused to endorse it. The letter gained practically no traction in Congress and generated heated controversy with Jewish organizations. Jewish leaders asserted that the letter unfairly singled out Israel and that the Christian leaders should have consulted them before crafting it. The Jewish leaders cancelled a regularly scheduled interfaith dialogue session. Given the combination of acute Jewish sensitivities about anti-Israel sentiment, the harsh conditions faced by Palestinians, and no or very slow progress in negotiations for peace, debates and tensions over how to understand the conflict and over strategies for advocacy both within and between our communities will continue and very likely intensify.

I believe our communities' access to diverse Arab and Israeli experiences and perspectives can be a rich resource to help all of us develop more holistic and nuanced understandings of the conflict and craft more constructive, politically effective advocacy. At the same time, I recognize that our connections to different sides of the conflict all too often pull us in opposite directions, creating painful tensions. I am also sadly aware of persistent anti-Jewish prejudice among American Christians, which Jews sometimes exaggerate and Christians too often deny. I am also aware of widespread ignorance about Islam and prejudice toward Muslims and Arabs among American Christians and Jews. I am reminded again of the moral and practical wisdom of one of NILI's most important founding principles:

> Recognizing and appreciating the deep, precious bonds many of us have with different sides of this conflict and how these bonds cause us to have different and sometimes conflicting viewpoints, we believe our areas of agreement are more important than our disagreements, and we commit ourselves to

work together conscientiously and sensitively to emphasize our common agenda for peace.[6]

The tensions caused by different views about the conflict and different advocacy strategies make the work of NILI more complicated and difficult. At the same time, as developments on the ground and failures of political leadership on both sides diminish chances for a two-state agreement, the need for strong public support of active, fair, and more determined American leadership for peace has increased. That makes the work of NILI more important and urgent.

NILI Leaders Trip to Israel and the West Bank

In December 2009 I organized and accompanied a NILI leaders' trip to Jordan, Israel and the West Bank, accompanied by senior leaders of the Roman Catholic Church, Greek Orthodox Church, Christian Church (Disciples of Christ), National Baptist Convention, Evangelical Lutheran Church in America, Episcopal Church, and United Methodist Church. The NILI delegation included leaders from Judaism's Reform and Reconstructionist movements and leaders of the Islamic Society of North America, the Palestinian American Muslim head of Clergy Beyond Borders, and Palestinian American president emeritus of the Council of Mosques USA. Participants on this trip sometimes experienced painful conflict with each other, as when people responded very differently and emotionally to a Palestinian's angry presentation about Gaza and the occupation; and at other times, participants experienced a convergence of views as when our delegation visited Yad Vashem and when we listened to a briefing on recent provocative expansion of Israeli settlements in East Jerusalem. These experiences reminded me again of how important it is for all of us to really listen to each other, especially when that is hard to do. Being engaged in relationships with each other and with each other's community is essential both for understanding the multiple narratives and truths about this conflict and for developing constructive and realistic advocacy strategies. I believe that participating in this trip reminded all of us that interfaith cooperation for peace is difficult, possible and worthwhile.

There are resources that can help nurture cooperation among our communities. In 2012, a small group of Israeli and Palestinian historians and teachers from the Peace Research Institute in the Middle East cooperated in publishing *Side by Side: Parallel Histories of Israel and Palestine,* which traces the two narratives of the Israeli-Palestinian conflict. Another interesting resource is Kai Bird's part memoir, part history, *Crossing Mandelbaum Gate: Coming of Age Between the Arabs and Israelis, 1956–1978.* Ari Shavit's 2014 book, *My Promised Land: the Triumph and Tragedy of Israel,* is a movingly honest Israeli account of modern Israel's history. David K.Shipler's

---

6. NILI "Principles of Cooperation."

1986 Pulitzer Prize winning book, *Arab and Jew: Wounded Spirits in A Promised Land*, in my view, is still the best book for deeply understanding both peoples.

On the last day of our trip, following a good meeting with the American ambassador to Israel, we gathered at a hotel in Tel Aviv for dinner, dialogue and to write the delegation's consensus statement to the Obama administration and members of Congress.[7] In our statement the religious leaders united in calling on the United States,

> to be a catalyst, in cooperation with Egypt and other parties, for achieving an effective, sustainable ceasefire in Gaza, including international measures for preventing resupply of rockets; for allowing the flow of urgently needed humanitarian and reconstruction assistance to the people of Gaza; for continuing good efforts to improve the capacity of the Palestinian Authority to increase security and economic development; and for further reducing the number of Israeli checkpoints and freezing all settlement expansion in the West Bank, *including in East Jerusalem.* (Italics added)

In the accompanying press release, Cardinal Theodore McCarrick, archbishop emeritus of Washington, DC and head of the NILI Delegation, said,

> We heard two messages repeatedly from Palestinians and Israelis with whom we met: first, that time is running out for a viable two-state solution; and second, that people on both sides are aware of difficult compromises that will be necessary to achieve a two-state peace agreement and, given a choice between peace and continued violent conflict, most people would likely be prepared to accept compromises.

Rabbi Paul Menitoff, commented,

> Even on the most emotional issues of refugees and Jerusalem, we believe most Palestinians understand that they will have to accept a negotiated solution regarding refugees that does not jeopardize the Jewish majority in Israel; and most Israelis understand that they will have to accept a negotiated solution for sharing Jerusalem that includes provision for both Israel and Palestine to have their capitals in the city.

In conclusion, Dr. Sayyid Muhammad Syeed added,

> Of course, Palestinians and Israelis themselves must make the negotiated agreements for peace, but most people we met believe that active, fully engaged US leadership is essential to making that happen. We are united in support of such US leadership for peace.

I sent the NILI statement and press release to several hundred media contacts and more than 500 local religious leaders on NILI's action alert list, encouraging them to send it, along with their own personal messages to their members of Congress.

7. NILI Leaders Delegation consensus statement.

The NILI national leaders uploaded the statement onto their organizations' websites, thereby potentially reaching thousands, if not tens of thousands of persons in all three religious communities who are actively concerned about Israeli-Palestinian peace. In March 2010, a small NILI delegation met with Under Secretary of State William Burns to present our report and lay the groundwork for a meeting with Secretary of State Hillary Clinton.

On the morning of September 29, 2010 I accompanied a NILI delegation of twenty-five Jewish, Christian and Muslim religious leaders to the White House for a morning meeting with General James Jones, then national security advisor to President Obama, and afternoon meetings at the State Department with Assistant Secretary Jeffrey Feltman and Secretary of State Hillary Clinton. It was clear that the Obama administration welcomed NILI's message and support, although it was also clear that the administration would not undertake a new initiative for peace at that time before the 2012 elections.

The Arab Spring and Unresolved Israeli-Palestinian Conflict

In 2011, popular, essentially nonviolent, uprisings erupted across the Arab world. Reminiscent of Prague in 1968, media labeled the uprising the "Arab Spring" and focused daily attention on these historic events. At the same time, the Arab-Israeli-Palestinian conflict remained unresolved. Former US Ambassador to Egypt and Israel, Daniel Kurtzer, whom Carol and I had known since the early 1980s, recognized the urgent need for progress toward peace. He reflected on how Egyptians and other Arabs perceived US policies in the region, including their resentment of decades of massive military aid to dictatorial Arab governments. He cautioned that the United States had very few assets in the current situation and wisely warned against any assertive, unilateral American initiatives, *except one*: a determined, pro-active, aggressive effort to achieve a breakthrough in Israeli-Palestinian peace negotiations. I was reminded of our 2002 family trip to the Middle East, when Carol and I visited Dan Kurtzer at the embassy in Tel Aviv. Dan told us then that he believed the United States should exert determined leadership for peace. In 2011, in the context of tumultuous events unfolding in the region, Dan spoke with an even greater sense of urgency.

During this period when it seemed there were no negotiations between Israel and the Palestinians, we should have remembered that not all progress toward peace takes place in public. As we learned in January 2011 from *Al Jazeera*'s release of the "Palestine Papers" and from Bernard Avishai's article, "A Plan for Peace That Still Could Be" in the February 7, 2011, *New York Times Magazine*,[8] significant progress in bilateral Israeli-Palestinian peace negotiations had occurred two years earlier. From the end of 2006 to September 2008, Israeli Prime Minister Ehud Olmert and

---

8. Avishai, "A Plan for Peace."

Palestinian president Mahmoud Abbas held thirty-six rounds of secret talks that came very close to producing a peace agreement. Not surprisingly, it included elements from the Clinton Parameters, the Taba Agreement, and the Geneva Accord. In 2008, Turkey hosted indirect negotiations between Israel and Syria, consistent with the 2002 Arab Peace Initiative and the principles developed in US-Syrian talks at the Wye Plantation in 1995 and later at Shepherdstown, West Virginia. Unfortunately, these encouraging developments were not pursued. In 2011, the Syrian government of Bashar al-Assad became preoccupied with violently suppressing a popular revolt, leading to catastrophic civil war. In 2012 Ehud Olmert became embroiled in financial scandal and resigned as Prime Minister.

Despite this discouraging context, in early March 2011, there was a positive breakthrough in Israel. A prestigious group of former senior Israeli government, intelligence and security officials including Danny Yatom, former head of the Mossad; Ami Ayalon, former head of the Shin Bet; Amnon Lipkin-Shahak, a former military chief-of-staff; Amram Mitzna, former leader of the Israeli Labor Party; and Yuval Rabin, son of the murdered prime minister issued an (unofficial) Israeli Peace Initiative.[9] They framed it as a response to the 2002 Arab Peace Initiative, which they argued represented an historic Arab offer that deserved a much more serious positive response from Israel than so far had been forthcoming. Taken together, these initiatives represented a very significant consensus on the elements of compromises required for comprehensive Arab-Israeli-Palestinian peace.

On April 14, 2011, thirty-three American Jewish, Christian and Muslim national religious leaders of NILI sent a letter to President Obama, with copies to Secretary of State Clinton and to every member of Congress, welcoming the new unofficial Israeli Peace Initiative and referencing the earlier Arab Peace Initiative and the Geneva Accord. We urged the president to go to Jerusalem and press for restarting peace negotiations focused on the benchmark principles and ideas in these three initiatives which could serve as the basis for compromises to resolve all of the final status issues.

Unfortunately, on May 18, 2011, American diplomatic engagement suffered a serious setback when, after serving for two very frustrating years as special envoy, former Senator George Mitchell resigned. Among other factors, Mitchell apparently was frustrated by independent initiatives taken by Dennis Ross, special assistant to the president, who at times negotiated with the Israeli government without consulting Mitchell.

On May 19, 2011, President Obama delivered a major speech on the Middle East in which he said a peace agreement between Israel and the Palestinians would have to be based on the 1967 boundary lines, with mutually agreed land swaps and security guarantees. While this was the longtime standard US position, supported by international agreement, Prime Minister Netanyahu complained publicly that Obama's position was new and would require Israel to return to "indefensible borders." To

9. Israeli (unofficial) Peace Initiative.

his credit, President Obama repeated his position in an address to AIPAC and held firmly to it despite a shameless show of support for Netanyahu during his speech to Congress, where he appeared to reject many of the elements widely assumed to be required for peace. NILI ran print and digital ads in Washington, with the headline, "Before It's Too Late," including a half page in Politico's daily *Capitol Hill* newspaper on the day Netanyahu addressed Congress. Digital images of the ad appeared on Politico's website 200,000 times during Netanyahu's visit.

Despite the positive encouragement of the unofficial Israeli Peace Initiative and pressure on the US to act in response to the new Palestinian strategy of seeking UN recognition for a state of Palestine, it seemed clear that the Obama administration would not undertake any significant action until after the 2012 elections. Responding to the lack of progress, NILI issued a statement in March 2012 endorsed by thirty Jewish, Christian, and Muslim leaders declaring that the momentous changes taking place in the Middle East as a result of the Arab Spring made Arab-Israeli-Palestinian peace "more urgent than ever." The leaders also urged candidates not to do or say anything that might harm chances for a negotiated two-state agreement.

Why I Still Work for Peace in the Middle East

It is not necessary for you to complete the work,

but neither are you free to desist from it.

RABBI TARPHON, SAYINGS OF THE FATHERS, CIRCA 200 CE

In 1982, when Carol and I accepted the assignment to represent Quaker service agencies as listeners in the Middle East, neither of us imagined that thirty years later I would still be working on this issue. On being asked how he chose his work, David Rockwell, a successful architect and designer of theatre sets, answered, "You never know the outcome of a particular project; you just have to decide on what journey you want to participate." Returning from three years living in the Middle East, crossing boundaries to listen to people on all sides, I clearly chose working for Arab-Israeli-Palestinian peace as the journey in which I wanted to participate. Besides a personality trait of stubborn idealism that I probably inherited from my mother and grandparents, there are two reasons related to my life experiences and one related to the strategic importance of resolving this conflict that help explain why I've continued for all these years doing this work.

First is the extraordinary and inspiring experience of living and travelling in the Middle East, making dozens of visits to Israel, the West Bank and Gaza, Egypt, Jordan, Syria and Lebanon, meeting many Israelis and Arabs as well as knowledgeable and dedicated US foreign service officers who believe peace is possible and that our nation has a special responsibility and indispensable role to help achieve peace. Second, are the equally extraordinary and inspiring experiences I have had working with American Jewish, Christian and Muslim religious leaders who, despite their deep personal connections to different sides of the conflict, share a profound moral commitment to advocate and support policies by our government to help make peace happen.

The third reason I continue to do this work is more political and strategic. I believe the goal of Arab-Israeli-Palestinian peace is integrally related to two other urgent, morally imperative global goals: reducing the threat of terrorism and abolishing weapons of mass destruction. While achieving a Palestinian state alongside Israel, with peace and security for both peoples, will not eliminate the threat of terrorism, it will greatly reduce the psychological, political and popular support for terrorist acts. Just as continuation of the conflict generates negative reverberations around the world, Israeli-Palestinian peace would make a major positive contribution to relaxing tensions in the region and generating positive ripple effects worldwide.

Arab-Israeli-Palestinian peace would also create a radically new context for addressing security issues in the Middle East, including the goal of eliminating nuclear and other weapons of mass destruction. Currently, Israel is the only Middle Eastern nation that possesses nuclear weapons. As long as the conflict continues, other countries in the region may be motivated to develop nuclear weapons. Since at present no other Middle East country possesses nuclear weapons, Arab calls for a nuclear-weapons-free Middle East are viewed as simply anti-Israel initiatives and never get off the ground. According to a 2002 study by the Carnegie Endowment for International Peace, several countries in the region do possess chemical and/or biological weapons; furthermore, Iraq, Egypt and Syria are known to have used chemical weapons in the past two decades. Given the region's volatility it seems almost inevitable that some party, including perhaps a non-state terrorist group, will use a weapon of mass destruction again, possibly with catastrophic consequences.

On November 24, 2013 an historic agreement was signed in Geneva between the United States, Russia, China, Britain, France, Germany (known as P5+1) and Iran to limit and reverse key elements of Iran's nuclear program and provide for strict monitoring and verification. This represented a major breakthrough in international efforts to assure that Iran does not develop nuclear weapons and to avert a nuclear arms race in the Middle East. Combined with the successful agreement to eliminate Syria's chemical weapons and an agreement to limit Iran's nuclear program, a two-state Israeli-Palestinian peace agreement would provide substantial momentum and public support, including potential US support, for negotiating a Middle East zone free of weapons of mass destruction. And that would be a major step toward the goal of eliminating such weapons worldwide. Ever since 1962, when I lived through the Cuban Missile Crisis while working with Jim Lawson in Memphis, I've believed that abolishing weapons of mass destruction is an urgent moral imperative; and it's a goal which evokes broad interreligious support. Peace in Jerusalem could inspire a cooperative global effort to accomplish that goal.

President Obama's Trip to Jerusalem and the Kerry Initiative

After his reelection in 2012, President Obama announced that he would visit Israel, the West Bank and Jordan, raising hopes that the United States would undertake a new initiative for peace. On January 25, 2013, four days after Obama's inauguration, thirty Jewish, Christian and Muslim national religious leaders issued a new NILI statement warning that "the window of opportunity for a two-state solution is closing." Expressing even more urgency than in past statements, NILI's leaders advocated bolder US leadership for Israeli-Palestinian peace.

> We fear the opportunity for a peaceful resolution is rapidly waning and the current stagnation encourages the rejectionists on both sides. Our nation has unique leverage and credibility in the region. Indeed, no past progress towards peace has occurred in this conflict without US leadership, facilitation or resolute support. Once again, we need active, fair and firm US leadership to help break the current deadlock and to achieve a two-state peace agreement now before it is too late.[10]

NILI also issued "Talking Points" recommending specific steps that the United States should take and advocating a comprehensive approach to final status negotiations that would include the US presenting a framework for peace, drawing on benchmark principles and practical ideas from earlier formal and informal Israeli-Palestinian negotiations, for resolving all the issues.

In February 2013, Daniel Kurtzer, former US ambassador to Egypt and Israel, wrote an article, "Toward A New American Policy" in the *Cairo Review of Global Affairs*[11]. Kurtzer warned that "the two-state solution . . . is on life support." He urged the Obama administration to undertake a bold, new comprehensive US initiative for Israeli-Palestinian peace, including presenting practical parameters to Israel and the Palestinians as terms of reference for negotiations to resolve all of the issues, including: "territory and borders, security, Israeli settlements and refugees, West Bank and Gaza safe passage, places of historical and religious significance, Jerusalem and water. . . .The time is now," Kurtzer concluded, "for confident American leadership to advance prospects of Israeli-Palestinian peace." Kurtzer's views closely paralleled NILI's January 25, 2013 public statement and talking points.

On his visit to Jerusalem in March 2013, addressing an audience composed largely of Israeli students and youth, President Obama offered strong confirmation of

---

10. NILI Statement January 25, 2013.
11. Kurtzer, "Toward A New American Policy."

American support for Israel and a compelling vision for a necessary, just and possible peace between Israel and the Palestinians.[12] The president declared,

> *Peace is necessary.* The only way for Israel to endure and thrive as a Jewish and democratic state is through the realization of an independent and viable Palestine. Given the frustration in the international community, Israel must address an undertow of isolation. And given the march of technology, the only way to truly protect the Israeli people is through the absence of war, because no wall is high enough, and no iron dome is strong enough, to stop every enemy from inflicting harm. . . .
>
> *Peace is also just.* . . . The Palestinian people's right to self-determination and justice must also be recognized. Put yourself in their shoes—look at the world through their eyes. It is not fair that a Palestinian child cannot grow up in a state of her own, and lives with the presence of a foreign army that controls the movements of her parents every single day. . . .
>
> *Peace is possible.* . . . Of course negotiations will be necessary, but there is little secret where they must lead: two states for two peoples. . . . (Italics added.)

Reflecting President Obama's commitment, Secretary of State John Kerry made several visits to Jerusalem and Ramallah, and consulted with Arab, European, Russian and Chinese leaders in an effort to restart negotiations. On July 30, 2013 standing between Israeli and Palestinian negotiators Tzipi Livni and Saeb Erekat, Kerry announced sustained, substantive talks with the explicit goal of achieving a two-state peace agreement over the next nine months. Nine months later, at the end of April 2014, following the breakdown of Israeli-Palestinian talks, I was reminded of Max Frankel's two controversial columns in *The New York Times* in November 1982, when Carol and I were living in the Middle East. Frankel's two columns reflected the views of prominent Israeli advocates for peace, including senior Labor Party leaders. In the first column he reflected their warnings that continued control of the occupied territories posed a threat to Israel's survival as a democratic, majority Jewish state; in the second, he reported that they urged US pressure on Israel's Likud government, including cutting non-military aid, to encourage more Israeli flexibility to enter negotiations for peace. With hope waning for a viable two-state solution, Frankel's prophetic messages were even more urgently relevant in 2014 than they were thirty-two years earlier.

On Sunday June 8, 2014, at the invitation of Pope Francis, Palestinian President Mahmoud Abbas and Israeli President Shimon Peres joined the Pope at the Vatican to pray for peace. On behalf of the National Interreligious Leadership Initiative, I sent out a nationwide action alert on May 30 encouraging local religious congregations and communities to join Pope Francis's initiative by offering prayers for Israeli-Palestinian peace in their worship services over that weekend. While the Vatican event

---

12. Obama, Speech in Jerusalem.

was not coupled with any political initiative, many hoped it might prompt Secretary of State Kerry to renew his peace effort. In 2014, many people concerned for Israeli-Palestinian peace were speaking with greater urgency. In early July, people's fears and sense of urgency became even more intense in response to kidnappings and gruesome killings of Israeli and Palestinian teenagers. Rioting erupted in and around Jerusalem. Hamas launched rockets from Gaza into Israel and the Israeli military unleashed air strikes and artillery attacks on Gaza, and another even more destructive ground invasion. As has been the pattern in previous flare-ups of violence, most of those killed were innocent civilians. The choice for both sides seemed even more urgent now, between negotiating a two-state peace agreement or condemning Palestinian and Israeli youth and children to a future of continued conflict, more violence, more suffering, and more death.

A day before the Vatican event, in a keynote address to the J-Street National Summit in San Francisco, former Ambassador Daniel Kurtzer, reflecting on consistent US declarations that Israeli-Palestinian peace is an American national interest, confessed he was dumbfounded by the lack of resolve in earlier US peace efforts. Kurtzer cited the failure of several administrations to achieve a halt to expansion of Israeli settlements and the US failure to build boldly and creatively on the historic Arab Peace Initiative. He spoke with more critical determination than I had heard from him before about what the US should do now.[13] Kurtzer advocated that the Obama administration should present a US framework for a two-state peace agreement, including ideas from previous official and informal negotiations for fair, realistic compromises to resolve all the issues. On June 30, in an op-ed article in Haaretz,[14] Kurtzer urged the Obama administration, "to declare as US policy a set of bold, forward looking terms of reference that would require both sides to look beyond their current comfort zones, and aim them toward a fair and reasonable negotiated outcome." Coupled with his suggestion at JStreet that as a next step the US present this framework for endorsement by the UN Security Council, this is the kind of balanced, bold, and determined American leadership I believe is needed to achieve an Israeli-Palestinian two-state peace agreement before it's too late. If the Obama administration decided to pursue this path, active, strong public support, especially from American religious communities, would be essential to assure the best chances for success. In a letter to Secretary of State Kerry, national Jewish, Christian and Muslim religious leaders of NILI wrote, "the time for peace is now;" and they again pledged to generate "support for determined US leadership for peace in synagogues, churches, and mosques across the country."

13. Kurtzer, Keynote address at the JStreet National Summit June 7, 2014
14. Kurtzer, "The US Must Inject Life into a Moribund Peace Process."

This prayer by Rabbi J. Rolando (Roly) Matalon, of Congregation B'nai Jeshurun in New York, one of several prayers I collected for the US Interreligious Committee is also my prayer.

> O God Source of Life, Creator of Peace . . .
> Help Your children, anguished and confused,
> To understand the futility of hatred and violence
> And grant them the ability to stretch across
> Political, religious and national boundaries
> So they may confront horror and fear
> By continuing together
> In the search for justice, peace and truth. . . .
> With every fiber of our being
> We beg You, O God,
> To help us not to fail nor falter.
>
> AMEN.[15]

---

15. Matalon, Prayer for Peace.

Lessons and Hope Going Forward

Listening to people in circumstances very different from our own; deciding about going to war; being committed to nonviolence; reflecting on the role of religion in generating and resolving conflict; relating the power of one to the power of many; the role of protest in changing policy; accepting that we may not complete the work, but we are bound to keep doing it; and appreciating the role of humor.

MOST OF WHAT I have learned on my life's journey is reflected in the preceding chapters. As readers you will draw your own conclusions, but here I want to share several of the most important lessons I learned and some of my hopes looking toward the future.

The first and most basic lesson from my life of "crossing boundaries" is the urgent importance—especially for western, white, middle class people—to find ways of dislodging ourselves from our relative comfort and safety, to walk with and listen to real people who face very different and much more difficult circumstances than our own. In fall 2011, while Congress was engaged in a dysfunctional debate over the federal debt, I was inspired by a news story about college students in the Midwest who spent a week visiting and interviewing impoverished African American families. Reflecting on their experience, one of the white students said, "This experience was the most important week of my life." Within days, a Pugh Research Center study[1] underlined the importance and timeliness of this experience when it reported that "the median wealth of white households in the United States is twenty times that of black families and eighteen times that of Hispanic families, larger gaps than ever recorded since the government started doing the survey." Studies have revealed that the gap globally between rich and poor is also widening.

Reading the Pugh Study, I was reminded of how deeply my life was affected by the year I spent living in the black community in Memphis, working with Jim Lawson.

1. "Social and Demographic Trends."

On-the-ground, boundary crossing experiences I had in Southeast Asia, Latin America, and the Middle East also profoundly shaped my ability to empathize with people in situations very different from mine. Simply reading data or hearing news about people facing difficult conditions and choices would not have had nearly the moral and motivational effects that these personal experiences had on me. I would strongly encourage young people to find a way to live and work in a community in the United States or abroad that is very different from their own. I would urge them to listen carefully to people's aspirations for themselves and their children, what obstacles they face; how prejudices, economic realities, and government policies affect their chances; and what they perceive to be their realistic options. I believe that real boundary crossing experiences provide essential moral motivation and practical guidance to help us imagine the kinds of initiatives and policies that could contribute concretely to improving peoples' lives and collectively enriching our life together.

On the importance of listening to people, I am reminded of what David Shipler said in the introduction to his 1997 book, *A Country of Strangers: Blacks and Whites in America*. Explaining his approach, David wrote, "My preference is to listen to real people . . . who are rarely heard by the larger public and have something to teach us."[2] If, as he suggests, we need to listen carefully to different experiences and perceptions of whites and blacks in our own country, we also need to listen to people in other countries and really hear both their praise and their criticisms of America and its policies. The experience Carol and I had living in the Middle East, listening to Arabs and Israelis, and my experience working with American Jews, Christians and Muslims convinced me that really listening to people with different experiences and perspectives than ours, including people with whom we might disagree, is an essential discipline in creative and effective work for progressive social change.

Crossing boundaries to listen to other people in conflict situations—African Americans, Vietnamese, Salvadorans, Palestinians and Israelis—it was naturally tempting sometimes to support one side against another. At a deeper level, really listening has taught me to try to stand *with people, not against* other people but against the situations and systems that are oppressing and doing violence to them. Witnessing the death and destruction caused by the US war in Vietnam, I sometimes felt tempted to support *the other side* against our side. Thanks to the examples and guidance of Jim Lawson, Martin Luther King Jr., A.J. Muste and Thich Nhat Hanh, I managed mostly to stay focused on opposing the war which was killing the people, destroying Vietnam, and robbing our own nation of precious human and limited economic resources that could help build a better society. In my many years working on the Arab-Israeli-Palestinian conflict, there was a seductive and powerful pull of the truth of each side's narrative. I am thankful for having had the Quaker-inspired assignment of really listening deeply to people on both sides. I'm also very grateful for having personal relationships with Israelis and Palestinians, including Matti Peled, Isam Sartawi,

2. Shipler, *A Country of Strangers, xi.*

Lova Eliav, Naomi Chazan, Mary Khass, Morela BarOn , Mohammed Milhem, and members of the Parents Circle-Bereaved Families Forum, who helped me resist the temptation to take sides, recognize that both peoples are victims of violence and extremism, and understand that the liberation of each of these two peoples is contingent on the liberation of the other. Neither Palestinians nor Israelis are the enemy: the conflict itself is the enemy of both peoples, and it must be resolved in a way that results in two viable, secure states and creates a context in which it is possible for people to build genuine, lasting peace and reconciliation.

A second message from my experiences relates to the imperative of thinking critically and acting effectively on issues in US foreign policy, especially in relation to our country's consideration of going to war. As a young boy in the late 1940s, I played war, pretending to be a soldier in America's good war, and naively believing America could do no wrong. As a teenager, I was a Boy Scout and active church member. To this day, I feel pride at having earned my Eagle Scout, and God and Country awards and having been president of my church Youth Fellowship. I remember how disoriented and dismayed I felt in June 1965, in the Dominican Republic, encountering proud American soldiers my age who probably had backgrounds similar to mine patrolling streets in Santo Domingo as part of the US military occupation that prevented the elected president from resuming his office. I also met many young idealistic Dominicans who angrily denounced the US invasion and occupation. If I had gone to West Point I might have been a young officer in the US occupation force. While I remain proud of America's principles and accomplishments, my personal experiences in the Dominican Republic, Vietnam and El Salvador strongly reinforced a basic lesson about how American ideals and actual policies are sometimes profoundly at odds.

Both as a Christian and as a citizen, I believe that support for US polices, especially a decision to go to war, should not be automatic or taken for granted. Being patriotic and loving my country doesn't mean giving blind acceptance to its policies. Indeed, today and into the future, I think loving America more often will mean publicly opposing war, and at times may require acts of nonviolent civil disobedience.

For me, and I think for a majority of Americans, the US invasion and occupation of Iraq underlines the urgent necessity for thinking critically and acting effectively to oppose going to war when we believe it is wrong. In 2003, if more Americans, including more members of Congress, had examined and acted on the available information that Iraq had nothing to do with the 9/11 terrorist attacks and that there was no real evidence that Iraq was developing nuclear weapons, I believe we might have prevented that disastrous war. In contrast to the relatively slow development of public opposition to the Vietnam War, it was encouraging to see more than a million Americans publicly protesting against the US invading Iraq even before any Americans were killed.

While the extraordinary pre-war public protests did not prevent the invasion of Iraq, they showed that many Americans learned valuable lessons from the Vietnam

War. I believe that the complex realities of global interdependence and the negative collateral consequences (both predictable and unpredictable) of modern warfare are convincing more and more people, including some military leaders, that war is not the solution to international conflict. In his May 2014 commencement address at West Point, President Obama quoted a line from General Eisenhower's commencement address there in 1947, just two years after the end of the so-called good war. Eisenhower declared, "War is mankind's most tragic and stupid folly."[3]

In 2012, President Obama's appointments of Senator John Kerry as secretary of state and Senator Chuck Hagel as secretary of defense were encouraging signs of a shift away from policymaking dominated by the hawkish views of Vice President Cheney and Secretary of Defense Rumsfeld during the George W. Bush Administration. In 2013–2014, the United States, the European Union, Russia, and Iran, in cooperation with the UN Security Council, successfully implemented a plan to rid Syria of chemical weapons. In 2014, the P5+1 (UN Security Council members plus Germany) reached a preliminary agreement and were negotiating a final agreement with Iran on limiting that country's nuclear program. At the same time, a crisis in Ukraine and the take-over by the extremist ISIS movement in areas of Iraq and Syria present new challenges. In Ukraine old US and Russian cold war attitudes and policies complicate the search for a necessary political resolution of the conflict. In Iraq and Syria, even as military force is being employed against ISIS, in the longer run it's clear that international efforts to choke off financial support and rebuild on-the-ground popular opposition to ISIS will be essential to its eventual defeat. Moreover, it's important to remember how the disastrous US invasion and occupation of Iraq, and US failure fully to support UN diplomatic initiatives to resolve the civil war in Syria contributed to the rise of extremism and greater violence in the two countries. Going forward, what's needed is much less reliance on military power and much more support for creative diplomacy and cooperative international efforts to address underlying causes for peoples' suffering. We're clearly not there yet, but there does seem to be a growing public consensus that this is the direction in which we need to go.

A third deeper personal learning from my experiences, particularly from working with Rev. Jim Lawson, Dr. Martin Luther King Jr. and A.J. Muste, and meeting Archbishop Oscar Romero, is my commitment to nonviolence. I believe that a principled commitment to nonviolence and the power of love is basic to being a Christian. At the same time, I appreciate that following Jesus and upholding a commitment to nonviolence in the midst of complex political realities is challenging for several reasons. First, Jesus did not lay down a set of laws or a blueprint for society. Jesus taught and modeled how we should live and how we should treat others, but he didn't extrapolate these teachings into a framework for what we should do in every situation or how society should be organized. Even in Judaism and Islam, which offer more detailed guidance for our life together, profound debates over interpretations of religious texts

3. Obama, Commencement address at West Point.

raise similar challenging ethical questions. Second, there is a temptation to treat Jesus' teachings as impossible ideals to be admired but not actually applied to messy everyday realities. In the 1960 revised edition of the iconic *New Testament Basis of Pacifism*, G.H.C. Macgregor subtitled his book, *The Relevance of an Impossible Ideal*. A third problem in applying Jesus' teachings to real world situations is that doing so can be dangerous, as demonstrated by what happened to leaders who tried. Jesus himself, Gandhi, King and Romero all seemed destined for early deaths. So, why am I committed to nonviolence and what does this commitment mean?

More than any abstract philosophical, theological or political argument, it is the influence and impact of persons committed to nonviolence whom I've known, or know about, that inspire and sustain my own commitment. The power of the real-life examples of Mahatma Gandhi, Jim Lawson, Martin Luther King Jr., Oscar Romero, and Nelson Mandela, how their lives affected others, and what they were able to accomplish, is more persuasive than any intellectual argument. Ironically, even those of us committed to nonviolence often underestimate how many individuals and social change movements have been inspired and influenced by the examples of Gandhi and King.

In 2011, I was surprised by the number of young Arab activists who cited Mahatma Gandhi and, even more often, Martin Luther King Jr., as inspiration for their commitments to nonviolence in the popular uprisings that overthrew decades-old authoritarian Arab regimes. I discovered that Gene Sharp's writings, including *The Politics of Nonviolent Action*, which I had viewed as overly academic, had significant influence on several Arab activists, as earlier Sharp's writings apparently had influenced key democracy activists in Eastern Europe. I was surprised to learn that two years before the Arab Spring, a young woman activist named Dalia Ziade translated *The Montgomery Story*— a comic book about the power of nonviolence, originally published in 1958 by the Fellowship of Reconciliation—into Arabic and distributed thousands of copies. On a trip to Cairo in 1984, I met an Egyptian father and son who were Muslim Brotherhood activists. I spoke very little Arabic and they spoke almost no English, but when I said that I had worked with Dr. King the father's eyes lit up and with an enthusiastic smile he said aloud, "*Aywah, Aywah* (Yes, yes), Martin Luther King *kwais kitir* (very good)." King modeled a way of viewing the world and a way of acting in the world that all of us can and should try to imitate.

In addition to famous persons, I have met dozens of Israelis and Arabs who are committed to working nonviolently for peace and reconciliation. Members of the Parents Circle-Bereaved Families Forum, despite losing family members in the conflict, are committed to rejecting violence and working for peace and reconciliation. I was privileged personally to meet Aziz Abu Sarah, a young Muslim Palestinian man whose older brother died after being beaten in an Israeli prison, and Robi Damelin, a white South African-born Israeli Jewish mother whose son was killed by a Palestinian sniper in the West Bank. They had powerful, personal reasons to become enemies, but instead they've chosen to work together as activist allies for peace.

Aziz Abu Sarah and Robi Damelin embody several elements that inform, inspire, and guide my own commitment to nonviolence. First is the basic recognition that as human beings, made in the image of God, even in extreme circumstances such as insult, mistreatment or even violence, we can and must choose how to act. It is easy to respond in kind, to seek revenge, and then to rationalize our violent reactions. But that would not necessarily be acting wisely or in our best interests. We should always try to achieve the best possible outcome in the situation, and as Aziz argues, choosing to act rationally and seeking the best possible outcome is a moral standard for action not just in times that are easy but in really tough times as well.

Another basic element in my commitment to nonviolence, so clearly reflected in Aziz' and Robi's examples, is acknowledging that the other, even the *enemy* other, is human, more like me than different. To realize and act on this recognition, I have to work hard to remove the stigma, shed stereotypes, and seek to know and understand the other person. This almost always involves overcoming fear. Whether someone is of a different race, nationality, religious tradition, or political orientation, freeing ourselves from fear is made much more difficult by the practice of many political leaders who often magnify and manipulate fear of others for their own personal or political advantage.

It is very important, in this context, to acknowledge a core teaching in the sacred scriptures of Jews, Christians and Muslims. The texts teach, "Fear not . . . for God loves you" or ". . . for God is with you." This teaching has been and still sometimes is interpreted in a narrow, selfish way, i.e., that God is with *us*, and not with or is against the *others*. I believe the more faithful and fundamental meaning of the teaching is that God's extraordinary love, God's Amazing Grace, *Shalom* (peace, or wholeness), *Bismallah al rahman al rahim* (God, who does and is mercy) extends toward us, not as whites or blacks, Americans or members of a particular religious tradition. Rather, God generously and relentlessly loves all people—indeed all creation—and our awareness of God's love can radically free us from fear of others, even those who are very different or who threaten us. Freed from fear of the other, we are free to act in fresh, creative ways.

Acknowledging the odds against which they struggle, Aziz and Robi believe they may never see the world restored to perfect humanity, but, paraphrasing King: they still feel obligated to believe that violence and hatred are not the tools of peace. More than this, they feel obligated to use their pain to spread peace. And they both are very much aware that this is not a one-time commitment, but a commitment they must make again and again. They believe that each day they must choose again to love and forgive those around them. So, if we decide to walk this path, we also must be prepared to choose, again and again, to love and forgive.

I am reminded of what Hannah Arendt wrote in her 1958 book, *The Human Condition* concerning the unique, creative power of forgiving.

> Forgiving, in other words, is the only reaction which does not merely re-act but acts anew and unexpectedly, unconditioned by the act which provoked it and therefore freeing from its consequences both the one who forgives and the one who is forgiven.[4]

Making a principled commitment to nonviolence and to its corollary, forgiveness, not only forces us to explore more options, but also offers the potential to break out of the cycle of predictable action-reaction, to begin something new. While some may dismiss this approach as an impossible ideal, I believe nonviolence actually represents a more creative kind of realism. Robi Damelin, the Israeli mother, clearly believes choosing this path can yield real results. Committed to nonviolence and to forgiving the Palestinian who killed her son, Robi told me that she believes a long term reconciliation process is possible. She believes it's possible in the Israeli-Palestinian context in part because she witnessed the extraordinary example of Nelson Mandela and the incredible, indeed miraculous, transformation between blacks and whites begun in her own birth country of South Africa.

In the Israeli-Palestinian context, both Aziz and Robi believe that nonviolence doesn't only mean refusing to use violence in the conflict, but requires working to address and resolve the underlying causes of the conflict by satisfying the legitimate aspirations of both peoples: to end the occupation and establish a viable, secure independent Palestinian state, and to achieve recognition and security for Israel coupled with normal peaceful relations with all of its Arab neighbors.

This larger, more challenging concept of nonviolence is related to a more comprehensive and complex definition of violence. A.J. Muste believed that to be a pacifist was not just a matter of rejecting violence as a means to resolve conflict. Muste believed, and I believe, we must be prepared to address and confront all the forms of violence, including the violence of economic as well as political and cultural systems that oppress people and block them from achieving their basic human rights and full potential as human beings.

It is very clear from their teaching and practice that both Jim Lawson and Martin Luther King Jr. not only rejected the violence of war but also the much more pervasive, often unacknowledged violence of the conditions in our own country and worldwide that prevent people from fulfilling universal human needs and rights. Both developed deep understandings of the relationship between US economic, political and military power—including our use of a hugely disproportionate percentage of the earth's resources—and the global conditions that oppress millions of human beings and threaten the planet itself. Given our country's contribution to these conditions, Americans have special responsibility for helping to alleviate them. In his "Time to

---

4. Arendt, *The Human Condition,* 216.

Break the Silence" speech on April 4, 1967 at Riverside Church in New York, I believe King was not simply speaking about the violence of the US war in Vietnam, but the broader problem when he declared, "the greatest purveyor of violence in the world today (is) my own government."

Radically critical as they were of the present global order, King and Lawson continued to be profoundly hopeful about the future. Their hope was grounded in their experience of God's extraordinary and powerful love for the world, their appreciation of American ideals and achievements, and their profound understanding of the fundamental and inescapable interconnectedness of humanity and, indeed of all creation. In 1964, back at Wesleyan University after my time living in Memphis, I remember being deeply inspired by Dr. King's baccalaureate sermon, particularly hearing him declare, "The arc of the moral universe is long, but it bends toward justice."

Three years earlier in a commencement address at Lincoln University, King spoke about his moral vision of mutuality and interdependence:

> All this is simply to say that all life is interrelated. We are caught in an inescapable network of mutuality; tied in a single garment of destiny. Whatever affects one directly, affects all indirectly. . . . Strangely enough, I can never be what I ought to be until you are what you ought to be. You can never be what you ought to be until I am what I ought to be. This is the way the world is made.[5]

Taken together, these are the most important elements of my commitment to nonviolence.

There are several good books and essays on nonviolence, including Dr. King's sermons and writings; Gene Sharp's writings over five decades; the *Annual John Howard Yoder Dialogues on Nonviolence* at Notre Dame; David Cortright's book, *Gandhi and Beyond: Nonviolence for a New Political Age;* and Erica Chenowith and Maria J. Stephan, *Why Civil Resistance Works: The Strategic Logic of Nonviolent Conflict.* In 2014, witnessing multiple conflicts in our country and around the world, the need for more widespread public understanding and application of nonviolence has never been greater. The challenge of applying nonviolence to real political issues and conflicts still needs a lot more academic and popular study and practical experimentation. That many younger people are engaging this challenge is a hopeful signpost for the future.

A fourth learning from my boundary crossings, particularly from my partnership with Jews, Christians and Muslims working for peace in the Middle East, relates to the role of religion in generating and in resolving conflict. Just as there is much evidence for how religion can cause, complicate, and exacerbate conflict, there also is plenty of evidence and experience for how religion provides inspiration and support for rejecting violence, and pursuing justice and peace. Judaism, Christianity and Islam have all been used as both destructive and constructive influences in the Arab-Israeli-Palestinian conflict.

---

5. Quoted in MartinLuther King Jr. "A Christmas Sermon for Peace," 254.

In his 1988 article entitled "Twice Promised Land," cited earlier, Rabbi Arthur Hertzberg addressed the issue of religion explicitly when he warned that defining the Israeli-Palestinian conflict in religious terms would make it more difficult, if not impossible, to resolve. He pointed out that if Jews (or fundamentalist Christians) advance the Jewish claim to the land based on God's promise to the ancient Israelites, "then instantly and immediately the answer from the Muslim point of view is a reciprocal (absolute) claim that nothing to which Islam applies, no piece of land to which Islam ever laid claim, is alienable."[6] As a student of Jewish history and editor of *The Zionist Idea*, Hertzberg pointed out that mainstream Zionism was never based on religious claims, but on the Jewish people's need and right to have a land where they would be the majority and the host people. Following the 1967 war, Hertzberg argued that this essentially secular, nationalist Jewish claim could and should accommodate Palestinian national aspirations in a negotiated two-state solution between the Jordan River and the Mediterranean Sea.

In his writings and in his work with the USICPME, Rabbi Hertzberg also stood firmly for the idea that Judaism, Christianity and Islam, rightly understood, could make powerful contributions to the pursuit of peace. At the same time, he recognized that there are supporters on each side who utilize religion to buttress their exclusive claim to the land and to justify violence against the other. Tragically, in recent years, several failed attempts to achieve a negotiated solution have fueled frustration and religious extremism on both sides.

In my years of living and traveling in the Middle East, I experienced the ways religion is used to fuel hatred and extremism, but I also witnessed how the ethical teachings of the three Abrahamic traditions provide powerful inspiration and practical support for ending violence and resolving the conflict. Having listened to Palestinian and Israeli advocates and supporters of peace, whether religious or secular, it is clear to me that moderate majorities on both sides draw deeply, whether explicitly or implicitly, on their religious traditions for wellsprings of inspiration for justice, peace and reconciliation. In my work for thirty years with American Jewish, Christian and Muslim leaders, I've been impressed and inspired by how, despite strong personal and communal ties to different sides in the conflict, they are committed in principle and practice to working together for peace. While extremist views are often expressed more loudly and gain more media attention, I believe for most Jews, Christians and Muslims, the core teachings of our religious traditions provide inspiration and motivation for progress toward peace.

At the Chautauqua Institution in my July 2000 morning lecture, "Religion: Source of Violence or Source of Peace?"[7] I addressed certain core texts and teachings in each of the three Abrahamic traditions that can inspire a sense of exclusivity, superiority and potential violence toward people of other religious traditions. I believe

6. Hertzberg, "Twice Promised Land."

7. Young, "Religion: Source of Violence or Source of Peace."

that these core teachings have to be addressed directly —not just by scholars but also by believers in the pews—and that ongoing, intense struggles over different interpretations are having profound effects on prospects for interreligious cooperation and world peace. Stated simply, core beliefs in the three traditions that need continuously to be critically examined include: the Jewish belief that Jews are God's chosen people; the Christian belief that accepting Jesus as savior is the only path to salvation; and the Muslim belief that, coming third of the three Abrahamic traditions, Islam represents the best and ultimate revelation. I believe we all need to acknowledge and critically examine teachings that are used to claim superiority for our tradition. We don't need to water down religious beliefs, but I am convinced by the way Jesus lived and what he taught that being a Christian does not require me to believe that my tradition is the exclusive way or superior to other paths. Late in his ministry, based on his experiences around the world meeting people of different religious traditions and none, and on his understanding of the wideness of God's mercy, the great Christian evangelical preacher Billy Graham came to the belief that there is more than one path.[8]

In my Chautauqua lecture I cited texts from the Hebrew Bible, the New Testament, and the Holy Quran, as well as several personal experiences which I believe reflect God's extraordinary, impartial love and mercy, teach us religious humility, inspire radical inclusivity, and encourage us to work for justice, peace and reconciliation. Three personal experiences exemplify what I believe are fundamental, blessed messages in all three traditions that call us to a spirit of radical openness and cooperation. In fall 1993, my two sons and I visited the Plymouth Colony in Massachusetts where actors imitating seventeenth-century villagers told us about how they had absorbed persons into their colony rescued from shipwrecks, and then added they were "very glad that so far we haven't had to rescue any Papists or Jews." In sharp contrast, that same afternoon, we three attended the groundbreaking ceremony for the Islamic Center of New England in Sharon, Massachusetts where Dr Mian Ashraf, founder and president, welcomed prominent local Jewish, Catholic and Protestant leaders to participate in the ceremony. Mian dedicated the Center to the study of Judaism and Christianity as well as Islam, explaining that because Islam arrived third of the Abrahamic traditions, he believed Muslims should study what it means to be a good Jew and a good Christian, on the path of becoming good Muslims.

A second example comes from my 1980 participation in an ecumenical delegation to El Salvador. As noted earlier, a day before he was assassinated, Archbishop Oscar Romero welcomed our delegation including Methodist, Quaker, Unitarian and agnostic participants, to Mass in the Basilica, and offered the bread of Holy Communion to every one of us. We all took the bread from his hand and ate it. A rabbi later commented that Romero's offering was a gracious invitation for all—regardless of our religious traditions—to join in God's work of *Tikkun Olam* (repairing the world). A third experience occurred at a Shabbat evening service at Temple Beth El in Boca

---

8. "Billy Graham Denies Jesus is the only way to the Father."

Raton, Florida. Following a dinner attended by local leaders of several different religious communities, a prominent Israeli spoke to a full sanctuary about his vision for peace with the Palestinians. Rabbi Merle Singer then invited responses from Heba Hechiche, a Muslim, and me, a Christian. When it came time to take the Torah out of the Ark, Rabbi Singer took three scrolls out instead of only one. Handing one scroll to Heba, and one to me, he invited us to join him in carrying the Torah through the congregation. After the service, Merle explained: "God didn't give the Torah *for* the Jewish people; God gave the Torah *to* the Jewish people *for* the healing the world. And it's clear," Merle said, "that Christians and Muslims can participate in the work of Torah just as much as Jews."

In these examples, a Muslim, Christian and Jew interpreted a core belief in a way that inspires humility and radical inclusiveness. From my experiences working for peace in the Middle East, I have learned that there are rich resources in the core teachings of all three Abrahamic traditions to inspire openness and interreligious cooperation. I believe it is an urgent imperative of our time that we discover or rediscover these resources, teach them in our communities and act on them in bold, practical, public ways.

A fifth lesson from my experiences is about the relationship between the "power of one" and the "power of many." On December 17, 2010 Mohamed Bouazizi, a Tunisian street vendor, set himself on fire to protest confiscation of his cart and his humiliation at the hands of government officials. He died three weeks later. His immolation inspired the democratic uprising in Tunisia and was a catalyst for the Arab Spring throughout the Middle East. Earlier I described how the immolations of Alice Herz, Norman Morrison and Roger LaPorte in 1965 haunted and inspired me and others to act more boldly to oppose the Vietnam War. We all know how Rosa Parks refusing to give up her seat to a white man and her being arrested inspired the Montgomery Bus Boycott. These stories reveal how one person's conscientious act can inspire others and significantly influence the course of events. These individual acts in context also teach us about, the essential importance of organizing to enlist the power of many. While an individual act of conscience can inspire change, it takes an organized movement of many acting together to actually achieve change. Organizing for progress, whether on the community, national or international level, is a complex process of motivating and uniting people with overlapping but not necessarily identical interests and assisting them to generate changes from which all benefit. The larger lesson we might take away from these examples is, "Act according to conscience, and organize, organize, organize!"

A sixth lesson concerns the intersection between protesting and changing policy. I have been involved in many protests over the years and believe deeply that demonstrations play a crucial role in promoting change. Indeed, achieving positive policy changes often cannot be achieved without protest. At the same time, I believe it is important that we work conscientiously and strategically to be clear and communicate effectively with others what immediate and longer term change(s) in policies we want to accomplish and why. While simple protest of wrongs can have value, without a clear, effectively communicated political strategy, protest is less effective. Especially when the change we seek is fundamental and far-reaching, it is important to link protest with immediate and intermediate steps toward the longer range goals we seek. In 2011 and 2012, while the "Occupy Movement" protests were inspiring and effective in generating public and media attention to growing inequalities in our nation, they could have done a better job to more clearly identify policies they wanted to change. Developing effective strategies that linked public protest with policy changes was an essential element of Martin Luther King Jr.'s genius and the civil rights movement's success. While the issues may be different and more complex, there is a lot we still can learn from King's life and the nonviolent civil rights movement about these relationships.

As I turn seventy-two in 2014, a seventh lesson from my life's journey draws on the wisdom and realism of Rabbi Tarphon's teaching almost 2,000 years ago: "It is not necessary to complete the work, but neither are you free to desist from it." I am deeply grateful for having had opportunities to participate in work that helped to advance civil rights and end the Vietnam War. Working for Arab-Israeli-Palestinian peace, for abolishing weapons of mass destruction, for achieving economic and ecological justice, and for reducing the scourge of violence in America and around the world goes on. While, hopefully, there will be progress toward these goals in my lifetime, I accept that they certainly will not be fully accomplished. I must gracefully accept that others will continue the work after I'm gone. In that context, I believe it's very important to engage with younger people, listen carefully to them, and share our hopes and our experiences working for change.[9]

The eighth and final lesson relates to the importance of humor in work for social change. I hope that some of my personal experiences show how humor plays a positive role in building a better future. I believe one of God's blessed gifts to humans is our ability to laugh and to cause others to laugh. From a very young age, I have appreciated that laughing at myself is both healthy and healing. To appreciate the humor in situations, including humor in our strivings and struggles for social change, doesn't in the least diminish the seriousness of our endeavors. Indeed, I believe audacity and humor are more effective tactics for achieving social change than rage and fury.

9. Harding, *Hope and History: Why We Must Share the Story of the Movement.*

Bibliography

Abu Sharif, Bassam and Uzi Manhaimi. *Best of Enemies.* Boston: Little, Brown and Company, 1995.

Ajami, Fouad. *The Arab Predictament: Arab Political Thought and Practice Since 1967.* Cambridge: Cambridge University Press, 1981.

Alexander, Michelle. *The New Jim Crow: Mass Incarceration in the Age of Colorblindness.* New York: New Press, 2010.

Arendt, Hannah. *The Human Condition.* New York: Doubleday Anchor, 1959.

Arnett, Peter. *Associated Press.* Online: http://en.wikipedia.org/wiki/Peter_Arnett.

Avishai, Bernard. "A Plan for Peace. That Still Could Be." *The New York Times Magazine* (February 7, 2011). Online: http://www.nytimes.com/2011/02/13/magazine/13Israel-t.html?pagewanted=all&_r=0.

Bernstein, Adam. "Alfredo Stroesner: Paraguyan Dictator." *The Washington Post* (August 17, 2006).

"Billy Graham Denies Jesus is the only way to the Father." Online: *You Tube,* April 20, 2007. http://www.youtube.com/watch?v=axxlXy6bLH0.

Bonhoeffer, Dietrich. *Papers and Letters from Prison.* Edited by Eberhard Bethge. New York: Macmillan Paperbacks, 1962.

Burg, Avraham. *The Holocaust Is Over: We Must Rise from Its Ashes.* Translated by Israel Amrani. New York: Palgrave Macmillan, 2008.

———. "Israel's Fading Democracy." *New York Times Sunday Review* (August 4, 2012).

Cronkite, Walter. *We Are Mired in Stalemate.* Commentary (television editorial). (February 27, 1968). Online: http://www.ushistoryatlas.com/era9/USHAcom_PS_U09_tet_R2.pdf.

Ezrahi, Yaron. *Rubber Bullets: Power and Conscience in Modern Israel.* New York: Farrar, Straus and Giroux, 1997.

Frankel, Max. "Looming Over Israel." *The New York Times* (November 15, 1982).

———. "Help Us By Cutting Aid," *The New York Times* (November 16, 1982).

Gitlin, Todd and Liel Liebovitz. *The Chosen Peoples: America, Israel and the Ordeals of Divine Election.* New York: Simon & Schuster, 2010.

Gray, Francine Du Plessix, "The Moratorium and the New Mobe," *The New Yorker* (January 3, 1970) 32–42. Online: http://www.newyorker.com/archive/1970/01/03/1970_01_03_032_TNY_CARDS_000294868.

Griffen, John Howard. *Black Like Me.* New York: Signet, 1962.

Hahn, Thich Nhat. *Vietnam: Lotus in a Sea of Fire.* New York: Hill and Wang, 1967.

Halberstam, David. *The Children.* New York: Random House, 1998.

——— , *The Making of a Quagmire.* New York: Random House, 1965.

Halevy, Efraim. "This Should Be the Beginning, Not the End of Israel Negotiating with Hamas." *New Republic* (October 24, 2011). Online: http://www.newrepublic.com/article/world/96457/gilad-shalit-release-netanyahu-hamas-negotiations.

Harding, Vincent. *Hope and History: Why We Must Share the Story of the Movement.* Second Edition. New York: Orbis Books, 2010.

Hentoff, Nat. *Peace Agitator: the Story of A.J. Muste.* New York: The MacMillan Company, 1963

Hershey, John. *Hiroshima.* New York: Alfred A. Knopf, 1946.

Hertzberg, Arthur. *A Jew in America: My Life and a People's Struggle for Identity.* San Francisco: Harper, 2002.

———. "Twice Promised Land." *Middlebury Magazine,* Summer, 1988.

Jerusalem Post. Editorial. (November 14, 1982).

"Israeli Dispute Erupts Over Columns in the Times," *The New York Times,* November 18, 1982.

Israeli (unofficial) Peace Initiative. (March 2011) Online: http://graphics8.nytimes.com/packages/pdf/world/IPI-English.pdf.

Johnson, President Lyndon. On Cronkite's *Commentary.* Online: http://www.britannica.com/EBchecked/topic/1312056/Walter-Cronkite.

Kahin, George McTurnin and John W. Lewis. *The United States in Vietnam: An Analysis in Depth of America's Involvement in Vietnam.* New York: A Delta Book, 1967.

Kahn, Herman. *On Thermonuclear War.* Princeton: Princeton University Press, 1960.

Khalidi, Walid. "Thinking the Unthinkable: A Sovereign Palestinian State." *Foreign Affairs* (Council on Foreign Relations) 56 no.4 (July 1978) 695-713.

King Jr., Martin Luther. "A Christmas Sermon for Peace." In *Testament of Hope: the Essential Writings of Martin Luther King Jr.* Edited by James M. Washington, 253-258. San Francisco: Harper & Row, 1967.

———. "Time to Break Silence." In *Testament of Hope: the Essential Writings of Martin Luther King Jr.* Edited by James M. Washington, 231-244. San Francisco: Harper & Row, 1967

Kurtzer, Daniel, Keynote at JStreet National Summit. (June 7, 2014). Online: https://www.youtube.com/watch?v=jaXLYv9Hxt0&list=PL4CViXUNRkO6zMLr6JrSKT8nQXGbXEEJW&index=2 (Kurtzer starts 45 minutes into video of Opening Night program.)

———. and Scott B. Lasensky. *Negotiating Arab-Israeli Peace: American Leadership in the Middle East.* Washington, DC: U.S. Institute for Peace Press, 2008.

———. "The US Must Inject Life into a Moribund Peace Process." *Haaretz,* (June 30, 2014). Online: http://www.haaretz.com/news/diplomacy-defense/israel-peace-conference/1.601474#!

———. "Toward A New American Policy." *Cairo Review of Global Affairs,* (February 2013).

Lens, Sidney. *The Futile Crusade: Anti-Communism As American Credo.* Chicago: Quadrangle Books, 1964.

Levertov, Denise. *Live in the Forest.* New York: New Directions, 1978.

Luce, Don. *The Tiger Cages of Vietnam* (April 2009). Online: http://www.historiansagainstwar.org/resources/torture/luce.html.

Matalon, Rabbi J. Rolando (Roly). "Prayer for Peace." From *Prayers for Peace in the Middle East.* US Interreligious Committtee. Online at http://www.nili-mideastpeace.org/prayers

Meacham, John. "The History of the American Dream: Is It Still Real?" *Time* 180 no.2 (July 2, 2012) 35-39.

"Middle East: Peace Plans." *Council on Foreign Relations.* Online: http://www.cfr.org/israel/middle-east-peace-plans-background/p7736.

National Conciliation Document of the Prisoners. Palestinian prisoners document May 2006. Online: http://unispal.un.org/UNISPAL.NSF/0/CE3ABE1B2E1502B58525717A006194CD.

NILI Leaders Delegation consensus statement. (December 2009) Online: http://nili-mideastpeace.org/downloads/2009_12_NILI_Trip_Statement.pdf.

NILI "Principles of Cooperation and "Twelve Urgent Steps for Peace." *National Interreligious Leadership Initiative for Peace.* Online: http//www.nili-mideastpeace.org.

NILI Statement. (January 25, 2013) Online: http://www.nili-mideastpeace.org/downloads/2013_01StatementwEndorsers.pdf.

Nusseibeh, Sari with Anthony David. *Once Upon a Country: A Palestinian Life.* New York: Farrar, Straus and Giroux, 2007.

———. *What Is a Palestinian State Worth?* Cambridge, Massachusetts: Harvard University Press, 2011.

Obama, President Barack. "Commencement address at West Point." (May 28, 2014). Online: http://www.washingtonpost.com/politics/full-text-of-president-obamas-commencement-address-at-west-point/2014/05/28/cfbcdcaa-e670-11e3-afc6-a1dd9407abcf_story.html.

———. Full Text of President Obama's Speech in Jerusalem. (March 21, 2013). Online: http://www.jpost.com/Diplomacy-and-Politics/Full-text-of-Obamas-Jerusalem-speech-307327.

Oglesby, Carl and Richard Shaull. *Containment and Change.* New York: The MacMillan Company, 1967.

Olmert, Ehud. "Two-State Solution or Israel Is Done For." Interview with *Haaretz.* (November 29, 2007). Online: http://www.haaretz.com/news/olmert-to-haaretz-two-state-solution-or-israel-is-done-for-1.234201.

Peoples Peace Treaty. Online: http://en.wikipedia.org/wiki/People's_Peace_Treaty.

"Prayers for Peace." *US Interreligious Committee for Peace in the Middle East.* Online: http://www.usccb.org/issues-and-action/human-life-and-dignity/global-issues/middle-east/israel-palestine/upload/prayers-for-peace-in-the-middle-east.pdf.

"Principles of Cooperation" and "Twelve Urgent Steps for Peace." *National Interreligious Leadership Initiative for Peace (NILI)* website: http://www.nili-mideastpeace.org.

"Programs for Broadcast." *Wartime Broadcasting Service.* Online: http://en.wikipedia.org/Wartime_Broadcasting_Service#Programsforbroadcast.

Report of the National Advisory Commission on Civil Disorders. New York: Bantam Books, 1968.

Romero, Archbishop Oscar. The Last Sermon (March 1980). Online: http://www.haverford.edu/relg/faculty/amcguire/romero.html.

Savir, Uri. *The Process.* New York: Random House, 1998.

Shipler, David K. *A Country of Strangers: Blacks and Whites in America.* New York: Alfred A. Knopf, 1997.

———. *Arab and Jew: Wounded Spirits in a Promised Land.* New York: Times Books, 1986.

"Social and Demographic Trends." *Pew Research Center Study.* (July 26, 2011). Online: http://www.pewsocialtrends.org/2011/07/26/wealth-gaps-rise-to-record-highs-between-whites-blacks-hispanics/.

Steinfels, Margaret O'Brien, "Death and Lies in El Salvador: the Ambassador's Tale." *Commonweal* 128 no. 18 (October 26, 2001).

Steinfels, Peter. "Mideast Initiative Pushes Beyond Platitudes," *New York Times,* (December 6, 2003). Online: http://www.nytimes.com/2003/12/06/nyregion/beliefs-interfaith-initiative-peace-middle-east-pushes-beyond-platitudes.html.

"The Blunt Reality of War in Vietnam." *Life Magazine* (November 26, 1965). Online: http://life.time.com/history/vietnam-war-life-magazine-covers-1961-1972/attachment/life-november-26-1965-2/.

"The Draft—Who Beats It and How." *Life Magzine* (December 9, 1966). Online: http://oldlifemagazines.com/media/catalog/product/cache/1/image/9df78eab33525d08d6e5fb8d27136e95/c/v/cv120966.jpg.

"The Top 100 Works of Journalism in the United States in the 20th Century." Study by *New York University Journalism Department* (February 1999),

The Zionist Idea: A Historical Analysis and Reader. Edited with an Introduction by Arthur Hertzberg. New York: Atheneum, 1984.

Wright, Robin. *Rock the Casbah: Rage and Rebellion Across the Islamic World.* New York: Simon & Schuster, 2011.

Young-Bruehl, Elizabeth. *Hannah Arendt: For Love of the World.* New Haven: Yale University Press, 1982.

Young, Ronald J. *Missed Opportunities for Peace: US Middle East Policy, 1981-86.* A Report Prepared for the American Friends Service Committee. Philadelphia: AFSC. 1987.

———. "Religion: Source of Violence or Source of Peace," *Chautauqua Institution.* (July 31, 2000). Online: https://www.thegreatlecturelibrary.com/flash/index.php?select=gllPreview,20-117.

Zinn, Howard. *Vietnam: the Logic of Withdrawal.* Boston: Beacon Press, 1967.

Appendix

Books I've read and recommend for
digging deeper on five subjects

Civil Rights Movement/Race Relations

Alexander, Michelle. *The New Jim Crow*. New York: The New Press, 2010.

Ahmann, Mathew, ed. *Race: Challenge to Religion*. Chicago: Henry Regnery Company, 1963.

Baldwin, James. *Nobody Knows My Name*. New York: Dell, 1961.

———. *The Fire Next Time*. New York: Dial Press, 1963.

Berry, Faith. *Before and Beyond Harlem, A Biography of Langston Hughes*. New York: Wings Books, 1995.

Bond, Julian. *A Time to Speak: A Time to Act*. New York: Simon & Schuster, 1972.

Branch, Taylor. *At Canaan's Edge: America in the King Years 1965-68*. New York: Simon & Schuster, 2006.

———. *Parting the Waters: America in the King Years, 1954-63*. New York: Simon & Schuster, 1988.

———. *Pillar of Fire, America in the King Years, 1963-65*. New York: Simon & Schuster, 1998.

Burns, Stewart. *To the Mountain Top*. San Francisco: Harper, 2004.

Campbell, Will D. *Race and Renewal of the Church*. Philadelphia: Westminster Press, 1962.

Carmichael, Stokely and Charles V. Hamilton. *Black Power*. New York: Vintage Books, 1967.

Cash, W.J. *The Mind of the South*. New York: Vintage Books, 1960.

Clark, Kenneth B. *Dark Ghetto: Dilemmas of Social Power*. New York: Harper & Row, 1965.

Cleaver, Eldridge. *Soul on Ice*. New York: Dell, 1968.

Cotton, Dorothy F. *If Your Back's Not Bent: The Role of the Citizenship Education Program in the Civil Rights Movement*. New York: Atria Books, 2012.

D'Emilio John. *Lost Prophet: The Life and Times of Bayard Rustin*. Chicago: University of Chicago Press, 2003.

Dollard, John. *Caste and Class in a Southern Town*. New York: Doubleday Anchor Books, 1957.

Dubois, W.E.B. *The Souls of Black Folk*. New York: Fawcett Publications, Inc., 1961.

Egerton, John. *Speak Now Against the Day: The Generation Before the Civil Rights Movement in the South*. New York: Alfred A. Knopf, 1994.

Fanon, Frantz, *Black Skin, White Masks*. Translated by Charles Lam Markmann. New York: Grove Press, 1967.

———. *Wretched of the Earth*. Translated by Frances Farrington. New York: Grove Press, 1963.

Garrow, David J. *Bearing the Cross, Martin Luther King Jr., A Personal Portrait*. New York: William Morrow and Company, 1986.

Griffin, John Howard. *Black Like Me*. New York: Signet Books, 1962.

Halberstam, David. *The Children*. New York: Random House, 1998.

Harding, Vincent. *Hope and History: Why We Must Share the Story of the Movement*. Second Edition. New York: Orbis Books, 2010.

Haselden, Kyle. *The Racial Problem in Christian Perspective*. New York: Harper Torchbooks, 1964.

Hentoff, Nat. *The New Equality*. New York: Viking Press, 1964.

King Jr., Martin Luther. *Strength to Love*. New York: Harper Collins, 1963.

———. *Stride Toward Freedom*. New York: Harper & Row, 1964.

———. *Where Do We Go From Here: Chaos or Community?* New York: Harper and Row, 1967.

———, *Why We Can't Wait*. New York: Harper and Row, 1964.

Lewis, John, with Michael D'Orso. *Walking with the Wind*. New York: Simon & Schuster, 1998.

Lincoln, C. Eric. *My Face is Black*. Boston: Beacon, 1964.

———. *The Black Muslims in America*. Boston: Beacon Press, 1961.

Malcolm X, with Alex Haley. *The Autobiography of Malcolm X*. New York: Grove Press, 1965.

Miller, William Lee. Of Thee, Nevertheless, I Sing. New York: Harcourt Brace Jovanovich, 1975.

Miller, William Robert. *Martin Luther King Jr.* New York: Weybright and Talley, 1968.

Myrdal, Gunnar. *An American Dilemma Vols. 1 and 2*. New York: Harper Brothers, 1944.

Report of the National Advisory Commission on Civil Disorders. New York: A Bantam Book, 1968.

Sellers, James. The South and Christian Ethics. New York: YMCA Association Press, 1962.

Shipler, David K. *A Country of Strangers: Blacks and Whites in America*. New York: Alfred A. Knopf, 1997.

———. *The Rights of the People: How Our Search for Safety Invades Our Liberties*. New York: Alfred A. Knopf, 2011.

Silberman, Charles E. *Crisis in Black and White*. New York: Random House, 1964.

Silver, James W. *Mississippi: The Closed Society*. New York: Harcourt, Brace & World, 1963.

Smith, Lillian. *Killers of the Dream*. New York: W.W.Norton & Company, 1949.

———. *Our Face, Our Words*. New York: W.W. Norton & Company, 1964.

———. *Strange Fruit*. New York: Harcourt, 1944.

Stringfellow, William. *Dissenter in a Great Society*. New York: Holt, Rinehart and Winston, 1966.

———. *My People Is the Enemy*. New York: Holt, Rinehart and Winston, 1964.

Washington, James M., ed. *A Testament of Hope: the Essential Writings of Martin Luther King Jr.* San Francisco: Harper & Row, 1986.

Waskow, Arthur I. *From Race Riot to Sit-in, 1919 and the 1960s*. New York: Doubleday & Company, 1966.

Nonviolence

Ackerman, Peter. *A Force More Powerful: A Century of Nonviolent Conflict.* New York: Palgrave/St. Martins, 2001.

———. *Strategic Nonviolent Conflict: The Dynamics of People Power in the Twentieth Century.* New York: Praeger, 1994.

Bondurant, Joan V. *Conquest of Violence,* Revised Edition. Berkeley: University of California Press, 1969.

Bruyn, Severyn T. and Paula M. Rayman, ed. *Nonviolent Action and Social Change.* New York: Irvington Publishers, 1979.

Chenowith, Erica and Maria J. Stephan. *Why Civil Resistance Works.* New York: Columbia University Press, 2011.

Cortright, David. *Gandhi and Beyond: Nonviolence for an Age of Terrorism.* Boulder: Pardigm Publishers, 2006.

Day, Dorthy. *By Little and By Little,* The Selected Writings of Dorothy Day. Edited by Robert Ellsberg. New York: Alfred A. Knopf, 1983.

Dellinger, Dave. *More Power Than We Know.* New York: Anchor Press Doubleday, 1975..

———. *Revolutionary Nonviolence.* New York: Bobs-Merrill Company, 1970.

Deming, Barbara. *Revolution and Equilibrium.* New York: Grossman Publishers, 1971.

———. *We Cannot Win Without Our Lives.* New York: Grossman Publishers, 1974.

Douglass, James W. *The Nonviolent Cross.* Toronto: The Macmillan Company, 1969.

Erikson, Erik H. *Gandhi's Truth.* New York: W.W. Norton & Company, 1969.

Finn, James. *Protest: Pacifism and Politics.* New York: Vintage Books, 1968.

Fischer, Louis. *The Life of Mahatma Gandhi.* New York: Harper & Row, 1950.

Gandhi, M.K. *Nonviolent Resistance.* New York: Schocken Books, 1951.

———. *Gandhi: An Autobiography.* Translated by Mahadeve Desai. Boston: Beacon Press, 1965.

Gregg, Richard B. *The Power of Nonviolence.* Second Revised Edition. New York: Schocken, 1966.

Hentoff, Nat. *Peace Agitator: The Story of A.J. Muste.* New York: The Macmillan Company, 1963.

———, ed. *The Essays of A.J. Muste.* New York: The Bobbs-Merrill Company, 1967.

Klein, Alexander. *Dissent, Power, and Confrontation.* New York: McGraw Hill, 1971.

Macgregor, G.H.C. *The New Testament Basis of Pacifism.* New York: Fellowship Publications, 1961.

Miller, William Robert. *Nonviolence: A Christian Interpretation.* New York: Association Press, 1964.

Muste, A.J. *Nonviolence in an Aggressive World.* New York: Fellowship Publications, 1944.

Nearing, Scott. *The Conscience of a Radical.* Harborside, Maine: Social Science Institute, 1965.

Oppenheimer, Martin and George Lakey. *A Manuel for Direct Action.* Chicago: Quadrangle Books, 1965.

Peck, Jim. *We Would Not Kill.* New York: Lyle Stuart, 1958.

Regamey, OP, P. *Nonviolence and the Christian Conscience.* London: Darton,, Longman & Todd, 1966.

Seifert, Harvey. *Conquest by Suffering: The Process and Prospects of Nonviolent Resistance.* Philadelphia: Westminster Press, 1965.

Sibley, Mulford Q. *The Quiet Battle.* New York: Anchor Books, 1963.

Sider, Ronald J. *Christ and Violence.* Scottdale, Pennsylvania: Herald Press, 1979.

Tolstoy, Leo. *The Kingdom of God is Within You.* Translated by Leo Wiener. New York: Noonday Press, 1961.

Tolstoy's Writings on Civil Disobedience and Nonviolence. New York: Bergman Publishers, 1967.

Trocme, Andre, *The Politics of Repentence.* Translated by John Clark, New York: Fellowship Publications, 1953.

Weinberg, Arthur and Lila Weinberg, ed. *Instead of Violence.* New York: Grossman Publishers, 1963.

Yoder, John H. *Nevertheless: Varieties of Religious Pacifism.* Scottdale, Pennsylvania: Herald Press, 1971.

Zinn, Howard. *Disobedience and Democracy.* New York: Vintage Books, 1968.

Vietnam War/U.S. Foreign Policy

Baker, Nicholson. *Human Smoke: The Beginning of World War II, the End of Civilization.* New York: Simon & Schuster, 2008.

Barnet, Richard J. *Intervention and Revolution: America's Confrontation with Insurgent Movements Around the World.* New York: The World Publishing Company, 1968.

———. *Roots of War: The Men and Institutions Behind U.S. Foreign Policy.* Baltimore: Penguin Books, 1973.

Baritz, Loren. *Backfire: Vietnam: The Myths that Made Us Fight, the Illusions that Helped Us Lose, the Legacy that Haunts Us Today.* New York: Ballantine Books, 1985.

Borton, Lady. *Sensing the Enemy: An American woman among the boat people of Vietnam.* New York: The Dial Press, 1984.

Branfman, Fred, ed. *Voices from the Plain of Jars: Life Under an Air War.* New York: Harper Colophon Books, 1972.

Cortright, David. *Soldiers in Revolt: The American Military Today.* New York: Anchor Press/ Doubleday, 1975.

Dudman, Richard. *40 Days with the Enemy: The Story of a Journalist Held Captive by Guerillas in Cambodia.* New York: Liveright, 1970.

Fall, Bernard. *Last Reflections on A War.* New York: Doubleday & Company, 1966.

———. ed. *Ho Chi Minh on Revolution: Selected Writings 1920-66.* New York: Frederic A. Praeger, 1967.

Fleming, D.F. *The Cold War and Its Origins. Vols. 1 and 2.* New York: Doubleday & Company, 1961.

Fulbright, Senator J. William. *The Arrogance of Power.* New York: Vintage Books, 1966.

Gettleman, Marvin, ed. *Vietnam: History, Documents, and Opinions on a Major World Crisis.* Greenwich, Connecticut: Fawcett Publications, 1965.

Gettleman, Marvin and Susan and Lawrence and Carol Kaplan, ed. *Conflict in Indochina: A Reader on the Widening War in Laos and Cambodia.* New York: Vintage Books, 1970.

Goodwin, Richard N. *Remembering America: A Voice from the Sixties.* Boston: Little, Brown and Company, 1988.

Halberstam, David. *The Making of a Quagmire.* New York: Random House, 1965.

Hanh, Thich Nhat. *Vietnam: Lotus in a Sea of Fire, A Buddhist Proposal for Peace.* New York: Hill and Wang, 1967.

Hassler, Alfred. *Saigon, U.S.A.* New York: Richard W. Baron, 1970.

Hayes, Thomas Lee. *American Deserters in Sweden.* New York: Association Press, 1971.

Hersh, Seymour M. *Mylai 4: A Report on the Massacre and Its Aftermath*. New York: Vintage Books, 1970.

In the Name of America. Seymour Melman, Director of Research. New York: Clergy and Laymen Concerned About Vietnam, 1968.

Kahin, George McTurnan and John W. Lewis. *The United States in Vietnam*. New York: A Delta Book, 1967.

Klare, Michael T. *War Without End, American Planning for the Next Vietnams*. New York: Vintage Books, 1970.

Lacouture, Jean. *Ho Chi Minh: A Political Biography*. New York: Vintage Books, 1968.

Lens, Sidnery. *The Futile Crusade: Anti-Communism As American Credo*. Chicago: Quadrangle Books, 1964.

Lifton, Betty Jean and Thomas Fox. *The Children of Vietnam*. New York: Atheneum, 1972.

Lowenfels, Walter, ed. *Where is Vietnam: American Poets Respond*. New York: Anchor Books, 1967.

Lynd, Staughton and Thomas Hayden, *The Other Side*. New York: New American Library, 1966.

Marr, David G. *Vietnam 1945: The Quest for Power*. Berkeley: University of California Press, 1995.

Martin, Earl S. *Reaching the Other Side: The Journal of an American who stayed to witness Vietnam's postwar transition*. New York: Crown Publishers, 1978.

McCarthy, Mary. *Vietnam*. New York: Harcourt, Brace & World, 1970.

O'Brien, Tim. *The Things They Carried*. New York: Mariner Books Houghton Mifflin, 1990.

Oglesby, Carl and Richard Shaull. *Containment and Change*. New York: The Macmillan Company, 1967.

Schurmann, Franz, Peter Dale Scott, and Reginald Zelnik. *The Politics of Escalation in Vietnam. Greenwich, Connecticut:* Fawcett Publications, 1966.

Shaker, Peggy and Holmes Brown. *Indochina Is People*. Philadelpia: United Church Press, 1973.

Sontag, Susan, *Trip to Hanoi*. New York: Farrar, Straus and Giroux, 1968.

The Pentagon Papers: The Defense Department History of United States Decisionmaking on Vietnam. Senator Gravel Edition. Vols. 1, 2, 3, and 4. Boston: Beacon Press, 1971.

Young, Alfred F., ed. *Dissent: Explorations in the History of American Radicalism*. DeKalb: Northern Illinois University Press, 1968.

Zaroulis, Nancy and Gerald Sullivan. *Who Spoke Up: American Protest Against the War in Vietnam 1963-1975*. New York: Doubleday & Company, 1984.

Zinn, Howard, *Vietnam: The Logic of Withdrawal*. Boston: Beacon Press, 1967.

Arab-Israeli-Palestinian Conflict

Ajami, Fouad. *The Arab Predicament: Arab Political Thought and Practice Since 1967*. Cambridge: Cambridge University Press, 1981.

Abu-Sharif, Bassam and Uzi Mahnaimi. *Best of Enemies*. Boston: Little, Brown and Company, 1991.

Assad, Dawud. *Palestine Rising*. New Jersey: Dawud A. Assad, 2010.

Ateek, Naim Stefan, *Justice, and only Justice: A Palestinian Theology of Liberation*. New York: Orbis Books, 1989.

Bailey, Betty Jane and J. Martin Bailey. *Who Are the Christians in the Middle East.* Grand Rapids, Michigan: William P. Erdmans, 2003.

Barghouti, Omar. *BDS (Boycott, Divestment, Sanctions): The Global Struggle for Palestinian Rights.* Chicago: Haymarket Books, 2011.

Bar-On, Mordechai. *In Pursuit of Peace: A History of the Israeli Peace Movement.* Washington D.C.: United States Institute of Peace Press, 1996.

Ben-Ami, Shlomo. *Scars of War, Wounds of Peace: The Israeli-Arab Tragedy.* New York: Oxford Unversity Press, 2006.

Burg, Avraham. *The Holocaust Is Over: We Must Rise from Its Ashes.* New York: Palgrave Micmillan, 2008.

Carter, Jimmy. *Palestine Peace Not Apartheid.* New York: Simon & Schuster, 2006.

———. *The Blood of Abraham: Insights Into the Middle East.* Boston: Houghton Mifflin Company, 1985.

———. *We Can Have Peace in the Holy Land: A Plan That Will Work.* New York: Simon & Schuster, 2009.

Chomsky, Noam. *Peace in the Middle East?* New York: Vintage Books, 1974.

———. *The Fateful Triangle: The United States, Israel & the Palestinians.* Boston: South End Press, 1983.

Cobban, Helena. *The Israeli-Syrian Peace Talks 1991-96 and Beyond.* Washington D.C.: United States Institute of Peace Press, 1999.

———. *The Palestinian Liberation Organization.* Cambridge: Cambridge University Press, 1984.

Dowty, Alan. *Israel/Palestine.* Malden, Massachusetts: Polity Press, 2005.

Eliav, Arie Lova. *Land of the Hart: Israelis, Arabs, the territories and a vision of the future.* Philadelphia: Jewish Publication Society of America, 1974.

———. *New Heart, New Spirit: Biblical Humanism for Modern Israel.* Philadelphia: Jewish Publication Society, 1988.

Elon, Amos. *Jerusalem: City of Mirrors.* Boston: Little, Brown and Company, 1989.

———. *The Israelis: Founders and Sons.* New York: Bantam Books, 1972.

Ezrahi, Yaron. *Rubber Bullets: Power and Conscience in Modern Israel.* New York: Farrar, Straus and Giroux, 1997.

Friedman, Thomas L. *From Beirut to Jerusalem.* New York: Anchor Books, 1990.

Gendzier, Irene L., ed. *A Middle East Reader.* New York: Pegasus, 1969.

Gitlin, Todd and Liel Leibovitz. *Chosen Peoples: America, Israel and the Ordeals of Divine Election.* New York: Simon & Schuster, 2010.

Grob, Leonard and John K. Roth, eds. *Anguished Hope: Holocaust Scholars Confront the Palestinian-Israeli Conflict.* Grand Rapids, Michigan: Willliam B. Erdmans, 2008.

Grossman, David. *The Yellow Wind. Translated by Haim Watzman.* New York: Farrar, Straus and Giroux, 1988.

Handy, Robert T., ed. *The Holy Land in American Protestant Life: A Documentary History.* New York: Arno Press, 1981.

Heller, Mark A. *A Palestinian State: The Implications for Israel.* Cambridge, Massachusetts: Harvard University Press, 1983.

Heller, Mark A. and Sari Nusseibeh. *No Trumpets, No Drums: A Two-State Settlement of the Israeli-Palestinian Conflict.* Washington, D.C.: Foundation for Middle East Peace, 1991.

Helmick S.J., Raymond G. *Why Camp David Failed: Negotiating Outside the Law.* London: Pluto Press, 2004.

Iyad, Abu with Eric Rouleau. *My Home, My Land: A Narrative of the Palestinian Struggle.* Translated by Linda Butler Koseoglu. New York: Times Books, 1981.

Jackson, Elmore. *Middle East Mission: The Story of a Major Bid for Peace in the Time of Nassser and Ben Gurion.* New York: W.W. Norton, 1983.

Khalidi, Rashid. *Brokers of Deceit: How the US Has Undermined Peace in the Middle East.* Boston: Beacon Press, 2013.

Kurtzer, Daniel C. and Scott B. Lasensky with William B. Quandt, Steven L. Spiegel, and Shibley Telhami. *Negotiating Arab-Israeli Peace: American Leadership in the Middle East.* Washington, D.C.: United States Institute of Peace Press, 2008.

Lerner, Rabbi Michael. *Embracing Israel/Palestine: A Strategy to Heal and Transform the Middle East.* Berkeley: North Atlantic Books, 2012.

Maoz, Moshe. *Asad: the Sphinx of Damascus, A Political Biography.* New York: Grove Weidenfeld, 1988.

Mendes-Flohr, Paul R. ed. *A Land of Two Peoples: Martin Buber on Jews and Arabs.* New York: Oxford University Press, 1983.

Miller, Aaron David, *The Much Too Promised Land: America's Elusive Search for Arab-Israeli Peace.* New York: Bantam Books, 2008.

Muasher, Marwan. *The Arab Center: The Promise of Moderation.* New Haven: Yale University Press, 2008.

Nusseibeh, Sari with Anthony David. *Once Upon A Country: A Palestinian Life.* New York: Farrar, Straus, and Giroux, 2007.

———. *What Is A Palestinian State Worth?* Cambridge, Massachusetts: Harvard University Press, 2011.

Peres, Shimon. *The New Middle East.* New York: Henry Holt and *Company,* 1991.

Quandt, William B. ed. *The Middle East: Ten Years After Camp David.* Washington, D.C.: The Brookings Institution, 1988.

———, Fuad Jabber, and Ann Mosely Lesch. *The Politics of Palestinian Nationalism.* Berkeley: University of California Press, 1978.

———. *Peace Process: American Diplomacy and the Arab-Israeli Conflict Since 1967.* Washington, D.C.: The Brookings Institution, 1993.

Ross, Dennis. *The Missing Peace: The Inside Story of the Fight for Middle East Peace.* New York: Farrar, Straus, and Giroux, 2004.

Said, Edward. *Peace and Its Discontents.* London: Vintage, 1995.

———. *The Question of Palestine.* New York: Times Books, 1979.

Saunders, Harold H. *The Other Walls: The Politics of the Arab-Israeli Peace Process.* Washington, D.C.: American Enterprise Institute, 1985.

Savir, Uri. *The Process: 1,100 Days That Changed the Middle East.* New York: Random House, 1998.

Shavit, Ari. *My Promised Land: The Triumph and Tragedy of Israel.* New York: Random House, 2013.

Shehadeh, Raja. *Occupier's Law: Israel and the West Bank.* Washington, D.C.: Institute for Palestine Studies, 1985.

———. *The Third Way: A Journal of Life in the West Bank.* London: Quartet Books, 1982.

Shipler, David K. *Arab and Jew: Wounded Sprits in a Promised Land.* New York: Times Books, 1986.

Smith, Charles D. *Palestine and the Arab-Israeli Conflict.* New York: St. Martin's Press, 1988.

Spiegel, Steven L. *The Other Arab-Israeli Conflict: Making America's Middle East Policy from Truman to Reagan.* Chicago: University of Chicago Press, 1985.

Tessler, Mark. *A History of the Israel-Palestinian Conflict.* Bloomington: Indiana University Press, 1994.

Tillman, Seth P. *The United State in the Middle East: Interests and Obstacles.* Bloomington: Indiana University Press, 1982.

Tolan, Sandy. *The Lemon Tree: An Arab, A Jew, and the Heart of the Middle East.* New York: Bloomsbury, 2006.

Wasserstrom, Bernard. *Israelis and Palestinians: Why Do They Fight? Can They Stop.* New Haven: Yale University Press, 2003.

Wyman, David S. *Abandonment of the Jews: America and the Holocaust 1941-1945.* New York: Pantheon Books, 1984.

Young, Ronald J. *Missed Opportunities for Peace: U.S. Middle East Policy 1981-1986.* Philadelphia: American Friends Service Committee, 1987.

Jewish/Christian/Muslim Cooperation for Peace

Abadi, Houda and Aaron Hahn Tapper, eds. *Abraham's Vision: Unity Program Teacher's Guide.* An Introduction to Jewish-Muslim Relations.

Abuelaish, Izzeldin. *I Shall Not Hate: A Gaza Doctor's Journey on the Road to Peace and Human Dignity.* New York: Walker & Company, 2010.

al Faruqi, Ismail Raji, ed. *Trialogue of the Abrahamic Faiths.* Washington, D.C.: International institute of Islamic Thought, 1982.

Arinze, Francis Cardinal. *Religions for Peace: A Call for Solidarity to the World's Religions.* New York: Doubleday, 2002.

Armstrong, Karen. *A History of God: The 4,000 Year Quest of Judaism, Chrisitianity, and Islam.* New York: Ballantine Books, 1993.

Borg, Marcus and Ross Mackenzie, eds. *God at 2000.* Harrisburg, Pennsylvania: Morehouse Publishing, 2000.

Carroll, James. *Constantine's Sword, The Church and the Jews: A History.* Boston: Houghton Mifflin, 2001.

Eck, Diana L. *A New Religious America: How A "Christian Country" Has Become the World's Most Religiously Diverse Nation.* San Francisco: Harper, 2001.

Ehrenkranz, Joseph H. and David L. Coppola, eds. *Religion and Violence, Religion and Peace.* Fairfield, Connecticut: Sacred Heart University Press, 2000.

Helmick S.J., Raymod G. and Rodney L. Petersen. *Forgiveness and Reconciliation: Religion, Public Policy, and Conflict Transformation.* Philadelphia: Templeton Foundation Press, 2001.

Herberg, Will. *Protestant, Catholic, Jew.* New York: Anchor Books, 1960.

Hick, John. *God Has Many Names.* Philadelphia: Westminster Press, 1980.

Johnston, Douglas and Cynthia Sampson, eds. *Religion, the Missing Dimension of Statecraft.* New York, Johnston Oxford University Press, 1994.

Juergensmeyer, Mark. *Terror in the Mind of God: The Global Rise of Religious Violence.* Berkeley: University of California Press, 2000.

Kimball, Charles. *Striving Together: A Way Forward in Christian-Muslim Relations.* New York: Orbis Books, 1991.

————. *When Religion Becomes Evil: Five Warning Signs.* New York: Harper Collins, 2008.

Lewis, Bernard. *The Jews of Islam.* Princeton: Princeton University Press, 1984.

Knitter, Paul F. *No Other Name? A Critical Survey of Christian Attitudes Toward the World Religions.* New York: Orbis Books, 1985.

Marty, Martin E. and R. Scott Appleby. *Fundamentalism and the State: Remaking Politics, Economics, and Militance.* Chicago: University of Chicago Press, 1993.

———. *When Faiths Collide.* Malden, Massachusetts: Blackwell Publishing, 2005.

McLaren, Brian D. *Why Did Jesus, Moses, Buddha, and Mohammed Cross the Road?* New York: Jericho Press, 2012.

Peters, F.E. *Children of Abraham: Judaism/Christianity/Islam.* Princeton: Princeton University Press, 1982.

———. *Jerusalem.* Princeton: Princeton University Press, 1985.

———. *Judaism, Christianity, and Islam: The Classical Texts and Their Interpretation. Volume 1: From Covenant to Community.* Princeton: Princeton University Press, 1990.

———. *Judaism, Christianity, and Islam: The Classical Texts and Their Interpretation. Volume 2: The Word and the Law and the People of god.* Princeton: Princeton University Press, 1990.

———. *Judaism, Christianity, and Islam: The Classical Texts and Their Interpretation. Volume 3: The Works of the Spirit.* Princeton: Princeton University Press, 1990.

Phillips, Kevin. *American Theocracy: The Peril and Politics of Radical Religion, Oil and Borrowed Money in the 21st Century.* New York: Viking, 2006.

Sachedina, Abdul Azziz. *The Islamic Roots of Democratic Pluralism.* New York: Oxford University Press, 2001.

Samartha, S.J. *Faith in the Midst of Faiths.* Geneva: World Council of Churches, 1977.

Smith, Wilfred Cantwell. *Toward a World Theology.* Philadelphia: Westminster Press, 1981.

Smith, Huston. *The World's Religions.* New York: Haper Collins, 1991.

———. *The Soul of Christianity.* San Francisco: Harper, 2005.

———. *Why Religion Matters: The Fate of the Human Spirit in an Age of Disbelief.* San Francisco: Harper, 2001.

Thiemann, Ronald F. *Religion in Public Life: A Dilemma for Democracy.* Washington, D. C.: Georgetown University Press. 2007.

Underwood, Kenneth. *Protestant and Catholic: Religious and Social Interaction in an Industrial Community.* Boston: Beacon Press, 1957.

Wasserstrom, Steven M. *Religion After Religion.* Princeton: Princeton University Press, 1999.